T0178819

Competitive Intelligence and Decision Problems

Competitive Intelligence and Decision Problems

Edited by
Amos David

First published 2011 in Great Britain and the United States by ISTE Ltd and John Wiley & Sons, Inc.

ISTE Ltd
27-37 St George's Road
London SW19 4EU
UK

John Wiley & Sons, Inc.
111 River Street
Hoboken, NJ 07030
USA

www.iste.co.uk

www.wiley.com

Library of Congress Cataloging-in-Publication Data

Competitive intelligence and decision problems / edited by Amos David.
    p. cm.
  Includes bibliographical references and index.
  ISBN 978-1-84821-237-4
  1. Business intelligence. 2. Decision making. I. David, Amos.
  HD38.7.C6593 2011
  658.4'72--dc23
                                                                            2011019568

British Library Cataloguing-in-Publication Data
A CIP record for this book is available from the British Library
ISBN 978-1-84821-237-4

Printed and bound in Great Britain by CPI Antony Rowe, Chippenham and Eastbourne.

MIX
Paper from
responsible sources
FSC® C013604

Table of Contents

PART 1

Models and Tools

Chapter 1

Model Use: From a Decision-Making Problem to a Set of Research Problems

1.1. Introduction: why model?

We "model" constantly in the course of everyday life: for each entity we encounter, be it an object, a person, or a process, we create an associated mental image that enables us to give meaning to its existence and behavior. As Valéry states in [VAL 77], "we only think using models". A model is a formal representation of an object or a set of associated phenomena, which we attempt to circumscribe. It may be seen as an analytical tool used to describe, in a reduced and formalized manner, a particular observed object. In this way, the model acts as an intermediary between the object and the questions we ask to understand the object. Thus, the value of the model resides not in its "reality", but in its use to explain a given object or a set of phenomena: it takes on a heuristic role in the process of generating knowledge about a given object.

We thus see that the concept of models is part of a "simplification/abstraction" dichotomy, containing aspects of both symbolic representation and reduction of the complexity of the observed object. However, although the model is only a partial representation of this object, or of a certain "reality" of the object (which implies that a large number of possible models exist for a given object), it enables us, in relation to our aims, to reduce this "reality" to a limited number of viewpoints that are intelligible and coherent for the modeler. For this reason, an "intentional" aspect is always present in the creation of a model. Modeling is a subjective activity,

Chapter written by Philippe KISLIN.

involving choices to which the user commits himself/herself. Another expression of this duality is given by Nouvel, who describes modeling as a "negligence strategy" [NOU 02]. Negligence, or the fact of not taking certain aspects of the object into account, is used intentionally to highlight other aspects of this same object. Depending on the refinement of the initial information at the base of the construction of the model, the model will appear, according to Terrasse [TER 05], as the result of a sophisticated strategy or as a form of negligence controlled by abstraction or simplification. Thus, the model plays a triple role, being subjective, projective, and intentional.

However, depending on the construction of the model and the aims of the user, a model may give a simplified or idealized vision of the reality being represented. For example, a model – in the fashion sense of the term – is chosen because he/she represents an ideal form, albeit one which is not representative of the average human physique. According to Thom [THO 03], it is thus easy, through excessive idealization or simplification, to pass from model use into the realm of "magical thinking". Depending on the degree of freedom allowed, the model may evolve and may be perceived in very different ways. Care is needed to avoid confusing properties of the model with those of the real world, particularly in the context of competitive intelligence where digital artifacts, approximations, extractions, and data visualizations are frequent sources of errors and illusions.

Although a model is, by its very nature, simplistic and "fake", it allows us to find answers to certain questions. A model is put to use through a process of questioning and testing. This process shows up misunderstandings and inadequate formulations that force us to reconsider the model, to look for other interactions, and/or plan new processes of observation. A main positive attribute of the model is the fact that it is a construct. Thus, we do not seek to know whether the model is "right", but to analyze its contribution to a process of understanding (and in our particular context, mutual understanding between a watcher and a decision maker) the object constituted by the decision-making problem. Does this mean, then, that a "good" model is a useful model? This is what we will attempt to demonstrate in this chapter, showing the usefulness of a model-based approach in the process of transforming and resolving a decision problem in the context of information gathering.

In the context of this resolution, the watcher acts as the modeler of his/her own activities, both in determining what actions are necessary for the resolution of the information problem and in reducing their cognitive load, which, thanks to a support model, may be concentrated on the essential, but also because the information problem is itself a model of the larger decision problem. This model, created by the watcher, acts as an intermediary, as a pivotal document, and as a support for social and cognitive exchanges between the watcher and the decision maker and between all actors and the model. The resolution of the decision problem will not involve comings and goings between actors and the real world, but follows a more complex pattern of three-way interactions between the actors, the model, and the context of the problem.

Based on Roy's work [ROY 85], we define the assistance provided by the watcher in resolving the decision problem in the competitive intelligence process as the activity which, based on clearly defined but not necessarily completely formalized models[1], helps us to obtain aspects of a response to questions posed by the decision maker in this process, to work together to clarify or simply to favor a behavior in a way that increases the coherence between the evolution of resolution on the one hand, and the aims and preference system of the decision maker for whom the watcher is working on the other hand.

The model that we will now present aims, in addition to promoting the transition from a decision problem to an information-gathering problem and the various comings and goings involved (as the problem does not have a single final definition), to act as an event memory, as past events and analogy play an important role in the decision process. In designing the model, we have aimed to remain as close as possible to Ockham's principle, that is, to avoid needless multiplication of elements of the model, while striving to be as faithful as possible to Boileau's formula in describing the model.

1.2. General presentation of the Watcher Information Search Problem model

The Watcher Information Search Problem (WISP) model is made up of a collection of 27 interlinked elements that correspond to different "objects" handled by the watcher in the course of the watching process. These objects, which act as both containers and links, enable the watcher to organize and coordinate different steps of the transformation process – from registering the request to the presentation of results. Each of these objects has a number of attributes (title, date, reference, etc.) that describe its characteristics and promote "cognitive traceability" [KIS 09] of information, activity monitoring, and reuse (Figure 1.1).

Although this model is presented as a flow chart in Figure 1.1, the WISP is not fixed, as its name suggests (taking the meaning of the word "wisp", and not just the WISP acronym). It is flexible and adaptable and allows for the addition of new elements, such as annotations. The square brackets [ ], which follow certain labels, indicate that the element is, in fact, a collection, that is, a group of objects.

---

1 For example, the two models developed by the SITE-LORIA team, namely MEPD and WISP [BOU 04, KIS 07].

For example, the element <Demand> is associated with a collection of objects, <Formulation>, which correspond to the registration of different formulations and reformulations of the demand produced by the decision maker and by the watcher.

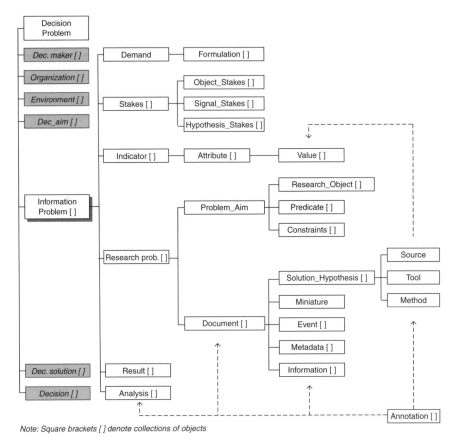

Note: Square brackets [ ] denote collections of objects

Figure 1.1. *General presentation of the WISP model*

1.3. Dimensions and aspects of the model

The WISP model is a three-dimensional, multifaceted model that incorporates the notion of the following points of view:

– an analytical dimension, which encompasses the understanding of demand, stakes, and context, the definition of information indicators and all knowledge creation and analysis operations that may be carried out by studying the memorized elements;

– a methodological dimension which, at the first level, is constituted by the capacity for transformation of the decision problem into an information problem (then into research problems), and on a second level by research strategies through which information is identified and knowledge acquired;

– an operational dimension, corresponding to the selection of action plans and the implementation of different steps of resolution of the methodology associated with the WISP model.

The "Need" aspect permits decision-based characterization of the expression of need (the formulated demand) suitable for the stakes and the context of the decision problem being considered; it is made up of the set of information produced by the model to explain the decision problem, the demand, and the associated stakes (Figure 1.2).

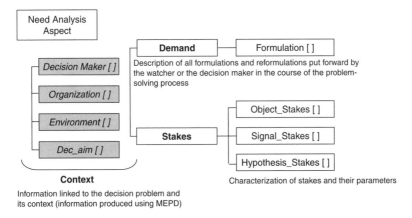

Figure 1.2. *The "Need" aspect: explanation of requirements and contextualization of demand*

The "Project" aspect links the demand to its transformation into information indicators, information problems, and their solutions, and the analysis and presentation of results to the decision maker (Figure 1.3).

The "Research" aspect connects information-gathering problems (through the formulation of the watcher's research aims and activities) with information elements (solutions) to show the value of indicators (Figure 1.4).

Finally, the "Knowledge" aspect is made up of annotations and analyses of both the results and the process itself by the watcher and by the decision maker. These aspects can be used to determine the boundaries of the model depending on different points of view, and in learning to use the model depending on the chosen aspects.

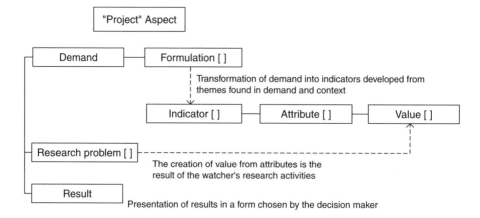

Figure 1.3. *The "Project" aspect: transformation of demand to produce information indicators*

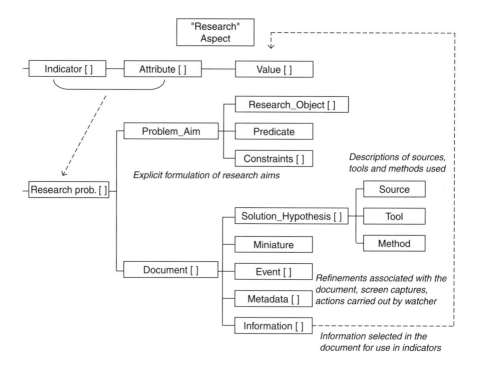

Figure 1.4. *The "Research" aspect: provision of indicator values through research*

1.4. Description of model elements

1.4.1. *Elements describing the decision problem and its context*

These elements of the model (Figure 1.5) carry information provided by both the decision maker and the watcher. Their purpose is to assist the decision maker in explicitly expressing needs and in formulating a request for information perfectly adapted to this need. The aim of the watcher is to register the facts that made the decision maker aware of the existence of the decision problem and to allow the decision maker to formulate the stakes linked to this problem. This step is carried out collaboratively with the aim of sharing the first intuitive ideas of both actors.

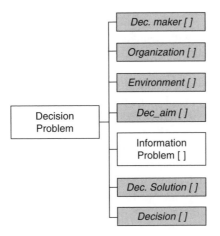

Figure 1.5. *Elements characterizing the decision environment*

The different information required for these elements is collected through guided interviews, by carrying out monitoring and by periodic research, the direction of which will be set out in the WISP model. Certain parameters included in these elements are destined for the decision maker alone; others may be shared with the watcher and may act as a basis for discussion.

The characterization of the decision problem involves seven elements, all of which appear at the same level in the hierarchical plan. These elements are object collections (represented by square brackets [ ]) that may contain one or more similar items. For example, several decision aims may be involved in a single decision problem, which may also spread over multiple environments and involve a group of decision makers. For a given problem, the elements *<Decision Maker>*, *<Organization>*, *<Environment>*, and *<Decision Aim>* define the context of the problem; if necessary, references to previous problems or to other problems being dealt with in parallel may also be included.

The information problem, or problems, is also found at this level. Each of these problems includes *<Demand>*, *<Stakes>*, *<Research Problem>*, *<Result>*, and *<Analysis>* elements, along with their derived elements and all associated dependencies. Finally, at the end of the information process, we find the elements *<Decision Solution>* and *<Decision>*, which encompass, respectively, the whole range of alternatives and possible solutions, and the chosen solution. Each of these elements has several parameters, which may be static, that is, which do not vary through different problems (e.g. the identity of a decision maker), or which may be dynamic, in which case their characteristic information changes in relation to given problems, is highly context dependent, or simply evolves, as when dealing with the level of experience of the decision maker. Transversal (invariable) parameters are imported as they are, will be duplicated for each new problem, and adapted as necessary and memorized.

The *<Decision Maker>* element contains individual characteristics of the decision maker: identity, initial training, functions, cognitive style, personality traits (such as Myers Briggs type indicator (MBTI)), and his/her level of expertise for the problem in question. Bouaka [BOU 04], taking inspiration from Hermann's work [HER 99], suggests adding an emotional dimension to take different emotional reactions into account, reactions that may influence the decision maker during the decision process. Although some of these parameters have not yet been completely formalized, they are mainly intended for use in self-diagnosis and are not intended to be transmitted. In addition to this information, we also find references to the decision problems under consideration. These operations are repeated for each decision maker involved in the decision project.

The *<Organization>* element contains information about the company. This includes not only data about the company (corporate name, site, legal status, sector of activity, clients, competitors, domains of expertise, resources, etc.) but also information on the way the company is perceived by the decision maker from his/her specific viewpoint. What, then, according to the decision maker, are the strengths and weaknesses of the company? What are its innovational niches? The main function of a business clearly depends not only on the company, but also on the points of view of the individuals that make up the company. The viewpoints of shareholders, employees, syndicates, and management have some similarities, but also palinodes and divergences, and may share doubts and uncertainties that should, in our opinion, be included in the model. In addition to these internal perspectives, we might add external impressions, for example, those of political and economic actors (the region, the state, etc.) and the viewpoints held by competitors and the media. The modeling of any of these different visions may be the subject of specific research in the framework of specialized scouting activities. They may be integrated into this element depending on the nature of the problem and of the aims. Other parameters may also be considered, the nature and number of which vary depending on the depth of the analysis desired. Examples of such parameters include the description of different operational functions of the business (production, service, sales, accounting, R&D, support, etc.), the identification of certain dysfunctional elements, the structure of the information system, its communication policies, its attitude to information in general (circulation, memorization, protection, patents, etc.), the measurement of its economic impact and various indicators (dashboard, indicators of direction, and performance, etc.), its originality, its history, and the way the company is managed. This element may be duplicated depending on the number of entities under consideration and the breakdown of the chosen structure (by subsidiaries, by departments, etc.) or in cases where the decision situation involves several organizations (e.g. an extended company), for example, in the case of a partnership.

The *<Environment>* collection of elements describes and defines the company's relationships with the outside world. It aims to identify the factors that the decision maker considers to be environment sensitive, to assist in capturing weak signals, and to identify opportunities and threats. This perception is highly subjective and is subject to implementation. This subjectivity is a source of interest to the watcher, as it is this which provokes strategic action from the decision maker and triggers the problem. This "problem premonition", which occurs before any decision-making activity, is made up of observations, interpretations, and incorporations of environmental stimuli, showing up filters and biases on the part of the decision makers and certain aspects of their preference system.

We will use Porter's five competing forces as parameters of the *<Environment>* element: the description (and perception) of competitors, partners, suppliers, the market, and the clients, to which the results of different specialized scouting activities may be added depending on the domain or domains under consideration. However, we will not attempt to divide the environment into sectors, but rather cover as many domains as possible. Using these parameters, it is also possible to characterize the environment in terms of turbulence, uncertainty, and complexity, and to define endogenous and exogenous indicators to measure and monitor the factors, which the decision maker considers to be critical. The information required to establish these indicators can come from different elements of the model, be the result of specific research activities, or have been collected using questionnaires that, coupled with a Likert scale, for example, allow us to measure the intensity of the revealed factors.

The *<Decision Aim>* element contains the aim or aims of the decision project or projects concerned. The decision aim, in our opinion, has a triple function: it is a particular and contextual expression of the strategy and current priorities of the business, a partial transformation of the stakes involved in the decision problem, and finally, the source of the information needs of the decision maker for this particular problem. This element may be broken down using a tree of intermediary aims and subgoals (operational, strategic, tactical, etc.) or be duplicated for each of the envisaged aims. It may also contain elements of the business plan that the decision maker considers to be useful.

1.4.2. *Chosen solutions and the final decision*

The two final elements, <*Decision Solution*> and <*Decision*>, regroup the different intentions and alternatives for solving the problem, which may be used by the decision maker. These elements allow the actors involved in the project to assess the project, adjust it by, for example, creating new demands, and "plan" the decision. They also aim to refine what Endsley calls "situation awareness" [END 00] for each actor, that is, the understanding of existing relationships between perceived elements of the environment and the mental projection of the evolution of these elements following specific envisaged solutions.

The <*Decision Solution*> element collection contains the description of different alternatives. It corresponds to the selection of possible choices for the problem being considered. The parameters (hypothesis, projection, and solution) of these elements contain projections of hypothetical futures based on different scenarios and allow the decision maker to define critical indicators, then to look for the variables that influence these indicators. The other parameters (resources, risks, cost, and validation) regroup the means available and those required to implement the envisaged solution. Each of these may also contain additional specifications; for example, within "resources", we may find human, financial, and temporal resources alongside raw materials.

The <*Decision*> element or elements contain the details of the chosen decision and, possibly, a plan of action. It, or they, also contains the link or links to the decision solution to implement (as presented in the previous element) and, in certain cases, the resulting negotiations.

These two elements only mark a provisional solution to the decision problem, as this problem may depend on another problem, be part of a larger problem, or, like the ouroboros, create new problems in a dynamic spiral process. Can we, then, truly believe that a "final" decision might exist, or that a problem could be solved once and for all, and "closed?"

1.4.3. *Supporting elements of the information problem*

The *<Information Problem>* or problems – more often the latter – are part of the decision problem through this collection of elements and constitute the point of origin for the transformation of a decision problem into information problems. Several information problems, then, are attached to one decision problem or demand for information. We will explain the reasons for this choice later on.

Six elements (Figure 1.6) are at the root of the problem: the *<Demand>* that contains the different formulations and reformulations of need in terms of information, the *<Stake(s)>* involved in the decision problem associated with the demand and its context, the group of information *<Indicator(s)>* that constitutes a validated expression of the demand, the *<Research Problem(s)>* that stem partly from the demand and partly from the assignment of values to indicators, and finally the *<Result>* and *<Analysis>* elements that contain, respectively, the information produced and the analysis carried out, both on the results and on the decision process.

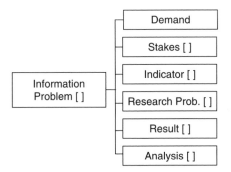

Figure 1.6. *Elements at the root of the information problem*

These elements will be filled in by the watcher and supervised by the decision maker. Additionally, some of these elements (particularly those included in, and derived from, the *<Research Problem>*) will benefit from computer support, which, due to its capacities for automization, will allow the association of data with certain parameters of these elements in a way easily understandable by the watcher.

1.4.4. *Demand, stakes, and context*

This first group, made up of 10 collections of elements, is the Demand–Stakes–Context (DSC) group (Figure 1.7). This links the four elements representing the context, imported from the decision problem, to two elements representing the demand and four others that will be used to define stakes. This group will also be superposed onto the "need" aspect of the model. The DSC group allows the watcher to contextualize the demands made of him/her (and, through the demand, the need for information that it expresses) and to link the two to the origin of the decision problem and to the environment.

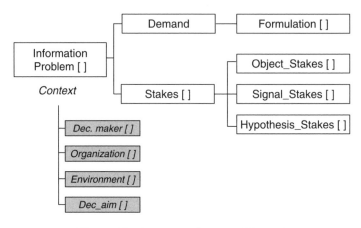

Figure 1.7. *Constituent elements of the DSC*

The *<Demand>* element has certain particularities: it alone plays the role of a "wrapper", acting as an "envelope" for the *<Formulation>* set of elements. For each decision problem, there is one single demand, but one that may be made up of several formulations. In the same way, a multiple demand would require the simultaneous coexistence of several decision problems. In our model, we will distinguish between "multiple" and "plural" demands. A multiple demand, which corresponds to multiple stakes, leads to the creation of several decision problems. For example, if a business wishes to improve its brand image and create new markets, it is easy to see that two decision problems may be involved. A plural demand, on the other hand, involves several demand elements. Thus, to improve brand image, a demand may encompass a study of the competition, a quality audit carried out at client level, and a media campaign project, the substance of which requires definition.

In reality, in our model, the decision problem and the associated demand pertain to the element *<Object of stakes>*. We have chosen a hypothesis where, for as long as the object of the stakes does not change, we are dealing with the same decision problem, of which different formulations will undoubtedly be necessary to outline the demand as clearly as possible. These formulations therefore correspond either to a development in the understanding of the problem or to changes in the context (or even the development of an unexpected situation), which lead to corrections, precisions, or modification of the demand. However, if the emergence of this situation, the detection of new signals, or the incorporation of new factors change the stakes involved in the problem (and thus the object), we consider that the decision maker is now faced with a new problem. Depending on particular cases, this may imply the cessation of activity on the current problem and transformation to deal with the new problem, or replication and division of the current problem into as many problems as proved necessary. Thus, when multiple stakes are involved (the objects of which may conflict), we will be able to look at different solutions to the decision problems and choose one, benefiting one aspect to the detriment of another (e.g. environmental stakes over economic stakes).

The *<Formulation>* element collection contains different formulations and reformulations of the demand by actors. Although we initially chose to create "formulation" and "reformulation" elements in the model, based on the understanding that the decision maker is responsible for formulation and the watcher for reformulation, in practice we decided to use only formulations, which are, nevertheless, distinguished by author and date information. Thus, in the case of a stipulated demand, the decision maker will be the first "formulator" of the demand. In the case of an implicit demand, the watcher may be responsible for the formulation of the demand based on what he/she understands of the need; the decision maker will then reformulate this first formulation, and so on. In our opinion, reformulation is necessary as it satisfies the need for mutual and shared understanding. It also allows specification of concepts and agreement on common meanings for each concept. From these formulations, the watcher identifies key concepts (or themes of the demand) that will be attached to the *<Demand>* element itself.

The *<Stakes>* collection of elements, itself made up of three collections, is used to characterize the stakes involved in the decision problem from the point of view of the decision maker and opposes them to the demand and the context.

The *<Object of Stakes>* is the target on which the decision maker wishes to act, the *<Signal>* is what incites the decision maker to begin considering the decision problem, and the *<Hypothesis>* corresponds to the perceived risks and gains and to the envisaged consequences of a lack of action on the part of the decision maker. These parameters justify the decision aims, and the attainment of this goal contributes to their fulfillment. The action taken by the decision maker is logical from his/her point of view, based on what the decision maker stands to gain or lose during the resolution of the project, that is, through the identified stakes. While these stakes are often multiple, ambiguous, and sometimes contradictory, we consider that these stakes relate to the quality of perceived information, to environmental constraints, to the preferences of the decision maker, and to the decision maker's value judgments. With a better perception of the stakes involved, the watcher is able to understand, via the formulated demand, which parameters of the decision problem hold the greatest importance for the decision maker. However, we are aware that part of these stakes will not be communicated to the watcher. Is the watcher, then, responsible for bringing forth results, based on personal reflection, from the hidden stakes of the decision maker? Does the watcher need to develop "psyops" [DAU 82] to "win over the heart and spirit" of the decision maker? These aspects are sensitive and the watcher must define the borders of his/her investigative territory and not overstep the limits. The relationships between actors themselves involve "risks and stakes which are decisive in self-image, defense of territory, maintenance or breaking of links" [PIC 06]. Thus, personal issues (concerning identity, territory, and position) always intervene as overlays to professional issues; once again, the watcher should act intelligently and show proof of good sense. Moreover, as Salomé emphasizes [SAL 02], it is difficult to establish a respectful and tolerant partnership when one of the two actors is not free (from hidden stakes in particular), as this will mean priority is given to former allegiances. Nevertheless, the decision maker must find the means of breaking free from the circle of prejudices; the formulation of stakes seems, to us, to be a suitable means of doing this.

After obtaining the titles of stakes involved, the watcher will establish a typology of stakes based on the different domains of the business (economic, strategic, commercial, social, etc.), depending on projections (short, medium, or long term) and, finally, based on the priority accorded to each by the decision maker.

1.4.5. *Information indicators*

The creation of a group of indicators constitutes the core of the WISP model and corresponds to the validated translation of the demand into a particular "documentary" language. The concept of indicators used here is not dissimilar to that of performance indicators used in the dashboard of the decision maker. However, it differs in that an information indicator does not measure performance, but characterizes, by its attributes, a notion for an individual and at a given moment ("what Z understands by X..."). Nevertheless, the similarities with performance indicators are not negligible, as they synthesize information in a limited data set with a presentation chosen to correspond to the decision maker's preferences. We will consider the information indicator as a meaningful document, the result of an element of information, a means of processing, or a method defined by attributes with observable and qualifiable properties and which may be evaluated in relation to an information demand formulated by the decision maker and analyzed in the light of stakes perceived by the watcher.

Several families of information indicators may be identified. The first, and most important, of these directly concerns the demand and is made up of "notional" information indicators. These indicators allow the description of key concepts associated with the demand and the characterization of notions used in breaking these concepts down by characteristics (which we will call "attributes"). We are therefore more interested in the particular meaning the decision maker gives to a term (the "notion") than in the general meaning of the term (which is more strongly attached to the concept). As Grise highlights [GRI 96], there are two well-determined and complementary fields of knowledge: the field of conceptual structures and the field of notional structures. Conceptual knowledge, which leads to logically structured provisional truths, is that used by scientists. In this case, it refers to thought structures built from axioms with logical conclusions where natural language merely plays a supporting role. Notional knowledge is constructed through communications, without necessarily having recourse to scientific truths, but with interpretations from personal experience which are more or less likely to be accepted by other parties as relevant. Notional knowledge also stems from culturally and psychologically determined beliefs present in each individual. A notional information indicator therefore contains the subjectivity of meaning (of a term) accorded by the decision maker in the particular context of the problem.

The second family brings together methodological information indicators. It concerns procedural knowledge, which the watcher transforms into indicators, mainly to enable their reuse in the research process. Examples include particular requests, sources to use in relation to a given theme, hints and tips to use to obtain information more quickly and securely, and so on. A methodological information indicator therefore encapsulates a certain *savoir faire* possessed by the watcher, with the aim of reusing this knowledge in other situations and for other problems. This knowledge is mainly oriented toward information gathering, but may also concern the characterization of notional indicators or any other element of the model.

The last family of indicators concerns reporting and results and is used in analyzing both the results of scouting and the process as a whole. It may contain performance indicators, such as a measurement of the costs (temporal, financial, etc.) involved in a given research activity, and the quantification of use of a search engine or information bank or even an inventory of sources consulted, broken down by nature (human, internet, databases, etc.) for the current problem. This may also consist of identifying a certain number of "quality" indicators referring to the process, for example, the time spent on research, financial cost of the information sources used or the number of requests carried out, fulfilled information demands, rejected documents, and so on, over a given period.

The characterization of (notional) *<Indicators>* is a two-step process. First, the watcher identifies the "titles" of these indicators and then creates a list of *<Attributes>* used in their definition. This list is presented to the decision maker for validation or rejection of various attributes. Second, the watcher, using an information-gathering process, assigns different *<Values>* to those attributes chosen for use.

The *<Attribute>* element collection contains different characteristics of notions linked to the decision maker's demand. For example, a competitor may be defined by looking for the name of its director, geographic location, sales figures, and sector of activity in a particular problem. In another case, information on partners and the number of patents obtained will be the determining factor. Each attribute has a status (validated, not validated, to be validated), a description, a type, an origin, and a priority level.

Each attribute can have one or more *<Values>*. These values generally take the form of information extracted from documents. For example, to assign a value to the attribute "sales", the watcher must look for this information for each identified competitor in various sources. These sources must be identified, and then the relevant information must be found and extracted from the source document(s). Sources should be compared if the data given are different, and the chosen value must then be assigned to the corresponding attribute. This research thus creates a certain number of research problems linked to the value assignment process. Each *<Value>* element, like *<Attribute>* elements, has a title, a status, a description, and a link to the document(s) in which it was found.

1.4.6. *Elements of research problems*

The elements of the *<Research Problem>* collection cover the research activity of the watcher in its entirety, from the explicit formulation of *<Research Aims>* to the extraction of *<Information>* from *<Documents>*. In the WISP model, the research problem is set apart from the research and information practices of the watcher. These practices (Figure 1.8) include the collection of data, mainly concerning different elements of the model and directly accessible data. At the end of this collection activity, the real information-gathering stage begins, involving an initial hunt for clues to define titles and attributes of indicators, and a "problem" activity that consists of finding values for these attributes.

Before beginning research, the watcher is invited to formulate his/her intentions, that is, to provide an expression of the research process in natural language. This explicit formulation of the research aims is another particularity of our model. This expression of aims gives meaning to the strategies used in its fulfillment (requests, surveys, database searches, etc.) and to the selection of documents to use. As Hameline [HAM 79] points out, for a research intention to become operational, "its content must be expressed as unequivocally as possible". The goal of this formulation of aims is to remove ambiguities, to provide explicit characterization of the object of the research, and to define requirements expressed through constraints.

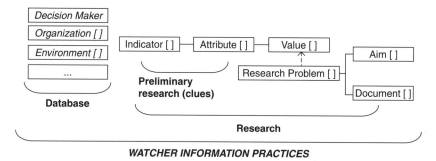

WATCHER INFORMATION PRACTICES

Figure 1.8. *Watcher information practices*

The *<Research Object>* element contains different objects sought after by the watcher. More often than not, this concerns a specific piece of information or the object containing this information (or an information network). To continue using the previous example, to provide a value for the attribute "sales", the research object may be "the sales figures of competitor X", but also "the register of commerce", "a telephone number for Paul (a college friend who works for X)", "open-access financial portals", "issue Y of review Z", and so on. All these objects will be connected to this attribute and will produce a corresponding number of research problems. We can therefore find problems and solutions that overlap, responding to intermediate goals, themselves defined by subaims but all generated to respond to one single goal: to find a value for the attribute concerned.

The *<Predicate>* is the predicative verb in the formulated aim. Given that aims are expressed following the structure "I want to *<Predicate>* + article + *<Research Object>*...", the predicative verb is always used in the infinitive. Examples of this include "define", "find", "consult", "question", "compare", "know", "check", and so on. The main interest of this is that these verbs are transitive and directly introduce the object of the research. The use of a particular verb may also lead to the acquisition of information by inference through retrospective analysis of the process. For example, "find" implies that the watcher is already aware of the existence of a piece of information; "check" suggests that the watcher already possesses the information but wants to check it against new facts or validate it. "Define" might suggest that the watcher already has vague knowledge of the object but requires clarification to avoid erroneous interpretation, for example.

Each objective may contain one or more <Constraints>. A <Constraint> element has a title and a type which define its nature. For example, we might find quantitative constraints (e.g. at least one, a maximum, more than 10), qualitative constraints (validated information, free source, etc.), or temporal constraints (time taken <1 h, before date T, etc.). These constraints are those imposed by the watcher in relation to the research problem or problems and are not attached to the information demand, although there may be a cause-and-effect relationship between the information demand and the constraints.

Following the formulation of aims, the watcher implements strategies to respond to these aims. These strategies are contained in the <Solution Hypothesis> element collection. Then, depending on the <Source>, <Tool>, and <Method> used, the watcher will obtain a collection of <Documents> which may or may not demand further attention. If the required information is found in the document, it is attached to the <Information> element. The registration of these documents and of the actions carried out using them (such as information extraction, annotations, or following hypertext links) may be done using computer-based tools for automation, extraction, and content management.

The information taken from the document will then be attached to the attribute of the corresponding indicator as a value. In this way, it becomes possible that a piece of information discovered (by serendipity or zemblanity) while looking for other information may be linked to the correct indicator at any time. In any case, we obtain "cognitive traceability" [KIS 07, KIS 09] and physical traceability of the element of information, from its extraction via the origins of the research up to the decision problem that justified its selection (Figure 1.9).

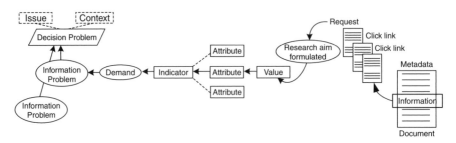

Figure 1.9. *Cognitive and physical traceability of information*

This traceability provides a number of access points for documents and information and, by its very existence, gives meaning to the nature of these links.

1.4.7. *Analysis and presentation of results*

At the end of the research process, we find the two last element collections of the model.

The *<Result>* element contains the results produced by scouting, presented in a way specified at the time the demand was made. This parameter will therefore be specified from the earliest formulations so that the information may be presented in the most suitable way possible, enabling easy interpretation and allowing the decision maker to make a decision. The solution to the information problem may take the form of an overview report, a contingency table, a series of histograms and various graphics, or a list produced by extracting certain elements of the model, presented in a more or less detailed manner.

In this model, we distinguish between two different forms of analysis: the analysis carried out on the results of the scouting process, produced by the decision maker with assistance from experts in the domain(s) concerned, and the analysis of the process itself presented in the form of reporting and result indicators. These two categories of analysis are associated with this element. However, if certain aspects of analysis are concerned essentially with the decision problem, it is best to include them in the *<Decision Solutions>* element instead. The *<Analysis>* element therefore contains both a collection of indicators (of performance, quality, etc.) and a link, which, like the *<Result>* element, directs the user toward one or more external documents containing the analytical reports.

1.4.8. *Common parameters for all model elements*

All elements of the model are dated and identified from the moment of their creation to allow users to refer to them at any point without ambiguity. Associated with a "date" parameter, it is thus possible to restitute an element in relation to another element or one part of the model in relation to a different part. The importance of chronology in identifying the order and succession of actions and events is therefore clear. The chronological record organizes events by data of occurrence, but also depending on the goals of the person responsible for creating the record. A chronology of the evolution of formulations, an overview of stakes and solutions, or the series of actions undertaken when processing documents would look different depending on whether the watcher or the decision maker created the chronology, for example. The use of these two parameters also allows this succession of facts and actions to be reviewed at a later date – as when reviewing the performance of an athlete or team captured on video – and gives a new understanding and unexpected knowledge of this succession.

In the same way, we may obtain a "paused" image giving access to all elements of a given moment: documents, information in the state in which it was found by the author, and information for recontextualization (what was the demand being processed? What was the company's perception of the environment at that moment? What information was available when making a particular decision?) and to measure development from the past situation to the present moment. This viewpoint on temporal evolution is at the heart of competitive intelligence, as it promotes understanding of the past and feedback, activities that may be grouped together, using Bickford's phrase, as "lessons learned" [BIC 00].

We have also chosen to harmonize element parameters that will, in the main, have a (type), an address (uri), a title or the contents of the element (text), a (description), and a (status).

1.4.9. *Knowledge building through annotation*

The use of annotations in the WISP model follows the methodological propositions set out in Explore, Query, Analyze, and Annotate (EQuA^{2}te), developed by David *et al.* [DAV 03]. EQuA^{2}te is a methodology developed for the exploration, analysis, and production of knowledge aimed principally at decision makers, and it aims to facilitate management and exploitation of a base of strategic data linked to a knowledge base concerning the system user. In this way, it covers the means used to give the decision maker the ability to explore, query, analyze, and annotate this knowledge base, built around previous personal activities. However, the same principle may be applied to the watcher who may also be confronted with (research) problems similar to others encountered in the past, which may be adapted to help with the current problem. Furthermore, knowledge production can surpass the factual and methodological aspects of research and apply to the whole competitive intelligence process. For this reason, we have planned for annotation of the scouting process itself as well as its results.

In the WISP model, the *<Annotation>* element is an independent element that may be inserted into any other element of the model. The defining characteristic of an annotation is the fact of being "anchored" (a link known as "uri" in our model) to a portion of the target document (structural text zone, word or group of words, image, etc.). If the model itself becomes a document, as is the case here, we can insert an annotation anywhere in the document; we must simply provide the element ID as the target of the annotation. The *<Annotation>* element contains the same parameters as the other elements of the model. We have, however, added a "rights" parameter to authorize or limit visibility of annotations for specific groups or categories of actors.

Using annotation, which promotes the production and exchange of knowledge, the model itself, through the process it represents, becomes a basis for communication and collaboration between the watcher and the decision maker. This support allows the two actors to "know what is really happening", thanks to scenarization of the competitive intelligence process. This contributes to the analysis of anomalies and incidents, the search for causes and consequences, and the definition of the means of correction and improvement. This formalization of the process assists the development of experience management within the company and provides a favorable environment for the creation and capitalization of knowledge based on this experience.

1.5. Conclusion: toward flexibility in the model

As with any model, this model is designed to be modified. As in cartography, it constitutes a "map" of elements and is used for orientation and progress; however, it also needs to be adapted to the stride and way of walking of the user, like a pair of shoes. Furthermore, as Korzybski states, "a map is not the territory" [KOR 98]. A model may be useful in understanding and outlining the space (or territory) of a decision problem, but it is not, nor will it ever be, universal in nature. In the same way that the demand is not the same thing as the need, the model is conditioned by the perceptions of the designer and is simply a material to be adopted and adapted by each user, who models it for their own usage and using their own representations.

The WISP model, which we have presented in this chapter, is based on two fundamental hypotheses:

– The decision maker must be convinced of the benefits of their information request and be certain that the information produced will not create a problem larger than that which he/she has to solve.

– The decision maker must be certain that the time invested in discussion with the watcher and, mostly, in discussions based on the reformulation of demands, the expression of stakes, and the definition of indicators will allow optimization of the research process and thus, in the long term, save time.

Throughout the testing of this model, we have noticed that in cases where these two hypotheses were fulfilled and as the information needs of the decision maker were better known and recognized, there was more scope for revision, free expression, and demonstrations of trust. However, the formulation of research aims for the watcher is based on new practices, requiring a learning process and solid collaboration based on confidence and on recognized and shared capabilities.

1.6. Bibliography

[BIC 00] BICKFORD J., "Sharing lessons learned in the Department of Energy", *AAAI-00 Intelligent Lessons Learned Systems Workshop*, Austin, Texas, USA, 31 July 2000.

[BOU 04] BOUAKA N., Développement d'un modèle pour l'explicitation d'un problème décisionnel: un outil d'aide à la décision dans un contexte d'intelligence économique, Thesis in ICT, University of Nancy 2, Nancy, December 2004.

[DAU 82] DAUGHERTY W.E., "Origin of Psyop Terminology", in MACLAURIN R.D. (ed.), *Military Propoganda: Psychological Warfare and Operations*, Praeger Publishers, New York, p. 257, 1982.

[DAV 03] DAVID A., THIERY O., "L'Architecture EQuA2te et son application à l'intelligence économique", *Proceedings of the Conference "Intelligence Économique: Rechercheset Applications"*, Nancy, France, April 2003.

[END 00] ENDSLEY M.R., GARLAND D.J., *Situation Awareness Analysis and Measurement*, LEA, Mahwah, NJ, USA, 2000.

[GRI 96] GRISE J.B., *Logique et langage*, Ophrys, Paris, 1996.

[HAM 79] HAMELINE D., *Les Objectifs pédagogiques en Formation Initiale et Continue*, ESF, Paris, 1979.

[HER 99] HERMANN N., *The Creative Brain*, Atlantic Books, New York, 1999.

[KIS 07] KISLIN P., Modélisation du problème informationnel du veilleur dans la démarche d'intelligence économique, Thesis in ICT, University of Nancy 2, Nancy, November 2007.

[KIS 09] KISLIN P., "Tracer, Annoter et Mémoriser: Trois Actions pour Asseoir la Collaboration-Confiance du Veilleur et du Décideur", *Actes de VSST'2009*, Nancy, France, 2009.

[KOR 98] KORZYBSKI A., *Une carte n'est pas le territoire: prolégomènes aux systèmes non-aristotéliciens et à la sémantique générale*, Editions de l'éclat, Paris, 1998.

[NOU 02] NOUVEL P., *Enquête sur le concept de modèle*, Collection Science, Histoire et Société, PUF, Paris, 2002.

[PIC 06] PICARD D., MARC E., *Petit traité des conflits ordinaires*, Le Seuil, Paris, 2006.

[ROY 85] ROY B., *Méthodologie multicritère d'aide à la décision*, Economica, Paris, 1985.

[SAL 02] SALOMÉ J., *Jamais seuls ensemble: Comment vivre à deux en restant différents*, Editions de l'Homme, Paris, October 2002.

[TER 05] TERRASSE M.N., SAVONNET M., LECLERCQ E., GRISON T., BECKER G., "Points de vue croisés sur les notions de modèle et métamodèle", *IDM'2005*, Paris, France, 30 June 2005.

[THO 03] THOM R., "Stabilité Structurelle et Morphogénèse: Essai d'une théorie générale des modèles", in THOM R., BOMPARD-PORTE M. (dir.), *Œuvres complètes*, CD-ROM, IHES, Bures-sur-Yvette, March 2003.

[VAL 77] VALÉRY P., *Cahiers*, NRF, Paris, 1977.

Chapter 2

Analytical Tools for Competitive Intelligence: from Data Collection to Data Processing

2.1. Introduction

Competitive intelligence (CI) emerged as a response to the upheavals caused by the global environment on our society. In an increasingly complex and fast-moving economy, companies must be able to develop new knowledge to maintain levels of innovation and gain a competitive advantage [OUB 05]. In addition to this, the use of information and communications technology (ITC) has introduced new constraints to which businesses must adapt to survive: a continuous flow of information, considerably faster circulation of information, and evermore complex techniques (it is more and more difficult to rapidly master new software) [COL 97]. There is a risk of "drowning" in this information, of losing the ability to distinguish between the essential and the superfluous. With the emergence of the new market-dominated economy, the industrial issues facing businesses have increased considerably in complexity. Now, to remain competitive, a business must be able to manage its intangible assets. CI is an approach and an organizational process that allows a company to be more competitive, through surveillance of the environment and of external changes alongside self-evaluation of internal changes.

In 2000, 6 years after the canonical definition put forward by Martre [MAR 94], the borders of the notion of CI were still unstable [SAL 00]. Over the last few years, more and more definitions of CI have emerged, with a perceptible shift

Chapter written by Ilhème GHALAMALLAH, Eloïse LOUBIER and Bernard DOUSSET.

from definitions based almost exclusively on CI processes and techniques toward definitions including the strategic aims of CI, and more recently toward definitions including notions of knowledge management, collective learning, or cooperation [SAL 00].

Our vision of CI is essentially strategic, an approach based on anticipation and forecasting [BES 96], which works by uncovering the links between actors in the same sector of activity. CI is based on individual and collective anticipation and on in-depth knowledge of the current environment and existing networks to act and react in relation to their development [BES 98], [REV 98], [LEV 01]. The coordination of actions, in the case of a common strategy, requires a strong capacity to seize on variations and environmental reactions each step of the way, to identify factors for change and account for these factors by suitable modifications [WIL 67], [LEV 96], [VAS 99], [GUI 03].

Table 2.1 presents a historical synthesis of the main themes in CI since 1961 [PAT 98]. It can be broken down into two tendencies: the core of the domain, which has been stable for over 15 years (including collection, processing, diffusion, interpretation, knowledge, coordination, decision making, and environment), and new, less consistent preoccupations, which have emerged in more recent years and essentially introduce the time factor (immediate, ulterior, continuous, anticipation, "right time", etc.). The time factor is of increasing importance and should always be taken into account in any strategic analysis.

In the context of our approach, we will use the definition set out by Martre [MAR 94], who defined CI as a group of coordinated research, data processing, and information distribution activities that allow actions to be carried out and decisions to be made. This goes further than the partial actions involved in Documentation. Watch in different skills (scientific and technological, competitive, financial, judicial, territorial, and regulatory) invites us to "move from individual processing of information toward information management and a collective action process" [MAR 94].

From now on, our work will consist of defining a model for data processing and management in the context of the CI cycle, including relational and temporal dimensions. Thus, our multidimensional analytical model will be based on the following four main steps of the CI process [JUI 05]:

– formulation of need,

– data collection and processing,

– analysis,

– presentation and interpretation of results.

Concepts \ Authors (Year)	Wilensky 1967	Baumard 1991	Martre et al. 1994	Martinet and Marti 1995	Levet and Paturel 1996	Colletis 1997	Revelli 1998	Besson and Possin 1998	De Vasconcelos 1999	Levet 2001	Paturel 2002	Guilhon and Manni 2003	Juillet 2005
Regrouping, research, collection, collections	x		x		x		x	x	x		x	x	
Processing, sorting, memorization, validation	x		x				x	x	x		x	x	
Knowledge, actors		x	x			x		x			x		x
Diffusion, distribution	x		x				x	x	x			x	
Interpretation, analysis, production	x				x			x		x	x		
Knowledge, strategic information								x	x	x		x	x
Coordination, collectives, connection, combination, communications, sharing		x			x	x			x			x	
Decision making, actions	x	x	x				x		x				x
Environment				x						x		x	
Understanding, adaptation				x						x			
Detection, active surveillance								x			x		
Immediate					x								
Ulterior					x								
Threats, opportunities								x					
Continuous									x				
Anticipation										x			
Right timing											x		
Creativity, new capabilities												x	
Protection													x

Table 2.1. *Synthesis of main themes in CI: gray shades highlight described concepts by authors over the time*

The main aim is the creation of new knowledge, often totally implicit and of strategic importance, which is most often found through the analysis of the development of networks of actors (authors, inventors, companies, towns, regions, countries, journals, etc.), semantic networks (keywords, free terms, multiterms, ontologies, etc.), and interactions (actor/semantics) [MAR 95].

2.2. Overview of the multidimensional analysis model

The proposed model may be described graphically, as shown in Figure 2.1.

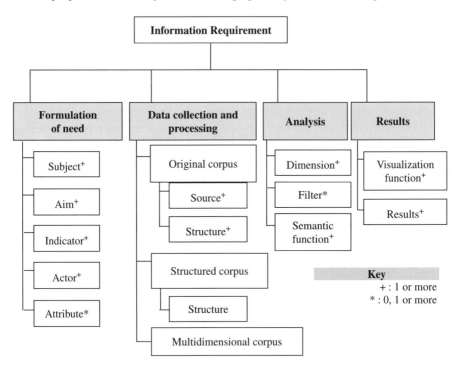

Figure 2.1. *Multidimensional analysis model*

– *Formulation of need*: this element contains the interpretation and identification of the decision aim. It is defined by five objects: <*Subject*>, <*Aim*>, <*Indicator*>, <*Actor*>, and <*Attribute*>. These elements provide a detailed description of the problem or information need connected to the aim of the analysis. In the case of an information need, we may identify one or more subjects, and for each subject, we define one or more aims, indicators, and actors. We may also assign several attributes to each actor.

– *Data collection and processing*: this element contains the sources of data chosen for use in relation to the information requirement [GOT 92], [RED 94]. It is described by the <*Body of source material*>, <*Body of processed material*>, and <*Multidimensional corpus*>. The body (or corpus) of the source material may be taken from one or more data sources. The body of processed material is most often obtained after formatting, retagging, and homogenizing the source material.

– *Analysis*: this element contains *<Dimension>*, *<Filter>*, and *<Semantic function>*. When analyzing a multidimensional corpus, we define one or more semantic functions based on one or more dimensions. For each dimension, filters may be applied to the dimension's attributes.

– *Results*: results are described by one or more *<Visualization function>* elements used for the visualization of each *<Result>*.

2.2.1. *Information process*

The main purpose of our model is the management and creation of knowledge in the context of a decision-making process. In this context, we will present the different steps of the information process supported by the model, from raw data to knowledge and the decision (see Figure 2.2).

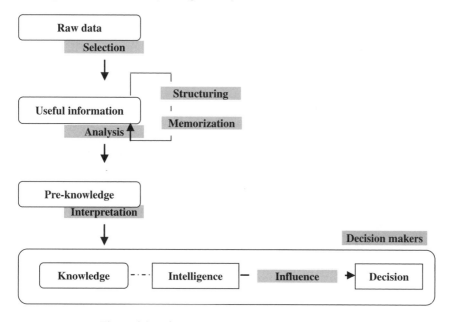

Figure 2.2. *Information process (based on [BOU 04])*

– *Raw data–useful information*: the relationship between data and information consists of selecting potentially useful information for analysis from among existing raw data, leaving aside any superfluous data. The data are therefore considered the origin of the information. The selected data are transformed into useful information by a value-adding process that consists of structuring and memorizing it to facilitate access.

– *Useful information–pre-knowledge*: this relationship consists of analyzing useful information and identifying various dependencies between pieces of information. The representation of useful information in the form of "pre-knowledge" is based on the restructuring and analysis of information based on relationships.

– *Pre-knowledge–knowledge*: this step is based on the interpretation of "pre-knowledge" by the decision maker via a synthetic vision of the information environment in the context of the decision. This relationship, therefore, describes the passage from explicit knowledge[1] (pre-knowledge) to implicit knowledge,[2] which belongs to the world of mental objects (decision maker).

– *Intelligence–decision*: intelligence is an interaction between the decision maker's personal knowledge and the knowledge deduced from "pre-knowledge" analysis, an interaction that can exercise influence on the decision maker in terms of the decision, that is, in terms of the choice among different possible solutions.

2.2.2. *Process architecture*

The process proposed for the implementation of our model can be presented following an architectural pattern over three levels (Figure 2.3):

– *Sources and extraction*: this level "feeds" the data stock from the available corpus of textual data. It allows us to pass from the initial representation of textual documents (qualitative data) to their synthetic form (quantitative data: occurrences, co-occurrences, etc.).

– *Data warehouse*: this is a storage space that provides both a unified view of the source corpus (documents) and a multidimensional representation of actors and concepts (relationships).

– *Analysis and presentation*: this level allows multidimensional analysis of the data taken from the warehouse and their presentation to the user using the reporting tools.

---

1 Explicit knowledge, contrary to tacit knowledge, is knowledge clearly set out in a written document or in a computer system; this knowledge is physically transferable, as it appears in a tangible form, whether in a document, a paper file, or a computer file.

2 Tacit, or implicit, knowledge is knowledge that belongs to the world of "mental objects", mental representations that often relate to personal life experience. It is generally difficult to put into words or "formalize", unlike explicit knowledge (source: Wikipedia). Michael Polanyi goes into more detail with regard to this distinction.

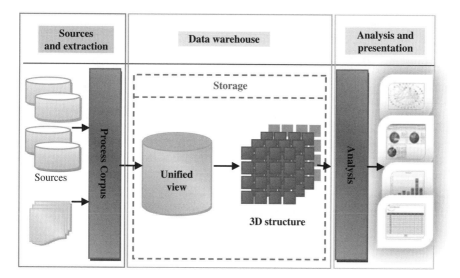

Figure 2.3. *System architecture*

2.3. Application of the multidimensional analysis model

We will present this analytical model using a study carried out on the domain of nanotechnology.

The field of nanoscience and nanotechnology represents a strategically important research sector, with high levels of competition and rapid growth. The domain has considerable economic potential in a number of domains, including computing and telecommunications, medicine and biology, materials, chemistry, energy and the environment.

Nanosciences and nanotechnology can be defined, in a basic manner, as the set of studies and processes involved in the fabrication and manipulation of structures, equipment, and material systems measured in terms of nanometers (nm). In this context, nanoscience is the study of phenomena and the manipulation of phenomena and materials on the atomic, molecular, and macromolecular scales, where physicochemical properties are significantly different from those observed at higher levels. Nanotechnology is the design, characterization, production, and application of structures, equipment, and systems by controlling forms on the nanometric scale.

Despite the relative simplicity and precision of these definitions, the terms "nanoscience" and "nanotechnologies" have several accepted meanings, linked to the transversal nature of this relatively new discipline.

These definitions refer to, and create new possibilities in domains such as optics, biology, mechanics, chemistry, and microtechnology.

The analysis that follows refers to a study of actors in the field of nanotechnologies. It is based on the results obtained by decision assistance tools, without going into the details with regard to their modes of operation.

Interested readers may refer to our research publications where the development and principles of these functions are covered in detail.

We will first consider the main actors in the domain, with the aim of identifying the key actors over the last 4 years. In the same way, we will investigate the existence of classes, their size, and, especially, their structure.

Next, we will identify those journals that are most characteristic of the domain. Finally, we will look at those countries where most work and collaboration in this domain are being carried out.

To do this, we will use the Tétralogie platform for strategic foresight, developed by the Institut de Recherche en Informatique de Toulouse (IRIT) Systèmes d'information Généralisée - Exploration et visualization d'Information (SIG-EVI) team, which allows macroscopic analysis of data on nanotechnologies. Tétralogie's graph creation module, VisuGraph, allows these data to be presented in a more intuitive form, facilitating the analysis of the structure and the evolution of these data.

The plan for this analysis is as follows. First, we will explain the preliminary data processing stage used to obtain the co-occurrence matrices from the textual data found in a database. Next, we will present a detailed breakdown of each step of the analysis. In conclusion, we will provide an assessment of the analysis of nanotechnologies.

2.3.1. *Preliminary data*

The data used for this analysis are taken from the Pascal database (see http://web5s.silverplatter.com/webspirs/start.ws?customer=tlseups3&language=fr&databas es=S(PASC)). The body of the material to be analyzed is made up of papers relating to the domain of nanotechnologies.

Once these documents have been retrieved, they are concatenated to form a single corpus of material in the form of a single text file. This text file is tagged to allow users to distinguish between and extract different types of data found in the file.

The bibliography of the Pascal database may be unpacked using either long or short tags.

In the first case, the tags are often made up of several words (e.g. CONFERENCE OR MEETING INFORMATION): this is a hindrance for the analyst and adds unnecessary additional weight to the corpus.

In the second case, it is no longer possible to differentiate between DESCRIBERS and IDENTIFIERS in English, French, and Spanish, a fact that poses problems for the processing of these fields. For this reason, we use a reformatting program written in Perl (Figure 2.4).

```
#!/usr/bin/perl -w
# <fich_In> : sera en general le dictionnaire.
# <fich_out>: nouveau dictionnaire.

unless (@ARGV == 2) { die "usage : $0  <fich_In> <fich_out> \n";}

open(IN, "$ARGV[0]");
open(OUT, ">$ARGV[1]");
#!/usr/local/bin/perl -w
# <fich_In> : sera en general le dictionnaire.
# <fich_out>: nouveau dictionnaire.

while ($_ = <IN>) {
   s/Notice /NO: /g;
   s/TITLE: /TI: /g;
   s/TRANSLATED TI: /TT: /g;
   s/PERSONAL AUTHOR: /AU: /g;
   s/AFFILIATION OF AUTHOR: /OR: /g;
   s/SOURCE \(BIBLIOGRAPHIC CITATION\): /SO: /g;
   s/CONFERENCE OR MEETING INFORMATION: /CF: /g;
   s/PUBLICATION YEAR: /DP: /g;
   s/COUNTRY OF PUBLICATION: /PA: /g;
   s/ABSTRACT: /AB: /g;
   s/ABSTRACT INDICATOR: /AI: /g;
   s/DESCRIPTORS ENGLISH: /DA: /g;
   s/DESCRIPTORS FRENCH: /DF: /g;
   s/DESCRIPTORS SPANISH: /DE: /g;
   s/IDENTIFIERS ENGLISH: /IA: /g;
   s/IDENTIFIERS FRENCH: /IF: /g;
   s/IDENTIFIERS SPANISH: /IE: /g;
   s/JOURNAL NAME: /JN: /g;
   s/LANGUAGE: /LA: /g;
   s/LANGUAGE OF AUTHOR SUMMARY: /LS: /g;
   s/BIBLIOGRAPHIC LEVEL: /BL: /g;
   s/LITERATURE TYPE: /DT: /g;
   s/MODE OR NATURE OF CONTENT TYPE: /CT: /g;
   s/NUMBER OF REFERENCES: /NR: /g;
   s/CLASSIFICATION CODES: /CC: /g;
   s/LOCATION OF PRIMARY DOCUMENT: /LD: /g;
   s/ACCESSION NUMBER: /AN: /g;
   s/SOURCE OF INDEXING: /SI: /g;
   s/COPYRIGHT: /CR: /g;
   s/ISSN: /IS: /g;
   s/LITERATURE TYPE: /PT: /g;
   s/ISBN: /IB: /g;
   s/PUBLISHER: /PU: /g;
   s/CODEN: /CD: /g;
   s/Full Text: /FT: /g;
   s/Links to Library Holdings: /LL: /g;

   print OUT $_;
}
print "\n******* Fin *******\n";
close(IN);
close(OUT);
```

Figure 2.4. *Reformatting the Pascal database in Perl*

This process has another advantage in that it allows us to assign standard names to certain common tags, allowing Pascal to be used in multibase analyses (fusion of databases such as SCI, Current Contents, Medline, Biosis, Francis, and Chemical Abstract).

To check the homogeneity of the corpus, we will enumerate, for each tag, the number of notices in which the tag is present. Thus, if a tag is found infrequently, we know that the information it contains is not sufficient for use in a reliable statistical study.

To do this, a filter is created to keep only those tags found in the corpus in its target format obtained after reformatting: TI:, AU:, AD:, SO:, NO:, ..., DE:, DF:,... and so on.

Once this filter has been established, we define specific metadata (Figure 2.5) to run the automatic tag counter. The file that corresponds to the metadata indicates a single tag, which is found at the beginning of each entry (the NO: tag). The names of other tags are considered to be attributes of this tag. The filter allows us to keep only that which concerns the tags. If a tag occurs several times in an entry, as in the Medline database, it is only counted once.

```
NO:
# descripteurs des champs de la base Pascal-CNRS #
# nom          abrev   champ   visible Separateurs  #
Notice         NO      NO:     True    b"\n"
FIN            FIN     FIN     FIN       "
```

Figure 2.5. *Specific metadata allowing tag counting*

From the "results" file, we can create a histogram showing those tags that occur most frequently.

From Figure 2.6, we can easily pick out those tags that occur most often: DP:, SO:, TI:, AU:, and so on. In our analysis, we will pay particular attention to authors (AU:), to heir origins (organizations, towns, countries, shown by the OR: tag), and to dates (DP:); this information is almost always present in the entries. Other fields, somewhat less frequent, such as English keywords (DE:), journals (JN:), and conferences and meetings (CF:) may also be very useful, but in processing them we must neglect certain documents.

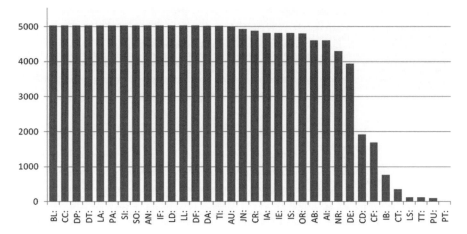

Figure 2.6. *Histogram showing the number of appearances of each tag in the corpus*

A second problem concerns the "cleaning" of some data fields, which are not important for our purposes. In the Pascal database, the "Author" field may be polluted by "parasite" information concerning editors, preface authors, directors, or translators (see Figure 2.7). This information, while useful in gaining a picture of particular social networks, is a hindrance when trying to identify research teams and their interactions. A filter may be used in this case to remove superfluous information. It is also possible to look only at this information or at the links between these individuals and the authors. To do this, we would create a virtual additional field to process these additional data.

After this "cleaning" stage, we must create a dictionary of items contained in each field and look for possible equivalences. Tétralogie includes a module for the automatic detection of synonymy (equivalence between terms) using several comparison algorithms. Manual validation is sometimes necessary, particularly for the names of authors of Asian origin, for names of organizations, or for certain keywords.

Figure 2.8 is an extract from the automatically generated synonymy file for the "Author" field. In this extract, we note that a false synonym has been created for the author ARNOLD-KLAUS and that the form ARNOLD-K is ambiguous, having two possible equivalents. The two synonymies to ARNOLD-KATHARINA must therefore be removed. Those for author AVOURIS-PHAEDON, however, seem to be perfectly correct (as do all the others).

```
NO: 1 de 5033 dans Pascal 2008/01-2008/07

TI:  Electrophoretic deposition : From traditional ceramics to nanotechnology. Developments in
Ceramic Sience and Engineering: The last 50 years.
AU:  CORNI-Ilaria; RYAN-Mary-P; BOCCACCINI-Aldo-R; EDIRISINGHE-Mohan, ed
OR:  Department of Materials, Imperial College London, Prince Consort Road, London SW7 2BP,
United Kingdom; Chair of Biomaterials, University College London, Department of Mechanical
Engineering, Torrington Place, London WC1E 7JE, United Kingdom
CF:  *Developments in Ceramic Sience and Engineering: The last 50 years. Meeting, *London United
Kingdom, *2008-04-10
SO:  Journal-of-the-European-Ceramic-Society. 2008; 28 (7) : 1353-1367
IS:  0955-2219
DP:  2008
PA:  United-Kingdom
LA:  English
BL:  Analytic
DT:  Serial; *Conference-Meeting
AB:  Electrophoretic deposition (EPD) is attracting increasing interest as a materials processing
technique for a wide range of technical applications. This technique enables the production of
unique microstructures and nanostructures as well as novel and complex material combinations in a
variety of macroscopic shapes, dimensions and arrangements starting from micron-sized or
nanosized particles. This review presents a comprehensive of relevant recent work on EPD
describing the application of the technique in the processing of several traditional and advanced
materials (functional and structural ceramic coatings, composite and porous materials, laminated
ceramics, functionally graded materials, thin films and nanostructured materials), with the
intention to highlight how EPD evolved from being a technique restricted only to traditional
ceramics to become an important tool in advanced materials processing and nanotechnology.
Moreover the fundamental EPD mechanisms and novel theories proposed to clarify the processes
involved are explained.
AI:  AB
NR:  195 ref.
CC:  001D08B04A; 001B80A05Z
DA:  Review-; Ceramic-materials; Technical-ceramics; Manufacturing-; Electrophoretic-deposition;
Nanotechnology-; Film-; Composite-material; Particle-suspension; Electroceramics-;
Structural-ceramic; Ceramic-coating; Porous-material; Scanning-electron-microscopy
DF:  Article-synthese; Ceramique-; Ceramique-technique; Fabrication-; Depot-electrophoretique;
Nanotechnologie-; Film-; Materiau-composite; Suspension-particule; Ceramique-electronique;
Ceramique-thermomecanique; Revetement-ceramique; Materiau-poreux;
Microscopie-electronique-balayage; 8105M-
DE:  Articulo-sintesis; Ceramica-; Ceramica-tecnica; Fabricacion-; Deposito-electroforetico;
Nanotecnologia-; Pelicula-; Material-compuesto; Suspension-particula; Ceramica-electronica;
Ceramica-termomecanica; Revestimiento-ceramico; Material-poroso; Microscopia-electronica-barrido
IA:  Ceramics-; Materials-science; Chemistry-; Applied-sciences; Materials-science; Physics-
IF:  Ceramique-; Science-des-materiaux; Chimie-; Sciences-appliquees; Science-des-materiaux;
Physique-
IE:  Ceramica-; Ciencia-de-los-materiales; Quimica-; Ciencias-aplicadas;
Ciencia-de-los-materiales; Fisica-
JN:  Journal-of-the-European-Ceramic-Society
LD:  INIST, Shelf number 21153, INIST No. 354000183351590050
AN:  080339012
SI:  INIST
CR:  <Copyright> 2008 INIST-CNRS. All rights reserved.
LL:  <img src=http://linksource.ebsco.com/images/LS.gif border=0>
http://linksource.ebsco.com/ls.AEA9986E-DF54-4CE2-929A-20BA0B17BAE6.true/linking.aspx?sid=SP:PASC
```

Figure 2.7. *Extract from an entry in the reformatted database*

AMIJI-MANSOOR	AMIJI-MANSOOR-M
ARMSTRONG-M	ARMSTRONG-MARK
ARNOLD-KLAUS	*ARNOLD-KATHARINA*
ARNOLD-K	*ARNOLD-KATHARINA*
ARSCOTT-S	ARSCOTT-STEVE
ATWATER-HARRY	ATWATER-HARRY-A
AUTH-C	AUTH-CHIS
AVOURIS-PH	**AVOURIS-PHAEDON**
AVOURIS-P	**AVOURIS-PHAEDON**
BACHELOT-R	BACHELOT-RENAUD
BAGLIONI-P	BAGLIONI-PIERO

Figure 2.8. *Extract from the author synonymy dictionary*

2.3.2. *Data visualization*

Once the filters and synonymy dictionaries are in place, the data are cross-referenced in the form of co-occurrence matrices. If our analysis is targeted toward the evolution of authors over the last 4 years, we obtain co-occurrence matrices based on cross-referencing the fields "Author X" and "Author X, Time". In this way, we can detect and analyze different structures and identify major players in the domain.

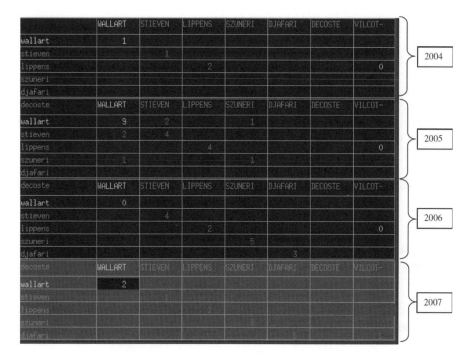

Figure 2.9. *Co-occurrence matrices for authors in the domain of nanotechnologies*

As our study is concerned with the development of nanotechnologies over the last few years, we will cross-reference authors for each of the years being studied to obtain four co-occurrence matrices (one per year), as shown in Figure 2.9.

From these four co-occurrence matrices, we can produce a time graph using the VisuGraph tool. The nodes and connections in this graph represent authors and collaborations between pairs of authors, respectively, collaborations that produced at least one co-publication.

On the development graph, reference points are distributed in a circular manner, like the hours on a clock, following the space–time analogy. Nodes, representing authors, are located in relation to these reference points depending on the period of their activity, that is, we use centroid bodies. Nodes, representing authors, are located in relation to these reference points depending on the period of their activity. We use centroid bodies to specify temporal characteristics. The nodes found closest to a reference point therefore correspond to authors who published their work only in the period under consideration. If a node is situated equidistantly from two reference points, then the author displays the same level of activity over two periods only. Authors in the center of the graph appear throughout the four periods and are therefore permanent contributors to the domain.

The study of the links between authors in each instantiation of the graph allows us to identify all of their collaborations over time. The graph in Figure 2.10 may be seen statically as a connate class showing collaborations at any given moment. If, however, we wish to consider a single period, then many authors will be absent and the graph is no longer connate.

We see, then, that the continuous study of instantiations of the graph produces a conclusion that is completely opposed to that produced by a static study as far as the essential notion of connexity is concerned.

In the case of a static analysis, the graph is seen to be connate, in spite of the fact that it was never connate in the four periods under consideration. This demonstrates the importance not only of the temporal component, but also of ignoring this component on occasion.

The global structure of the graph is already difficult to perceive using a static study; this problem arises in the same way when trying to understand any macroscopic or specific structure (collaboration networks, new arrivals, rapprochements, fusions, breakaways, progressive restructurings, etc.).

Looking at Figure 2.10, we see that teams were essentially present in a single period: they are found in the four corners. Those present over two periods are found in the middle of the sides. Those present over three periods are found between the three relevant reference points, and those present over all 4 years are found in the center of the graph. From this initial breakdown, the graph may be redrawn to make each team easier to read and to facilitate analysis of the internal structure and relationships with other teams.

A morphing algorithm may then be used to animate the graph, with progressive development from one moment to the next. We can, therefore, detect structural changes and interpret their strategic implications.

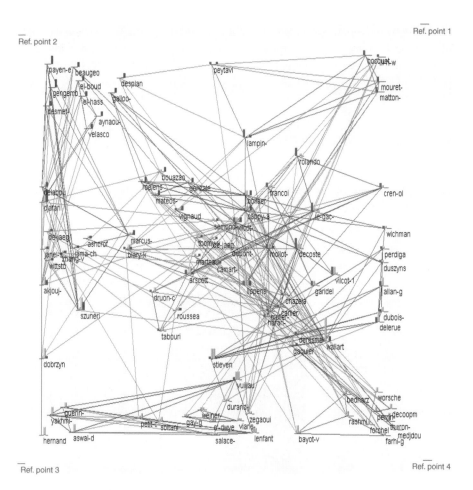

Figure 2.10. *Graph showing evolution of research teams*

Finally, using segmentation, transitive unfolding, and K-core threshold functions, it is possible to either focus on a detail or obtain a simplified view of the global structure.

In addition to Tétralogie and VisuGraph, our team was responsible for the development of a third tool, XPlor, which allows more detailed exploration of structures, updated via a data warehouse concerning relationships. The data warehouse is uploaded to an Internet portal. To add to a macroscopic study of the evolution of the authors, for example, we might extract the *n* best authors over the four periods, the first *n* for a given period, produce a histogram showing their evolution or compare their dynamics. In the same way, we can obtain knowledge of the full environment of their static and dynamic interactions with all the other information presented in the corpus. This tool is very useful when zooming in on targeted data, such as a competing team, a potential partner, new arrivals, leaders in the field, and so on.

To illustrate these capabilities, we have produced Figure 2.11, showing the top 20 authors in the static case, and Figure 2.12, showing the top 20 authors in dynamic mode.

Using the same procedure, we might study which countries produce the most work in the domain of nanotechnologies or which countries show the most interest in one particular application of nanotechnology.

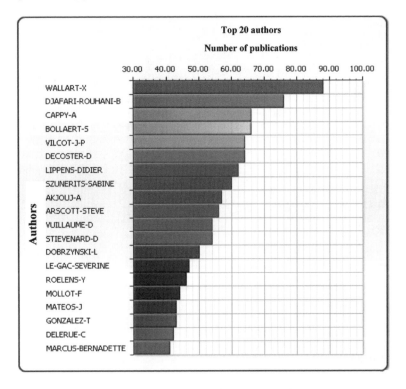

Figure 2.11. *Histogram showing top authors*

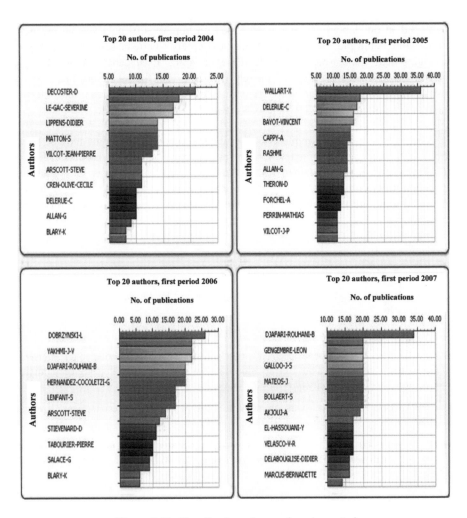

Figure 2.12. *Visualization of top authors by period*

2.4. Conclusion

We have seen that the results produced by our three tools were obtained using different, but complementary, approaches. Tétralogie was used to prepare data (reformatting, synonymies, filtering, and cross-referencing) and for global analysis (macroanalysis). VisuGraph allowed us to look at the relationship aspects of the data and to study its development, specifically in terms of author networks. XPlor made it easier to look at data in depth (targeted microanalysis), providing all the information needed to validate the knowledge we discovered. This set of tools, developed in our laboratory, has been tested on hundreds of data sets (using both single and multiple databases) from extremely varied sources, including bibliographical databases, patent databases (Uspto, Esc@cenet, Wipo, Google patents, Patents.com, Derwent, Wpil, etc.), directories (for medicine, pharmacies, businesses, etc.), Webpages, Weblogs, streaming and press databases, and latterly, databases in Unicode UTF-8 (Chinese, Korean, Japanese, Arabic, etc.).

As the tools used are completely generic, all forms of textual data may be used, after a very short period of adaptation, to support decision making by the revelation of implicit knowledge contained within the data. Work is underway to extend this extraction process to other, non-textual sources (audio, video, films, images, genes, encrypted data, etc.); conclusive tests have already been carried out on .mp3 files and animated films.

2.5. Bibliography

[BES 96] BESSON B., POSSIN J.C., *Du Renseignement à l'intelligence économique*, Dunod, Paris, 1996.

[BES 98] BESSON B., POSSIN J.C., *L'audit de l'intelligence économique*, Dunod, Paris, 1998.

[BOU 04] BOUAKA N., Développement d'un modèle pour l'explication d'un problème décisionnel: un outil d'aide à la décision dans un contexte d'intelligence économique, Doctoral Thesis, University of Nancy 2, Nancy, 2004.

[COL 97] COLLETIS G., "IE: vers un nouveau concept en analyse économique?", *Revue d'intelligence économique*, no. 1, 1997.

[GOT 92] GOTTHARD W., LOCKEMANN P., NEUFELD A., "System-guided integration for object-oriented databases", *IEEE Transactions on Knowledge and Data Engineering*, pp. 1–22, 1992.

[GUI 03] GUILHON A., MANNI C., "L'intelligence économique comme processus de création de savoir: le cas de Mecaplast", in GUILHON B., LEVET J.L., *De l'intelligence économique à l'économie de la connaissance*, Economica, Paris, 2003.

[JUI 05] JUILLET A., *Commission nationale consultative de la formation de l'IE, référentiel de formation en intelligence économique*, SGDN, Paris, 2005.

[LEV 96] LEVET J.L., PATUREL R., L'intégration de la démarche d'IE dans le management stratégique, Acte de l'Association Internationale de Management Stratégique, Lille, 1996.

[LEV 01] LEVET J.L., *IE: mode de pensée, mode d'action*, Economica, Paris, 2001.

[MAR 95] MARTINET B., MARTI P., *L'IE: comment donner de la valeur concurrentielle à l'information*, Editions d'Organisation, Paris, 1995.

[MAR 94] MARTRE H., *IE et stratégie des entreprises, Œuvre Collective du Commissariat au Plan*, La Documentation Française, Paris, 1994.

[OUB 05] OUBRICH M., La création des connaissances dans un processus d'IE, Doctoral Thesis, University of the Mediterranean, Aix-Marseille II, Marseille, 2005.

[PAT 98] PATUREL R., "Panorama général et synthétique des thèses françaises en management stratégique", *Actes des XIV journées des IAE Nantes,* France, pp. 37, 15–16 Mai 1998.

[RED 94] REDDY M.P., PRASAD B., "A methodology for integration of heterogeneous databases", *IEEE Transactions on Knowledge and Data Engineering*, vol. 6, no. 6, pp. 920–933, 1994.

[REV 98] REVELLI C., *Intelligence stratégique sur Internet, comment développer efficacement des activités de veille et de recherche sur les réseaux*, Dunod, Paris, 1998.

[SAL 00] SALLES M., CLERMONT P., DOUSSET B., "Une méthode de conception de système d'IE", *Presentation at the IDMME'2000 Conference*, Montréal, Canada, 2000.

[VAS 99] VASCONCELOS C.R.M., L'intelligence économique et la stratégie de développement de la PME, Doctoral Thesis, University of Grenoble 2, Grenoble, 1999.

[WIL 67] WILENSKY H., *Organizational Intelligence: Knowledge and Policy in Government and Industry*, Basic Books, New York, 1967.

Chapter 3

The Synergy of Knowledge Management and Competitive Intelligence

3.1. Introduction

The capitalization of knowledge is an essential condition to ensure the growth of organizations and their continued viability. It cannot be separated from human agents. Knowledge of individuals or groups of individuals and of their actions constitutes a precious resource, a resource that should be preserved to optimize the realization of organizational aims. These aims are often manifested in the form of decision-making problems. Decision making starts with the adoption or construction of a decision strategy, followed by controlled progress until the decision is made. It is therefore essential for any organization, institution, or government to define and attain strategic means of reinforcing the decision process. This work aims to design and develop user-centered methods for knowledge management (KM) to assist in tactical and strategic decisions concerning processes in organizations.

Competitive intelligence (CI) emerged as a specialized domain offering tactical and strategic processes for decision making. In this context, the approach of facilitating decision making differs from the conception of shared decision support systems (DSS). Most DSS focus heavily on the technological dimension. Furthermore, CI aims to facilitate decision making by recognizing the fact that automated products can be used as a complement to human intervention. In the context of CI, an efficient decision process is the product of coordinated action between human actors. The process also concerns the activities involved in

Chapter written by Bolanle OLADEJO and Adenike O. OSOFISAN.

obtaining relevant and validated information to satisfy the needs of the organization. Precious resources, both human and material, are involved in the process of facilitating strategic decision making. For example, the competences of an actor responsible for the analysis and structuring of a decision-making problem, or of the person responsible for research, are human resources. Material resources may take the form of documents, information, and so on. These resources act as triggers in attaining organizational goals, and more specifically in obtaining an advantage over competitors. Consequently, material resources should be stored to capitalize and use them in resolving future problems. This requirement falls into the domain of KM.

Knowledge is defined as an indispensable resource in acquiring advantages in terms of competition and innovation. Publications in this domain [POH 00, MIL 02] distinguish between data and information. As information is essential to the operation of the organization, so knowledge is also an important economic asset for organizational productivity. This statement is justified by the use of information in research and development (R&D), in industry, and so on. Effective information use of this kind is made possible by applying KM methods. A system must be put into place for the organization, conservation, and transmission of existing knowledge, whether factual or implicit, and it is vital to anticipate needs in terms of new knowledge. Consequently, KM strategies are essential in the context of CI. These two notions are linked in the matter of processing information and knowledge.

3.2. Theoretical context

We will provide a brief overview of our field of research over the following sections.

3.2.1. *Definitions of knowledge*

Several definitions of knowledge may be found in published literature on the subject. From a philosophical viewpoint, knowledge is defined as a justified, true belief. However, belief is defined as a mental attitude or a state of mind, personal conviction, or acceptance of a particular fact or idea. Most contemporary philosophers instead use the term "propositional belief". Belief may not be considered to be knowledge simply because it concerns a decision [EDW 06]. Moreover, Blackburn [BLA 99] suggests that no form of belief may be considered to be knowledge. Thus, in epistemology, it is defined as a perception or observation of an object or event, or as experience exercising a particular activity. Knowledge is seen as a form of capital that has an economic value and constitutes a resource of strategic importance in increasing productivity [MAT 02]. In [STA 89], Stata describes knowledge as the main source of wealth in industry and traditional sectors of the economy. We will conclude by noting that knowledge refers to the meaning transmitted when information is placed into context, with reference to the environment or associated events. Different types of knowledge exist, which have an impact on the method necessary for capitalization.

3.2.1.1. *Types of knowledge*

Knowledge can be broken down into classes, whether explicit or tacit or theoretical and practical [NON 95]. Explicit knowledge may be expressed in the form of a theoretical or practical experiment. It may be transmitted easily, formally, and systematically, via individuals. Tacit knowledge, on the other hand, is a form of personal competence and is difficult to formalize or share with other actors. Tacit knowledge needs to be transformed into explicit knowledge, rendering it representable and useable in a KM system.

3.2.2. Competitive intelligence

The decision-making process involves three kinds of images: values, aims, and plans. The image of value is a representation by decision makers (or DMs, economic actors who initiate decision problems (DPs)) of beliefs, values, and opinions on what is appropriate. The aim image is a representation of the DM's vision of what should be attained. The plan image is a representation of actions and results [DAV 03]. CI provides a platform for the integration of these DM images to provide a basis for the resolution of DPs.

Information is required at different stages of a decision process in a company or community to develop and implement a coherent strategy and the tactics necessary to attain objectives set by the business, with the aim of improving the position of the company in relation to its competitors. CI emerged as a process to fulfill these needs. At single-company level, CI may be defined as the capacity of the DM to make good use of new knowledge and experiences, while reusing existing knowledge and experience, to resolve a DP as successfully as possible [KIS 02]. It is "the set of coordinated research actions, processing actions and the distribution of information to economic actors in the aim of using this information. These various actions are carried out legally, with all necessary guarantees to protect the capital of the company, within the best time and cost conditions" [MAR 94]. CI seeks to develop methods for the identification of relevant sources, analysis, collection, and use of information to respond to the needs of users in making decisions. There are four main types of actors involved in the process:

– The *DM* formulates an exact description of the DP.

– The *watcher* localizes, supervises, validates, and specifies the strategic information needed to solve the problem.

– The *information systems analyst* analyzes the information gathering process to understand its impact on company or institutional strategy.

– The *project coordinator* acts as a link between the DM(s) and other actors [KNA 07].

All actors cooperate to optimize the sharing of strategic knowledge. The CI process is a systematic approach in which seven steps are taken to solve a DP. [BOU 04a], following [BOU 04b], it includes the phases presented in Figure 3.1.

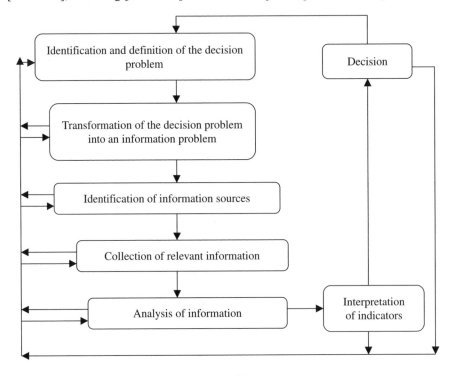

Figure 3.1. *CI process*

Each step in the process may be traced back to the validation phase. What follows is a list of some existing models for the representation of knowledge in relation to the CI process:

– the Model for Explicit Definition of Decision Problem (MEDP) [BOU 04b];

– the Watcher's Information Search Problem (WISP) model [KIS 07];

– the Model for Information Retrieval query Annotations Based on Expression (MIRABEL) [GOR 06];

– the Model for Representation of Information Search Problem in Economic Intelligence (MORPRI^{2}E) [AFO 07];

– the Annotation Model for Information Exchange (AMIE) [ROB 07];

– the Representation of User's needs at the time of Interrogation of Information system (RUBICUBE) model [PEG 06];

– the Specification of the Competence of the Coordinator of Regional EI (CADRIE) model [KNA 07].

The first phase of the CI process involves the definition of a DP and the analysis of its context in terms of internal and external environmental factors that impact upon the organization. The DM (or manager) applies the MEDP model in defining the DP. Their profile and the internal and external environment of the organization are then analyzed. Consequently, stakes are expressed and hypotheses formulated, showing risks or threats (things that stand to be gained or lost) in relation to the DP. MIRABEL is applied to validate the activity so that the project coordinator, DM, and watcher can check concepts while connecting them to laws or theorems to clarify the supposed stakes. Hypotheses are examined to confirm the elements to which they correspond according to the context of the organization. This provides the watcher with a better understanding of the information needs of the DM (by applying the WISP model). The DP is transformed into a precise and sufficient information problem that assists in identifying the most relevant sources of information. The watcher, in collaboration with the information systems analyst, begins a process of research, collection, and analysis of information. The MORPRI^{2}E assists in the acquisition of relevant information according to the context of the demand. The AMIE model facilitates traceability using annotations made by the actors (editors/commentators) linked to a piece of information. The project coordinator and the DM(s) validate results and information indicators in relation to the DP before any decision is made. Knowledge capitalization (KC) is required for all actors during all phases of the CI process.

Models for CI are proposed separately. To exploit the experiences and results gained from past DPs, we must integrate and represent these models. We will consider the KM approach in CI as being based on the roles of actors in the CI process.

3.2.3. *KM in CI*

The explicit and tacit knowledge present in an organization must be captured and stored to facilitate access, sharing, and reuse of this knowledge. KM involves all of these activities. Reference is occasionally made to KC, but the two phrases are often used interchangeably. In a subtle way, KC is the major service provided by KM, as stated by Dieng-Kuntz and Matta: "Knowledge Management is a global process in the enterprise, which includes all the processes that allow capitalization, sharing an evolution of the knowledge capital of the firm" [DIE 02].

KM allows us the knowledge present within an organization to be capitalized in a way which permits its reuse in connection with future problems. To be capitalized, knowledge must be stored in databases or repositories often known as "corporate memory" (CM) or "organizational memory". CI requires the integration and reuse of knowledge from past and ongoing projects to help with the strategic decision-making process. The application of KM principles and techniques to CI, in this research, prevent the loss of individual or collectively acquired knowledge. Throughout all phases of the CI process, such knowledge, by its acquisition, organization, integration, and preservation, may be used, reused, and distributed to different economic actors, such as DMs, research specialists (watchers), or project coordinators.

KM has been applied in several domains of activity, of which we will consider a number of examples in the following section.

3.2.3.1. A generic model for CM: application to industrial systems

Admane suggests that industrial activities should be represented in the form of "cases", producing reusable resources with roles dependent on the context, considered with assistance from models to allow KC within a context of systematic reuse. The aim of this project is to assist the designers of future industrial systems to transform tasks as quickly as possible to contribute to the design phase [ADM 05]. The system model takes into account two types of knowledge: knowledge linked to abilities and themes of knowledge. Knowledge linked to abilities refers simply to the basic capabilities of the company. Themes represent domains of knowledge. The component parts of a theme refer to specifications for product installation and are modeled from graphical and textual descriptions. The name of the CM model is ReCaRo (Resource Cases and Roles): it has a multiple-memory architecture containing sets of five memories. The model was validated by use in a renovation, maintenance, and extension project in a hydrocarbon transport network. All experiments carried out and all the knowledge acquired throughout the different phases of the project were capitalized.

Organizational memory is a set of models and resources, used in the form of a set of databases. The reuse principle is based on the collection (inventory) and classification of roles and resources. As mentioned above, KM deals with both tacit and explicit knowledge. We acknowledge that this work is limited as it only covers the acquisition of explicit knowledge, that is, knowledge concerning industrial products and processes. It does not take the tacit knowledge of employees of the organization involved in the project into account. However, the use of case-based reasoning (CBR) techniques facilitates the organization of saved solutions and simplifies access to the required knowledge.

3.2.3.2. *KC in an equipment repair and diagnostics system*

The aim of this system was to create a specialized CM for maintenance services [CHE 05]. A model was developed by Grundstein [GRU 94] to describe the KC cycle for a given application, as illustrated in Figure 3.2. The cycle shows the four phases applied for an e-maintenance system according to Brigitte *et al.*:

– Information detection: the practices of maintenance experts in repair and diagnosis in industrial zones were observed. Observation was combined with an analysis of the maintenance process presented in [RAS 04].

– Classification of knowledge: the design of a system of this kind demanded the application of appropriate tools for modeling knowledge.

– KC: capitalization was carried out based on a maintenance platform developed by project partners specializing in information technology. The platform was used as a medium for the diffusion of information. Web services were developed to take the acquisition of knowledge into account depending on the expertise considered.

– Knowledge update: this step was carried out using a CBR method. Access to the diagnostic service was opened up to all maintenance actors. Modifications that might be carried out on this knowledge were validated using the authority of experts, designated by theme.

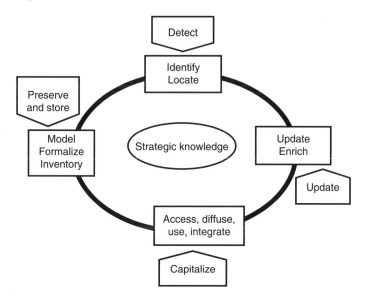

Figure 3.2. *KC cycle [GRU 94]*

The system is modeled by a Web portal architecture, assisted by a CBR tool. The CBR module uses Belfort's site ontology in addition to the generic maintenance ontology. A new problem was processed from saved cases, chosen following criteria of similarity with the problem considered. The solution suggested by these saved cases was adapted (or reused) based on the new situation and tested to increase its chance of success.

This approach is similar to our proposals as it also uses a CBR system in the context of a working memory destined for cooperative use. The evaluation and evolution of CM based on the reuse of knowledge were not included in this system.

3.2.3.3. *Knowledge acquisition and modeling for CM: lessons learned*

This project was put to use in the field of metallurgy, with a focus on characteristics of knowledge reuse from capitalization systems. This knowledge reuse supplied general methods, tools, and techniques [SIM 96]. It permitted storage and reuse of knowledge and abilities within the company concerning descriptions of steel production and metallurgical problems arising during this production. The technique chosen for use was CBR. The first phase of work involved the creation of common synthesis documents covering all geographical sites of the company. The uniform format used in these documents allowed the development of a communication medium for the group of experts involved. The second phase focused on the use and diffusion of the set of models of synthesis documents for the implementation of the CM of the information system. The author proposed a general system architecture that supports representations of CM to allow reuse of capitalized information based on the fact that the architecture establishes a set of general constraints induced by all capitalization systems according to [CAU 95].

3.2.3.4. *Software engineering for KC using CBR: case structure*

The main task carried out involved the capitalization of experience created by software engineering projects through the construction of CBR systems. The main case study used was named "intelligent computer-aided design for information systems" (*Conception intelligente assistée par ordinateur de systèmes d'information*) [NGA 04]. The authors specified two types of knowledge: knowledge of software artifacts and knowledge of the development process. The artifacts represent information and models generated during the development of a given program, including all steps of the software development project and knowledge relating to bridging activities. The knowledge considered was essentially explicit in nature. The case structure used to represent and store knowledge for a project was developed using a software life-cycle model [BOU 01]. The case structure was modeled in the form of a relational, hierarchical, and object-oriented database. The authors simply improved the representation of knowledge produced during different steps of the design process. Other knowledge concerning the exploitation and evaluation of software, also linked to the problem of KC, was not processed. Thus, the authors focused on the technological dimension alone; however, KM also involves social and cultural aspects linked to the final users of the product, the information system or the design system.

3.2.3.5. *Information security systems and KM*

Belsis *et al.* [BEL 05] focus on the identification of certain dimensions: types and sources of knowledge inherent to activities associated with an information security system as a basis for the development of a specialized KM system. The authors discuss factors of motivation affecting KM needs associated with the security of an information system. They propose a model for illustrating the knowledge structure of an information security system. This model describes explicit knowledge in the form of security policy and instructions. The developers of the model refer to the introduction of broad guidelines to assist staff in making decisions affecting the security system. In addition, steps taken later on indicate the security strategies of members of the organization. The third component of the model concerns "measures", that is, specific actions required for the installation of the information system. The model also covers risk analysis for the implementation of the system. The knowledge identification and acquisition method is based on person-to-person contact or on expert opinions. The authors also propose a "knowledge-capture" function for the documentation and analysis of knowledge in case of incidents, but which does not disturb the work of security experts.

In conclusion, this model offers less improvement in terms of knowledge sharing and exploitation techniques among the employees considered. Moreover, the project only covers a very specific domain of KM, that of information security.

3.2.3.6. *Business process modeling through KM*

In this section, we will provide an overview of a research project considering the role of business process modeling (BPM) as a KM tool [KAL 06]. This project fits into the context of the broader issue of accounting for and understanding an increasingly complex environment, with mounting national and international competition, where the rapid development of technology often means that growth is proportional to the demands made by a company's current and potential future clients.

Another important reason that justifies interest in BPM concerns the considerable potential advantages an organization stands to gain from the explanation and formalization of its knowledge and abilities to exploit, communicate, and/or locate this knowledge more effectively. BPM involves the description of business processes (all relevant processes involved in the creation of added value), which constitute a base of available and potentially exploitable knowledge throughout the production system of the business in question. Authors who have worked on this question affirm that BPM may be considered a KM tool, as it allows tacit knowledge to be identified and converted into explicit knowledge throughout the process. Their approach focuses on the creation of networks of concepts, in which BPM concepts are categorized and linked to other concepts relating to the life cycle of products and services associated with the Business Process (BP). BPM concepts are categorized by activity and "behavior models".

These researchers developed a theoretical framework to illustrate how BPMs capture and allow sharing of knowledge associated with business processes. They propose a model for a KM process, which relates to the externalization and internalization of knowledge of two participants in a process (tacit knowledge); this is then transformed into artifacts (explicit knowledge). They also highlight the impact of culturally shared knowledge (e.g. knowledge shared by a community) for the understanding or interpretation of a formal process model. This research work recognizes the capitalization of technology knowledge concerning and takes account of social and cultural questions. However, the scope of the written work concerning this research is limited to business processes and the fact of making explicit knowledge available. For the moment, no evaluation of exploitation seems to have been taken into account.

3.2.3.7. *KM: planning for the future*

In this section, we will consider [RAN 06], which highlights the necessity of protecting knowledge in KM systems. The author of the work defends the idea that knowledge acquired in the KM system should include security measures and policies that allow access to and use of this knowledge to be controlled. He makes a distinction between the security of knowledge and data security and considers that knowledge is dynamic in nature and that a demand is non-deterministic.

Based on this idea, the author proposes an implementation of security levels for different identified types of organizational knowledge. The functions proposed for all secure KM systems are as follows:

– creation or reinforcement of trust among organization personnel, creating a culture of knowledge sharing;

– protection of main knowledge assets;

– monitoring knowledge transfer;

– eliminating risks of imitation by competitors.

This structure focuses on technical aspects (artifacts) to best identify the most appropriate knowledge and its source(s). For example, knowledge linked to the evolution and use of a document belonging to the organization may be protected by artifacts such as a secure connection, verification of the information involved, and so on.

In the case of moderators in discussion forums, these artifacts may take the form of time stamps and identification of authors of sources of annotations, and so on.

This research work focuses essentially on the security of KM systems rather than on their implementation.

3.2.3.8. *KM in industry and government: security versus sharing*

Zannes [ZAN 00] discusses the security requirements of an organization in relation to knowledge assets. The author picks up on the reluctance of government agencies and national laboratories to install KM systems, for fear of the risks involved in knowledge sharing. It highlights the following points associated with organizational security:

– use of copyrights in digital products or other documents in the industrial publication process;

– installation of KM systems for secure networks;

– use of secure ID cards for internet access and distance knowledge sharing;

– long-distance maintenance of Web sites and databases, that is, from outside the organization.

In the conclusion, Zannes [ZAN 00] recommends that trust in the tool and in individuals should be estimated when sharing knowledge. This work highlights a major demand concerning the installation of KM systems. However, it does not go into detail concerning the stages of planning and development of such a system.

3.2.3.9. *KC in research and design projects: an integrated and diversified approach*

Simon [SIM 03] is concerned with KC methodology and considers lessons learned from the observation of design projects in a multinational company to formulate a theory regarding the impact of social and organizational factors on KC in this context. The author looks at different dimensions of knowledge, such as its social, organizational, and cognitive aspects. The work includes an analysis of the diversification of dimensions of knowledge in KC practices.

To do this, the author took the general methodology for management of systematically assembled and analyzed data set out in [STR 94] as a base. The approach was based on the iterative analysis of data produced by case studies (supported by opinions from the research and study office) and may be used in conjunction with the theory of CBR described in [EIS 89].

This study aims to evaluate different KC methods used in R&D projects and the factors that affect KC practices.

3.2.3.10. *Overview: classification of works*

The publications described above may be split into three distinct categories: methodologies, applications, and principles of KM.

Methodologies refer to the structure and organization of knowledge and knowledge transmission during the different stages and tasks involved in KC.

KM principles concern characteristics (or functions) recommended for the development or implementation of KM systems.

Applications refer to KM systems developed for specific domains. Tables 3.1, 3.2, and 3.3 provide a synthetic presentation of these three categories.

Evaluation criteria / Author	User-oriented	Adaptability to different domains	Dating	Feedback on reused knowledge
[DAV 98]	*[1]	*	-[2]	-
[DIE 98]	*	*	-	*
[ALA 97]	-	*	-	-
[HOL 02]	-	*	-	-

[1] * signifies positive

[2] - signifies negative

Table 3.1. *Evaluation of KM methodologies*

3.2.3.11. *Evaluation criteria for methodologies*

– User oriented: this indicates whether or not the needs of users guide the main aims and operations of the KM system.

– Adaptability to different domains: criterion for flexibility of the structure of the KM system enabling application in other domains.

– Dating: this indicates whether or not the system attaches dates to knowledge, introducing temporal contextualization.

– Feedback on reused knowledge: indication concerning the evaluation of relevance of knowledge used, guaranteeing the evolution of the KM system.

3.2.3.12. *Application evaluation criteria*

The following list provides a summary of evaluation criteria for KM applications, as described in Table 3.2:

– Specificity of the domain: this represents the application object of the KM system as, for example, its adaptability to other domains.

– Type of knowledge: typology of knowledge identified for capitalization.

– Main technological focus: this shows the high dependence of the system on the technological infrastructure and on techniques involving little or no human intervention.

– Socioeconomic target: economic orientation of the KM system.

– Respecting and adapting to the culture of the domain: involvement of rules, languages, and standards present in an organization or group of individuals.

– Level of socialization: the weight of human interaction in the explanation, acquisition, and sharing of knowledge.

– Representation and exploitation of temporal attributes: integration of spatiotemporal data on knowledge managed by the system and reasoning concerning these attributes.

– Evaluation of reused knowledge: evaluation of the relevance of knowledge used while solving a new problem.

– Dynamism: continuous research and recording throughout the new problem and contextualization using a rate of relevance for knowledge used.

Evaluation symbol / Application	1	2	3	4	5	6	7	8	9
Process design	H^3	E	H	M^4	A	H	A	A	L^5
Business experience	H	B	H	M	H	L	A^6	A	L
Business processes	M	E^7	H	L	A	H	A	A	L
Equipment diagnosis	H	B^8	H	M	A	H	A	A	L
Steel process	M	B	H	M	M	H	A	A	L
Software project(s)	H	E	L	L	L	H	A	A	L
Information systems	H	B	H	M	M	M	A	A	L

[3] H → High
[4] M → Moderate
[5] L → Low
[6] A → Absent
[7] E → Explicit knowledge
[8] B → Both Explicit and Tacit knowledge

Table 3.2. *Evaluation of KM systems*

3.2.3.13. *Evaluation criteria based on principles*

The principles of KM are evaluated using the following criteria, as set out in Table 3.3: focus, the main slant chosen by authors; strength, the contribution made by the recommended principles; and limits, other, less developed constraints of the KM system.

Evaluation criteria / Authors	Focus	Strength	Limits
[KAL 06]	Modeling business processes	Formalization of knowledge based on the BMP	Exploitation and evaluation of knowledge
[RAN 06]	Knowledge protection	Security of dimensions and artifacts	Development of KM systems
[ZAN 00]	Knowledge protection	Techniques and examples for securing knowledge	Development of KM systems
[SIM 00]	Expression of KM theory covering social and cultural factors	Evaluation and analysis of case studies	Effect technology

Table 3.3. *Summary of principle-based evaluation*

3.2.3.14. *Summary of evaluation of KM methodologies, principles, and systems*

We note that three particular functions are less developed in existing work on the subject:

– orientation toward use,

– temporal attributes,

– integration of feedback.

These functions would provide the following benefits if used in a capitalization system:

– satisfaction of user needs,

– generation of procedural knowledge for a new problem,

– facilitation of knowledge development through the analysis of feedback from knowledge reuse.

There is a need to identify, acquire, and record all knowledge involved in a CI project and the capabilities of actors. This must be converted to explicit knowledge to allow representation for capitalization. CI models are used to represent the procedural knowledge of actors. These assist in the transformation of tacit knowledge into explicit knowledge. These models must be integrated to form a single model to capture and record knowledge in a decision-problem resolution project. We will apply the principles of KM to capitalize on and date knowledge, thus facilitating the decision-making process. The first stage in this process is to identify and acquire knowledge.

3.3. Knowledge acquisition strategy

Our methods for the acquisition of knowledge generated by a CI project may be classified as follows:

– Studies of CI models: these models represent knowledge concerning the activities of each actor.

– Rendering actor knowledge explicit: observation of activities and interactions of actors.

– Real-time identification of knowledge applied during different phases of the decision-problem resolution process (e.g. the definition of stakes of a DP, specification of a research problem, and information sources).

3.3.1. *Action-based knowledge acquisition*

In this case, the acquisition strategy takes users into account. A DM may, for example, initiate a DP by expressing a problem or an initial demand, its context, the time frame, and so on. Our approach aims to help actors to concentrate exclusively on what is relevant for them at a given moment. Consequently, the provision of information and knowledge suitable for the problem becomes their sole focus. Appendix A shows a process of knowledge acquisition based on the roles of actors, implemented using a prototype knowledge repertoire devoted to CI.

3.4. Formalization of knowledge

Our approach to the formalization of knowledge identified as resources in the context of CI is as follows:

– a structure for KC for CI projects;

– an architecture for the representation of CI knowledge;

– conceptual and relational modeling of knowledge.

3.4.1. *KC structure for CI projects*

Our approach consists of designing an adaptable structure (Figure 3.3) for the capitalization of CI projects. For example, problem domains that require the solution of various management problems may properly be taken into account. The structure acts as a platform for the development of a knowledge repertoire.

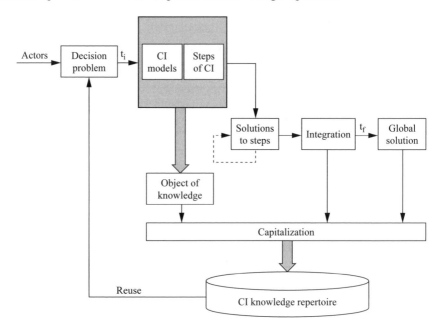

Figure 3.3. *Model for KC in CI projects*

The heterogeneity of existing models is a factor, which must be taken into account and which poses major difficulties in this work. Currently, we must deal with models designed entirely independently, with the exception of the WISP model that includes part of the Model for Explicit Definition of Decision Problem (MEDP) model. However, all models include shared references to economic actors involved in a CI process. Consequently, we suggest that models should be harmonized to facilitate direct acquisition and use of knowledge from a system.

The general structure proposed shows the different components that feed into the capitalization system and the relationships that connect them. Actors present a DP at a given moment. Their problem-solving activities, based on models, are identified and recorded. The solutions produced are also recorded, with reference to the time frame, and integrated into a knowledge repertoire.

The knowledge repertoire, used to represent and organize knowledge, is modeled using a conceptual model that takes account of relationships.

3.4.2. Architecture for KM in CI projects

Figure 3.4 shows a possible architecture for the representation of knowledge in the context of CI. Our approach consists of modeling the above framework from the point of view of the user, to respond to the questions: "who" does "what", "when", "why", and "how". The architecture presents a platform for the presentation of knowledge with timestamps for decisions in a CI decision project. This facilitates the generation of implicit inferences in reasoning concerning temporal properties (marked t for timestamp, and i, l, and f, for the initial, later, and final phases, respectively) of knowledge resources. We will illustrate the application of the architecture to a decision-making problem scenario in Appendix B.

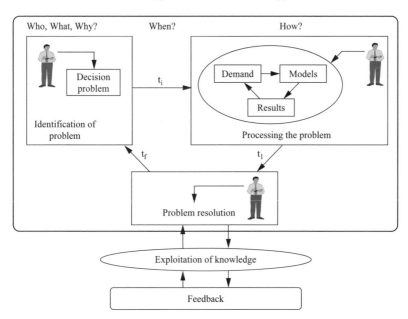

Figure 3.4. *Architecture for a CI knowledge repertoire*

3.4.2.1. *Case study of a DP: moral decadence among young people*

This framework provides a model for KC for case studies. The objects of knowledge of actors in the CI process are identified and acquired using different models. The following scenario provides an example of knowledge objects in the first phase of the CI process.

3.4.2.1.1. Scenario

The DM presents the DP as concerning moral decadence among young people.

– the context of the DP is the education sector in Nigeria;

– understanding the DP: what does the DP mean?;

– the terms or concepts of the DP are defined by the DM as follows:

- morality refers to principles or rules of correct behavior;

- decadence is a state of moral decline;

- moral decadence implies a state of decline or deterioration in conformity to the principles or rules of correct behavior.

Thus, moral decadence among young people implies a state in which adolescents, or the general teaching college, present a decline (reduction) in the respect of rules (authorities) for correct behavior among individuals (of the population).

Definition of the interest of the DP:

– object: moral decadence;

– signals: unauthorized absences, violence, crime, and immorality;

– hypothesis: if moral decadence among young people is not restrained, then there will be:

- a high school dropout rate;

- bad signs for the future leadership of the country;

- a social threat.

The meanings of the DP are thus interpreted by the watcher. The two actors evaluate their individual points of view and finally agree on a specific definition of the DP. Appendix B shows the knowledge objects to harness in relation to the first phase of the CI process. Later, these knowledge objects may be reused in solving another DP.

3.4.2.2. *Action-based knowledge use*

The aggregation of knowledge objects in CI is carried out using a relationship-based modeling schema. This acts as a support for the classification of knowledge objects. Acquired knowledge is presented as elements in the knowledge repertoire. The architecture and the relationship model assist in organizing knowledge objects with the aim of enabling actor-centered exploration of the repertoire. An actor may explore the knowledge repertoire based on his/her role; for example, a DM may have access to stored knowledge on past projects to find knowledge and information on the identification, evolution, and definition of DPs, or on actors. We have developed a prototype, in the form of a knowledge portal, of the client–server environment to validate our research aims. The research mechanism for knowledge use is implemented using the CBR approach and *Explore, Query, Analyze, Annotate* (EQUA^{2}TE). The appearance algorithm is oriented according to the role of the user. Case studies on solving DPs in the sectors of education, economy, and social issues were used to test the developed prototype.

3.5. Conclusion

The resolution of a DP using strategic CI processes, coupled with a KM model linked to the activities and capabilities of actors, should, in our opinion, render organizations more competitive. We have designed and developed KM models to assist the DM in the decision process, whether the decision is tactical or strategic. Our proposed model is user-centered and can be adapted for different types of knowledge resources within the CI process. The architecture is based on a knowledge repertoire, which harmonizes available knowledge linked to a decision project. We thus offer a basis for the acquisition and exploitation of knowledge linked to the CI process, contributing to knowledge reuse tools in terms of availability and accessibility with the aim of accelerating the decision process for economic actors.

3.6. Appendices

3.6.1. *Appendix A: knowledge acquisition based on actor activities*

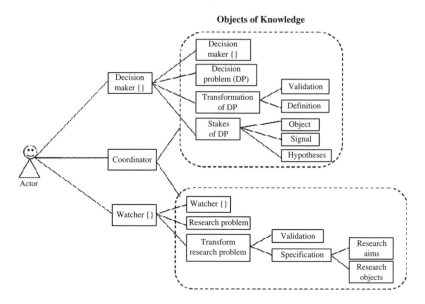

3.6.2. *Appendix B: capitalization scenario in decision making*

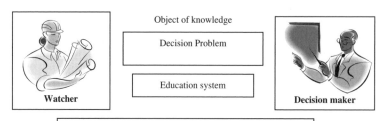

Identify knowledge to capitalize in relation to
- the decision problem
- CI actors.

Decision Problem
The transformation of the decision problem is based on:
- the identification of definition of keywords in the DP
- the relationships between keywords in the context
- the date of the DP.

CI Actors
Information on actors according to profile:
- domain of specialization
- years of experience
- training received, etc.

3.7. Bibliography

[ADM 05] ADMANE L., "A generic model of corporate memory: application to the industrial systems", *IJCAI'2005: Workshop on Knowledge Management and Organizational Memories*, pp. 55–66, 2005.

[AFO 07] AFOLABI B., La conception et l'adaptation de la structure d'un système d'intelligence économique par l'observation des comportements de l'utilisateur, Doctoral Thesis, University of Nancy 2, Nancy, 2007.

[ALA 97] ALAVI M., *One Giant Brain*, Harvard Business School, Boston, MA, 1997.

[BEL 05] BELSIS P., KOKOLAKIS S., KIOUNTOUZIS E., "Information systems security from a knowledge management perspective", *Information Management and Computer Society*, vol. 13, no. 3, pp. 189–202, 2005.

[BLA 99] BLACKBURN S., *Truth: A Guide*, Oxford University Press, Oxford, 1999.

[BOU 01] BOURQUE P., DUPUIS R., ABRAN A., MOORE J., TRIPP L., "The emerging consensus on the software engineering body of knowledge", *SPIN-Ottawa*, Ottawa, Ontario, Canada, p. 51, 18 October 2001.

[BOU 04a] BOUAKA N., DAVID A., "Proposal of a decision-maker problem model for a better understanding of information needs", *Proceedings of International Conference on Information and Communication Technologies: From Theory to Applications*, pp. 551–552, 2004. *IEEE*, pp. 1–5, ISBN: 0-7803-8482-2.

[BOU 04b] BOUAKA N., Développement d'un modèle pour l'explicitation d'un problème décisionnel: un outil d'aide à la décision dans un contexte d'intelligence économique, Doctoral Thesis, University of Nancy 2, Nancy, 2004.

[CAU 95] CAULIER P., HOURIEZ B., "Apports de la modélisation des connaissances et du raisonnement à partir de cas à la capitalisation et la réutilisation de connaissances", *Actes des Journées Acquisition Validation Apprentissage*, Grenoble, France, pp. 331–345, 1995.

[CHE 05] CHEBELMORELLO B., RASOVSKA I., ZERHOUNI N., "Knowledge capitalization in system of equipment diagnosis and repair help", *IJCAI'2005: Workshop on Knowledge Management and Organizational Memories*, pp. 55–66, 2005.

[DAV 98] DAVENPORT T.H., PRUSAK L., *Working Knowledge: How Organizations Manage What They Know*, Harvard Business School Press, Boston, Cambridge, 1998.

[DAV 03] DAVID A., THIERY O., "L'architecture EQuA²te et son application à l'intelligence économique", *ISDM NO 11*, Article No. 98, pp. 1–8, available online at www.isdm.org

[DIE 99] DIENG-KUNTZ R., CORBY O., GIBOIN A., RIBIERE M., "Methods and tools for corporate knowledge management", *International Journal of Human-Computer Studies*, Vol. 51, No. 3, pp. 567–598, 1999. Also in http://ksi.cpsc.ucalgary.ca/KAW/KAW96/KAW98/dieng/

[DIE 02] DIENG-KUNTZ R., MATTA N., *Knowledge Management and Organizational Memories*, Kluwer Academic Publisher, Boston, 2002.

[EDW 06] EDWARD N.Z. (ed.), *The Stanford Encyclopedia of Philosophy*, 2006, available online at http://plato.stanford.edu/entries/epistemology/.

[EIS 89] EISENHARDT K., "Building theories from case study research", *Academy of Management Review*, vol. 14, no. 4, pp. 532–550, 1989.

[GOR 06] GORIA S., Proposition d'une démarche d'aide à l'expression des problèmes de recherche d'informations dans un contexte d'intelligence territoriale, Doctoral Thesis, University of Nancy 2, Nancy, 2006.

[GRU 94] GRUNDSTEIN M., *Développer un Système à Base de Connaissances: un Effort de Coopération pour Construire en Commun un Objet Inconnu*, CP2I, Paris, 1994.

[HOL 02] HOLSAPPLE C.W., JOSHI K.D., "A knowledge management ontology", in HOLSAPPLE, C.W. (ed.), *Handbook on Knowledge Management*, Springer-Verlag, Berlin, vol. 1, pp. 89–128, 2002.

[KAL 06] KALPIC B., BERNUS P., "Business process modeling through the knowledge management perspective", *Journal of Knowledge Management*, vol. 10, no. 3, pp. 40–56, 2006.

[KIS 02] KISLIN P., DAVID A., THIÉRY O., "A model of information retrieval problem in Economic Intelligence context", *SCI'2002*, Orlando, Florida, USA, 14–18 July 2002.

[KIS 07] KISLIN P., Modélisation du probleme informationnel du veilleur, Doctoral Thesis, University of Nancy 2, Nancy, 2007.

[KNA 07] KNAUF A., Caractérisation des rôles du coordinateur – animateur: émergence d'un acteur nécessaire à la mise en pratique d'un dispositif régional d'intelligence économique, Doctoral Thesis, University of Nancy 2, Nancy, 2007.

[MAR 94] MARTRE H., Intelligence économique et stratégique des entreprises, Results of a workgroup led by Henri Martre, La Documentation Française, Paris, 1994.

[MAT 02] MATTA N., ERMINE J., AUBERTIN G., TRIVIN J., "Knowledge capitalization with a knowledge engineering approach: the MASK method", in DIENG-KUNTZ R., MATTA N. (ed.), *Knowledge Management and Organizational Memories*, Kluwer Academic Publisher, Boston, pp. 17–28, 2002.

[MIL 02] MILLER F., "I = 0 (Information has no intrinsic meaning)", *Information Research*, vol. 8, no. 1, pp. 1–13, 2002.

[NGA 04] NGANTCHAHA G., NKAMBOU R., BEVO V., "Software engineering knowledge capitalization using CBR: case structure", *Proceedings of the IASTED International Conference, Artificial Intelligence and Applications (AIA)*, Innsbruck, Austria, February 2004.

[NON 95] NONAKA I., TAKEUCHI H., *The Knowledge-Creating Company: How Japanese Companies Create the Dynamics of Innovation*, Oxford University Press, Oxford, 1995.

[PEG 06] PEGUIRON F., Application de l'intelligence économique dans un système d'Information stratégique universitaire: les apports de la modélisation des acteurs, Doctoral Thesis, University of Nancy 2, Nancy, 2006.

[POH 00] POHL J., "Transition from data to information", *Collaborative Agent Design Research Center (CADRC) Technical Paper*, Cal Poly San Luis Obispo, CA, USA, pp. 1–8, November 2000. www.cadrc.calpoly.edu. www.cdmtech.com

[RAN 06] RANDEREE E., "Knowledge management: securing the future", *Journal of Knowledge Management*, vol. 10, no. 4, pp. 145–156, 2006.

[RAS 04] RASOVSKA I., CHEBEL-MORELLO B., ZERHOUNI N., "A conceptual model of maintenance process in unified modelling language", *Proceedings of INCOM'2004 – 11th IFAC Symposium on Information Control Problems in Manufacturing*, Salvador-Bahia, Brazil, 2004.

[ROB 07] ROBERT C., L'annotation pour la recherche d'informations dans le contexte d'intelligence économique, Doctoral Thesis, University of Nancy 2, Nancy, February 2007.

[SIM 96] SIMON G., "Knowledge acquisition and modeling for corporate memory: lessons learnt from experience", in GAINES B., MUSEN M. (eds.), *Proceedings of KAW'96*, Banff, Canada, html page: http://ksi.cpsc.ucalgary.ca/KAW/KAW96/simon/KAW96US.htm

[SIM 03] SIMONI G., "Knowledge capitalization in research and design projects: an integrative and diversified approach", *13th European Summer School in Technology Management*, EIASM – European Institute for Advanced Studies in Management, WHU, Vallendar, Germany, 2003. Also in http://www.lest.cnrs.fr/lesdocumentsdetravail/simoni/knoledge.pdf

[STA 89] STATA R., "Organizational learning – the key to management innovation", *Sloan Management Review*, vol. 30, pp. 63–73, 1989.

[STR 94] STRAUSS A., CORBIN J., "Grounded theory methodology", in DENZIN N.K., LINCOLN S.Y. (dir.), *Handbook of Qualitative Research*, Sage, Thousand Oaks, CA, 1994.

[ZAN 00] ZANNES E., "Knowledge management in industry and government: the conflict between security & knowledge sharing", *IEEE*, 2000. Computer Security, Emerald Group Publishing Limited, vol. 13, pp. 160–169.

Chapter 4

Collaborative Information Seeking in the Competitive Intelligence Process

4.1. Introduction

In a world undergoing perpetual social and economic transformation, decision making demands permanent reactivity, particularly in light of the globalization phenomenon. Decision making is the core of competitive intelligence (CI) and requires us to seek information that could help in resolving a decision problem (DP). In most books on decision support, emphasis is placed on the importance of clarifying a DP and on information seeking (or gathering), which are the primordial phases in solving a DP.

Going from the phase of clarification of the DP to the information seeking phase requires that the DP be first transformed into an information problem (IP). Thus, an IP can be considered to be a derivative of a DP [KIS 07, ODU 09].

An IP demands that we seek and retrieve information, indispensable activities in solving a DP following the CI process. However, it has been shown that the final goal of information retrieval is the production of knowledge, and that this is a collaborative task[1] [KAR 98]. Several studies have shown that information retrieval is both a cognitive and a social process that requires collaboration between users.

Chapter written by Victor ODUMUYIWA.
1 "It is argued that the fundamental intellectual problems of information retrieval are the production and consumption of knowledge. Knowledge production is fundamentally a collaborative labor, which is deeply embedded in the practices of a community of participants constituting a domain" [KAR 98].

In fact, users' information behavior reveals that they manifest collaborative information seeking (CIS) patterns when attempting to solve IPs.

Based on the fact that the overall effectiveness of a group is not the same as the sum of its individual parts, we surmise that IPs, particularly in the context of CI, may be better and more rapidly resolved if a CIS approach is used.

We consider that, whether in designing methods or developing tools, information seeking and retrieval should not be seen as an individual activity but rather as a collaborative act. We will therefore attempt, in this chapter, to demonstrate the *importance* of CIS, on the one hand, and, on the other, *a way of managing* CIS in solving IPs, particularly in today's world where collaborative watch is beginning to gain ground in socioeconomic sectors.

To explain what we mean by CIS and how this may be applied to the CI process, we will begin by presenting CI processes as seen by the SITE research team at LORIA laboratory. Second, we will present the evolution of information retrieval toward collaborative information retrieval (CIR). Based on the information behaviors of users, we will consider the CIS, and retrieval as a social and cognitive activity that leads to knowledge sharing. The third section will focus on approaches for facilitating and managing CIS.

4.2. The CI process

CI can be defined as the set of coordinated actions of seeking, processing, and disseminating useful information to economic actors susceptible to use this information. These actions are carried out legally, with all necessary guarantees for the preservation of business patrimony, in the best possible quality, time, and cost conditions [MAR 94]. According to Revelli [REV 98], CI is the process of collecting, processing, and disseminating information with the goal of reducing uncertainty in any strategic decision making process.

CI is linked to various similar concepts, such as economic intelligence (which is the term commonly used in French), business intelligence, and knowledge management. It is a process that embodies decision making. Decision making can be regarded as an outcome of mental processes (cognitive processes) leading to the selection of a course of action among several alternatives [THI 02]. CI is also considered to be an information process, made up of the following phases [DAV 09]:

a) identification of a DP;

b) transformation of the DP into an IP;

c) identification of relevant sources of information;

d) collection of relevant information;

e) analysis of collected information to extract indicators for decision making;

f) interpretation of indicators;

g) decision making.

Our focus here is not to elaborate on the CI process but rather to highlight the level of involvement of CIS in the CI process. We are interested in phases *b*, *c*, *d*, *e*, and *f* which are the phases in which the CIS activities are carried out by CI actors. However, it is important to note that there are four invariable factors in CI processes: the decision maker, the DP, information, and the protection of material and immaterial patrimony [DAV 09]. In a CI project, three main actors cooperate to ensure the success of the process: the decision maker, the watcher, and the coordinator.

The decision maker, who sits at the top of the process, is capable of identifying the DP to be solved in terms of stakes, risks, or threats to the company. The watcher, on the other hand, is responsible for the collection, analysis, and dissemination of information throughout the company. The coordinator acts as an intermediary between all CI actors and is responsible for managing workflow in the CI process, and for coordinating interactions among actors [KNA 07].

Philippe Kislin, in his PhD thesis [KIS 07], analyzed the cooperation process that may likely be established between a decision maker and a watcher in transforming a DP into an IP. Indeed, an IP may be resolved through a collaboration process involving internal watchers of an organization and, if necessary, with external watchers. This approach may also involve cooperation with other information workers. The question we are thus faced with is: how can we facilitate and manage collaboration in information seeking and retrieval to help solve an IP, with minimum cost and delay, while protecting the information patrimony of the company?

4.3. From information retrieval to CIR

4.3.1. *Information retrieval*

Information retrieval, as defined by Fidel *et al.* [FID 01], may be interpreted in a broader sense to include processes such as problem identification, analysis of information needs, query formulation, retrieval interactions, evaluation, presentation of results, and applying results to solve an IP.

An issue that is ever-present in the domain of information retrieval is that of relevance of the information found in relation to the information need of the user.

This problem of relevance calls for reflection in the design and development of information seeking methods and tools. Possible reasons for the problem are as follows:

– incoherencies between an IP and its representation as a query;

– differences between terms used for indexing preexisting documents in information retrieval systems (IRSs) and the terms used by the user to express an information need;

– inability to capture the semantics of a user's query;

– differences between the context of production of information and the context of final use [MAG 08];

– differences between the user's mental model of an IRS and the functional model of the IRS;

– differences between user information behavior and user representation in IRSs.

The need to personalize the response of the IRS for each user, taking into account the variations in user preferences, is one of the developments that have emerged in the information retrieval domain. This gave birth to the idea of modeling users to better satisfy their information needs [BUE 01a, DAN 03].

Another development in IR is collaborative filtering and recommendations. This idea is not only concerned with personalizing responses but also with using what others have already found and evaluated. This hypothesis supposes that what is judged to be relevant by some users might be relevant for another user working on a similar IP [BUE 01b, GOH 05, JIN 06].

In spite of these developments, the problem associated with the semantic interpretation of user information needs expressed as a search query is still in want of a solution. For example, Google (www.google.fr) has introduced a system of automatic suggestion of search terms to users while they are typing their query. This constitutes progress on the part of Google, but potential problems arise from the inadequacy of a keyword or free text query to effectively represent user information need. If the typed query is a false representation of the user's information need, the suggestions provided by the search engine might be considered to be an edifice built on a faulty foundation. A similar example of collaborative recommendation is proposed on the amazon.com (www.amazon.com) Web site, where a user searching for a book receives, as a response to his/her query, a list of suggestions based on books that were bought by other users who had formulated a similar query in the past. These developments are based on an approach of inferring users' information needs based on their activities, profile, and queries through the use of algorithms.

From the cognitive viewpoint of information retrieval, we believe that it is, in fact, impossible to dissociate the problem of satisfying user information needs, and that of the relevance of information found in relation to the IP from the user's understanding of the problem, and his/her level of knowledge of available information retrieval methods (or systems). This problem is strongly linked to the cognitive capacity of the user. This cognitive lack may be made up for by collaborating with other users, implying the notion of explicit collaboration in information retrieval and seeking [FOL 09, ODU 09, SHA 09].

4.3.2. *Collaborative information behavior*

CIR is a research domain that interests various disciplines including information and communication sciences (ICS), computing, linguistics, cognitive psychology, and artificial intelligence. Each discipline tackles the subject using its own set of rules. In ICS, the starting point is to study the information behavior of users to understand their information practices, before designing and developing IRSs and tools.

We will extend Wilson's nested model of information behavior [WIL 99] to explain the three associated concepts involved in CIS. These concepts, as shown in Figure 4.1, are collaborative information behavior (CIB), CIS, and CIR.

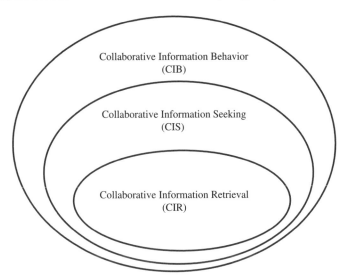

Figure 4.1. *A nested model of CIB (adapted from [WIL 99])*

In the outer circle of Figure 4.1, we find CIB, which concerns all information practices or behaviors of users seeking information in a collaborative manner, generally in more or less digital environments. CIB therefore includes CIS and CIR. CIB includes both active and passive information seeking and also includes the avoidance of information.

The second level, CIS, designates the context in which a group of users is found at the moment of choosing relevant information sources to respond to their information need (in this case, a shared information need).

The core, CIR, concerns the context of querying an IRS, that is, the collaborative formulation of queries and the collaborative evaluation of the relevance of the information found.

In the context of CI and watch activities in particular, observation of user behavior in collaborative information search situations shows that:

– users always find themselves in a loop made up of their IPs, information sources, and other users;

– users make use of several information systems in solving their IPs;

– users give more credit to information provided by an expert than to that found on an information system;

– users follow the evolution of an expert in their domain;

– users exploit the networks of other users they consider to be more experienced in their domains;

– users monitor the evolution of an information source, which they consider to be a good source of relevant information;

– users depend greatly on their social and professional networks in solving their IPs.

Figure 4.2 is an abstraction of these CIBs. Note that the trust factor is essential for determining with whom a user will collaborate or to what extent a user will express the totality of his/her IP and objectives.

Ihadjadene and Chaudirron conclude, in [IHA 09], that "information retrieval is at the heart of a process integrating search and navigation, collaboration, serendipity,[2] tagging, reading, or writing, all of which serve to complicate the modeling of information practices".

---

2 Serendipity is the fact of discovering something by accident and sagacity while in pursuit of something else (definition given by Walpole H. (1754) - source: www.intelligence-

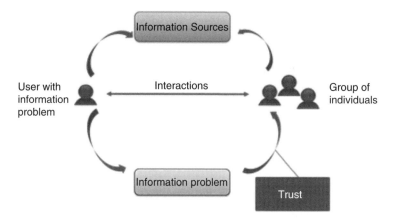

Figure 4.2. *Modeling collaborative behavior*

4.3.3. *CIS and retrieval*

In the previous sections, we looked at information retrieval and CIBs, but we have not yet defined the word "collaboration" or the concept of CIS.

We define "collaboration" as the act of working jointly with shared objectives. Collaboration can be distinguished from cooperation, as in [LON 03]. In a context of "collaboration", actors have a common goal, whereas in the context of "cooperation" this is not necessarily the case.

In Figure 4.1, we see that CIR is embedded in CIS, which means that CIR activities are subsets of CIS activities. We will henceforth stick to the term CIS to explain all information seeking and retrieval activities carried out in a collaborative manner. We thus define CIS as consisting of methods and systems for managing the collective activities of users in an information seeking and retrieval process to facilitate direct collaboration among them (the users) thereby enabling knowledge sharing [ODU 08a]. This definition highlights two important concerns in CIS:

– management of collective activities;

– facilitation of direct collaboration for sharing knowledge.

---

creative.com/354_serendipite_definition.html). According to [MAR 95], it is the art of finding the right information by accident. In competitive intelligence, "it allows us to identify the 'blind spots' of a strategy or unfounded but widely accepted beliefs, which may help a competitor or a new entrant to create a breach in a market".

The aim of CIS is to share knowledge and to create new knowledge. In terms of knowledge sharing, the questions to ask are as follows: What knowledge should be shared in CIS? In what activities is this knowledge shared, and how may this knowledge be shared? In response to these questions, we will list the various forms of knowledge that may be shared [ODU 08b]:

– domain knowledge,

– competence in search methodology,

– system knowledge,

– knowledge of information sources,

– knowledge of collaborators.

4.3.3.1. *Domain knowledge*

Domain knowledge reflects the degree to which a user understands a search topic. It covers knowledge of facts, concepts, and terminology in a specific domain. High domain knowledge gives a user better access to relevant search results and gives the user the ability, through a richer set of concepts and terms, to formulate queries more effectively [SUT 98].

4.3.3.2. *Competence in search methodology*

The capacity of a user to plan his/her search depends on his/her competence in search methodology, which consists of search strategies, system selection, the use of operators, parentheses, truncation marks, formulation, modification, and expansion of search queries [ZHA 05].

4.3.3.3. *System knowledge*

Our knowledge of the functionalities of an IRS is very important in attaining our search goals. These functionalities may include a thesaurus, a list of keywords, a library of reusable queries, support for Boolean queries, visualizations of result summaries, visualization of the search process, and so on.

4.3.3.4. *Knowledge of information sources*

This knowledge relates to the ability of a user to find online databases, web resources, or IRSs that may be useful in solving a given IP [ZHA 05].

4.3.3.5. *Knowledge of collaborators*

All the types of knowledge mentioned above are possessed by users in differing proportions. The first question to ask when attempting to collaborate is with whom can we collaborate, that is, who are our prospective collaborators.

Determining a prospective collaborator is a function of how best a user can mine the histories of other users and their models so as to determine their level of domain knowledge and other forms of knowledge mentioned above. The ability to mine and discover potential collaborators constitutes another form of knowledge that can be shared. We agree with the hypothesis that the best way of obtaining good information is to identify the person who possesses it.

To respond to the second question, "in which activities is knowledge shared?", we will give an overview of these activities while at the same time identifying the knowledge to be shared in each of them:

– IP identification and clarification: the first activity in CIS is to identify the IP. Identifying a problem necessitates the clarification of the problem. Considering the fact that a user's knowledge of his/her problem increases over time and that the problem may not be well understood initially, collaboration with another user may, therefore, help in clarifying the problem. The knowledge shared in this collaborative activity is domain knowledge.

– Articulation of the information need: the identification and clarification of an IP lead to the articulation of information need by formulating a search objective. Sharing domain knowledge is also very important in this activity.

– Choice of an information system to use: the articulation of search objectives leads to the choice of information sources to use for search. This activity requires sharing knowledge of information sources and competences in search methodology.

– Query formulation, reformulation, and clarification entail representing the information needs in terms of queries that are sent to the IRS. These activities require sharing domain knowledge, competences in search methodology, and system knowledge.

– Evaluation of results: this reflects the user's judgment of the relevance of information found for their information need. This judgment is intrinsically linked to the user's domain knowledge. Observation has shown that a document judged relevant today by a user may be judged irrelevant tomorrow by the same user with respect to the same IP and vice versa. This can be explained by the fact that a user's knowledge of his/her problem increases over time. It also shows the importance of collaboration in evaluating the results of information search activities. For example, we might encounter a situation where a domain expert assists a user in determining whether a document is relevant or not to his/her information needs.

– Communication: communication among collaborators is required to share the knowledge in all the activities outlined above. This provides a response to the question of *how* knowledge can be shared. We will go into more detail with regard to this aspect in the following sections.

4.4. Facilitation and management of CIS

We will propose a conceptual framework and a communication model for managing CIS. The conceptual framework assists in understanding CIS and shows the four main aspects involved in managing CIS. The communication model is a model of the collaborative context for knowledge sharing.

4.4.1. *The conceptual framework*

Managing CIS involves the following four main aspects:

– communication,

– modes of collaboration,

– coordination of user interactions,

– management of knowledge involved in collaboration.

We are, effectively, considering a case where we *communicate* to *collaborate*, requiring *coordination* of interactions to successfully *manage* the knowledge involved in the collaboration.

These four elements are presented below.

4.4.1.1. *Communication*

For collaboration to be possible in the process of solving an IP, the actors involved must communicate. We will consider this aspect using the following questions:

– Why?: The "why" of the communication is the reason for the collaboration or the need for sharing, which can be seen as the objective of communication.

– What?: The "what" of communication concerns the communication object, whether audio, text, or video. These objects are knowledge expressed as queries, search results, annotations, and so on.

– How?: This aspect concerns the style of interaction that may be in either synchronous or asynchronous mode.

– Who?: The sender and receiver of the communications object (collaborators).

– When?: The date and time of communication, useful in contextualizing the expressed knowledge and in analyzing the evolution of users.

Communication is also considered a form of coordination of user interactions in the case of an information transfer – for example, the transmission of a document from one user to another.

4.4.1.2. *Modes of collaboration*

Two modes of collaboration may be found between actors involved in CIS:

– observation mode,

– interaction mode.

In observation mode, one or more users observe another user (expert or otherwise) carrying out search activities or attempting to solve an IP. Observation mode is represented by the graph in Figure 4.3a.

In interaction mode, two or more users attempt to resolve an IP conjointly. They share and exchange information and competences, each contributing to the resolution of the IP.

The graph in Figure 4.3b shows this mode of collaboration, with each user represented by a node.

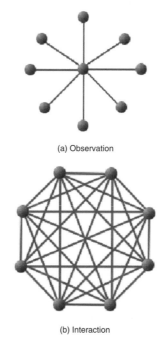

(a) Observation

(b) Interaction

Figure 4.3. *Graphs showing different modes of collaboration*

4.4.1.3. *Coordination of user interactions*

Coordination, in the context of CIS, is the management of dependencies between the information seeking activities of collaborating users. We support the notion expressed by Malone [MAL 94], who categorized possible dependencies between users into three general groups:

– flow dependency,

– sharing dependency,

– fit dependency.

Flow dependency occurs when the activities of a user become a resource for the activities of another user. For example, the query formulated by one user may become a starting point for another user with a similar information need.

Sharing dependency occurs when a resource is shared between two or more users.

Fit dependency occurs when the activities of two or more users must adjust to produce a resource. When two watchers work together on an IP, for example, their activities must be adjusted to fit together to produce a single resource.

4.4.1.4. *Managing knowledge in collaboration*

As mentioned in section 4.3.3, CIS involves knowledge sharing among users. This implies the need to manage the various types and forms of knowledge involved in CIS.

Knowledge to be shared includes queries, search results, annotations, dialogs between users, and shared documents. To manage this knowledge, we should consider the following:

– user modeling,

– knowledge acquisition,

– knowledge exploitation.

User modeling is carried out based on a user's profile and activities. Knowledge acquisition entails capturing, encoding, and storing the different forms of knowledge expressed during collaboration, as set out above.

To exploit this knowledge, we will adopt the $EQuA^2te$ model [DAV 02]:

– Explore: to discover objects of the domain of study.

– Query: to access objects in the domain of study, from knowledge already acquired concerning the desired objects.

– Analyze: to obtain information with added value to discover the phenomena of the domain of study.

– Annotate: to create new knowledge. An annotation is seen as value added to information.

In the context of CIS, the $EQuA^2te$ model can be extended to include a syndication phase. After exploiting the knowledge base, a user may discover other users in his/her domain who constitute potential collaborators. The user may form a network with such potential collaborators, whence the term syndication.

4.4.2. *Communication model for CIS*

Successful collaboration depends on both collaboration technologies and a culture of openness among actors. Collaboration can, therefore, be said to be an interaction between technology and culture. Given these two factors, there is a need to model the collaborative context for interaction. Thus, for successful collaboration, integrating both collaboration technology and actors' openness, there is a need for a knowledge sharing model, and a coordination mechanism for managing possible interactions in the collaboration.

From our previous studies of existing CIR and CIS systems and our own conception of CIS, we see CIS as communicating to share knowledge and acquire new knowledge [ODU 08a, ODU 08b, ODU 09]. The communication can take place in the interactions between two or more users passing by the IRS. It can also be manifested in the interaction between a user and the IRS as he/she formulates a query and sends it to the IRS, and the IRS provide him/her with results of relevant documents that correspond to his/her query. Summarily, we see every interaction process in CIS as a communication process because at any point in time, there is an information object being communicated from a sender to a receiver. The communication may be bidirectional as the receiver may also send an information object to the sender. We must also note that for every exchange, there is a context that necessitates the exchange as stated above (collaborative context). Based on this, we may model the process of communication in CIS. This model is known as the Communication model for Collaborative Information Retrieval (COCIR). The model is made up of four elements as shown in Figure 4.4.

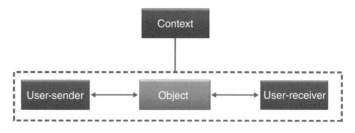

Figure 4.4. *COCIR model*

As we stated earlier, we consider communication to be a means of collaboration and coordination; therefore, this model can be used to share knowledge and manage interactions among collaborators.

Each element of this model is made up of subelements which describe it. Both sender and receiver are users so they will have the same subelements. A user can therefore play both roles in a CIS session. Thus, when we make reference to the user, it may be either the sender or the receiver. The three elements of the COCIR model are made up of subelements presented in Figure 4.5.

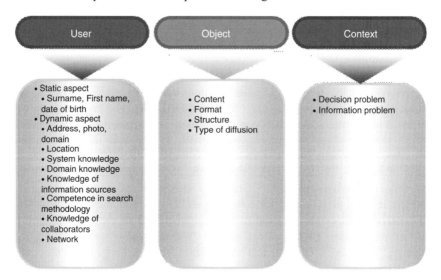

Figure 4.5. *Three elements of COCIR and their subelements*

4.4.2.1. *User*

Modeling users allows us to manage expressed knowledge during a collaborative session. It also allows us to link users with similar models. In modeling users, we combine the implicit and the explicit approach. Some information is explicitly provided by the user while other information is derived from his/her activities. Some of this information is static because it does not change, while other information is dynamic and may change with time. We combine the static and dynamic elements in representing a user. The user model contains information such as identity (surname and first name), date of birth, photo, and domain. The "location" subelement concerns the geographical location of the user during collaboration. This can be obtained from the internet protocol address of the computer used by the user. From the activities of the user (queries, annotations, consulted documents, etc.), we can obtain information on his/her domain knowledge, system knowledge, competence in search methodology, information source knowledge, and knowledge of collaborators. The "network" will contain information about users with whom the user had already collaborated.

4.4.2.2. Object

The object of communication represents all information exchanged among collaborators whether such information is expressed by them or comes from other existing artifacts. It is made up of four subelements: content, structure, format, and diffusion type. The content is the message to communicate. The message can be in different *formats* (text, audio, or video). The type of diffusion can be unidirectional or conversational. It is unidirectional when an information object is sent by one user to one or more others without expecting a reply. It is conversational when an object is sent to one or more users and produces a response. For example, when a user's activity is automatically captured and sent to his/her partner during a direct synchronous collaboration for awareness purposes [ODU 10 p. 211–214], the diffusion type is unidirectional. Meanwhile, when two or more users engage in interpersonal communication during the course of the collaboration, the diffusion type becomes conversational.

Since one of the main aspects of CIS is the management of expressed knowledge, it is therefore necessary to capture and store this knowledge in the knowledge base. For knowledge to be stored, it must be structured. The subelement "structure" thus concerns the representation of information on the organization of the information object in the knowledge base. The structure varies according to the type of information object to be communicated.

4.4.2.3. Context

The third element of the COCIR model concerns the context of collaboration. Every exchange in collaboration applies to a specific context. In the framework of CI, the first subelement of "context" is the DP. As explained earlier, a DP can be translated into an IP. CIS activities are centered on IP. Thus, the second subelement is the IP, which can also comprise a set of IP that is, an IP may be broken down into various IPs. To model the DP, we adopt the *Model for expressing a decision problem* proposed by Bouaka [BOU 04, ODU 10]. Our major focus in CIS is the derived IP from the DP. Modeling the IP allows clarification of the problem to be solved and also allows collaborators to have a clear representation of the context initiating their interactions. IP will therefore contain subelements such as expression of IP, objective of search, keywords, information sources, domain, and temporal attribute [ODU 10].

This model can be used to facilitate CIS and the capitalization of knowledge expressed during the collaboration. An implementation of this model in developing a CIS system is seen in [ODU 10].

4.4.3. *Application context*

There are two possible cases of collaboration in information seeking. The first case corresponds to a situation where a user with an IP seeks another person with whom he/she can collaborate to solve the problem. The second case corresponds to a situation where a predefined group of users works together to solve a shared IP.

When discussing knowledge sharing in information seeking, three categories of knowledge should be captured to help users to:

– know other users better (potential collaborators);

– develop the necessary trust to begin collaboration;

– improve their social cognition;

– find already expressed knowledge that may be used to solve their problems;

– describe their metacognitive capacities.

These three categories of knowledge consist of:

– initial knowledge and competences,

– mental knowledge and competences,

– applied knowledge and competences.

Initial knowledge and competences are knowledge expressed and captured during the signing up of the user to the CIS system. They are deduced from the responses given by the user to a series of questions posed during registration.

Mental knowledge and competences are expressed during the definition, analysis, and clarification of the IP. They demonstrate the level of understanding a user has of his/her IP. They also describe how a user proposes to approach and solve his/her problem. In cases of collaboration where the problem is shared between several users, each contribution to the definition, analysis, and clarification of the problem via annotations and interpersonal communications falls into this category.

Applied knowledge and competences are derived from the information seeking activities and from interactions between users during resolution of an IP. They are expressed in the form of sources of information used, searches carried out, links visited, annotations made, users contacted, networks exploited, documents found, evaluations of these documents, and so on. This knowledge shows how users really succeed in solving a shared IP.

Let us begin by examining the first situation. A user connects to a CIS environment and defines an IP according to the attributes given in the problem definition interface. This definition relates to the user's understanding of the IP. The user may progress to the level of information retrieval by connecting to an IRS and beginning to launch queries. However, since we are concerned with collaboration and faced with a situation where the user does not know with whom to collaborate, the user may attempt to exploit the collaborative knowledge base to find other problems similar to his/her own and the users who expressed such problems and who succeeded in solving them. This approach aims first at reusing potentially helpful preexpressed knowledge. However, the user may also want to identify users who possess, or have expressed, this knowledge. The goal is to enable direct collaboration to share tacit knowledge. This interest may be justified as follows, using an extract from a course given by Le Dantec [LED 07]: "The implementation of cognitive functions and processes is not the same for all subjects. However, at performance level, we regularly observe relative intra-individual, intra-task stability (particularly when tasks are of a similar nature), whereas the implementation of cognitive processes and functions does not necessarily work in the same way for the same subject in different tasks."

Once the user has identified a potential collaborator, the user with the IP sends a collaboration request to the other user. If this user accepts the request, the IP becomes a shared problem for the two users and they begin a process of integrating and differentiating their understanding of the problem, aiming to obtain a shared understanding of the IP, and information sources to use.

From the instant when the problem is shared, the collaborative process that follows is the same in both cases discussed. The potential difference between the two is linked to the social cognitions of collaborators. We suppose that these cognitions are more developed in a predefined group where the members know each other.

Starting from a shared understanding of the IP, users begin to connect to information sources. This may be done in one of three ways:

– Each user connects to different sources then shares gathered information. User activities (navigations and searches) are also captured, providing the possibility for sharing them too.

– A user can observe another user in real time during navigation or searching. The user follows the activities of the other user and engages in interpersonal communication with this user to obtain explanations or clarifications about his/her actions when retrieving information. The first user may also express opinions to contribute to the actions of the other user. This is a learning process in collaborative working. For example, a user with considerable experience in the use of a specialized database may take the lead while others observe.

– All users (collaborators) formulate queries collaboratively and simultaneously. This is a more pronounced form of interaction. Users connect to the same IRS, formulate, clarify, and reformulate queries together. They evaluate the relevance of information together. They combine their queries and suggest keyword synonyms to use to find more relevant information. They engage in interpersonal communication and, at the same time, create annotations to express their knowledge on objects (a query, a document, a URL, a source of information, etc.).

Another interesting thing is to go from instant collaboration to user syndication, a process that creates networks of collaborators.

4.5. Collective information seeking scenario

To illustrate our approach for the facilitation of CIS, we will take the example of a student preparing a final dissertation on the subject "The impact of social unrest in the Niger Delta region of Nigeria on the international crude oil market".

The student connects to an IRS (e.g. Google) and begins to look for information on the subject. He/she finds a large amount of information with a lot of background noise; his/her information need remains unsatisfied, as he/she is not prepared to sift through all of this information. In this example, the student uses the search engine alone by placing a search term.

Following our approach, he/she first defines the context as follows:

<Problem> The impact of social unrest in the Niger Delta region of Nigeria on the international crude oil market <Problem>

<Objective>Write dissertation </Objective>

<Date time> 25 April 2007, 15:00hr (automatic) </Date time>

<Search engine> Google, ask.com </Search engine>

<Keywords>social unrest, international crude oil market, Niger Delta, Nigeria </Keywords>

<Databases> </Databases>

<Other sources of information> </Other sources of information>

This definition shows the student's mental knowledge of the problem. By sharing this problem with another user, the two users begin a differentiation and integration process to establish a shared understanding of the problem. In this example, the student, initiator of the problem, decides to connect with a user who knows the domain better than he/she does, and who has more knowledge of information sources. For the rest of this illustration, we will refer to the student as SU and to the second user as CU.

First, CU provides details concerning the domain: he/she gives a list of the states which make up the Niger Delta region of Nigeria. He/she then explains the forms of social unrest occurring in the region. Next, he/she highlights various possible categories of impact. This leads to a clearer understanding of the domain.

<Problem>
        <Constituent states of the Niger Delta region>
                Akwa Ibom
                Balyesa
                Rivers
                Cross-river
                Delta
                Edo
        </Constituent states of the Niger Delta region>
        <Social unrest>
                Kidnappings of foreign expatriates
                Bombing oil wells
                Attack by militant group
                Conflict between militant group and the army
        </Social unrest>
        <Impact>
                Social
                Economic
                Military
        <Impact>
      <Problem>

> *<Objective>*
> > *State of the art*
> > *Type of diploma*
> > *Discipline*
> *</Objective>*
> *<Information source>*
> > *www.shell.com/home/content/nigeria*
> > *www.nigeriaworld.com*
> *</Information sources>*

Following these clarifications, interpersonal communications take place between the two users through the CIS system so that they may harmonize their understanding of the problem.

Based on a shared understanding of the problem, SU and CU may begin navigating through information sources, and formulating queries to express the shared information need.

CU: "Now, I'll formulate queries and you can see what happens: use of quotation marks, the need to break up keywords into several queries, etc."

SU observes CUs activities in real time through the ISS using WISIWYS (What I See Is What You See) technology. In the course of this process, SU learns better ways of formulating queries in line with the document representation model of the IRS in question. Seeing the results found by CU, SU may express an opinion on the relevance of the documents found. Based on the knowledge acquired in the observation mode, he/she may also begin to launch queries.

At the end of the process, SU succeeds in acquiring knowledge of the domain (clarification of the region of Nigeria), and competences in search methodology (how to formulate targeted queries in Google). All the knowledge expressed during the collaboration process is capitalized for future reuse.

4.6. Conclusion

We have demonstrated that the information seeking is indispensable in the CI process aimed toward resolving DP. Several studies have shown that information seeking, which is both a cognitive and a social process, requires collaboration among users. This chapter has focused on managing collaboration activities of users in solving an IP derived from a DP.

CIS involves the management of collective activities and sharing of knowledge among users. The knowledge to share includes domain knowledge, competence in search methodology, system knowledge, knowledge of information sources, and knowledge of collaborators.

To facilitate knowledge sharing and to manage the collective activities of users, we proposed a conceptual framework for CIS and a communication model.

4.7. Bibliography

[BOU 04] BOUAKA N., Développement d'un modèle pour l'explicitation d'un modèle décisionnel: un outil d'aide à la décision dans un contexte d'intelligence économique, Doctoral Thesis, University of Nancy 2, Nancy, 2004.

[BUE 01a] BUENO D., DAVID A., "METIORE: a personalized information retrieval system", in BAUER M., GMYTRASIEWICZ P.J., VASSILEVA J. (eds), *User Modeling 2001*, Springer-Verlag, Berlin and Heidelberg, pp. 168–177, 2001.

[BUE 01b] BUENO D., CONEJO R., DAVID A., "METIOREW: an objective oriented content based and collaborative recommending system", *Proceedings of the Twelfth ACM Conference on Hypertext and Hypermedia*, pp. 310–314, 2001, available online at http://citeseer.ist.psu.edu/482403.html.

[DAN 03] DANILOWICZ C., NGUYEN H.C., NGUYEN N.T., "Model of user profiles and personalization for web-based information retrieval systems", in ABRAMOWICZ W. (ed.), *Knowledge Based Information Retrieval and Filtering from Internet*, Kluwer Academic Publisher, Norwell (MA), pp. 121–136, 2003.

[DAV 02] DAVID A., THIERRY O., "Application of "EQuA^{2}te" architecture in economic intelligence", *Information and Communication Technologies Applied to Economic Intelligence – ICTEI'2002*, Ibadan, Nigeria, pp. 32–38, 2002.

[DAV 09] DAVID A., "Relevant information in economic intelligence", in PAPY F. (ed.), *Information Science*, ISTE Ltd, London and John Wiley & Sons, New York, 2009.

[FID 01] FIDEL R., BRUCE H., PEJTERSEN A.M., DUMAIS S., GRUDIN J., POLTROCK S., "Collaborative information retrieval (CIR)", *The New Review of Information Behavior Research: Studies of Information Seeking in Context*, vol. 1, pp. 235–247, 2001.

[FOL 09] FOLEY C., SMEATON A.F., JONES G.J.F., "Combining relevance information in a synchronous collaborative information retrieval environment", in CHEVALIER M., JULIEN C., SOULE-DUPUY C. (ed.), *Collaborative and Social Information Retrieval and Access: Techniques for Improved User Modelling*, IGI Global, Hershey, PA, pp. 140–164, 2009.

[GOH 05] GOH D.H., FU L., FOO S., "Collaborative querying using the query graph visualize", *Online Information Review*, vol. 29, no. 3, pp. 266–282, 2005.

[IHA 09] IHADJADENE M., CHAUDIRON S., "Electronic information access devices: Crossed approaches and new boundaries", in PAPY F. (ed.), *Information Science*, ISTE Ltd, London and John Wiley & Sons, New York, 2009.

[JIN 06] JIN R., SI L., ZHAI C., "A study of mixture models for collaborative filtering", *Information Retrieval*, vol. 9, no. 3, pp. 357–382, 2006.

[KAR 98] KARAMUFTUOGLU M., "Collaborative information retrieval: toward a social informatics view of IR interaction", *Journal of the American Society of Information Science*, vol. 49, no. 12, pp.1070–1080, 1998.

[KIS 07] KISLIN P., Modélisation du problème informationnel du veilleur dans la démarche d'intelligence économique, Doctoral Thesis, University of Nancy 2, Nancy, 2007.

[KNA 07] KNAUF A., Caractérisation des rôles du coordinateur-animateur: émergence d'un acteur nécessaire à la mise en pratique d'un dispositif régional d'intelligence économique, Doctoral Thesis, University of Nancy 2, Nancy, 2007.

[LED 07] LE DANTEC C., Psychologie différentielle PSP2DF4_S4 - Interaction cognition/conation, Class given at the university of Rouen 2006–2007, available online at www.univ-rouen.fr/servlet/com.univ.utils.LectureFichierJoint?CODE=1172696611874&LANGUE=0.

[LON 03] LONCHAMP J., *Le Travail Coopératif et ses Technologies*, Hermes, Paris, 2003.

[MAG 08] MAGHREBI H., DAVID A., "Open system for indexing and retrieving multimedia information", *Actes du 36e congrès annuel de l'Association canadienne des sciences de l'information (ACSI)*, University of British Columbia, Vancouver, Canada, 5–7 June 2008.

[MAL 94] MALONE T.W., CROWSTON K., "The interdisciplinary study of coordination", *ACM Computing Surveys*, vol. 26, no. 1, pp. 87–120, 1994.

[MAR 94] MARTRE H., *Intelligence économique et stratégie des entreprises*, La Documentation Française, Paris, 1994.

[MAR 95] MARTINET B., MARTI Y.M., *L'intelligence économique*, Editions d'Organisation, Paris, pp. 27–28, 1995.

[ODU 08a] ODUMUYIWA V., DAVID A., "Collaborative information retrieval among economic intelligence actors", *The Fourth International Conference on Collaboration Technologies (Collab Tech 2008)*, Wakayama, Japan, pp. 21–26, 2008.

[ODU 08b] ODUMUYIWA V., DAVID A., "A communication model for knowledge sharing in collaborative information retrieval", *International Conference on Knowledge Management (ICKM 2008)*, Columbus, Ohio, 23–24 October 2008.

[ODU 09] ODUMUYIWA V., DAVID A., "A user centered approach to collaborative information retrieval", *Proceedings of the 2009 International Symposium on Collaborative Technologies and Systems*, Baltimore, Maryland, 18–22 May 2009.

[ODU 10] ODUMUYIWA V., La gestion de la recherche collaborative d'information dans le contexte du processus d'intelligence économique, Doctoral Thesis, University of Nancy 2, Nancy, 2010.

[REV 98] REVELLI C., *Intelligence stratégique sur Internet*, Dunod, Paris, 1998.

[SHA 09] SHAH C., MARCHIONINI G., KELLY D., "Learning design principles for a collaborative information seeking system", *Proceedings of CHI 2009*, Boston, MA, 4–9 April 2009.

[SUT 98] SUTCLIFFE A., ENNIS M., "Towards a cognitive theory of information retrieval", *Interacting with Computers*, vol. 10, pp. 321–351, 1998.

[THI 02] THIERY O., DAVID A., "Modelling of the user in strategic information systems and economic intelligence", *Journal of the Association for the Development of Software* (ADELI), vol. 47, p. 12, 2002.

[WIL 99] WILSON T.D., "Models in information behaviour research", *Journal of Documentation*, vol. 55, no. 3, pp. 249–270, 1999, available online at http://informationr. net/tdw/publ/papers/1999JDoc.html.

[ZHA 05] ZHANG X., LI Y., "An exploratory study on knowledge sharing in information retrieval", *Proceedings of the 38th Hawaii International Conference on System Sciences*, Hawaii, 2005.

Chapter 5

Study of Risk Factors in Competitive Intelligence Decision Making: A Cognitive Approach

5.1. Decision making and decision problems

5.1.1. *Introduction*

Decision making is a process undertaken by a person, a group of people, several groups, or a company. It is a "living" process: any form of decision making has consequences that determine the success or failure of other actions [WAN 04]. This process may be simple (personal decisions) or complex (decisions involving large organizations or governments); the weight attached to these decisions, expressed in the form of a risk, varies in the same way. Human knowledge is enriched through experience and reasoning capacities that allow us to bring order to a mass of available information. In this context, it is imperative that the decisions resulting from this process be controlled [ONI 08a]. The capacity for decision, which we might call "decisionability", is determined by numerous factors including judgment, experience and, in particular, cognitive capacities. As decisions are taken based on information, the mode and methods used to obtain this information are as important as the decision itself [TOD 00, RED 98]. Our perception of the world is limited by the lack of a suitable lexicon, by imprecision, and by the incompleteness of the "measurements" we carry out [SIV 07]. The formulation and implementation of the

Chapter written by Olufade F.W. ONIFADE, Odile THIERY, Adenike O. OSOFISAN and Gérald DUFFING.

decision process has a significant impact on the result of the decision; this can be linked to the cognitive capacities of the decision maker (DM) and to risk factors (RFs). Decision making, with the aim of improving organizational performance, is the focal point of competitive intelligence (CI).

According to Martre [MAR 94], CI is defined as a group of coordinated research, data processing, and information distribution activities that allow actions to be carried out and decisions to be made. The author indicates that these actions are carried out legally, with the aim of protecting company assets, within optimal quality, cost, and time limits. Revelli [REV 98] defines CI as a process of collection, processing, and diffusion of information with the aim of reducing uncertainty in a strategic decision process. CI has been defined, in a given organizational context, as the capacity of the DM to exploit new or recently acquired knowledge and experience to solve a new decision problem. Another vision, put forward by [KAR 03], considers CI as the global process through which DMs obtain a clear understanding of the environment in which they operate.

By synthesizing these views, we can easily identify recurring themes: "information", "actor or user", and "DM". These aspects form the basis of CI, while the cognitive capacity of the DM determines the possibility of RFs in the decision process.

In the following section, we will look at the question of decision making and decision problems using typical examples of the CI process.

5.1.2. *Fundamental aspects of the decision problem*

There may be multiple reasons for a given decision, but we will use two main categories:

– Decision based on a choice between alternatives: the decision is seen as a study, then identification and choice of alternatives based on the values, and preferences of the person concerned [HAR 98]. Therefore, there are several possible choices in the decision process. This implies not only that *several alternatives* should be identified but also that a *choice* between these alternatives must be made to find the "best solution" based on given desires, aims, values, lifestyles, and so on.

– Decision based on a reduction of choice: we have already highlighted factors we consider to be important in the process. In this case, we must reduce incertitude and doubt concerning possible alternatives as far as possible to facilitate selection of the best option. It is important to note that very few decisions are made with absolute certitude, as complete understanding of all possible alternatives is rarely attainable. For this reason, we talk of "reduction", and not "removal", of doubt.

We may also consider a decision problem in relation to different types of decision. While all living things make decisions, humans are the most developed, creating complex operations with the aim of reaching a logical conclusion. Figure 5.1 gives some examples of decisions, based on linguistic expression.

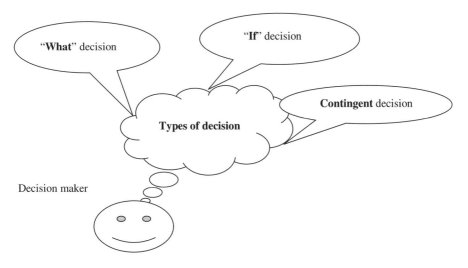

Figure 5.1. *Types of decision*

The "what" decision corresponds to a choice of one or more alternatives from a set of possibilities. In most cases, the selection results from the level of satisfaction of several predefined criteria. The "if" decision is simply Boolean: yes or no. It requires consideration of arguments *for* and *against* a choice. A "contingent" decision is, in fact, a provisional decision, conditioned by an exterior element. The decision is considered to have been made, but it "waits" for the completion of the associated condition [HAR 98]. For example, "I'll go back to university if I can save enough money to pay the fees". In actual fact, human beings often have decisions "ready" to be made, but must wait for an environment, a trigger, or an opportunity to validate this decision.

We have presented a number of definitions and concepts that are useful in decision making. Goals, alternatives, and incertitude have been identified and used to define the notion of decision making. We have also discussed three types of decisions: "what", "if", and "contingent". We will now consider the different components of the decision-making process.

5.1.3. *Decision and cognitive capacity*

Instinct, conscious or subconscious beliefs, values, and intuition have been identified as major elements having an effect on modes of decision making [BAR 06]. Figure 5.2 shows different modes and the factors that affect them.

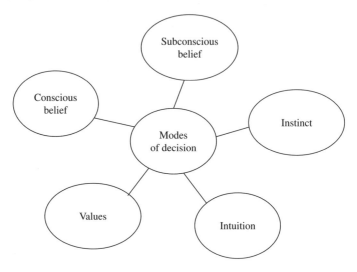

Figure 5.2. *Components of the decision-making process which determine modes*

Decisions based on instinct. This method of decision making has its origins in our genetic makeup. It is mostly associated with problems affecting survival. A typical example is the suckling and crying reflex observed in newborn babies. Distinctive properties of this type of decision include actions that precede any deep reflection or decisions taken based on recognizable past experiences (and which maintain an internal stability or balance). An individual may be said to have little control over these decisions; it is the decision that controls the human being.

Decisions based on subconscious belief. This decision context is similar to that described above, the difference being that the decision is founded on personal memories. Once again, action precedes thought and is an expression of emotional factors that may be negative (blame, competition, rivalry, mistrust) or positive (openness, trust, etc.) [BAR 06].

Common examples of decisions based on subconscious beliefs include tears of joy, the feeling of pride, and feelings of spontaneous happiness. Main characteristics of these decisions include the fact that action precedes thought, that decisions are based on past experience, and that the DM has no direct control over their actions and behavior, that is, emotional or rational stability. Decision-making operations of this kind occur at the first three levels of consciousness [HAR 98].

Decisions based on conscious belief. The subconscious does not allow rational decision making, necessitating passage to a conscious mode of decision making. This means that there will be a time lapse between the construction of meaning and the decision itself. This period is used for reflection, reconsideration of ideas, and the implementation of a logical and thought-out process, in the aim of understanding the "work in progress". In this mode, thought precedes the decision, and time is set aside for discussion before the final decision is made. There is, however, a similarity between decisions based on subconscious beliefs and those based on conscious belief: both are founded on information acquired from past experiences (that which is "known"), reused to deal with new and future problems.

Value-based decisions. In this case, we are once again dealing with conscious decisions, but with a certain input from emotional attachment that may obstruct the decision process. A major question raised in this type of decision is: "Is this decision rational, and does it correspond to our values?" The response to this question may lead to reconsideration of the problem or to a final decision being made. A decision that runs contrary to the values of an organization will reveal a lack of integrity. In a similar manner, a decision that does not reflect the personal values of the DM will lack authenticity. In both cases, there is a noticeable absence of cohesion. Value-based decision allows decisions to be made concerning a preestablished "mission" and differs in this respect from decisions based on conscious belief; the construction of meaning is less important. Value-based decision means our behavior is guided by our values, but not by our beliefs. Values, considered to be universal, transcend all contexts, whereas beliefs are local and contextual [JUN 04].

Decisions based on intuition. This type of decision is described through particular characteristics. The collection and processing of data are carried out as usual, but the judgment stage is absent: there is no in-depth reflection, whether conscious or subconscious. Reasoning and beliefs are not involved; the mind delves into a collective subconscious and thoughts emerge, reflecting knowledge, wisdom, the common interest, and deeply rooted values with long-term applications.

There is therefore an important contrast between analytical decisions (where attention is given to details) and intuitive decisions (where attention is focused on broad themes). Consequently, instinct, conscious and subconscious beliefs, values, and intuition determine the mode of decision making [BAR 06]. Several concepts have been identified [HUN 89]: the DM is seen as a stable individual with beliefs, predispositions, competences, and experience that define and describe their personality. The decision task (DT) itself merits special attention: first, it falls within a particular decision situation (DS) associated with contextual, conceptual, and circumstantial factors. It is based on the decision process (DP) and the decision produces a result or decision object. The aim of this study was to show the relationships between the characteristics of the DM and the DP, with an ill-defined DT. Figure 5.3 illustrates these relationships.

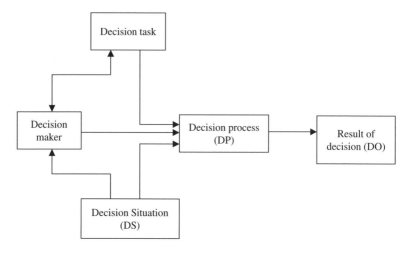

Figure 5.3. *The decision model proposed by Hunt et al. [HUN 89]*

Studies have been carried out examining the consequences of this on managerial decision making [ROB 81]. Aspects concerning the collection and evaluation of information have also been the subject of study [MCK 74], concentrating on the characteristics of DMs: some are essentially analytical (collection, analysis of sensitivity) [OSO 07] while others work in a more intuitive manner (filtration of data). This allows us to better define the cognitive characteristics of actors and to see how these traits are used in the process of solving a decision problem.

5.1.4. *Decisions in the context of CI*

DMs may rely on intuition to either solve their problem or rationalize the problem. Normally, the decisions we find in CI are linked to financial considerations, the importance of which determines the size of the challenge facing the DM.

In this context, we use a well-defined process, beginning with the identification of the decision need. The watcher then assists the DM in transforming this need into an information problem (IP), before carrying out the necessary research. This requires precise mutual understanding of the problem and the stakes involved.

The final decision is based on the information obtained in this way. The process is, therefore, relatively robust and theoretically takes account of all elements that are useful in making an effective decision.

CI is thus presented as a coordinated research and information use action, which aims, in time, to enable strategic decision making [MAR 94, REV 98]. Bouaka and David [BOU 04] and Thiéry and David [THI 02] present a model that combines the context of the problem with a representation of the DM and the stakes involved in the decision problem. The aim is, on the one hand, to facilitate identification and representation of the problem and, on the other hand, to prepare for the information-seeking process that follows. This is made possible by the identification of user characteristics and by evaluating the stakes involved in the problem.

A proposal aiming to assist the DM in defining the problem was established by Bouaka and David [BOU 04] with particular emphasis on data linked to the environment, to the organization, and to actors. The goal of this proposal was essentially to clarify relationships between actors to know who asked a given question and why the question was asked. In this case, we presume that a relationship of trust has been established between actors.

Figure 5.4 shows the actors, information, and processes implemented in the context of CI. David and David [DAV 01] present a model that allows the process to be adapted to the actors. It includes a stage for understanding the process, leading to the production of interpretable indicators useful in decision making and constructed using available information. The authors highlight the importance of considering risks and threats posed by the decision itself, leading to more precise consideration of the profiles of two key actors: the DM and the watcher (seen as an information seeking specialist). We propose a new information seeking system, named METIORE, based on a double filtration process. The first stage of this system consists of capturing research aims, formulated using natural language. Following this stage, the user may construct simple or complex requests, based on a set of available research functions. In this situation, we presume that the user already has an idea of the information required.

In terms of decisions, another approach focuses more specifically on management issues and presupposes the existence of a data repository [DUF 05]. This work highlights the importance of data quality and looks at all stages of information processing: the identification of useful data, processing and the inclusion of data in the database are considered first, followed by reflection concerning its effective use.

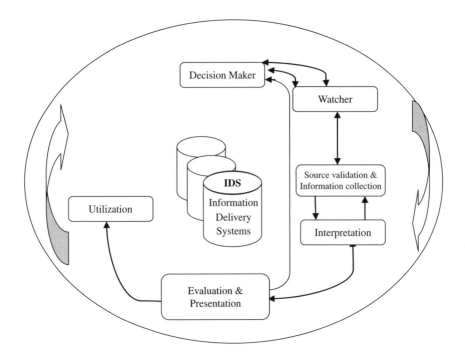

Figure 5.4. *Circular representation of the decision process*

The DM must choose how to act based on relevant indicators connected to their particular problem(s) [THI 02]. The consequences of any decision are seen as expected benefits. The sense of judgment and other cognitive factors play an important role in characterizing the "capacity" of a DM to make the right decision [TOD 00]. Insufficiency in these respects may have significant consequences.

We have given a brief overview of decisions and decision problems, which take account of the cognitive capacities of the DM in the context of CI. We will now look at the concepts of risk and RFs, based on possible interactions between different elements of CI.

5.2. Risks and RFs in CI

5.2.1. *Introduction*

Risk is generally seen as the existence of an unwelcome occurrence triggered by a threat and a level of vulnerability [ALL 07]. A risk is not necessarily a danger, but the indication of a dangerous situation that may result from an action, voluntary or otherwise, applied to a weakness of the system in question. Coras [COR 00] offers a platform for the analysis of security risk in critical systems. This context is, however, different from that of CI, which mixes information systems with decision theory. The work identifies two types of risks: business risks, associated with the organization, and technical risks, which relate to the information processing practices used in the organization (often those which pertain to the operation of a database). The associated risk model may be two-dimensional, with both structural and behavioral axes [MOU 06]. In this section, we will explore notions of risk in the context of CI.

5.2.2. *Actors and their interactions in CI*

CI is made up of a set of processes used in series for decision assistance [EDE 94, RUB 90]. The main users of this system, known as actors, are the DM and the watcher (although other categories of actors exist). These users interact to identify a decision problem, reinterpret it as an IP, process and present the results obtained, and, finally, make a decision based on this newly available information. Although this sequence of operations allows us to build a robust decision assistance process, a certain number of risks, linked to data quality in particular, must not be ignored. The issue of data quality has attracted the attention of a number of researchers; for the moment, no definitive solution to the problem has been found, and the number of different actors involved does not make things any easier [TOD 00, RED 98].

Decision making, based on the processes described above, requires interaction between the actors involved. The DM is confronted with a decision problem that must be solved through the use of relevant indicators. The DM is responsible for the identification, analysis, and deductions they produce before reaching a final decision [DUF 05]. Tasks may be shared: a watcher deals specifically with questions linked to the provision of information from various different systems, both within and outside of the organization.

Figure 5.5 illustrates the relationships and interactions between CI users along with the risks involved. These risks arise from the need to make a decision based on observation and interpretation of the real world (made up of the organization and its environment). To model this world, we use entities, that is, objects or events represented symbolically by identifiers and the values of their attributes. In this, we presume that these values relate to the symbolic representation of things, events, states, and environmental factors which must be taken into account and which may change the context in which the decision must be made, and/or the results of operations, and/or the actions required for a successful implementation of the resulting decisions [ONI 08a].

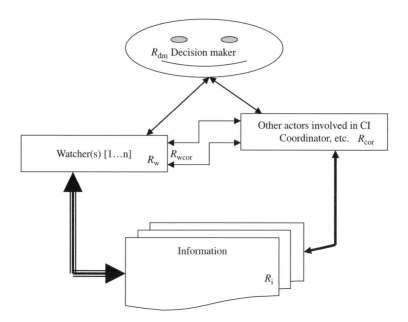

Figure 5.5. *Relationships and risks between actors*

5.2.3. *Risks and RFs*

The identification and quantification of consequences of a risk is not easy. Duffing, David, and Thiery [DUF 05] show several modes of occurrence, the existence of which means that a unique and inflexible approach is not suited to the changing context of CI. Considering the importance of cognitive style in the decision process and the notion of risk in CI presented in [ONI 08a], we note that the effectiveness of a decision is a measurement of the level of risk attributable to this process. To determine the level of risk inherent in a particular decision, we make use of another concept: RFs [ONI 08b].

A *RF* is a concept, thing, circumstance, or factor, which increases the level of vulnerability to a threat and to its consequences in a given situation. This RF may be inherent or be a consequence of non-habitual actions. A RF may, therefore, be defined as any individual action, interaction, or process capable of reducing the performance of an operation. An RF may be the result of action or inaction, of a process already described or of an activity carried out in the life cycle of processed information [ONI 08b]. These RFs are linked to "information" and are therefore represented by the symbol R_i; RFs linked to the watcher are R_w, to coordinators or other actors are R_{cor}, to interactions between the watcher and the coordinator are

R_{wcor}, and to the DM are R_{dm}, as set out in Figure 5.5. We may consequently define every risk using the following variable parameters:

– R_{dm} risk:

- individual characteristics relating to cognitive style, personality traits, and experience;

- false presumptions in the definition of aims and stakes;

- incapacity for satisfactory expression in establishing mutual understanding between the watcher and the coordinator;

- unsatisfactory breakdown of the decision problem into an information/research problem;

- unsatisfactory characterization of stakes in terms of threats, vulnerabilities, and consequences;

- lack of experience and intuition;

- cognitive capacities unsuited to the environmental and organizational parameters;

- bad judgment;

- bad analysis and presentation of data.

– R_w and R_{im} risks:

- inability to correctly understand the DM during the phase of transformation of the decision problem into an IP;

- unsatisfactory breakdown of the problem in relation to the formulation of research aims;

- partial or erroneous characterization of stakes and their transformation;

- research based on ill-defined aims;

- bad information sources;

- inability to validate information sources;

- inaccessibility of data sources (access authorization);

- lack of validation of obtained information, which may arise from:

- incomplete data,

- incorrect data (bad calculations, aggregations, duplicate elements, false, or falsified information),

- incomprehensible data (fields containing multiple values, incorrect formatting, unknown codes, unsuitable models),

- incoherency (linked to coding used, to applicable management rules, to the model used, or to the violation of integrity constraints),

- conflicting names (different terms for the same thing); these incoherencies may produce homonyms, synonyms, or polysemes,

- structural conflicts linked to modeling (conflicting types, dependences, etc.).

– R_{im}, R_w, and R_{wim} risks:

- poor analysis of hypotheses;

- inappropriate transformation of data (e.g. rounding);

- limited access to confidential information;

- inappropriate processing (data discordance, wrong application context);

- faulty interpretation of results due to a lack of experience, intuition, environmental factors, and so on;

- partial or irrelevant presentation of facts through omission, supposition, and so on.

From Figure 5.5, we also note the following:

– R_i: risk involved in the acquisition of information, heterogeneity of sources, their representation, extraction, or use. These RFs are linked to the extraction, transformation, and loading process. Examples include date format: dd-mm-yyyy or mm-dd-yyyy.

– R_w: risk involved in the way the watcher links the decision problem to corresponding IPs. For example, with the problem "we need a car", what other properties might be used to describe the car?

– R_{cor}: useful for representing potential maladaptations resulting from the activities of the coordinator, constituting a risk for the DM. Example: availability of information at the right time.

– R_{wcor}: represents the potential risk arising from collective action (or inaction) on the part of watchers and coordinators. Examples: presumption, omission, and delegation.

– R_{dm}: risks created by the definition and presentation of the decision problem, to its interpretation and to the final inference process – for example, faulty observation and presentation of the problem.

We may then define the risk R:

$$R = \Pi \ \{R_{dm}, R_{wcor}, R_{cor}, R_w, R_i\} \tag{5.1}$$

The above risk may be interpreted as a conditional probability, that is, the information seeking process will be valid (B) if information acquisition (A)

$$\text{Pr (error\_free)} = \text{Pr } (B/A) \tag{5.2}$$

The context of CI is characterized by complex strategic decisions linked to performance demands. The ability to identify and model possible RFs in an appropriate manner should allow us to determine the effectiveness of a decision.

We have now presented the notions of risk and RFs and seen how their effect on the decision performance of the DM may be determined. As DMs are somewhat risk averse, we made proposals concerning the notion of RFs, with emphasis on the fact that risk only becomes clear when vulnerability is involved. We will now attempt to show the importance of cognitive capacities in the decision process.

5.3. Cognitive capacity, a risk, and decision factor

5.3.1. *Introduction*

One fundamental question that needs to be asked is whether the quality of a decision should be evaluated on the basis of the process involved in its construction or by looking at its results (and their consequences). Following the process approach, "almost all decisions are made amid uncertainty". Thus, a decision is a "bet" that must be taken, considering its stakes and odds, and not just looked at in terms of its results. However, it is widely accepted that a good decision structure should include possible results, in that these results affect the attainment of the aims of the DM (consequentialism). A typical example used to demonstrate this idea is that of a surgeon talking of an operation as successful in spite of the fact that the patient died. This is clearly unsatisfactory for all concerned, as the final consequence is much more important than the fact the process went smoothly and according to plan [BUL 03]. In this section, we will demonstrate the importance and the effect of individual cognitive capacities in knowledge collection operations [ONI 08b].

5.3.2. *Cognitive capacity and its effects on decision making*

Decision making is one of the cognitive processes associated with human behavior; it involves the choice of options or of series of actions from a set ofalternatives established from criteria [MOU 06]. This decision-making process is one of 37 fundamental cognitive processes, according to the layered reference model of the brain (LRMB). There are two main categories:

– Descriptive theories are based on empirical observation and on experimental studies of choice behaviors.

– Normative theory supposes that a rational DM makes decisions based on clearly defined preferences, which conform to certain axioms of rational behavior: the utility paradigm and Bayesian theory.

Figure 5.6 shows the relationship between the act of deciding and other processes in the LRMB [RUB 90]. The cognitive capacities of DMs may refer to different capacities depending on their level of exposition, the environment, and other factors. However, the basic cognitive processes of the human brain share and demonstrate similar and recursive characteristics and mechanisms. The complexity of definition of a problem is a result of differences in the interpretation of each actor in a given situation. This produces different levels of understanding of an event and different explanations of influences between events. This is at the base of a concept known as "knowledge collection" [ONI 08b]. Differences in interpretation should be connected to the personal values of individuals. In the same way, explanations of influences are linked to the life experiences of individuals which allow them to construct different belief systems [EDE 94].

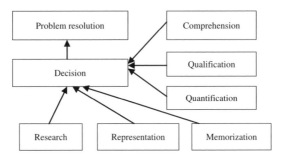

Figure 5.6. *Relationship between decision processes and other processes in the LRMB*

The bulk of work concerning decisions is normative and dominated by rationalist perspectives. Commonly studied decisions are said to be programmed and structured. There are decisions for which the notion of process itself is not relevant, implying that the decision is the result of an immediate mechanical connection between behavioral results and certain environmental conditions [HUN 89].

Practical decisions based on formal models and methods applied to complex and poorly structured situations, forms of representation of users in a situation and their aims and interests, always constitute a relevant aspect for the solution of a problem [ABR 08]. Thus, most decisions and information seeking systems that support these aspects are largely characterized by different forms of incertitude seen as risks [OSO 07].

Figure 5.7 shows quite clearly that the act of decision is far from being uniquely mechanical. It is evident that this process, which results from the capacity for resolution of the problem, proceeds from two factors, involving the following:

i) the processes of understanding, qualifying, and quantifying the decision to be made; a false representation of one of these processes will certainly produce bad judgments or perceptions, leading to failure;

ii) subsequent research, representation, and memorization processes.

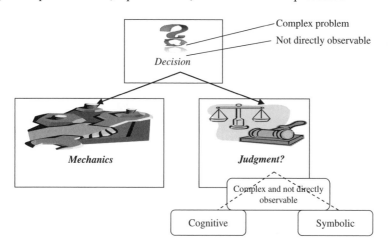

Figure 5.7. *Complexity of the decision process*

As users are classified as actors and each has particular tasks to carry out, stage (i) above may be carried out by different people. The variety of personalities, individual intuition, and experiences, coupled with organizational factors, biases, and other misinformation risks, unequivocally demand a reliable knowledge collection process for use by all actors involved.

5.3.3. *Cognitive model of RFs*

Most human decisions are not mechanical but are based on judgment, implying and explaining the different steps proposed in CI processes. That which we call a "decision" is, in fact, a set of fairly complex processes that are not directly observable (i.e. cognitive and symbolic processes) through which actors develop and share models of their own realities, which they then apply to particular cases to organize their actions. Bullen and Sacks [BUL 03] state that cognitive style is the way in which individuals process and organize information to reach a judgment or a conclusion based on their observations [EDE 94].

Several reasons have been put forward in defense of the idea that a decision and its qualities are difficult things to measure. They are seen to be too vague and ill-defined, preventing the definition of a systematic or concise manner of processing them. Moreover, decision making is multidimensional, and the resulting classes require different judgment criteria. Finally, we should highlight the existence and the importance of a decision that may be made in relation to another decision or a decision of the "second order". We may then pass recursively to higher levels [EDE 94].

The fact that DMs do not always base their decisions on the exact reality (as this is hard to comprehend and never *totally* known) means that a decision is a complex problem. DMs operate using available representations of reality. We can, therefore, state that a DS involves an inventory of that which is known to the DM (data) and that which must be discovered (information). Afterward, rules of reasoning (knowledge) must be applied to guarantee optimal effectiveness [HUN 89, JUN 04]. To attempt to demonstrate the importance of this phase of knowledge collection in the decision process, we offer a causal model taken from [ONI 08a] in the form of an Ishikawa diagram.

In a "fishbone" diagram (Figure 5.8) (which makes no claim to be exhaustive), each "bone" corresponds to a cause that may affect the quality of the result of the following step. The multiplicity of occurrences of these RFs is due to imprecision, which is itself linked to the difficulty of adequately transforming the decision problem – as perceived and presented by the DM – into the equivalent IP. It is this IP that is used in the information seeking process. One commonly accepted quality problem associated with data is "actionability", that is, the degree of credibility accorded to these data from which the DM may wish to act [BUL 03].

The presentation of decision problems to other actors by the DM, with the aim of reducing risk in the entire process, should allow us to guarantee an acceptable level of information action among participating entities. Based on Figure 5.7, we have aimed to integrate both tangible factors (problems linked to database techniques) and intangible factors (bias) to demonstrate the importance of the knowledge collection process in decision making. Up until now, these two types of factors have been dealt with in isolation, and it was difficult to understand their joint effects on the quality of data produced by these processes. Their treatment as a pair will facilitate a balanced approach to risk detection and management, thanks to the identification and reduction of RFs. This is made possible by an appropriate integration of cognitive and environmental factors with organizational needs, the technical constraints of information systems, biases, and problems associated with faulty information.

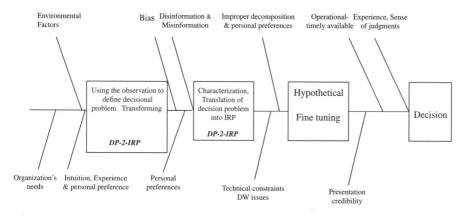

Figure 5.8. *Cognitive architecture of RFs for decision making in CI*

5.4. Conclusion

We have presented a useful model for the identification of RFs in interactions between actors involved in the CI process. We highlighted the importance of the cognitive capacities of the DM, based on the capacity to adequately discern events requiring a decision. Globally, we have presented a cognitive architecture of RFs for decision making in the context of CI, with the idea of identifying and formatting tangible and intangible components that are the sources of risk for the DM.

A popular French saying states that "deciding not to decide is not the same thing as indecision". However, it is important to know what factors lead a DM to not want to make a decision or to know what factors may affect their decision. Although a certain aversion to risk is understandable, it is evident that risk-free projects rarely produce great benefits! Consequently, we have concentrated on the decision process, taking account of the reasons behind a decision and associated risks. In the context of CI, we enumerated a number of possible RFs and the point at which they occur in different CI concepts. This allowed us, in particular, to cover data quality issues in the form of RFs.

We feel that the introduction of a cognitive perspective into the study of RFs linked to decision making in CI will not only facilitate determination of decision capacity but also act as a guarantee of quality for the decision, thus providing precious assistance to actors needing to make strategic decisions.

5.5. Bibliography

[ABR 08] ABRAMOVA N.A., KOVRIGA S.V., "Cognitive approach to decision-making in ill-structured situation control and the problem of risk", *Human System Interactions Conference*, Krakow, Poland, pp. 485–490, 25–27 May 2008.

[ALL 07] ALLAN G.M., ALLAN N.D., KADIRKAMANATHAN V., FLEMING P.J., "Risk mining for strategic decision making", in WEGRZYN-WOLSKA K.M., SZAZCEPANIAK P.S. (eds), *Advances in Intelligent Web System*, ASC 43, Springer-Verlag, Berlin and Heidelberg, pp. 21–28, 2007.

[BAR 06] BARRETTE R., Building a value driven organization – A whole system approach to cultural transformation, 2006, available online at www.valuecentre.com/docs/fivemodels. pdf, accessed on 6 October 2008.

[BOU 04] BOUAKA N., DAVID A., "A proposal of a decision maker problem for a better understanding of information needs", *IEEE Explore*, pp. 551–552, 2004, available online at http://ieeexplore.ieee.org/iel5/9145/29024/01307879.pdf.

[BUL 03] BULLEN G., SACKS L., *Towards New Modes of Decision Making Complexity of Human Factors*, Version 1, Issue 1a, University College London, pp. 1–5, 29 August 2003.

[COR 00] CORAS, A platform for risk analysis of security critical systems, IST-2000-25031, 2000, available online at http://coras.sourceforge.net.

[DAV 01] DAVID B., DAVID A., "METIORE: A personalized information retrieval system", *Proceedings of the 8th International Conference on User Modeling*, pp. 168–177, 2001.

[DUF 05] DUFFING G., DAVID A., THIERY O., "Contribution de la gestion du risque à la démarche d'intelligence économique", *Fouille de Données Complexes, EGC' 05*, 2005.

[EDE 94] EDEN C., "Cognitive mapping and problem structuring for system dynamics model building", *System Dynamic Review*, vol. 10, no. 2–3, pp. 257–276, Summer/Fall 1994.

[HAR 98] HARRIS R., "Introduction to decision making – Virtual Salt", July 1998, available online at www.virtualsalt.com/crebook5.htm.

[HUN 89] HUNT R.G., KRZYSTOFIAK F.J., MEINDL J.R., YOUSRY A.M., "Cognitive style and decision making", *Organizational Behavior and Human Decision Process*, Harvard Business School Press, Boston, MA, vol. 44, pp. 436–453, 1989.

[JUN 04] JUNG W., "A review of research: an investigation of the impact of data quality on decision performance", *International Symposium on Information & Communication Technologies* (ISITC'04), Las Vegas, NV, pp. 166–171, 2004.

[KAR 03] KAREN G., BRUINEDE BRUIN W., "On the assessment of decision quality: consideration regards utility, conflict & accountability", in HARDMAN D., MACHI L. (eds), *Thinking Psychological Perspectives on Reasoning & Decision Making*, John Wiley, Chichester, pp. 347–363, 2003.

[MAR 94] MARTRE H., Intelligence économique et stratégie des entreprises, Report by the Commissariat Général au Plan, La Documentation Française, Paris, pp. 17–18, 1994.

[MCK 74] MCKENNY J., KEEN P., "How managers' minds work", Harvard Business Review, vol. 52, pp. 79–90, 1974.

[MOU 06] MOUZHI G., MARKUS H., "A framework to assess decision quality using information quality dimensions", Proceedings of the International Conference on Information Quality, ICIQ, Boston, 2006.

[ONI 08a] ONIFADE O.F.W., "Cognitive based risk factor model for strategic decision making in economic intelligence process", GDR-IE Workshop, 16–17 June 2008, available online at http://s244543015.onlinehome.fr/ciworldwide/wp-content/uploads/2008/06/nancy_onif adeofw.pdf.

[ONI 08b] ONIFADE O.F.W., THIÉRY O., OSOFISAN A.O., DUFFING G., "Ontological framework for minimizing the risk of non-quality data during knowledge reconciliation in economic intelligence process", Proceedings of the International Conference on Information Quality, ICIQ, Boston, 2008.

[OSO 07] OSOFISAN A.O., ONIFADE O.F.W, LONGE O.B., LALA G.O., "Towards a risk assessment and evaluation model for economic intelligent systems", Proceedings of the International Conference on Applied Business & Economics, Piraeus, Greece, October 2007, available online at www.icabeconference.org.

[RED 98] REDMAN T.C., "The impact of poor data quality on the typical enterprise", Communications of the ACM, vol. 41, no. 2, pp. 79–82, 1998.

[REV 98] REVELLI C., Intelligence Stratégique sur Internet, Dunod, Paris, 1998.

[ROB 81] ROBEY D., TAGGART W., "Measuring managers' minds: the assertiveness of style in human information processing", Academy of Management Review, vol. 6, pp. 375–383, 1981.

[RUB 90] RUBLE T.L., COSIER R.A., "Effect of cognitive styles and decision setting on performance", Organizational Behavior and Human Decision Process, vol. 46, pp. 283–295, 1990.

[SIV 07] SIVANANDAM S.N., SUMATHI S., DEEPA S.N., Introduction to Fuzzy Logic using MATLAB, Springer, Berlin, Heidelberg, NY, 2007.

[THI 02] THIÉRY O., DAVID A., "Modélisation de l'utilisateur, systèmes d'informations stratégiques et intelligence économique", La Lettre de l'Adeli, no. 47, April 2002.

[TOD 00] TODD P., BENBASAT I., "The impact of information technology on decision making: a cognitive perspective", in ZMUD R.W. (ed.), Framing the Domains of IT Management, Pinnaflex Educational Resources, Cincinnati, OH, pp. 1–14, 2000.

[WAN 04] WANG Y., LUI D., RUHE G., "Formal description of the cognitive process of decision making", Proceedings of the Third IEEE International Conference on Cognitive Informatics (ICCI'04.), Washington DC, 2004.

Chapter 6

Multimedia Information Seeking Through Competitive Intelligence Process

6.1. Introduction

Value-added information is widely considered a strategic asset for any decision maker or company able to find, use, and reuse it. Advances in information and communication technology have led to improvement in the quality and increases in the quantity of mutimedia information.

Given this increase in the volume of multimedia information, and the complexity attached to its structure, information seekers may need assistance in searching and efficaciously accessing multimedia information. Rapidly obtaining relevant information may be difficult, but nevertheless this remains indispensable in responding to user information needs and, consequently, in resolving decision problems.

The connotative nature of multimedia information does not in any way facilitate its search and retrieval. The task of multimedia information retrieval is rendered delicate given the fact that multimedia information supports a wide variety of viewpoints, readings, and interpretations. Multimedia information representation and indexing is complex, and this complexity also extends to the expression of a user's need for multimedia information. We have observed [MAG 08] that a semantic gap may emerge between the user, their information needs, and the information solution proposed by the information system. This semantic gap is, in our opinion, caused

Chapter written by Hanène MAGHREBI.

by problems associated with the notion of user needs and by the specificities of multimedia information.

Competitive intelligence (CI) can be used to provide approaches and tools for solving these problems. In this chapter, we will present our methodology, based on CI, for facilitating research and access to multimedia information.

6.2. The two dimensions of CI: decisions and information

For [LEV 01], "Competitive intelligence can be regarded as a mode of thinking and acting in the new economy"; this concerns not only the material economy but also the "immaterial" economy: information and knowledge. The report produced by the French General Planning Commission, led by Henri Martre, in 1994 [MAR 94] defines CI as "the set of coordinated research, processing and distribution actions involving useful information and economic actors susceptible to use this information. These actions are carried out legally with all the necessary protection for the safeguard of the company's patrimony and with the best quality, delay and cost". This definition, therefore, describes not only those operations in which CI may be of assistance but also the way in which these operations should be carried out.

We will consider CI under two main aspects: first, the decision aspect and second, the information that is at the root of, and which justifies, the decision [MAG 07].

CI is a form of "decision intelligence". It may be defined not only as "the action of judgment in relation to a point of contention" but also as "the judgment that produces a solution". The decision process is therefore complex, but produces solutions.

A decision problem may be seen as a gap established between a given situation and a desired situation, considered to be stable. To reduce this gap, a decision problem solving process must be put in place. This process elicits different possibilities for problem resolution, measuring the points for and against each possible solution. The adoption of a solution proposed by the decision-making process allows us to resolve a decision problem with little or no risk. Consequently, a "good" decision is unenvisageable without intelligent information use.

CI is also, by and large, a form of "informational intelligence" in that it professes mastery of an insightful approach to research and information processing and promotes intelligent usage of value-added information.

Many authors [DAV 03, DOU 95, MAR 94, REV 98, SAL 00, CAR 03, LES 06] consider CI as an information process that exists with the aim of assisting the decision process.

In our research, we have adopted a fairly explicit approach put forward by David [DAV 06] who considers CI as an eight-step process:

1) identification and definition of a decision problem;

2) transformation of the decision problem into an information problem;

3) identification of relevant sources of information;

4) collection of relevant information;

5) analysis of collected information to extract indicators for decision;

6) interpretation of indicators;

7) decision;

8) capitalization and protection of assets.

Capitalization and protection of patrimony are transversal steps that should be applied to all other stages of the process.

The CI process presented above emphasizes the link that exists between a decision problem and an information problem (Figure 6.1). It represents a set of

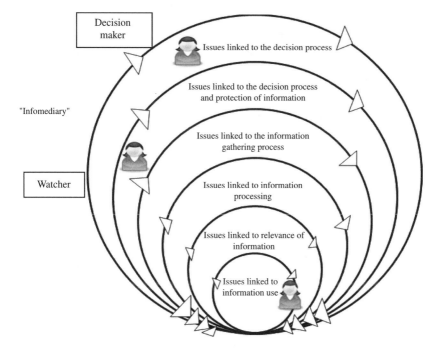

Figure 6.1. *Spiral of issues in CI*

decision and information issues that are interconnected by logical relationships and exchanges between actors (decision maker, watcher, and infomediary) aiming to resolve these problems.

The explicit expression of a decision problem allows us to deduce the information need(s) of users/actors (decision makers). Based on this statement, we will look at the representation of multimedia information not only from the information process view but also as an element of a decision problem.

6.3. Multimedia information: between complexity and accessibility

As explained above, multimedia information is a rich type of information that may provide elements of solution to any information problem and thus constitute a useful basis for decision making. However, the richness of multimedia information – the combination of a set of elements rich in meaning – may complicate or restrain user access to this information.

For instance, the polysemic nature of an image and its ambiguity can pose problems for information seekers. The image may have many meanings and can be interpreted in various ways. Yet, "a sign may express not only several meaning but a quantity of meanings as the image only takes on its quality of signification in relation to the context and implications it assumes". The interpretation of visual signs – that is, an image – is therefore a delicate matter as it varies from one individual to another.

Information seeking, indexing, and representation are also difficult activities. Questions may be raised concerning which elements to take into account in the representation of this kind of information.

6.4. The information seeking process: an overview of paradigmatic evolution

We will tackle the question of information seeking as a process. The expression "information seeking process" refers to all stages and methodology that provide access to information.

Little after the invention of computers, models and tools were proposed with the aim of facilitating the progress of information seeking processes. In 1985, following the first international Conference on Scientific Information, dedicated to "information seeking", and Peter Luhn's demonstration of his indexing system (KWIC). The first conference on scientific information held in 1985 and dedicated to "Information Seeking" (which with Peter Lunhn's demonstration of his indexing system, from this time information seeking) are standing tradition. Since the first conference, the chain, or documentary process, which consists of collection, storage, processing, and diffusion of documents has passed from a simple design to a more systemic approach.

The notion of "System Relevance" emerged at during this period. Indeed, the first models and studies of the information seeking process focused on systems as technical equipment based on the general theory of systems[1] developed by Von Bertalanffy (1937) and on the systemics of these models.

The process of information retrieval in computer systems is based on three fundamental steps: the representation of the request, the representation of information, and the establishment of a relationship between the two. Over time and with technological developments, work has focused on perfecting these steps.

Since then, many studies concerning information seeking systems and processes have been published. The first studies on the subject of the information seeking process looked at the technical aspects of information retrieval systems. In the 1990s, a second approach emerged, involving the user in the information seeking process. This new focus, known as "the user-oriented cognitive paradigm", led to modifications in the perception of performance of an information seeking process and/or an information seeking system by taking into consideration the user, with his/her specific cognitive characteristics and information needs.

6.5. Actors involved in information seeking processes and problem solving

To solve an information problem or decision-making problem, a person is given the responsibility and the charge of carrying out the necessary research activities. In a CI process, this may be the watcher [BOU 04, KIS 07], the "infomediary" [KNA 07], the archivist, the librarian, a consultant, or the person requesting the information [GOR 06].

The watcher is responsible for information seeking and for monitoring of information sources. The "infomediary" plays a role of coordination and mediation between actors involved in the CI process. The watcher, "infomediary", information officer, or consultant are all actors involved in the information seeking process with the aim of providing necessary relevant information for solving a decision problem.

---

1 Systems theory is a principle according to which everything is a system, or everything can be conceptualized following system-based logic. This principle led to the establishment of systemics as a scientific method. Durand's 1979 work, *La systémique*, constitutes an essential reference for understanding systems theory.

For Goria [GOR 06], the person who is responsible for solving a decision problem or making the decision must create "a sequence for the transformation of the problem, enabling the transformation of problem data, in relation to the initial state envisaged, which helps define a path towards a solution to the problem".

This definition is interesting and attractive because the actor seeking information must possess some knowledge, not only in relation to the decision problem but also in connection with the information problem. Although knowledge relating to the decision problem is mainly communicated by the decision maker – who identifies and formulates the decision problem – the person in charge of information seeking will transform the decision problem into an information problem. This transition from decision to information problem is carried out by combining information sources that may contain relevant information that can solve a decision problem.

The information problem may also be approached in the form of a communication problem, where CI actors are not the final users of the information. In this case, a request is made to a human intermediary – a search specialist. In the context of CI, this may be the watcher responsible for information retrieval. The clarification of the decision or information problem by the decision maker and the watcher is, therefore, essential before any use of a computerized information seeking system. The CI actors must have a common understanding of the terms used, their meaning, and their interpretation. This is absolutely critical to avoid difficulties linked to the expression of the problem. Work may be needed to reformulate the problem with the participation of both the decision maker and the watcher.

Before presenting our approach of multimedia information seeking through CI processes, we should clarify our choices in terms of terminology. Researchers working on information retrieval issues and access use generally varied vocabulary; the variety of terms used is probably due to reference points from different contexts. Thus, the terms used in information and communication sciences in connection with information seeking are not necessarily the same as those used by a computer scientist. It is therefore important to clearly explain our choices and our intended meanings before going any further.

6.5.1. *Terminology: the notion of the user*

A user is a person who uses a product or a service. The elements used, in this context, subsist after use. A person becomes a user after a single use of a service, product, or fragment of information, but their relationship with these items may change with repeated and/or frequent use.

Depending on the context of research and the type of study, the "user" may be defined using different situations. In the context of our work, information seeking is seen as the use of an information system with the aim of accessing multimedia information, and also the use of the retrieved information. The user may, therefore, be defined as an information seeker interacting with the information system, an interaction that may itself be presented as a communication situation.

6.5.2. *Terminology: the notion of use*

In terms of terminology, "use" and the less frequent variant "usage" are presented as more or less synonymous.

In the *Petit Robert* dictionary [PRO 05] (in French, but the definitions and distinctions made remain relevant in English), two main meanings are given to the term "usage". The first refers to "the social practices which age (or frequency) renders normal in a given culture". The second refers to "the use of an object, natural or symbolic, to particular ends".

According to [LEC 97], "use is an action and a means of putting something into service in order to attain a specific result".

The term "usage" is more widely encountered in the fields of information and communication sciences and sociology. From a sociological standpoint, Breton and Pro [BRE 06] and Ihadadene and Chaudiron [IHA 08] describe the insertion of new technologies into society. The observation of the way in which individuals interact with technological innovations was at the core of research on users and gratification in the American functionalist approaches of the 1960s and 1970s. "What people do with media" was the main slant of this research, based on the assumption that people actively use media to obtain specific elements of satisfaction that correspond to their psychological or psychosociological needs.

The notion of "usage" is, therefore, found in the context of study of interactions between humans and new technologies.

By focusing on the notion of "usage", the individual ceases to be considered first and foremost as an epistemic subject, that is, as a learner faced with knowledge constituted as mental representations. Attention is instead focused on the socio-technical knowledge the user puts into action to access this knowledge. This somewhat changes the perspective of the user. Although no such distinction exists in English, in French the words "utilisateur" and "usager" are used to differentiate between the former and latter cases, as stated in [IHA 08]. There is also a shift in perspective in that work on the user not only no longer concentrates exclusively on the cognitive dimension of person/system interactions but also on social and symbolic dimensions. "Usage" is thus found in a socio-technical framework as "a stabilized use of an object, a tool to obtain an effect".

Cognitive approaches have been proposed for the study of usages of objects and techniques and their appropriation by individuals. However, if we focus our research on the sphere of mediation studies, we must place these approaches at social rather than technical mediation level. We must remember that, before belonging to collective units, users are individuals in their own right.

In this chapter, we will place an emphasis on the interaction of the individual (user) with the information seeking system, aiming to go beyond the technical aspects of interaction, by treating the information retrieval system as a "partner" in the cognitive activity of individuals, giving it the status of a cognitive artifact.[2]

When considering the use of multimedia information, we subscribe to the point of view set out in [IHA 08], where "use" refers to the interaction between the human individual and the way in which an individual "uses" equipment based on their own competences, cognitive style, and habits. This does not mean that the user is free from the influence of their environment (private, social, symbolic, etc.) but simply that emphasis is placed on the interaction aspect.

Three main principles stand out in the definitions presented above: precision, repetition of the use action, and the socio-psychological and technical contextualization of the action of use. In this work, we will consider the user to be any person who interacts with an object; this object may be an "information system", where the information is the object sought by a person for a particular use.

6.6. Applying a user-centered approach to facilitate multimedia information seeking

The representation of information is a key step in ensuring the success of an information seeking process. An examination of literature on the subject of standards in the representation of multimedia information and a study of the needs of users on the empirical approach[3] have shown us that the user is barely present, if not absent, in considerations of representation of this information; there is a clear

---

2 For Norman, an artifact is a tool designed to conserve, expose, and process information with the aim of satisfying a representation function. The artifact is used to compensate for the lack of necessary objects.

3 We carried out a study among students at the *Institut Européen du Cinéma et de l'Audiovisuel* to study their needs in terms of audiovisual information.

lack of balance between the representation of information on the one hand and the effective needs of users on the other.

In recent times, however, new technologies have reached a degree of maturity which, in our opinion, allows us to place the user and their information needs at the center of considerations. We, therefore, offer a new approach dedicated to the representation of multimedia information, centered on the user and on the use of the information. Our approach allows us to re-establish balance by integrating the information needs of users. An approach of this kind is "open" as it brings together a group of information elements concerning not only the information itself but also elements that characterize its production and use. The aim of this approach is to adapt the representation of multimedia information to the user's information needs and expectations to personalize the seeking process for each user.

Our methodology for a multimedia information seeking process highlights two elements which, from our point of view, are essential in developing a multimedia information representation in that they best ensure access to this type of information. The first of these elements is the multimedia information itself and its characteristics; the second is the user and their information needs.

We suggest that user parameters and those parameters linked to their information needs be used to enrich the representation of standardized information (e.g. by Dublin Core initiation). The user's information needs are determined by the user, by the multimedia information available, and by the context of use of the information.

Contextualization involves the interaction of three elements: multimedia information, the user, and the information need (shown in the form of attributes representing the context of use of the information sought – see Figure 6.2).

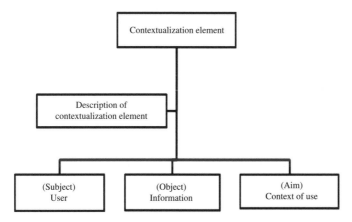

Figure 6.2. *Context model representation in mulitimedia information seeking approach*

The "multimedia information" element represents the object of the information needs of the user. The representation of this element is standardized.

The "user" element corresponds to the subject interacting with the object (the information). The user also interacts with the information system, which facilitates access to multimedia information. As we intend to adapt the representation of information to the user and their information needs, a representation of the user must be established as a vital phase of our suggestions.

The "context of use" element refers to the aims of the subject (the user) concerning the object (the information). This element also reflects the information needs of the user. The context of use of the information represents the end results of an information seeking process from the user's point of view. We consider that every usage is contextualized.

Contextualization, which brings together these three interactive elements, is a "package" that characterizes the information needs of the user and can provide context for different adaptation processes linked to the user's information needs. Each of these three elements possesses a group of attributes for illustration and specification. These attributes are based on the CI approach as they consider the notion of the user's information and decision problems. We will provide specific details of this later on.

6.6.1. *Multimedia information granulation to support multimedia information seeking processes*

Multimedia information presented following different approaches in published literature on the subject: we encounter low-level, high-level, and structural approaches [MAG 06]. The use of standard description forms set up by the community of information officers and computer scientists aims to provide tools for the description of the contents and structure of a document. It would seem, however, that these approaches do not give sufficient consideration to the information needs of the user or to the context of use of research results.

In specialist proposals for indexing and representing information, the usual approach consists of describing a given document using a standard bibliographic notice or description form. These forms, also known as "metadata" – that is, structured data about other data (http://dublincore.org/resources/faq/# whatismetadata) – give access to documents by representational attributes (date, authors, abstract, etc.).

Two standards have emerged which are useful for the representation of multimedia information: the Dublin Core and the International Association of Sound and Audiovisual Archives (IASA) standard.

The Dublin Core is an international standard for the definition of bibliographical elements. Hillman [HIL 01] defines the metadata standard of the Dublin Core as "a set of simple but effective elements for the description of a wide variety of network resources". This standard is made up of 15 fields or elements: cover, description, type, relationship, source, subject, title, collaborator, creator, editor, rights, date, format, identifier, and language.

According to Weibel [WEI 99], the Dublin Core defines a list of fundamental properties capable of providing basic descriptive information for any and all types of resources, independently of format or type. It is essential that the model should remain independent from the platform on which the resources are found. Unfortunately, this standard does not include a "user" field or a field referring to the context of use.

The IASA standard, created by the International Association of Sound and Audiovisual Archives, was set up in 1969 in Amsterdam as a standard for international cooperation between archives holding sound and audiovisual recordings. As with the Dublin Core, the IASA standard contains the following specific descriptive elements:

1) title and responsibility relationships,

2) edition, issue,

3) publication, production, distribution, transmission and date of creation,

4) copyright,

5) physical description,

6) series,

7) notes,

8) note and limits of availability.

An analytical or multilevel description is then used for the first five elements. As with the Dublin Core, use and the user are absent from this standard.

The work of Weibel [WEI 99], Lelong [LEL 00], Hillman [HIL 01], Roussi [ROU 06], and Auffret [AUF 00], in continuing reflections on standards (such as those of the AFNOR or the ISO (International Standard Organization)), attempts to demonstrate and explain the positive and negative points of various standards.

We are forced to recognize that approaches to the representation of multimedia information, whether the result of academic research or consensus-based institutional considerations (such as the AFNOR[4] or the ISO (www.iso.ch)), the Dublin Core (http://dublincore.org/documents/usageguide/) or the IASA), barely consider the user and/or the user's information needs. This is due to the contents of the standards themselves. Despite occasional claims to the contrary (in terms of operability, reusability, etc.), these standards are not used in relation to the user; we must conclude that their missions are the object of incomplete and often implicit definitions on the part of the user.

6.6.2. Integration of the representation of the user into the multimedia information retrieval process

The notion of representing the user is fairly recent. The interest of the notion lies in the information seeking process and in information retrieval systems devoted to the user, which then allow users to find required multimedia information.

The representation of a user is an explicit and simplified model of their characteristics. The use of a representation leads to a strategy for integration of the user in the information seeking process and allows exploitation of necessary knowledge concerning the user and their behaviors. User representation is a fairly complex method that requires us to "borrow" from different branches of science.

The representation of the user in an information retrieval system is generally undertaken with the aim of improving the operation of the system. A more specific aim is to personalize the responses of the information system and reduce the level of complexity, which may "shut in" a user in their interactions with an information seeking system during the information seeking process. In the context of our study, the user (the information seeker) aims to find a particular fragment of multimedia information. Therefore, the user has an information need that is at the root of their engagement in the research process.

Representation of the user allows us to personalize the information retrieval process and develop a flexible information system, one capable of behavioral modification and personalization of responses in relation to the information needs of specific users.

The architecture of an information retrieval system that adapts the representation of the user is based on the cognitive development of users. The abilities and

---

4 Afnor: *Association française de normalisation*, French standardization organization (www.boutique.afnor.org/NEL1Accueil) NormeEnLigne.aspx).

knowledge of users in relation to specialist fields and to the types of problems they can solve are recorded to refine the information seeking process and functions of the information system. The collection of information concerning users allows us to apply an information filtering procedure, whether thematic or functional. After representation, thematic filtering is used to store information that may be used to solve decision problems in the system. Functional filtering is based on the profile of the user and the information proposed corresponds to the user's preferences.

Representation of the user may be carried out using several criteria. User characteristics may be broken down into two categories: static characteristics (representing static parameters) and dynamic characteristics (which are changeable). In the context of our work, we will predetermine characteristics as described in the following sections.

6.6.2.1. *Representation of user characteristics*

This parameter, used to identify a user, contains elements that distinguish the user (a decision maker or watcher in the context of CI). It is presented as a list of attributes concerning the identity and training of the user: for example <surname, first name, postal address, email address, telephone number, status, training>. The <training> attribute contains the name of the course followed by the user and the highest level attained in this training.

The identity parameter may be shared by different users. We include references to contexts of use in this parameter, that is, references to decision and information problems posed by the user and processed by the information system, along with associated annotations.

6.6.2.2. *Representation of user knowledge*

We draw a distinction between theoretical knowledge and practical knowledge, or "know-how". A user may have practical abilities without necessarily possessing theoretical knowledge, or, in the opposite case, have theoretical knowledge, but very little idea of practical applications.

A second distinction should be made between knowledge of the information seeking system and knowledge of the domain concerned by research. The user knowledge parameter allows us to determine what the user does or does not know concerning the operation of the information seeking system and concerning the domain of research.

6.6.2.2.1. Representation of user knowledge of the system used

Knowledge of the system has an impact on the information seeking system; it influences the formulation of the intention of the user, the expression of an information need, and the execution of tasks by the user. The integration of user knowledge within a representation of the user is a particularity often found in the domain of adaptive hypermedia.

Two types of representation are used. The first is a group model, based on the classification of a user among a group of users using a fuzzy matrix associating the user with a group. User preferences are deduced directly from the preferences of other members of the same group. The second type of representation is an individual model, based either on annotation of the user or on the detection and identification of the activities of the user during the information seeking process.

We will look at both types of representation. From our perspective, we consider that it is possible to deduce a user's preferences from their requests (level of granularity of the information concerned by the research, vocabulary used in expressing the request, etc.), from definition of the context of use of information gathered by the user, and from the annotations made by the user.

In our representation of this parameter, knowledge of the system is represented by an attribute using value pairing. A first attribute concerns the precision of user knowledge of operators used in formulating information seeking equations (e.g. Boolean operators). A second attribute concerns the success of an information seeking task in an information seeking system or (Internet) search engine over a series of 10 cases. The third of these attributes concerns the success of an information seeking task. This presumes mastery of information seeking operators and of the conversion of an information requirement into a search request.

6.6.2.2.2. Representation of user knowledge in the research domain

The characteristics of this parameter concern the knowledge of patterns of reading multimedia information (including knowledge of the structure of audiovisual elements, technical characteristics of audio and video elements, fixed images, etc.). Following the example of the representation of knowledge of the system, knowledge of the domain of research is represented as an attribute-value pairing. A first attribute describes the name of the research domain, and a second gives detail as to the knowledge the user has of the domain. With this aim, we have chosen to study the number of information seeking tasks successfully carried out by a user in a particular domain over a total of 10 cases.

6.6.2.3. *Representation of user competences*

Competence may be considered an "internalization" of a set of knowledge and practical abilities or as a judgment of this internalization. There is always a form of "ability" and knowledge above and beyond competence. Judgment of competence is either a judgment of our own abilities or of those of others.

The user competence parameter refers both to competence in a domain and to competence in using a system. System competence reflects the ability of the user to formulate a request, clarify a need in the form of a context of user, and successfully carry out an information seeking task. We consider that a user has information seeking competences in a specific domain if they have both the necessary knowledge (practical and theoretical knowledge of the specificities of the domain of research) and the ability to mobilize this knowledge successfully to use the information seeking system.

Competences are built up through learning. In our case, the user acquires competences (system competences and competence in the domain of multimedia information) by carrying out information seeking tasks using information systems. Competence is, therefore, acquired by working on real information seeking tasks. To build competence, therefore, we must valorize the set of meaningful research situations.

6.6.2.4. *Representation of user preferences*

The user preference parameter allows us to determine the preferences and perceptions of the user concerning:

– The representation of multimedia information (the nature of attributes used by the user during the information seeking process, using attributes concerning denotation, connotation, symbolism, etc.).

– The way in which research results are presented by the system. A user might, for example, prefer the most recent documents. Other considerations include the language in which results are displayed, the number of results shown by the system, and appreciation of the way in which the user gathers information (in this case, we aim to know whether the user prefers the PULL or PUSH method).

– In gathering information, does the user take an intuitive, analytical, discursive, or sensory approach? Does the user treat the information in a reflective, methodical, or affective way? Finally, are the user's preferred sources formal or informal in nature?

The representation of user characteristics is a key aspect of our proposals. The following section looks at the representation of user information needs concerning multimedia information. Clarification of the notion of information need is therefore necessary.

6.6.2.5. *Representation of information needs*

The notion of information needs is crucial in information seeking. An information need is, on the one hand, a transformation of the information and decision problem and, on the other, the cornerstone of information seeking systems, as the information need determines the relevance of items of information.

The information need is part of the cognitive process whereby the user becomes aware of a need and expresses this need not only in a particular language, but also when the user engages in an information seeking process and interacts with an information system. According to [LEC 08a], "the information need corresponds to a lack of knowledge by an individual in a situation, where this lack of knowledge prevents the individual from understanding or from acting in an optimal manner in the situation".

The information need "is born of a cognitive impulse" [LEC 08] but also from a psychological impetus [TRI 04a]. Since the 1980s, cognitive psychologists have been interested in the notion of information need, relating it to a state of gaps in knowledge. An individual responsible for information seeking begins an information seeking process to fill this knowledge gap, thus creating the ability to solve an information problem. By defining the information need, it becomes easier to identify sources and find relevant information later on.

6.6.2.5.1. Awareness of the information need

The user may become aware of their information need by setting it out in two ways: either through interaction with an entity responsible for information seeking (which may be a human intermediary) or by interaction with an information seeking system, through the transformation of an information need (in natural language) into an information request (language used by the information system) that takes the form of a research equation. Tricot [TRI 04b] states that the dawning of awareness of an information need is not always as obvious as it might seem, but it is necessary for the definition of a research goal.

Each user encounters his/her own difficulties in expressing an information need. Each expresses a need using their own vocabulary and in connection with a set of parameters including culture, language, professional experience, and so on. A single word may have many meanings and connotations depending on context and on the person using the word.

Given the complex nature of the question of information need, interview techniques have been developed to evaluate the process by which a user becomes aware of a need.

6.6.2.5.2. Information needs and knowledge: paradoxal or complementary?

Researchers in the domain of psychology consider that awareness of an information need presumes knowledge of the object of research (connected subject and themes) and the ability to find and use information. In our opinion, the user should also possess knowledge concerning the formulation of information needs and of methods used to obtain information. Knowledge of the operation of information systems is also essential.

The fact of launching an information seeking process is positively influenced by the fact of having previously sought information. Thus, a study carried out by Joo and Grable [JOO 01] on information demands concerning retirement showed that those retired individuals who sought the most information on financing their retirement were the richest and the best informed.

Information that is suitable to respond to an information need is said to be relevant. However, a certain level of knowledge of the information language is required to make use of this information. Le Coadic [LEC 08b] highlights the paradox of information needs and the knowledge concerning these needs. According to the author, "an information need shows the state of knowledge in which an information seeker finds himself when confronted with a demand for information he does not have, a piece of information which is necessary for him to continue his research work. It is thus born of a cognitive impulse".

The information need, an important factor in the information seeking process, may be perceived from the perspective of cognitive style. According to Legendre [LEG 93], "cognitive style is a personal, global and relatively stable approach which characterizes the distinct manner in which one person prefers to think, learn, organize their experiences and knowledge, perceive and process information, comprehend perceptual elements or solve a problem in a wide variety of situations". For this reason, the question of information need takes on various dimensions according to the information seeking situation of the user.

Information needs may be seen as falling into the following three categories:

– Information need/acquisition of new knowledge: This first category is the broadest of the three. The user seeks information that he/she needs but does not possess. Tricot [TRI 03a] [TRI 03b] assumes that "we only seek if we know what we don't know, and we know that we may find".

– Information need/confirmation of preexisting knowledge: the user identifies a need, links it to what they already know, and determines what knowledge must be acquired to enrich their knowledge with additional and precise information.

– Information need/exploration of knowledge: in this case, the user takes an exploratory approach. The information need is absolute and does not relate to the first two aspects.

We support the idea expressed by Le Coadic [LEC 08a] that an information need is "extensible", as one information requirement can produce another. Thus, a need to acquire new knowledge may lead to a need to confirm this knowledge.

In our opinion, an information need presupposes two things:

– A hope, a perspective in that each user has their own interpretation of the information they require.

– A use or usage for this information. The user has certain intentions that direct their information need. The gathered information will be used for a precise aim in a particular context. For these reasons, we can say that the information need is a connection between a user and an item of information with the intention to use. To find this information, each user carries out at least one contextualization operation, with the possibility of modifications.

The question of information need only has meaning in relation to information, that is, as an interaction between an individual requiring certain information and a source that does or does not provide a response to this need.

6.6.2.5.3. Transformation of the information need in the context of information use

Multimedia information is viable in any decision situation on the condition that it is able to respond to information needs. The information system should not only facilitate but also personalize access to information. The final use to which information will be put has early implications; we must be able to bring out information through its representation, and this information must be useful in the creation and transfer of knowledge.

In our opinion, the value and relevance of information may be measured by its effective use by final users. The value of information is, therefore, determined late in the process by its use, and earlier in the process by a set of specific characteristics (the content of the information, its author, the sources of the information, and so on).

The user needs a piece of information in relation to their specific situation. The achievement of this aim necessitates a very precise approach from each user. At this point, the CI process that aims to clarify the information problem to improve perception and delivery of relevant information is useful.

The notion of information use is fairly prevalent in definitions of CI (e.g. [DAV 02, MAG 07, MAR 94]. To assist the user in the information seeking process, we propose that the user should clearly set out their information needs in the context of use parameter.

In accordance with our definition of the information need, the satisfaction of this need must involve the establishment of a relationship between a user and a piece of information in the context of use, with each user providing the necessary context as required.

In our proposals, the context of use is represented as a dynamic interaction between different elements (user, information, and use), representing the user's information needs as more than just an external characteristic of the user. The specification of an information need is, by its very nature, dynamic, as it may evolve over the course of the information seeking process or through the interactions of a user with the information. This being the case, the nature of the context demands a precise goal, and the user is the person best placed to specify their needs in terms of representation of information.

The information need of a user is the product of an information problem. The information problem is a transformation of a decision problem, following the CI process suggested by David [DAV 06]. We will represent the information need as an attribute stemming from the <information_problem> attribute, which itself flows from the <decision_problem> attribute.

The <decision_problem> attribute is modeled by the name of the decision problem, the date of formulation of the decision problem, the domain to which the problem pertains, the aim of the decision problem, the name and identifier of the decision problem, and the identifier of the user who formulated the decision problem.

The <information_problem> attribute is represented by the name of the information problem, the date of formulation of the information problem, the domain to which the problem pertains, the aim of the information problem, and the identifier of the user who formulated the information problem.

The <information_need> attribute is modeled by the following elements:

– the cultural context of the information need;

– the spatial context of the information need;

– the temporal context of the information need;

– the physical context of the information need;

– the name of the context of use of the information sought by the user;

– the subname of the context of use;

– the data defining the context of use;

– the identifier of the user who defined the context of use;

– the domain relating to the context of use and the specificities of this domain;

– the aim of the user in using the sought information and the stake element;

– stakes are represented by three subelements: object, signal, and hypothesis.

We have taken inspiration from the proposals set out in [BOU 04] in the context of research into modeling decision problems. This inspiration is most clear in what follows; in particular, we borrowed Bouaka's "stakes" element. This corresponds to the aim of the user. The "stakes" element is made up of three subelements that characterize it: "object", "signal", and "hypothesis". The "object" subelement corresponds to the object of the problem. The "signal" subelement corresponds to the decision environment triggered by observation of the object. The "hypothesis" subelement is linked to the level of signal of the object. The signal corresponds to that which leads the user to seek information. The "stakes" element may be resumed as follows: "if I do not act on "object" in spite of "signal", I run the risk of "hypotheses"".

The context of use element and its subelements aim to render the information needs of the user distinct. Once the context of use has been clarified, it becomes easier to save this information for future reuse. The representation of the information problem in this form enriches the information seeking phase as it allows us to find out if other users have formulated the same context of use, and what information was used.

The integration of representations of the user and their information needs on the same level as the representation of the characteristics of multimedia information is done with the aim of reducing the gap between user information needs and the representation of information, thus facilitating access to multimedia information.

6.7. Conclusion

The goal of an information seeking approach is to satisfy the expectations of an information seeker by fulfilling their information needs. Key notions of information seeking, such as representation, recording, and information needs are taken into consideration in our approach. The integration of user information needs via the context of use of research results in the representation of multimedia information seems, to us, to be the cornerstone of a successful information seeking process and is central to any "intelligent" information seeking system.

6.8. Bibliography

[AUF 00] AUFFRET G., "Structuration de documents audiovisuels et publication électronique. Constitution d'une chaîne éditoriale pour la mise en ligne de collections audiovisuelles", Computer Science Thesis, Compiègne University of Technology, Compiègne 2000.

[BOU 04] BOUAKA N., "Développement d'un modèle pour l'explicitation d'un problème décisionnel: un outil d'aide à la décision dans un contexte d'intelligence économique", Thesis, Information and Communication Sciences, University of Nancy 2, Nancy, 2004.

[BRE 06] BRETON P., PRO S., L'Explosion de la Communication. Introduction aux Théories et aux Pratiques de la Communication, La Découverte, Paris, 2006.

[CAR 03] CARAYON B., Intelligence Économique, Compétitivité et Cohésion Sociale, La Documentation Française, Paris, 2003.

[DAV 02] DAVID A., THIERY O., "Application of EQuA²te architecture in economic intelligence ICTEI", IERA, Ibadan, Nigeria, 2002.

[DAV 03] DAVID A., THIERY O., "L'architecture EQuA²te et son application à l'intelligence économique", IERA, Nancy, France, 2003.

[DAV 06] DAVID A., "La recherche collaborative d'information dans un contexte d'intelligence économique", Le Système d'Information de l'Entreprise, Algérie-Télécom, Alger, Algeria, 2006.

[DOU 95] DOU H., Veille Technologique et Compétitivité, Dunod, Paris, 1995.

[GOR 06] GORIA S., Proposition d'une démarche d'aide à l'expression des problèmes de recherche d'informations dans un contexte d'intelligence territoriale, Doctoral Thesis, University of Nancy 2, Nancy, 2006.

[HIL 01] HILLMAN D., Guide d'utilisation du Dublin Core, 2001, available online at: www.bibl.ulaval.ca/dublincore/usageguide-20000716fr.htm.

[IHA 08] IHADADENE M., CHAUDIRON S., L'étude des Dispositifs d'Accès à l'Information Électronique: Approches Croisées, Hermès, Paris, 2008.

[JOO 01] JOO S., GRABLE J.E., "Factors associated with seeking and using professional retirement-planning help", Family and Consumer Sciences Research Journal, vol. 30, pp. 37–63, 2001.

[KIS 07] KISLIN P., Modélisation du problème informationnel du veilleur dans la démarche d'intelligence économique, Doctoral Thesis, University of Nancy 2, Nancy, 2007.

[KNA 07] KNAUF A., Caractérisation des rôles du coordinateur-animateur: émergence d'un acteur nécessaire à la mise en pratique d'un dispositif régional d'intelligence économique, Doctoral Thesis, University of Nancy 2, Nancy, 2007.

[LEC 97] Le COADIC Y.F., Usages et Usagers de l'Information, Nathan, Paris,1997.

[LEC 08a] Le COADIC Y.F., La Science de l'Information, 3rd edition, Que sais-je?, no. 2873, PUF, Paris, 2004.

[LEC 08b] Le COADIC Y.F., *Le Besoin d'Information: Formulation Négociation, Diagnostic*, ADBS, Paris, 2008.

[LEG 93] LEGENDRE R., *Dictionnaire Actuel de l'Éducation*, 3rd edition, Guérin, Montréal, 1993.

[LEL 00] LELONG B., MALLARD A., "La Fabrication des Normes", *Réseaux*, vol. 18, no. 102, 2000.

[LES 06] LESCA H., "Veille stratégique pour le management stratégique de l'entreprise". *Economie et sociétés*, Séries sciences de gestion, vol. l5, no. 20, pp. 31–50, 1994.

[LEV 01] LEVET J.L., *L'Intelligence Économique Mode de Pensée, Mode d'Action*, Economica, Paris, 2001.

[MAG 06] MAGHREBI H., DAVID A., "Toward a model for the representation of multimedia information based on users' needs: economic intelligence approach", *IV International Conference on Multimedia and Information and Communication Technologies in Education (m-ICTE)*, Spain, 2006.

[MAG 07] MAGHREBI H., DAVID A., "Integrating users' needs into multimedia information retrieval system", *3rd International Conference on Computer Science: ATINER*, Athens, Greece, 2007.

[MAG 08] MAGHREBI H., DAVID A., "Open system for indexing and retrieving multimedia information", *36th Canadian Association for Information Science Conference (CAIS/ACSI)*, Vancouver, Canada, 2008.

[MAR 94] MARTRE H., CLERC P., HARBULOT C., *Intelligence Économique et Stratégie des Entreprises*, La Documentation Française, Paris, 1994.

[PRO 05] PROULX S., "Penser la conception et l'usage des objets communicationnels", in SAINT-CHARLES J., MONGEAU O., (eds), *Communication. Horizon de Recherches et Depratiques*, Presses de l'Université du Québec, Québec, pp. 297–318, 2005.

[REV 98] REVELLI C., *Intelligence Stratégique sur Internet*, Dunod, Paris, 1998.

[ROU 06] ROUSSI S., "Standardisation de l'indexation de documents numériques: le cas des questionnaires pour l'évaluation des connaissances", *Indice, Index, Indexation*, ADBS 2006.

[SAL 00] SALLES M., "Problématique de la conception de méthode pour la définition de système d'intelligence économique", *Revue d'intelligence économique*, no. 6–7, Association française pour le développement de l'intelligence économique, October 2000.

[TRI 03a] TRICOT A., "IHM, cognition et environnements d'apprentissage", in BOY G., (ed.), *L'Ingénierie Cognitive: IHM et Cognition*, Hermès, Paris, pp. 411–447, 2003.

[TRI 03b] TRICOT A., "Pour une approche ergonomique de la conception d'un dispositif de formation à distance utilisant les TIC", *Revue STICEF*, vol. 10, pp. 1–27, 2003.

[TRI 04] TRICOT A., "Besoin d'information", *Argos*, no. 36, pp. 36–39, 2004.

[WEI 99] WEIBEL S., "The state of the Dublin core metadata initiative", *D-Lib magazine*, April 1999, available online at: www.dlib.org/dlib/april99/04weibel.html.

Chapter 7

Strategies for Analyzing Chinese Information Sources from a Competitive Intelligence Perspective

7.1. Introduction

Mastery of information has become an essential issue for organizations, whether state departments or private structures, in the field of politics, of business, or of scientific research. In recent years, the scientific research sector has experienced increasing pressure with mounting stakes in political, ideological, and commercial terms, and presents major strategic issues. Scientific research has accelerated and flourished with the development of awareness of a real planetary emergency in certain sectors, particularly those of renewable energy and environmental protection, but also in other fields important for human survival, such as medicine, agriculture, and water treatment. Technical and high-tech sectors are also concerned by new patents that create strategic monopolies. Given that intellectual property rights lock down all scientific discoveries and depend on the fact of being first to register a patent, we are now dealing with a "research race" on an international scale. This is as true in industrialized countries as for major emerging powers, such as India and China. We can no longer afford to ignore these new players, who are gaining rapidly in importance in all domains.

In this context of heightened competition, with alliances between businesses and government and genuine engagement in scientific research, there is a clear need for

Chapter written by Nadège GUENEC.

high-performance tools to harness useful information in record time. It is therefore essential to find tools that ally performance, rapidity, and multilingual capabilities to carry out extremely fine watching activities. Faced with a growing mass of information of varying nature and in the context of an unstable economy, decision makers need increasingly high-performance tools to assist them in comprehending their environment.

These tools must have an extremely fine capacity for exploration to obtain the most relevant information for the decision maker, on the one hand, and to assist decision makers in refining their own analysis of the environment, corresponding as closely as possible to the user's own logic and to their domain of study.

This chapter focuses on Chinese scientific information, as this is more or less unknown territory for our organizations. Chinese researchers, on the other hand, who generally have a strong grasp of English, have access through their laboratories to worldwide scientific databases. They are, therefore, able to access the totality of scientific information available from around the world, whereas Western researchers have no means of accessing Chinese scientific information (unless Chinese researchers publish in English). Scientific and technical information are essential for any researcher wishing to carry out relevant scientific watch; it is also a crucial component of the strategic information needed to carry out a competitive intelligence process, whether this be done by decision makers in the private sector or at government level, mostly in the context of industrial applications of research. Competitive intelligence and the practices involved may be defined as an analysis of the status quo with the aim of anticipating possible developments, allowing correct orientation of future actions [MAR 94]. Mastery of this type of information is, therefore, an absolute necessity in all economic domains linked to the rapidly developing technical sector: pharmacology, genetic engineering, chemistry, energy, physics, aeronautics, nuclear technology, and so on.

In the context of this work, we aim to demonstrate what may be achieved in terms of automatic processing of Chinese scientific information, using largely validated information processing and analysis tools generated by the French research sector. Our main task was to adapt these tools to the Chinese information environment. After a discussion of the indispensable nature of Chinese scientific information, our analytical strategy will show how Chinese strategy is developing at international level (section 7.2). We will then consider means of harnessing Chinese information (section 7.3) and create a first level of value-added strategic information (section 7.4).

7.2. Chinese scientific information as an essential source of information

Although Deng Xiaoping launched a new era of openness between China and the rest of the world at the beginning of the 1980s, internationalization and the economic boom truly occurred only in the mid-1990s, institutionalized by the establishment of the "socialist market economy". The 2000s marked a new turning point; in 2001, China joined the world trade organization and, by this act, entered into worldwide competition. Increasing numbers of foreign companies have created bases in China and the entire country was connected to the Internet in the space of a few years. Although the first decade of the new millennium was marked by new issues for the Chinese government, their strategy remains essentially the same: reconquer the position of leader in Asia and gain recognition as a major power on the world stage.

Transfers of knowledge and technology are therefore crucial. Nonetheless, China, following its strategy of economic domination, cannot focus exclusively on this method of acquiring scientific knowledge, and must develop its own power in terms of scientific innovation. On January 9, 2009, a national prize giving ceremony was held in Beijing to honor achievements in science and technology in the presence of the President, Hu Jintao, the Prime Minister, Wen Jiabao, and a number of other political and scientific heavyweights. The Prime Minister declared that it is the strength of research that will decide the destiny of the country, exhorting scientists to place themselves at the service of businesses and to themselves invest in the development and commercialization of new products.

According to the latest Biennial Report of the Observatory of Science and Technology (OST)[1] [OST 08], internal expenditure on R&D in China more than doubled between 2000 and 2005. In 2006, China reached the number two position worldwide in terms of R&D expenditure, with a cash injection of $136 billion [OCD 06], an increase of more than 20% in 1 year. R&D expenditure in 2008 was around $101 billion[2] [OST 08]. In 2005, China became the preferred destination for Western industrialists hoping to globalize their R&D [UNE 05]. The Chinese government, aiming to increase the attractiveness of the country in terms of R&D, created special zones by theme. Furthermore, the number of researchers in China increased by 77% between 1995 and 2004; today, China is second only to the USA in terms of numbers of researchers, with 926,000 individuals involved in this activity [OCD 06]. *Nature* journal considers [BUT 08] that scientific development in China is progressing even more rapidly than economic development (Figure 7.1).

---

1 The OST (*Observatoire des sciences et techniques*) is an inter-institutional platform founded and administered by major actors in the French system of research and innovation.
2 USA: $280 billion. EU: $199 billion. Japan: $113 billion.

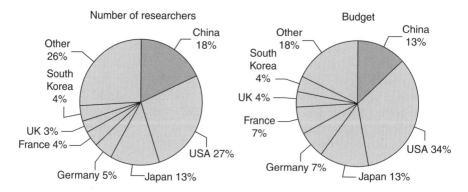

Figure 7.1. *Part played by China in worldwide research and development (source: Les Echos, July 6, 2007)*

The emergence of Chinese authors in the international scientific press has been gradual, beginning in the early 2000s, but there has since been a major explosion in English language scientific publications by Chinese authors in international journals with a high impact level, particularly in the first semester of 2007. In 2004, Chinese researchers contributed to the production of 6.5% of all worldwide scientific publications, and attained second place in terms of publications linked to nanotechnology research [VIL 08]. In 2005, China reached number five in world rankings in terms of the number of international scientific publications [ZHO 09]. The 1.1 million Chinese researchers (out of a total of six million worldwide) increased the number of their scientific publications by 96% between 2001 and 2006, putting their country in third place worldwide with 7% of all publications recorded by the science citation index (SCI) (in all disciplines) [OST 08]. The number of publications of which the first author is based in China has also increased dramatically. In 2007 alone, the journal *Science* published around 30 articles by Chinese authors or co-authors. China is also second on the world stage in terms of presentations at major conferences, with 10.1% of the total according to ISPT rankings[3] [IST 08]. Chinese authors, therefore, have a major presence, and the quality of their work is on a par with its quantity. The number of patents and journal articles produced by both Chinese scientists and engineers are increasing rapidly.

The medium- and long-term national program for the development of science and technology (2006–2020), launched on February 9, 2006, sets out a 15-year strategy for scientific and technological development in China. The declared aim of this plan is that science and technology and their direct applications should contribute at least 60% to the development of the Chinese economy. Over the same

3 ISTP: *Index to scientific and technical proceedings*. This index relates to communications at major international conferences.

time period, dependence on foreign technologies should be reduced by at least 30%. The number of patents and academic scientific publications should place China in one of the top five positions worldwide. Through this plan, the Chinese government has encouraged big businesses to set up R&D centers, either alone or in collaboration with public bodies. Analysis of the dichotomy between private and public research in China should not follow the same lines as in Western countries. In reality, everything in China is considered to be public; in other words, everything belongs to the Party. A Chinese company is never really private. Even if it is managed in the same way as a private company, links with the state remain very strong. The circulation of knowledge and decision-making networks have evolved very little, as the Communist Party is ever-present and all-powerful not only in the political sphere but also in economic, scientific, and other domains. Moreover, a brief look at the CVs of the heads of Chinese companies reveals a great deal. The more a business is involved in a sensitive sector or has important dimensions, the more its directors are likely to hold important strategic positions within the Party. An individual may easily be a member of the national people's assembly and the director of a company. Knowledge, patents, and technologies, therefore, belong "to the Chinese people".

Furthermore, plans have been made to overhaul the current system of scientific and technical management by bringing together the military and the civilian research organizations, with the aim of creating common research programs and producing commercial applications to cover research expenditure. All major axes of technical research are included in the 15-year plan, but certain domains are given priority: energy research, use of biological resources, and the development of space and laser technologies. Thus, four major research projects have been defined for the next 15 years in the aim of increasing China's international competivity through major breakthroughs in science and technology: protein studies, quantum control, nanotechnology research, and genetics. In terms of budget, the program aims to double contributions to R&D as a proportion of China's gross domestic product (GDP), which is itself increasing at a rate of 9–10% per annum; investment may, therefore, potentially triple over 15 years. New technologies thus constitute a major strategic axis of Chinese policy.

As major strategic domains have been clearly defined by the government, the direction to be taken by the country is already fixed and, from here, attention is focused on the concrete application of these aims. New banking and fiscal policies aim to support innovative start-ups alongside R&D departments in existing companies.

Furthermore, one of the main concerns of this plan is the protection of intellectual property and the registration of patents, which form part of a strategic plan at national level. The Chinese government considers scientific advances as part of a national integrated system of innovation. It is therefore interesting to look at the position of Chinese actors in terms of numbers of patents registered worldwide. China has also accelerated the internationalization of its research system, thanks to an increased visibility in international journals and conferences, and to a vast network of international cooperation, although – as we see in Figure 7.2 – the number of triadic patents remains low.

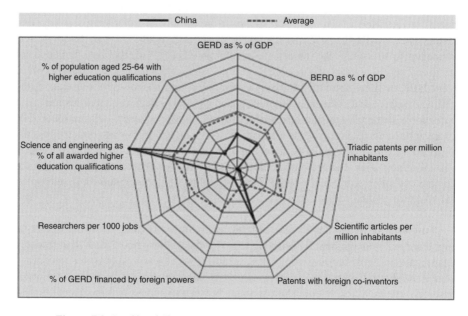

Figure 7.2. *Profile of China in science and innovation (source: OCDE 2008)*

To complete this presentation of the growing scientific power of China and demonstrate how our method for the analysis of Chinese scientific information is connected to a wider approach to competitive intelligence, we will now look at the sector of agriculture and biotechnologies in China. This sector includes the question of hybrid wheat, which will be the focus of our demonstration.

A plan has already been set out according to which research domains in biotechnology will count for 5% of Chinese GDP in 2020 (a total of around $250 billion) [QUO 07]. The main applications of this domain will be in the fields of pharmaceutics, genetics, protein engineering, human tissue engineering, and new-generation industrial biotechnologies. The Chinese government wishes to encourage research in this domain and hopes, in particular, to accelerate the implementation of transgenic technologies that it considers to be crucial for durable agricultural development and for increased competitivity in agriculture. "The stated objective is to obtain a stock of genes with high added value, while avoiding, as far as possible, paying intellectual property rights. The Prime Minister, Wen Jiabao, highlighted the urgency and strategic importance of this technological program and asked those responsible to move as quickly as possible. An additional four billion Yuan (just under $570 million) has been assigned to research on genetically modified rice and wheat (part of which will go to fulfilling security conditions linked to these crops)" [VIL 08]. At the present moment, around 150 agricultural biotechnology laboratories at national and local level are spread among over 50 research institutes and universities across the country. Over 100 laboratories across the country are working on the genetic sequencing of plants, animals, and humans and more than 50% of third-world investment in plant biotechnologies is directed toward China. In 1999, Chinese expenditure on vegetal biotechnologies was around $112 million. In 2000, this reached $120 million and, in 2001, $360 million. Of the tests carried out in agricultural biotechnology, 90% concern resistance to insects and to disease.

All these figures serve to show that China has entered into a phase of scientific research clearly oriented toward aims of economic domination, part of a strategy to gain political power on the international stage.

7.3. A global vision of the sector through patent analysis

To look at the position of China in a given domain at international level and, therefore, to measure the country's capacity to gain a scientific and economic monopoly of a technology, we must begin by studying patents registered in the domain worldwide. On an international level, only three patent offices are important: those of the USA, Europe, and Japan. The OST report shows that the increase in Chinese patent registrations was +124% for the European Patent Office, and +261% for the American office.

As patents are an important indicator of the technological dynamism of a country, we must begin any analysis of the position of China in a given sector by studying patents concerning that sector. To do this, we use Matheo Patent, an automatic patent analysis tool developed by the Université Aix-Marseille. Matheo Patent is directly connected to Espacenet, the European Office's online database of global patents.

To obtain all patents relating to the hybridization of wheat, we chose to search for keywords in titles and abstracts rather than using the ICP code[4], having noticed that the patents that interested us fell into various different ICP categories.

---

4 *International Patent Classification*, hierarchical system for the classification of patents and models by the domain of technology concerned.

Our research equation, based on recommendations from experts in the domain, was as follows: [(HYBRID AND WHEAT) AND MALE AND STERILE].

Matheo Patent, after detecting the corpus of patents corresponding to this request, downloads all linked bibliographical entries, abstracts, claims, and even pages of drawings if these are included in the patent. 79 patents were found for the period January 2000–October 2008. We were then able to establish a preliminary map of author locations.

It is interesting to note that the two countries with most entries were the USA and China (with several organizations registering patents: Hebei Normal University, Crops Institute of Sichuan Provincial Academy, and the Hunan Agricultural College). The different countries registering patents were placed into groups to obtain more information on national orientations in terms of research strategies and actors (Figure 7.3).

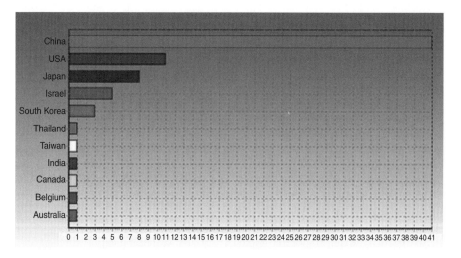

Figure 7.3. *Countries classed by number of patents registered*

China thus takes a very clear lead in terms of the number of patents held in this domain. Although, Chinese patents do not always follow the same information structure in terms of format (Chinese patents are often shorter than global, European, or American patents), their large number shows that Chinese researchers are extremely active in this domain.

We now move on to a deeper analysis of these different groups to study levels of cooperation between different actors in the domain. This information is important in the sphere of scientific research. Cooperating leading groups share research domains, and thus information, technologies, and capabilities which increase scientific efficiency. To obtain this information, we will look at the network links between different groups (Figure 7.4).

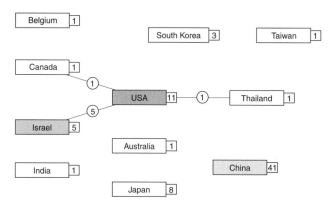

Figure 7.4. *Cooperation between countries*

We note that in spite of a high number of patents, China has not developed cooperative links in terms of patent registration (Figure 7.4), confirming the direction of Chinese government strategy as described above. In comparison, the USA has cooperative links with three other countries – Canada, Israel, and Thailand. This may also indicate that reflection has already taken place concerning a research strategy and that a choice in terms of research directions has already been made. To deepen our analysis, we may establish a diagram of IPCs by country, allowing us to visualize different research techniques used by different countries (Figure 7.5).

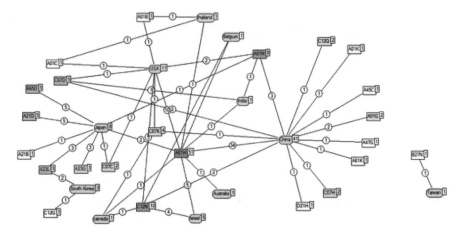

Figure 7.5. *Technologies used by different countries*

Specific technologies (ones not shared with other countries) are particularly present in China and Japan. For the other countries included (with the exception of South Korea and Taiwan), technologies used are shared by two or more countries. This analysis is interesting as it highlights the orientation of research in this domain by ASEAN member states. This analysis may be taken even further by using the IPC to its full extent (with more precise eight figure codes).

Research orientations within the "China" group can be shown easily using a matrix within the group to cross-reference "inventor" and "IPC" fields (Figure 7.6).

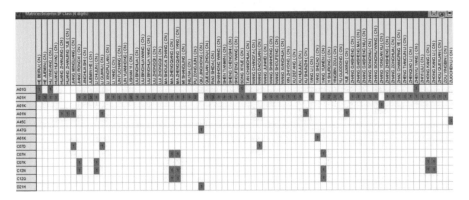

Figure 7.6. *Research focus of Chinese inventors in relation to IPC*

Global information on key technologies is obtained by creating a network between the different IPCs found in each patent. This produces a network map that indicates the key domains (network nodes), main research orientations, and areas that are detached from the bulk of the networks, and which may indicate innovative technologies (Figure 7.7).

Figure 7.7 shows three main research orientations, one of which constitutes a separate group from the other two orientations. It also clearly indicates a research domain that seems to be an innovative approach (as it does not participate in all networks). This is also the case for techniques that are linked to a network by their IPC code without being connected to other technologies.

The use of Matheo Patent thus provides us with a first visualization of the domain of hybrid wheat at international level, clearly showing that scientific research orientations in Western countries (the USA, Canada, etc.) are very different from those observed in the same domain in Asia, and in China in particular. The use of this first tool in our watch process confirms the previously unproven suspicions of experts in the domain: first, that active scientific research is underway in the domain of wheat hybridization in China, and second, that the country has not yet developed cooperative links between its institutions or businesses and those in other countries. This analysis, carried out using data from the European patent office, does not reflect the totality of Chinese activity linked to hybrid wheat. However, it clearly demonstrates China's position as leader in terms of the number of patents registered. We must, therefore, dig deeper to obtain a more precise vision of the realities of Chinese scientific research in this domain, along with the technological applications of the domain and the associated economic issues, not only in China but also in the near future, at international level.

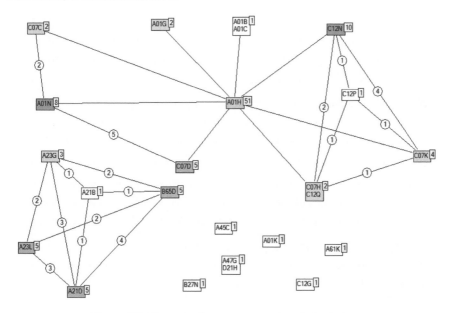

Figure 7.7. *Key technologies in research on hybrid wheat*

7.4. Chinese sources of scientific information

A vast amount of information on China can be found on the Internet. This is evident in scientific domains where Chinese researchers, seeking global recognition, are publishing increasing numbers of articles in international journals with a high impact factor. Thus, as we saw above, an analysis of databases such as SCI, PubMed, and others can be very instructive, and constitute a veritable goldmine of information when beginning a scientific watch process concerning China.

At this point, a quick experiment to compare the numbers of Chinese publications in English and those in Chinese may be interesting. We will use the Google Scholar search engine, which indexes the contents of certain scientific article databases, and is the only search engine of its kind to also process articles in Chinese characters.

We launched a search using the expression "male sterility gene", then a second search with the same expression in Chinese: 雄性不育基因. We chose to restrict our search to the period 2000–2009. We were then able to make the following rapid observations:

– There were more responses for the Chinese search term, with 1,320 against 938 in English.

– Of the five key authors in the English language version of the search, three had Chinese surnames (WANG, TAO, and DONG). These authors do not appear as key authors in the Chinese version of the search, where the "top five" are FANG, WANG, ZHU, SUN, and YUAN.

Although we would not wish to use this type of approach to carry out relevant watch, this brief experiment shows that the potential research capacity of China is far beyond that which we might deduce from analysis of English language scientific documentation alone. In our opinion, English language publications are just the tip of the iceberg where Chinese research is concerned; these publications relate to the most successfully completed fields of research, but reveal little on work in progress. Scientific and technical information are important sources of strategic information for decision makers in a competitive watch process, used to plan decisions and competitive intelligence actions. This information is also important for researchers, who can subsequently effectuate complete global watch on the state of the art and scientific developments in their field of study. As far as the database industry is concerned, China has been part of the International Committee on scientific and technical databases since 1984. In 1987, China gained an international information center, initially responsible for the creation of 134 major databases. Less than 10 years later, the center had over 1,300 databases. Currently, almost half of all databases are developed by public bodies and may be consulted over the Internet [MA 05].

Any competitive intelligence and information seeking process aiming to facilitate business decisions must, in China as in any other part of the world, include a source verification aspect with qualification of the degree of reliability of information depending on the source. We must pay particular attention to various forms of manipulation of information that may be encountered: "information poisoning", unfounded rumors, erroneous predictions, imprecise, or false factual data, and so on. We provide a qualification of the various different Chinese information sources available online, which is given in Table 7.1. In our opinion, scientific articles present the same level of credibility in China as in other countries. We will therefore use the Chinese scientific and academic article database, China national knowledge infrastructure (CNKI), to access the totality of Chinese research and define an approach for the reading and analysis of the dynamics of the hybrid wheat market in China.

Type of site	Credibility of contents
Government websites	Propaganda
Online newspapers	
Company websites	Incomplete
Financial information websites	
Discussion boards	Require checking
University websites	Imprecise information
Professional associations	Good product information
The SIPO Chinese patent database	Credible
Scientific databases	

Table 7.1. *Qualification of information depending on source*

The CNKI portal is a project developed by universities, bringing together various Chinese databases. Its development was, and still is, strongly supported by the Chinese government, which aims to use this portal to stimulate growth of a "culture of information" in China and develop information-based intelligence in China. In addition to Chinese databases, CNKI is now open to foreign databases; for example, an agreement was signed with Springer in 2008, giving the latter a foothold in the Chinese market. Consultation of bibliographical notices is free, but full text downloads must be paid for and require a subscription. At the end of 2007, CNKI contained references to over 25 million articles.

The Internet in general in China is undergoing a permanent process of improvements. In few months, the entire configuration of CNKI changed [GUE 08]. In addition to the collection of a corpus, which is always labor-intensive (this process cannot be done automatically), two new problems have emerged:

– One line of Chinese text contains up to three fonts, which alternate from one character to the next. This is not noticeable when reading, but creates noise in coding.

– Keywords disappear when downloading the corpus; they are no longer present in the description fields of an article, restricting bibliometric analysis.

However, online bibliometric tools have been integrated into CNKI, allowing us, for a request, to see lists of authors by frequency of publication, organizations, keywords, and so on. Essentially, CNKI provides bibliometric data but does not allow users to create their own data (at best, possibilities for this are limited).

We are, therefore, obliged to make new modifications to process this information automatically using our tools.

To keep our demonstration simple, we have deliberately restricted the collected corpus. A more relevant analysis would involve the collection of all articles in the database containing the word "wheat". This request would provide us with a visualization of research on hybridization as a proportion of all work concerning wheat. However, this request produces almost 30,000 responses. The analysis of a corpus of this size would be beyond the scope of this article, hence our restriction of the corpus; our aim here is to demonstrate the feasibility of analysis of Chinese information. Our extracted corpus, therefore, focuses on male sterility, a major condition for hybridization, and covers all articles from the period 2000 to 2008. We thus obtain 302 responses (Figure 7.8) and, by analyzing this corpus, we are able to observe the development of research on wheat hybridization over this 8-year period.

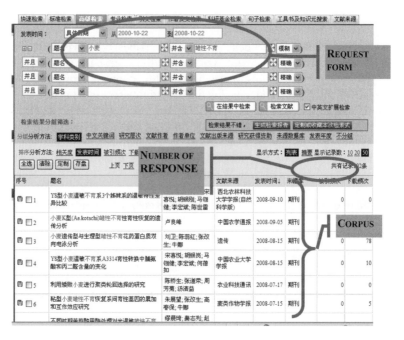

Figure 7.8. *Request process in the CNKI database*

The next step after sending the request is to download the corpus. Notices can be downloaded in pages of 50. Note that the database is extremely well structured (Figure 7.9). We can then carry out a certain number of analyses on the metadata of the database to extract a first level of information.

Figure 7.9. *Page of 50 notices extracted from the corpus*

7.5. Automatic processing of information by bibliometrical analysis of metadata

7.5.1. *Specificities of a Chinese-language corpus*

Our work takes place in the context of analyzing an economic environment to provide strategic knowledge to support a decision process. The first set of information to obtain, therefore, concerns the actors in the domain and their reciprocal actions. This type of information may be extracted from our corpus, but it is not immediately apparent from simple reading of the corpus; we must use a specific tool to cross-reference and count fields. We do not aim to simply model information based on its contents, but in relation to the use to be made of the information [DAV 05].

From this extracted corpus, we can carry out a first level of analysis on the metadata contained within the bibliographical notices of articles. The structure of the database allows us to carry out the necessary cross-referencing.

The Tétralogie program, developed by the *Institut de Recherche en Informatique* in Toulouse, France, is used for data mining [DOU 03] and allows us to show networks of actors and their dynamics, the development of concepts and subjects of study and to detect weak signals [LOU 07] present in a corpus of material. Its use has been widely proven to be valuable; our aim is to use Tétralogie in a new linguistic environment.

It was therefore necessary to add a software development phase to our work to adapt Tétralogie to the Chinese linguistic environment, on the one hand, and to the structure of the CNKI database on the other hand. Each database has its own structure, and we needed to make modifications for the new format of CNKI. To do this, we first created a basic "structure describer".

This describing tool defines different basic fields, identifying their banners, separators, use, and the various types of information they contain (Figure 7.10). It also allows us to identify the beginning of each notice and the physical structure of recording (format and number of occurrences of banners).

To enable automatic processing of Chinese characters, we used Unicode to transform and tag metadata fields. All identifiers for Unicode characters may be found in Unicode tables in hexadecimal or decimal form (Table 7.2).

This permits automatic processing of all bibliographical notices in the corpus and, in the long run, will produce strategic analyses of Chinese-language information which are perfectly accessible to readers with no knowledge of the language.

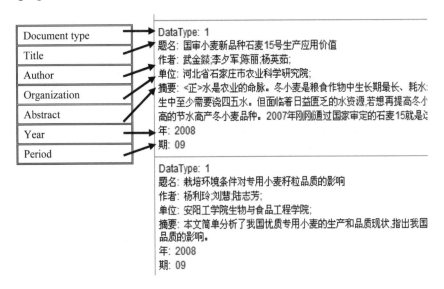

Figure 7.10. *Description of fields in a bibliographic notice*

Chinese	English translation	Decimal numeric bell codes
题名	Title	题名
作者	Author	作者
单位	Organization	单位
摘要	Abstract	摘要
年	Year	年
期	Period	期

Table 7.2. *Correspondence between Chinese characters and Unicode for metadata fields*

The Unicode converters available online (Figure 7.11) are insufficient for the conversion of an entire corpus with tens of thousands of characters. We must therefore carry out minor modifications to our corpus to show up codifications. The entire corpus will be saved in text mode to process characters directly. However, a problem emerges in analyzing the structure of the document; in text mode, the character font changes constantly. A single phrase may contain up to three different fonts, increasing noise in the coding and rendering processing more complex.

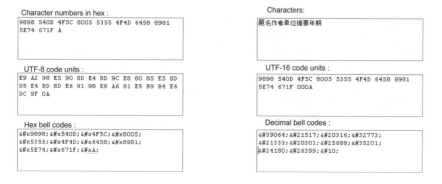

Figure 7.11. *Visualization of character coding using different standards: Unicode code convertor (source: http://hapax.qc.ca/conversion.fr.html)*

Take, for example, the following notice. The title field (题名) contains two characters. The first uses the SimSun font and the second is in MS UI Gothic (Figure 7.12).

```
??'>DataType:  1<br>
</span><span lang=ZH-CN style='font-size:9.0pt;font-family:SimSun;mso-bidi-font-family:
SimSun'>&#39064;</span><span lang=ZH-CN style='font-size:9.0pt;font-family:
"MS UI Gothic";mso-bidi-font-family:"MS UI Gothic"'>&#21517;</span><span
```

Figure 7.12. *Visualization of coding for characters* 题名 *("title")*

If we want to process data directly from the code for Chinese, we need to reformat data to "clean" notices and remove the noise generated by formatting (Figure 7.13).

The results of this first process should contain only the Unicode coding of Chinese characters and of bibliographical fields (Figure 7.14).

The reformatter contained within Tétralogie "cleans" notices to produce a result more suited to bibliometric treatments.

```
??'>DataType:  1<br>
</span><span lang=ZH-CN style='font-size:9.0pt;font-family:SimSun;mso-bidi-font-family:
SimSun'>&#39064;</span><span lang=ZH-CN style='font-size:9.0pt;font-family:
"MS UI Gothic";mso-bidi-font-family:"MS UI Gothic"'>&#21517;</span><span
style='font-size:9.0pt;font-family:??'>:  </span><span lang=ZH-CN
style='font-size:9.0pt;font-family:"MS UI Gothic";mso-ascii-font-family:??;
mso-hansi-font-family:??'>&#19981;&#21516;</span><span lang=ZH-CN
style='font-size:9.0pt;font-family:SimSun;mso-bidi-font-family:SimSun'>&#26102;</span><span
lang=ZH-CN style='font-size:9.0pt;font-family:"MS UI Gothic";mso-bidi-font-family:
"MS UI Gothic"'>&#26399;&#33545;&#33673;&#37240;&#30002;</span><span
lang=ZH-CN style='font-size:9.0pt;font-family:SimSun;mso-bidi-font-family:
SimSun'>&#37231;&#22788;</span><span lang=ZH-CN style='font-size:9.0pt;
font-family:"MS UI Gothic";mso-bidi-font-family:"MS UI Gothic"'>&#29702;</span><span
lang=ZH-CN style='font-size:9.0pt;font-family:SimSun;mso-bidi-font-family:
SimSun'>&#23545;</span><span lang=ZH-CN style='font-size:9.0pt;font-family:
"MS UI Gothic";mso-bidi-font-family:"MS UI Gothic"'>&#20809;&#28201;&#25935;&#38596;&#24615;&#19981;
style='font-size:9.0pt;font-family:??'>BS366</span><span lang=ZH-CN
style='font-size:9.0pt;font-family:SimSun;mso-bidi-font-family:SimSun'>&#39062;</span><span
lang=ZH-CN style='font-size:9.0pt;font-family:"MS UI Gothic";mso-bidi-font-family:
"MS UI Gothic"'>&#33457;</span><span lang=ZH-CN style='font-size:9.0pt;
font-family:SimSun;mso-bidi-font-family:SimSun'>&#24320;</span><span
lang=ZH-CN style='font-size:9.0pt;font-family:"MS UI Gothic";mso-bidi-font-family:
"MS UI Gothic"'>&#25918;&#30340;</span><span lang=ZH-CN style='font-size:
9.0pt;font-family:SimSun;mso-bidi-font-family:SimSun'>&#35825;&#23548;</span><span
lang=ZH-CN style='font-size:9.0pt;font-family:"MS UI Gothic";mso-bidi-font-family:
"MS UI Gothic"'>&#25928;</span><span lang=ZH-CN style='font-size:9.0pt;
font-family:SimSun;mso-bidi-font-family:SimSun'>&#24212;</span><span
style='font-size:9.0pt;font-family:??'><br>
```

Figure 7.13. *Visualization of coding of a notice title. In Chinese:*
题名:不同时期茉莉酸甲>酯处理对光温敏雄性不育小麦颖花开放的诱导效应

```
&#39064;&#21517; &#19981;&#21516; &#26102; &#26399;&#33545;&#33673;
&#37240;&#30002;&#37231;&#22788; &#29702;&#23545; &#20809;&#28201;
&#25935;&#38596;&#24615;&#19981;&#32946;&#23567;&#40614; &#39062;
&#33457;&#24320;&#25918;&#30340;&#35825;&#23548;&#25928;&#24212;
```

Figure 7.14. *Visualization of coding of Figure 7.13, after reformatting*

7.5.2. *Analysis and results*

After "cleaning" the corpus in text mode, we can finally process the data. We will supply a few results here, but the reader is invited to consult previous publications on Tétralogie to gain a better idea of the wide range of cross-referencing and analytical activities the program provides. In what follows, we will present some results produced using Tétralogie to process the corpus of material on "male sterility".

From a representation of actor networks in the "male sterility" corpus, we rapidly observe that a number of very distinct research teams exist, with very little connection between these teams; some of these teams only contain three authors. We will not devote much time to these groups and will instead focus on the largest group (Figure 7.15). In this group, author collaborations are widespread, demonstrating the existence of a real research team with fruitful exchanges; it is also easy to identify the most prolific authors, as their associated nodes are larger.

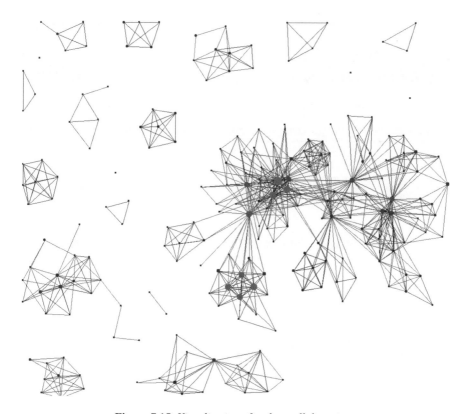

Figure 7.15. *Visualization of author collaborations*

Having targeted the main network, we can now use a matrix to identify authors and to follow their development over the period concerned by our corpus.

It appears that at the height of its activity, in 2006, the network included 15 major authors (Figure 7.16).

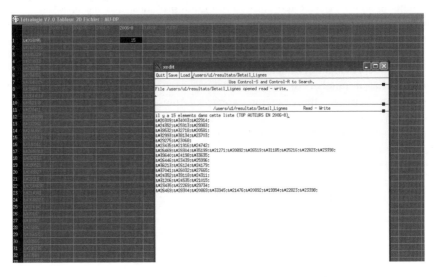

Figure 7.16. *Visualization, in Unicode, of author names in the target group*

Unicode	Chinese	Pinyin transcription
张改生	张改生	ZHANG Gaisheng

Table 7.3. *Conversion of decimal numeric codes into Chinese characters*

It is then easy to carry out conversions in the opposite direction to obtain the corresponding Chinese character (Table 7.3).

The name of the first person in the group thus appears in a relatively simple manner. Repeating the same operation for other names rapidly allows us to identify the most active Chinese researchers in the domain of hybrid wheat. It is then easier for decision makers to carry out searches on these names to contact the author, follow their work, and/or enter into negotiations with the person or group in question.

Particular attention is required when dealing with the names of Chinese authors, as a large number of names are similar, particularly when transliterated into pinyin.

By analyzing Chinese information directly without prior translation, Tétralogie is able to limit confusion in this domain.

7.5.3. *Validation and comparison*

The author list produced by Tétralogie has been validated by experts in China and ties in with our own on-the-ground experience. We note that these authors are not only major actors in Chinese research into hybrid wheat but also key players at national level from a political standpoint. Tétralogie allows us to identify these actors in a simple manner, based on a mass of articles where not all authors have the same importance and level of influence.

If we continue our validation process by looking at the author ZHANG Gaisheng alone, CNKI provides us with 236 articles by this author, including 19 from 2008. This author is therefore particularly prolific. However, if we search for "ZHANG Gaisheng" as an author in PubMed, we obtain no results. The INIST French database proposes four articles, but only two actually correspond to the target author. A Google Scholar search for the author for the year 2008 produces two articles, the first referenced by Elsevier and the second by Wanfang Data.[5]

We should add that the results provided by this analysis effectively allow us to identify key elements of Chinese research on hybrid wheat. The scope of the present chapter does not allow us to cover the entire study in detail, but we have shown that decision makers are able to target key actors rapidly and relevantly. The possibilities offered by Tétralogie do not stop here; many other analyses are possible which we were not able to discuss here. We have demonstrated the feasibility of analysis of a corpus of Chinese scientific information, and invite the reader to consult the numerous publications available concerning Tétralogie to gain an insight into the full potential of the program [DOU 03].

7.6. Conclusion

Any analysis of an environment in the context of a competitive intelligence process begins with in-depth analysis of the actors in the target domain. In China, the sectors of research, economics, and politics are more closely linked than in the West. A research partnership with a Chinese organization, even if the organization is institutional, itself opens doors into the Chinese market. It is therefore absolutely

---

5 Wanfang Data is a Chinese database of scientific articles and a competitor of CNKI. It covers fewer articles but, for the Chinese public, presents the advantage of giving access to major international databases and portals, allowing it to maintain control of a certain part of the Chinese information provider market.

essential to accurately identify actors and their ways of working, including those who dominate given sectors, before deciding on any action involving approaches and negotiation.

Our work is anchored in the context of competitive intelligence and decision assistance. The final results of this should be the acquisition of useful knowledge, leading to subsequent action. Faced with the phenomenal growth of China on the international stage in all sectors (political, economic, and scientific), we believe that no watcher can go without access to Chinese information in carrying out full global watching. Our work therefore focused first on the modification of classic information processing and analysis tools to cope with the Chinese information environment. We have proposed a complete approach to information analysis, including the choice of sources, extraction of a corpus, preparation for processing, and facilities for the visualization of results.

High-performance data mining tools have been developed by French researchers. These enable us to identify major and emerging actors, to observe collaborations between authors and groups and to study the development of these interactions over time, based on a very large corpus of source material. These techniques are incredibly useful and merit regular use by decision makers. Up until now, these tools were applicable to any corpus of material in Indo-European languages, not only mostly in English but also in French, Spanish, and Portuguese. The novelty of our approach is that all processing is carried out on the Chinese text and that only the results are translated. This process is applied to selected and reliable elements. The method therefore enables any decision maker, even those with no knowledge of Chinese, to analyze the Chinese environment for a particular domain.

Our approach then allows real-time watching of knowledge, based on the capitalization of knowledge in the domain. Once again, our contribution allows the use of Chinese sources and provides ideas for further development of tools. Although the final documents are proposed in their original language (in this case, Chinese), watchers may easily identify documents to translate. Translation is an expensive business[6], but waste is avoided as the watcher chooses articles based on concepts expressed in the article and not simply using keywords. This translation phase occurs in the very final stages of analysis and applies to specific, targeted information that will clearly be useful to the watcher.

We have thus shown how large quantities of Chinese-language documents may be used efficiently and demonstrated the way in which we can extract information with a real value in terms of knowledge. This may be integrated into a strategic

6 Between €200 and €300 for a scientific article for a Chinese-to-English translation carried out by an agency in Beijing.

scouting process to support decisions concerning planned actions in new territories, which are often difficult to understand and which present a commercial risk. At the end of this process, the real work of negotiation begins.

7.7. Bibliography

[BUT 08] BUTLER D., "China: the great contender", *Nature*, vol. 454, 23 July 2008, available online at: www.nature.com/news/2008/080723/full/454382a.html.

[DAV 05] DAVID A., Organisation des connaissances dans les systèmes d'information orientés utilisation – contexte de veille et d'intelligence économique, PU Nancy, Nancy, April 2005.

[DOU 03] DOUSSET B., Intégration de méthodes interactives de découvertes de connaissances pour la veille stratégique, HDR, University of Toulouse III, Toulouse, 2003.

[GUE 08] GUENEC N., DOU H., "Intérêt et méthode d'extraction de l'information scientifique Chinoise", *Cahiers de la Documentation*, Association Belge de Documentation, no. 2008/4, 2008, available online at: ww.abd-bvd.be/index.php?page=cah/rc-2008-4&lang=fr.

[IST 08] ISTIC 年中国和世界十大科技进展新闻评出 (2008 China and the world's top ten scientific and technological progress in selected news), 27 November 2008, available online at: www.chaxin.org/EducationDetail.aspx?ArticleID=86505.

[LOU 07] LOUBIER E., BAHSOUN W., DOUSSET B., "La prise en compte de la dimension temporelle dans la visualisation de données par morphing de graphe", *Colloque Veille Stratégique Scientifique et Technologique* (VSST 2007), IRIT, Marrakech, Morocco, 21–25 October 2007.

[MA 05] MA J., Bibliothèque et document numérique en Chine, summary for the RTP-DOC, CNRS, June 2005.

[MAR 94] MARTRE H., CLERC P., HARBULOT C., "Intelligence économique et stratégie des entreprises", *Commissariat général du plan*, La Documentation Française, Paris, 1994.

[OCD 06] OCDE, Perspectives de l'OCDE de la science, de la technologie et de l'industrie, OCDE, Paris, 2006, available online at: www.oecd.org/document/61/0,3343,fr_2649_33703_37743997_1_1_1_1,00.html.

[OST 08] OST, Edition of the report of the observatoire des sciences et techniques, OST, Paris, 2008, available online at: www.obs-ost.fr/dossiers/article/publication-de-ledition-2008-du-rapport-de-lost.html?tx_ttnews[backPid]=5&cHash=7008cb6c80.

[QUO 07] QUOTIDIEN DU PEUPLE, "La Chine dresse les grandes lignes d'un projet de développement de la bio-économie", *Quotidien du Peuple*, 28 June 2007, available online at: http://french.peopledaily.com.cn/Economie/6200702.html.

[UNE 05] UNESCO, Science Report 2005, UNESCO Reference Works series, UNESCO Publishing, 2005.

[VIL 08] VILLALONGA A., La Chine se hisse dans le peloton de tête du classement des publications scientifiques, ADIT, BE Chine 56, 8 January 2009, available online at: www.bulletins-electroniques.com/actualites/57207.htm.

[ZHO 09] ZHOU P., LEVDESDORFF L., "The emergence of China as a leading nation in science", *Research Policy*, vol. 35, no. 1, pp. 83–104, February 2006, available online at: http://users.fmg.uva.nl/lleydesdorff/ChinaScience/ChinaScience.

Chapter 8

Generic Tagging Strategy Using a Semio-Contextual Approach to the Corpus for the Creation of Controlled Databases

If we want relevant knowledge, we need to link, contextualize and globalize our information and knowledge, and thus seek complex knowledge.

Edgar Morin [MOR 99]

8.1. Introduction

Research carried out in competitive intelligence covers a wide variety of fields of investigation: strategic watching, mastery of information, data and system protection, and so on. We are particularly interested in information mastery, that is, knowledge management based on an audited database relevant to economic actors. This approach consists of processing and organizing documentary resources and contents produced by strategic watching. While information gathering is essential in economic intelligence, it is also necessary to sort, select, and organize the information obtained to adapt it to the strategic aims of users. This is the aim of the generic tagging strategy we propose using a semio-contextual approach to corpora (*Approche Sémio-Contextuel des Corpus* [ASCC]).

Chapter written by Lise VERLAET.

ASCC-based modeling was developed with the aim of fulfilling the expectations and needs of researchers in terms of scientific information and was implemented in a so-called adaptive journal. As information seeking aims to fill a gap in the knowledge of the user, the results produced should not only effectively solve the problem but also direct the user to the most interesting directions to take in continuing their reasoning. As we will see, a model using ASCC allows categorization of relevant information for a reader seeking information. This categorization corresponds to the main cognitive processes used by humans to comprehend meaning and, through this, understand and solve problematic situations.

8.2. The adaptive journal concept

Unlike a classic digital scientific journal, which generally operates using three interdependent levels of information (the journal, themes, and articles), an adaptive journal increases reader research possibilities by adding a fourth level of information based on concepts. An adaptive journal gives users direct access to the conceptual universe of the domain, thus increasing their semantic competences. As Eco points out [ECO 88], this semantic competence may be assimilated to an encyclopedic knowledge, regrouping knowledge of the world, and linguistic information. This new mode of accessing information constitutes the main added value of an adaptive review.

The first level of information is subjacent to the constitution of a journal and to the editorial policies applied. The editorial committee informs readers of the intellectual orientation of the journal. This first level of information has a clear impact on all other information presented within the journal. We will refer to this first level of information, which covers all other levels of information, as the macro-level. The macro-level determines the angle taken by all other information published within the journal.

A scientific review is made up of different themes. These themes constitute the second level of information and are clearly linked to the editorial policy of the journal. This second level of information is known as the meso-level. In our case, these themes are submitted to readers via calls for papers, presentations that allow the outline of the theme to be traced and aims to be specified, and so on. Calls for papers present readers with rules to follow if they wish to participate in thematic debates launched by the journal.

This takes us to the third level of information, the micro-level, where readers contribute to the thematic debate by means of an article. Through an article, the reader–actor shares their knowledge and experience of the theme.

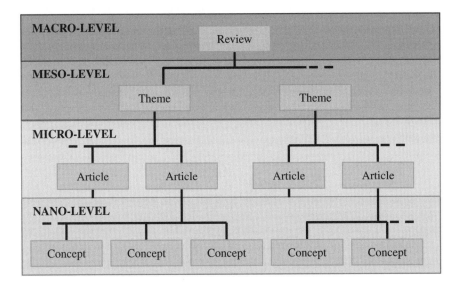

Figure 8.1. *Levels of information in an adaptive journal*

An adaptive journal adds a fourth information level, the nano-level, which covers concepts brought up by the contents of articles. This information level provides readers with an encyclopedic vision of the journal and of the domain that it covers.

An adaptive journal therefore includes four levels of information, corresponding to its hierarchical structure, which may be represented in a tree diagram. These levels are interlinked and interdependent. Concepts at nano-level are used to specify the articles at micro-level, which themselves form part of the meso-level, that is, themes; these themes flow from the journal, that is, macro-level. Nonetheless, each of these levels provides readers with a specific type of information and in this way offers a different context of reading. Every communication situation and each information level should provide readers with a specific mode of access. To optimize the relevance of information searches, all levels of the adaptive journal will be subject to semantic tagging.

8.2.1. *The notion of semantic tagging: selection of relevant information*

Berners-Lee *et al.* [BER 01] state that the Internet of tomorrow will aim to establish greater cooperation between man and machine, and this notion may be expanded to cover information systems in general. Among other factors, this cooperation works through indexing or semantic tagging that is both understandable for human users and interpretable by machines. The particularity associated with research based on the semantic Web is essentially due to the capacities of its descriptive language, XML. XML is a meta-language that allows us to tag resources using natural language. It thus facilitates the creation of languages with specialized tags. It is, in fact, no longer necessary to use artificial languages. The main effect of this has been to considerably facilitate indexing and, subsequently, the development of new methods for describing content that had previously been ignored due to the vast amount of work involved.

XML allows the free creation of metadata concerning the contents of texts. It promotes the emergence of "annotation" or "comment" type metadata, which may be considered "interpretative" or "subjective". This metadata can be used to tag resources and their contents in relation to the intentionalities expressed at the moment of creation of the information system. The use of metadata is therefore no longer restricted to the formulation of an "objective" index and can now be used in response to different contexts of use. Amar [AMA 04] notes that "although methods of linguistic or structural indexing have blossomed with the expansion of the Web, they are still not perfectly adapted to the needs of users". We agree wholeheartedly with this statement, and we are convinced that to satisfy user needs we must take new approaches to digital resources, and particularly to semantic tagging.

From our point of view, semantic tagging is at the heart of the concept of adaptation and therefore of mastery of information. Semantic tagging is an intentional process that varies depending on the domain of application or the particular project involved. Tagging should be thought out in such a way as to provide users with a qualitative tool, able to supply effective assistance in information seeking and the construction of knowledge, by offering a reading of information adapted to their stakes. We therefore pass from "objective and formal" indexing to a notion of "contextual" semantic tagging, where the idea of contextual meaning is linked to a research intention. Semantic tagging, then, consists of analyzing a corpus to bring out meaningful passages for users in light of their research aims. This requires the freeing up, conceptualization, and contextualization of the different information resources under study.

8.2.2. *Modeling knowledge: organizing relevant information*

Semantic tagging allows us to select and qualify fragments of information that are relevant for the reader. In other terms, semantic tagging is used to conceptualize documentary resources and their contents. However, simple conceptualization of the corpus is not enough; we must also organize the set of obtained data through semantic tagging. The intention subjacent to this organization is to give computer systems the ability to "recognize" and relate resources to carry out "reasoning" based on this information, with the aim of providing the user with a better quality of service.

Organizing data is no mean feat. Nevertheless, we have access to high-performance tools that have been used over a long period in philosophy, information sciences, documentation, or knowledge management, among other things. These "tools" are ontologies. Ontologies are partial and shared conceptualizations that aim to clarify and organize a domain of knowledge. Ontology consists of studying what exists in the domain and the system of relationships that predominates in that domain. This representation of knowledge should allow sharing and the reuse of these data by computer systems, and consequently by human users of these systems.

The generic term "ontology" covers two modes of formulation and representation of knowledge. The first mode is that of formal ontologies, characterized by a formal hierarchical structure showing specification relationships. The second mode is that of informal ontologies, which form a network of varied relationships of associative type. To avoid ambiguity between these two categories, we will reserve the term "ontology" for formal ontologies and use the term "semantic network" to refer to informal ontologies.

These models of knowledge allow readers to consult information in more or less direct relation to their initial research, guaranteeing a better construction of knowledge.

8.2.3. *Recomposed documents: sorting and presenting relevant information*

Semantic tagging applies to the contents of documentary resources and consists of the identification and qualification of fragments of information that correspond to units of meaning. The information fragments referenced in this way may then be extracted from their initial contexts and manipulated to form new documents, which we will call as "recomposed documents". Recomposed documents are thus based on the principle of extraction and recomposition of information fragments to constitute documents with their own meaning. The final meaning of recomposed documents correlates with the communication strategy to establish within an information system and subsequently determines the scenarization offered to readers. In practice, the methodology used to adapt recomposed documents always has an effect on the semantic tagging applied. The recomposition of documents is interdependent with information fragments that are tagged to satisfy their formulation and the coherence of their layout for the reader.

8.2.3.1. *The extraction–recomposition principle*

The process of creation of a "recomposed document" makes use of the capacities of XML technologies and their extensions, particularly XSLT style sheets. Once the source document has been tagged using XML, these languages give us the possibility of extracting fragments of articles from their original supports to collect them, in a coherent manner, within a new document. This new document, the recomposed document, brings together all selected tagged fragments, organized using XSLT style sheets. XSLTs act as filters, and only the desired information is extracted for presentation to the user. The recomposed document, the result of the association of one or more XML documents and one or more XSLT style sheets, is made up of various fragments of information, selected and organized following the strategy of the project. These functions lead us inexorably toward new approaches to digital textuality.

8.2.3.2. *The decontextualization–recontextualization principle*

The extraction–recomposition principle in relation to the creation of documents is not without significance. The fact of extracting information fragments from their source document and decontextualizing them to recompose them in a new document with recontextualization involves copying entire passages written by specific authors to put this information to a new use. In this way, the decontextualization–recontextualization principle has a tendency to contravene the intellectual property rights of authors.

This violation of intellectual property rights is even more significant when a tagging strategy aims to generate a new document with its own narrative structure. In this case, extracts are assembled with no reference to the original authors. Of course, authors may grant rights of modification or derivation of their work to information systems. However, without distinct points of reference concerning the recomposed document, the reader cannot know where ideas came from originally and thus make undiscerning use of them. This may be a source of misunderstandings in relation to author rights. Of course, standards exist for citing this information using the name of the information system as a reference, but it remains difficult, if not impossible, to go back to the sources of ideas and to identify their authors. The problem, therefore, remains unsolved.

In our research work, we concentrate on scientific writings. We start from the premise that any and all decontextualization of information fragments linked to scientific production cannot be carried out without explicit source references being attached to these fragments. Moreover, studies carried out by Guinchat and Skouri [GUI 96] support our vision. They insist that a part of a document, whether a "documentary unit" or an information fragment, can only be used in cases where extracts mention their origin to guarantee traceability. Citing the source documents of extracted passages presents the double advantage of respecting author rights and of ensuring recontextualization, allowing readers to consult the initial sources of these fragments if the need arises. The principle of recontextualization thus covers two distinct fields. First, it operates on the effective recomposition of information fragments for their organization within recomposed documents. Second, it participates in allowing retroaction between information fragments and their original context, that is, the source resources.

Thus, the decontextualization–recontextualization principle inherent in the creation of recomposed documents is based not only on the semantic tagging strategy chosen for extraction–recomposition but also on indications concerning the source documents that guarantee the traceability of information fragments.

8.3. A generic tagging strategy: models using the ASCC

The purpose of an adaptive journal is to offer readers relevant information in connection with their research intentions. As we have just explained, to do this, the creators of an adaptive journal must select, organize, and present useful information to readers. Our proposals for a semantic tagging strategy result from the creation of an initial prototype for an adaptive journal. In this case, the tagging strategy was based on purely conceptual tagging of the contents of articles, which is the main added value involved in an adaptive journal. The development of this first prototype allowed us to observe that readers want greater precision concerning concepts uncovered through tagging, explanations that must be extracted from information inherent to the corpus. Those interviewed suggested bases for categorizing information, consisting of distinguishing information fragments concerning definitions and examples linked to concepts, but also specification and association relationships (in relation to the ontology and the semantic Web) created between concepts. These last two categories of information proved particularly interesting in our subsequent work, as they raise questions concerning the whole process of formulation of models of knowledge and the very interest of these models for the reader. Studying reader expectations and desires led us to rethink the creation of knowledge models, which should no longer be constituted *a priori* by a community of experts, but should instead be formulated using the information contained in the documentary corpus. The final aim of readers is to understand the relationships between concepts and thus to have access to the information fragments setting out this information.

The results of evaluation of the first adaptive journal prototype refocused our attention onto the following questions:

– What categories of information will be relevant for a reader seeking information?

– Which information categories will be best able to solve the reader's research problems?

– How will these categories contribute to the emergence of meaning and to a better construction of knowledge for the reader?

8.3.1. Categorizing meaning

A multidisciplinary research process, bringing together ICT [MOR 04, LEC 04], cognitive psychology [PIA 67, GAR 04, LEN 05], social psychology [VYG 97, BRU 91], education sciences [BAR 04a, BAR 04b], and philosophy [WIT 04, WIT 06], allowed us to confirm the categorization set out by readers during evaluation of the first prototype of the adaptive journal. This research also brought us into the domain of information and communication sciences, as cognitive activities are built through communication situations experienced by the actor. When we speak of communication, we do not simply refer to the transmission of messages. We define communication as the set of expressions – language, interactions, and human behaviors – which contribute to the construction of a common sphere of references. This raises a question: Which cognitive activities do we use to interpret and understand a communication situation, and how does meaning emerge in a communication situation?

These issues are at the center of research work carried out by Mucchielli [MUC 98, MUC 00, MUC 05] on the genesis of meaning. Among the various theoretical contributions of this author, situational semiotic theory (or semio-contextual theory) is particularly well suited to our needs. First, this theory looks at the construction of meaning by actors by studying the processes inherent in any communication situation. Second, the communication processes put forward correspond almost perfectly to the recurring elements of categorization of information observed during our research on the creation of a semantic tagging strategy.

Situational semiotic theory is a method of contextual and cognitive analysis of a communication situation. Situational semiotics is based on seven inter-related contexts that are found in any communication situation: standards or domains, stakes, positions, relationships, and the temporal, spatial, and physic-sensorial dimensions. The theory postulates that all communication situations are, on principle, problematic. Understanding the contexts which make up a situation allows us to solve the problem or problems created and thus to act in an appropriate manner. We have therefore made use of the contextual breakdown used in situational semiotics, which we transposed and backed up for use in a semantic tagging strategy [VER 08]. We were thus able to define a series of nine basic questions to use to bring out meaning in an information seeking situation.

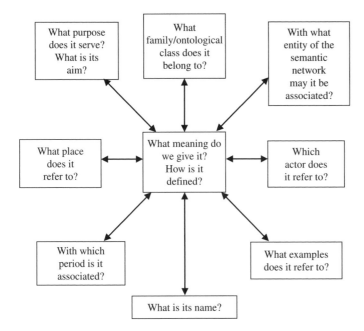

Figure 8.2. *Basic questions for the emergence of meaning*

Each question coincides with a possible information seeking problem. This set of questions ensures the contextualization of relevant information on a subject and allows us to identify text fragments that may provide a response to problems encountered by the reader. These questions are interlinked and interdependent. However, the question "what does it mean?" takes a central place. The study by Mucchielli and Morizio allows us to highlight the importance of the normative context, or the question "what?" We consider that other contexts and questions emerge based on the values commonly accepted to qualify and represent a subject – that is, the meaning, the definition we give it. Our language system includes a large number of polysemic or plurivocal terms. Contextualization therefore depends on the standard used, as it is in light of the meaning given to a term that we may determine other contexts.

These basic questions enabled us to develop a generic tagging model through a ASCC. As we will see, these questions, which we transformed into semantic tags, fit perfectly with each of the information levels found in an adaptive journal. For clarity, we will start by providing explanations and details of ASCC-based models at nano-level in an adaptive journal and move progressively toward the macro-level.

8.3.2. *The ASCC at the nano-level of information in an adaptive journal*

The nano-level is at the core of our adaptive journal and constitutes the main value added by our study. ASCC tagging at nano-level of the journal, that is, of the contents of articles, allows us to pick out fragments of information linked to the concepts used at this level (Table 8.1). Each ASCC tag highlights a category of information relevant for a reader seeking information on encyclopedic or terminological problems. This categorization of information should allow readers to better understand the ins and outs of the selected concept.

ASCC tags	Problems posed	Category of information to tag
Identity	What is its name?	Identification of significant passage on concept
<*norme*id="concept X">	What are the properties of the concept?	Information fragment with definition of concept
<*enjeux*id="concept X">	What are the stakes of the context?	Information fragment explaining stakes and aims of concept
<*position*enfant="concept X" **parent**="concept X">	How is the concept situated in the ontology to which it belongs?	Information fragment marking specification relationships between concepts
<*relation* a="concept X" **b**= "concept Y" **type**="lien">	With what other concepts in the semantic network might it be associated?	Information fragment showing relationship (not linked to specification)
<*temps*id="concept X" date="2009">	What period is associated with this concept?	Information fragment giving chronological indications concerning the concept
<*spatial*id="concept X" lieu="France">	Which places does the concept refer to?	Information fragment showing relationship between a place and a concept
<*citation*id="concept X" auteur="auteur" reference="reference">	Which author is linked to this concept?	Information fragment showing a citation from an author regarding a concept
<*cas*id="concept X" titre="titre_cas">	In what cases is the concept used?	Information fragment pertaining to cases of use of a concept

Table 8.1. *ASCC tag table for use at nano-level in an adaptive journal*

First, we notice that there is no "identity" tag to respond to the question "what is its name?" The aim of tagging at nano-level is itself to identify information fragments setting out a concept. For this reason, the identity of the concept is necessarily included within the other ASCC tags.

The <norme> tag is used to signpost information fragments concerning the value, properties, or characteristics given to a concept. Thus, any text fragment including explicit definition of a concept will be highlighted using this tag, filled in by the tagger who identified the concept in question as <norme id="concept X">.

A concept does not exist without a function or an intention. It was created to respond to a need, which determines its purpose. The tagger must therefore identify and qualify information fragments setting out the purpose or purposes linked to a concept. To do this, the tagger uses the tag <enjeux id="concept X">.

The <position> tag refers to the place of the concept(s) within an ontological tree diagram. This tag is used to identify information fragments that describe specification relationships via a parent–child tag: <position parent="concept X" enfant="concept Y">. This tag is made up of two attributes: the "parent" attribute, the semantic value of which is the strong or dominant concept, and the "enfant" (child) attribute, representing the weaker concept. This means that once a tagger has identified a passage formulating a specification relationship between two concepts, they must evaluate the respective positions of these concepts in accordance with what is set out in the passage. The conglomeration of the set of data obtained using <position> tags is used in the constitution of an ontology.

The <relation> (relationship) tag is used to identify information fragments revealing an associative type relationship between two concepts. The document passages tagged in this way are used in the formulation of a semantic network. These fragments are brought out using the tag <relation a="concept X" b="concept Y" type="qualité de la relation">. This tag allows us to identify a relationship between a concept "a" and a concept "b" and to typify it ("type"), that is, to explain what kind of relationship exists between the two concepts.

The <temps> (time) tag is used to identify all indications of a temporal nature attached to a concept. The aim is to position a concept in a chronology, identifying the time of its creation, and so on. To identify temporal indices linked to a concept, we use the tag <temps id="concept X" date="date">.

The spatial indices linked to a concept are identified using the <spatial> tag. To identify places that may be associated with a concept, we use the tag <spatial id="concept X" lieu="lieu">, where "lieu" means "place".

The information fragments that show that a citation has been "borrowed" from a specific author are highlighted using the <citation> tag. In addition to the identity of the concept, this tag contains two other attributes that allow us to highlight the cited author and to indicate the reference of their work. The full tag therefore takes the following form: <citation id="concept X" auteur="nom de l'auteur"

reference="reference dont est extraite la citation">, where "nom de l'auteur" is "author name" and "reference dont est extraite la citation" is a reference to the original work from which the citation is taken.

The last tag in the ASCC model is <cas>, "case", which concerns text fragments relating to an example of use of a concept. For each example identified by the tagger within an article, this tag is used to stipulate the name of the concept and the title of the example: <cas id="concept X" titre="titre du cas">.

The tagger therefore selects relevant information fragments on concepts included in review articles based on ASCC tags. These fragments are then sorted and presented to readers in the form of a recomposed document devoted to a conceptual search term.

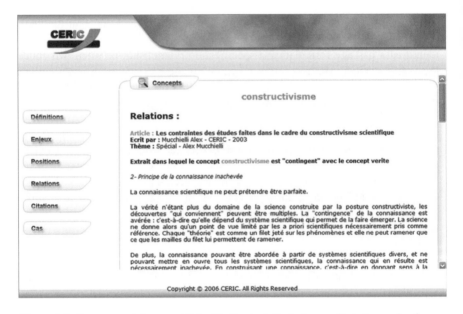

Figure 8.3. *Recomposed document linked to the <relation> tag applied at nano-level. Concept page for the French term "constructivisme"*

8.3.3. *ASCC at micro-level in an adaptive journal*

The micro-level of information in the journal is concerned with the scientific articles making up the journal. As with any information and reading situation, the micro-level itself presents certain problems for the reader. The problems encountered by a reader looking for articles are essentially linked to article choice. Our work consists of providing the reader with the necessary information to make a choice between articles at micro-level. We therefore need to know how best to assist the reader in selecting articles, and how to tag the information included in an article in a way that makes sense to the reader, thus facilitating research.

In a similar way to that observed at nano-level, ASCC tagging at micro-level highlights all meaningful elements of articles. The ASCC user model applied to micro-level also allows us to qualify and categorize relevant information on articles and, subsequently, solve the main problems of the reader (Table 8.2). We will see that the norms applied to writing scientific articles have already contributed a good deal to the tagging process, and that this context is particularly favorable to our model.

ASCC tags	Problems posed	Category of information to tag
<titre>	What is the name of the article?	Article title
<resume>	What is the key problem dealt with in this article?	Key problem as set out in the abstract
<resume>	What is the aim of this article?	Aim of the article as set out in the abstract
<theme>	What theme does this article fall under?	Reference theme of the article
<motcle>	With what other article(s) may it be linked?	Article key words
<date>	What is the publication date of the article?	Date of publication
<lieu>	With which geographic location is the article connected?	Organization and address connected with the article
<auteur> *<reference>*	Who is the author of the article? What are their references?	Author name, bibliographical references used in the article
<concept>	What concepts are applied in the article?	Key concepts as set out in the abstract

Table 8.2. *Tag table for ASCC at micro-level of an adaptive journal*

As we see from the micro-level tag table, we chose new names for micro-level tags that are close to the vocabulary used in the breakdown of a scientific article.

Every article has a title, identified using the <titre> tag. It is essential to identify the name of the micro-level element, in this case the article title. This tag has no exact equivalent in nano-level tagging; at nano-level, the identity of concepts is obtained through the qualification of ASCC tags. The tagger is responsible for the identification of concepts based on the contents of the article.

We then pass to the <resume> tag, which refers to the *résumé*, summary, or abstract of the article. This tag is used to represent questions relating to both norms and questions concerning the aims of the article. Although these represent two distinct categories of information, both are found in the abstract. Current writing norms make no difference between that which relates to the domain itself and that which relates to the purpose of the article. These two categories of information are thus mixed within the abstract; in this way, all abstracts cover the standards and the aims of the article. In practice, the tagging of both categories most often coincides. We have therefore chosen to use just one tag, the <resume> tag, although we advise authors of scientific articles to distinguish clearly between the norms of an article and its intentions. Moreover, we strongly suggest that the editors of an adaptive journal make it clear in author recommendations that a summary should be written in two parts: the first setting out the norms of the article and the second clarifying intentions and aims. This would facilitate decision making for readers in search of relevant articles.

The <theme> tag is used to situate the article in question in relation to its original theme. This tag thus links the article to the meso-level of the journal and consequently to other articles with the same theme.

We use keywords present in an article to connect sets of articles presenting identical concepts, whatever the initial theme of the article may be. <motcle> (keyword) tags allow readers to link the chosen article with other articles displaying shared semantic traits.

We also encounter <date> and <lieu> (place) tags referring to temporal and spatial questions in the ASCC tag tables. The first of these tags gives the date of publication of the article, and the second sets out the institution or organization to which the author, and therefore the article, is connected.

The <reference> and <auteur> (author) tags are used to identify the author and their bibliographical references. Thus, at the micro-level of the journal, the author and references context is broken down into two parts. The <auteur> tag gives the name of the author of the article, and the <reference> tag indicates the bibliographical references used by the author as a basis for reflection. This context cannot be covered by a single tag at micro-level as it concerns two different blocks of information.

Finally, the <concept> tag highlights several key concepts, set out in the summary, which the author uses in their demonstration. These are the concepts that are applied in the article. The <concept> tag therefore refers to the context of the example and links back to the nano-level of information in the journal. These concepts are shown in the contents of the article and will therefore be encountered by the reader. This tag thus links the micro- and nano-levels of the journal. If the reader does not possess knowledge of one of the concepts described in the abstract, they may refer to the description file for the concept in question.

Figure 8.4. *Recomposed document synthesizing micro-level content*

Looking at the ASCC tag table for micro-level, we notice that the tagging approach is different from that used at nano-level. At nano-level, the approach was centered on the creation of meaning, whereas at micro-level, we are essentially concerned with valorization. In other terms, at nano-level, we "create"; at micro-level, we "renovate". We therefore have a high degree of freedom at nano-level, whereas we experience more limitations at micro-level.

8.3.4. *ASCC for authors in an adaptive journal*

We have seen how the generic tagging model through ASCC is applied at the micro-level of information in an adaptive journal. However, from our perspective, a level of information was lacking regarding the authors participating in a journal. Authors occupy a key place in information resources such as scientific journals. The journal itself is made up of the research carried out by these scientific actors. Without their input, the journal would not exist. It therefore seems inconceivable to tackle an article without consideration of its author, as the two are intrinsically linked. An article is a reflection of the thought processes of its author, and it is through the article that the author communicates with readers of the journal. To fully understand the scientific scope of an article, it is often necessary to know who the author is, what their intentions are, and so on.

However, traditional journals often leave authors in the background, giving priority to their creations (creations from which, moreover, certain journals made a considerable profit without paying their authors). It is clear that certain journals blatantly make profit from their authors; this is particularly evident in the case of teaching researchers, who are obliged to publish their research, if only to move up the career ladder. In other terms, not only do traditional journals not remunerate their authors, but also they allow them very little of the space they need to raise the profile of their research work.

In general, the only information presented to the reader concerning the author is that which accompanies the article. ASCC at micro-level provides information that allows the reader to "contextualize" the author (Table 8.3). As the article cannot be dissociated from the author, relevant information on the article is also relevant information about the author. From the information inherent to the micro-level, we know that a given scientific actor is the author of a specific article written in a specific year, belonging to a specific laboratory in a specific geographic location, and that they used specific bibliographical references to develop a given concept. Although this information is usually satisfactory for experienced users, it is far from sufficient to cater to the needs of newcomers to a domain.

ASCC tags	Problem posed	Category of information to tag
<auteur>	What is the name of the author?	Author name and surname
<parcours>	What is the domain of the author?	Author discipline
<theme>	What are the author's centers of interest?	Themes on which the author has worked
<statut>	What is the status of the author?	Author status
<publication>	Which other authors does the author work with?	Collaboration with other authors on works or articles
<date>	What dates are connected with the author?	Date of writing of the article found in the journal
<lieu>	What organization does the author belong to?	Name and address of the organization with which the author is affiliated
<publication>	What are the author's publications?	Publications by the author
<titre>	What publications by the author are available?	Articles by the author present in the journal

Table 8.3. *ASCC tag table for authors at micro-level*

Furthermore, readers may experience relatively simple problems in relation to authors: Who is the author? What field does he/she work in? What has he/she written? and so on. These problems on their own do not attract particular attention in standards on scientific writing and, consequently, are largely ignored in traditional journals. To respond to this issue, we have added a new communication situation to the journal, concentrating on actors at the micro-level. By doing this, we restore authors to their rightful place within the journal and, subsequently, provide readers with a new possibility in terms of modes of access to information. We are thus confronted with the question of what relevant information concerning actors will be useful to an information-seeking reader.

ASCC tagging at the micro-level of the journal enables us to obtain a certain amount of relevant information on the author, particularly in relation to the <identite> (identity) tag (name and surname), the <spatial> tag (associated organization), and the <titre> (title) tag (the article), to cite the most obvious examples. We will see that other elements at micro-level can add to this information concerning the author.

First, according to different writing norms, authors may or may not be required to state their status or rank. In cases where this occurs, the relevant information can be selected using the <statut> (status) tag.

Second, and again in accordance with different norms, authors may or may not be required to specify their domain of activity. The domain of activity is the only relevant element we can find concerning the norms of the author within the micro-level (<parcours> tag). On this subject, it is regrettable that certain editorial norms leave aside the status and discipline of authors, as this information is crucial to a reader seeking information. The status gives an idea not only of the level of abstraction but also of the intellectual standing of the author. Reference to a specific discipline allows the reader to understand the angle from which the author approaches a subject.

The intentions of an author may also be deduced from the micro-level. If an author participates in a debate launched by a journal on a given theme, it is obvious that the author has an interest in that theme. Micro-level tagging reveals certain information on the research interests of the author (<theme> tag). However, the scientific interests of an author are not limited to the themes proposed by the journal, no matter how many topics the journal covers. Nevertheless, this information allows us to follow the problems an author is interested in within the journal.

Social networks (the <relation>, relationship, tag) formed by authors may also be inferred based on micro-level tags via bibliographical references. Tagging these references allows us to identify authors who have collaborated on projects. This is, moreover, one of the strategies used in bibliometry to construct images of social networks. However, while intellectual and methodological affinities between authors are interesting, rivalries and enmities are just as interesting, and cannot be detected from bibliographical references. This represents a gap in our tagging system. Nevertheless, the ability to visualize networks is useful for the reader, as a tool for identifying other relevant authors in relation to a given problem.

The bibliographical references contained in articles can also allow us to extract information to respond to the needs of the <publication> tag. By tagging resources used within the micro-level, we can call up titles of publications by different authors. In doing this, we are able to find all references to an author and present these references to the reader. The only limit to this is that the publications of the author in question must be used as bibliographical references within the journal. This information allows readers to gain knowledge of other work produced by the author, and in this it valorizes the work of the author concerned.

Finally, the <temporal> tag covers chronological elements that may be linked to the scientific activities of the author. The dates of publication of articles in the journal therefore belong to this chronology.

All categories of relevant information concerning the author are thus brought to the fore via ASCC author tags. Each of these tags participates in the emergence of meaning concerning the author of an article at the micro-level of information in the journal. The tags allow us to extract relevant information about an author to respond to the main problems that may be encountered by a reader.

8.3.5. ASCC at meso-level in an adaptive journal

The meso-level of information is the result of calls for papers put out by a journal to generate progress in the domains of research it covers. Meso-level therefore concerns the different themes studied within the journal. The micro-level and nano-level of the journal flow from this meso-level of information.

Like the other levels of information in the journal, the meso-level can be analyzed and tagged via the user model by ASCC. Any reading situation must be made up of contexts of reference, which ensure the emergence of meaning for the reader. We have therefore produced an ASCC tag table for the meso-level of an adaptive journal, to bring out relevant information concerning the themes present at this level.

Unlike the previous levels, the meso-level has its own documentary resource. For this reason, we have chosen to name our tags in accordance with the contexts/questions they represent, thus facilitating the naming of tags (Table 8.4).

ASCC tags	Problem posed	Category of information to tag
<identite>	What is the name of the theme?	Name of theme
<norme>	What is the domain of the theme?	Definition of theme
<enjeux>	What are the aims/intentions of the theme?	Aims of theme
<position>	From what viewpoint is the theme dealt with?	Field of application of theme
<relation>	What other themes is it linked to?	Relationships to other theme(s)
<temps>	What dates are connected to the theme?	Date of appearance of theme
<spatial>	What organization is linked with the theme?	Organization responsible for launching the theme
<auteur>	Who are the scientific guarantors of the theme?	Members of the scientific committee and their references
<cas>	What articles refer to the theme?	Articles on the theme

Table 8.4. *ASCC tag table at meso-level in an adaptive journal*

Each ASCC tag poses a question to which we must respond by tagging information at meso-level. The first of these questions refer to the name given to the theme, its definition, and its aims, corresponding to the <identite> (identity), <norme> (domain), and <enjeux> (aims). This significant information will necessarily influence reader choices in selecting an element at meso-level.

A theme is chosen by the editorial committee of the journal and therefore corresponds to the intellectual orientations of the committee. However, a theme may be tackled from different perspectives and with attention to different aspects; it is not, for example, rare to find calls for papers which subdivide a theme into several subcategories. The <position> tag is used to indicate, if need be, relevant information inherent to different fields of application supported by the theme.

The <relations> (relationships) tag concerns possible links between different themes and aims to satisfy the information needs of a reader seeking new themes with shared characteristics. Tagging this information allows the reader to direct their attentions, in a constructive manner, toward other themes of research. The processing of <relation> tags also allows us to generate networks of themes. The <temps> (time) tag is attached to the date of appearance of the theme, allowing the reader to situate the theme and its contents chronologically. Given that our journal must be "fed" by calls for papers, which should, in this particular case, lead to a conference or symposium, the date of appearance of the theme may well coincide with the date of these presentations. On the other hand, a conference is always organized by one or more institutional structures, which have an interest for the reader in the same way as the organization to which the author belongs. This information is therefore highlighted using the <spatial> tag. Another element that is useful to the reader is the list of members of the scientific committee, which ensures the validity and the scientific quality of the contents of themes and thus of the positions of the journal. This information is selected using the <auteur> (author) tag.

To conclude this section, we note that a theme can only exist through articles that illustrate it, articles picked out by the <cas> (case) tag. This information directs the reader to the micro-level of the journal. In a similar way to what we saw with micro-level tagging, the tagger should highlight the most relevant information for the reader to assist with decision-making processes.

8.3.6. *ASCC at macro-level in an adaptive journal*

ASCC at the macro-level should provide readers with responses to problems subjacent to the journal, and, in this way, present useful information concerning the journal. We must therefore determine what macro-level information is meaningful to a reader seeking a scientific journal.

The ASCC tagging table underlies several questions that may be asked by the reader and for which responses must be found in information at macro-level (Table 8.5). Seen from the point of view of the ASCC model, the macro-level should display certain information, beginning with the name of the journal, essential for identification and highlighted using the <identite> (identity) tag. It should show the norms of the journal, that is, the collective and shared definition linked to editorial policy and intellectual orientations (the <norme> tag). The aims found at macro-level should also be stipulated along with the domain concerned. The <enjeux> (stakes, issues, or intentions) and <position> tags inform the reader of the main research interests of the journal in a given field of scientific activities. These scientific activities may be shared with other journals, including other adaptive journals; these links are expressed in the <relation> tag at macro-level. Other relevant information concerns spatiotemporal considerations demonstrated using the ASCC, including possible contacts with the journal, a postal and email address for the journal (the <spatial> tag), but also the date of its creation and various news items (<temps> (time) tag). The macro-level also covers authors and their references, brought together to form an editorial committee (<auteur> (author) tag). These authors act as guarantors for the journal, and they are partly responsible for the subjacent intellectual project. Finally, every journal needs a theme and scientific debate. The <cas> (case) tag serves this purpose, setting out the themes covered by the journal.

ASCC tags	Problems posed	Category of information to tag
<identite>	What is the name of the journal?	Journal name
<norme>	What are the domains covered by the journal?	Intellectual orientations of journal
<enjeux>	What is the aim of the journal?	Stakes of journal
<position>	What position does the journal take?	Domain or discipline of journal
<relation>	What other journals are linked to it?	Partnerships with other journals
<temps>	When was the journal created?	History of the journal (date of creation and news)
<spatial>	Where is the journal found?	Contacts for the journal
<auteur>	Who are the authors of the journal?	Journal edition committee
<cas>	What themes are covered by the journal?	Themes of journal

Table 8.5. *ASCC tag table at macro-level in an adaptive journal*

All of this information provides the reader with a global vision of the macro-level, formed by the "journal" entity and by its scientific activities. This is, therefore, the central information that any adaptive journal should provide to its readers.

8.4. Conclusion

We have seen that the user model by ASCC displays relevant information at every level of the journal. ASCC contexts allow us to categorize and organize the contents of these levels to adapt information to readers. Each category of information tagged using ASCC aims to respond to a problem that may be encountered by a reader in an information seeking situation. Any piece of information is, by its very nature, a source of problems; ASCC contexts allow us to find the meaning of information and thus participate in the solution of research problems encountered by readers.

Table 8.6 provides a summary of the categorization of information corresponding to the ASCC user model of a scientific journal. Whatever the level of information considered, the nine questions included in ASCC can be used to qualify and organize relevant information to present it to the reader, bringing out the inherent meaning. Each level of an adaptive journal constitutes a separate mode of access, within which information is clarified and ordered to facilitate research, promote understanding of the information, and, finally, suggest a constructive approach to information from the point of view of meaning.

Questions	Macro-level	Meso-level	Micro-level	Nano-level	*Author*
Identity	Name of journal	Name of theme	Name of article	Name of concept	*Name of author*
Norms	Definition of journal	Definition of theme	Definition of article	Definition of concept	*Discipline of author*
Aims	Aims of journal	Aims of theme	Aims of article	Aims of concept	*Theme on which author is working*
Position	Domain of journal	Field of application of theme	Reference theme of article	Specification relationship between concepts	*Author status*
Relationships	Partnerships with other journals	Relationship to other themes	Relationship to other articles	Associative relationships between concepts	*Collaborations with other authors*
Time factors	History of journal	Date of appearance of theme	Date of publication of article	Chronology of concept	*Dates of published articles*
Spatial factors	Journal contacts	Organization behind theme	Organization and address linked with article	Place linked to concept	*Name and address of organization of author*
Author and references	Journal edition committee and references	Scientific committee and references	Author and bibliography used by article	Citation from an author on the concept	*Author publications*
Example	Themes of journal	Articles on the theme	Concepts of the article	Cases of use of concept	*Articles by the author in the journal*

Table 8.6. *Generalized ASCC tag table for adaptation to readers of a scientific journal*

We thus offer a generic tagging model for controlled databases, a model that we have applied to the case of a scientific journal. Each level of information making up the communication approach of a journal can be broken down into nine contexts, which highlight relevant elements of information for a reader in a research situation. Contrary to appearances, the generic ASCC tagging table, generalized for the whole of a journal, is based on just 20 semantic tags. As far as possible, we attempted to keep the same tags for all levels of information in a journal, with the aim of facilitating the appropriation of the ASCC user model.

8.5. Bibliography

[AMA 04] AMAR M., "L'indexation aujourd'hui", *La fonction documentaire au cœur des TICE*, Les Dossiers de l'Ingénierie Educative, vol. 49, December 2004.

[BAR 04a] BARTH B.M., *L'Apprentissage de l'Abstraction*, Editions Retz, Paris, 2004.

[BAR 04b] BARTH B.M., *Le Savoir en Construction*, Editions Retz, Paris, 2004.

[BER 01] BERNERS-LEE T., HENDLER J., LASSILE O., "The semantic web", *Scientific America*, May 2001.

[BRU 91] BRUNER J.S., *Car la Culture Donne Forme à l'Esprit: de la Révolution Cognitive à la Psychologie Culturelle*, Edition Eshel, Paris, 1991.

[ECO 88] ECO U., *Le signe. Histoire et Analyse d'un Concept*, Edition Labor, Brussels, 1988.

[GAR 04] GARDNER H., *Les Intelligences Multiples. La Théorie qui Bouleverse les Idées Reçues*, Editions Retz, Paris, 2004.

[GRU 93] GRUBER T., "A translation approach to portable ontology specifications", *Knowledge Acquisition*, 5, 1993.

[GUA 97] GUARINO N., "Understanding, building and using ontologies: a commentary to 'using explicit ontologies in KBS development'", *International Journal of Human and Computer Studies*, 1997.

[GUI 96] GUINCHAT C., SKOURI Y., *Guide Pratique des Techniques Documentaires*, Edition Edicef, Vanves, 1996.

[LEC 04] LECOADIC Y.F., *Usages et usagers de l'information*, Coll. Information Documentation 128, Armand Colin, Paris, 2004.

[LEN 05] LENY J.F., *Comment l'Esprit Produit du Sens*, Odile Jacob, Paris, 2005.

[MOR 99] MORIN E., "Les défis de la complexité", *Le défi du XXIe siècle: Relier les Connaissances*, Le Seuil, Paris, p. 456, 1999.

[MOR 04] MORIZIO C., *La recherche d'informations*, Coll. Information Documentation 128, Armand Colin, Paris, 2004.

[MUC 98] MUCCHIELLI A., CORBALAN J.A., FERNANDEZ V., *Théorie des Processus de la Communication*, Armand Colin, Paris, 1998.

[MUC 00] MUCCHIELLI A., *La Nouvelle Communication*, Armand Colin, Paris, 2000.

[MUC 05] MUCCHIELLI A., *Etude des Communications: Approche par la Contextualisation*, Armand Colin, Paris, 2005.

[PIA 67] PIAGET J., *Psychologie de l'intelligence*, Coll. Agora, Armand Colin, Paris, 1967.

[SOW 00] SOWA J.F., "Ontology, metadata and semiotics", in GANTER B., MINEAU G.W. (eds), *Conceptual Structure: Logical, Linguistic, and Computational Issues*, Springer-Verlag, Berlin, pp. 55–81, 2000.

[VER 08] VERLAET L., Modèle communicationnel de balisage générique pour la sémantisation des informations: le cas d'une revue scientifique, Doctoral Thesis in Information and Communication Sciences, CERIC, Montpellier, 2008.

[VYG 97] VYGOTSKI L., *Pensée & Langage*, La Dispute, Paris, 1997.

[WIT 04] WITTGENSTEIN L., *Recherches Philosophiques*, Gallimard, Paris, 2004.

[WIT 06] WITTGENSTEIN L., *De la Certitude*, Gallimard, Paris, 2006.

Chapter 9

Design and Development of a Model for Generating and Exploiting Annotation in the Context of Economic Intelligence

9.1. Introduction

The contribution of this chapter aims at the design and development of an annotation model for users (in the context of economic intelligence (EI), economic actors) that could assist them to add annotations to documents of interest. A user reads a document, either electronic or hard copy, for many reasons. One of such reasons is interpreting the document content. When used as a user's interpretation of document content, annotation is regarded as value-added information. Document in this context is anything that serves as a source of information of interest to the user. The major formats of document are text, video, and images. Different users employ different *annotation forms* such as underlining an object of interest, writing on the margins, making a comment, and using some marks such as asterisk, question mark, and so on. Annotation may have explicit or implicit meaning. With explicit annotation, the intention of the annotation is explicitly made available to at least a community of users. Unlike explicit annotation, the intention of implicit annotation is known only to the annotator. This chapter focuses on the need to design and develop a model for creating annotations as value-added information in the EI process aimed toward decision problem resolution. The next section discusses the annotation concept.

Chapter written by Olusoji B. OKUNOYE and Charles O. UWADIA.

9.2. Annotation as a concept

The definition and use of annotation are closely linked with the objectives, context of use, and available source of information. Information sources available to users can be put into two categories: open sources and official sources. With the open sources, information is freely, directly, and lawfully accessible with little or no access restriction. Examples of information in this category include published information on the Web. The official sources, on the other hand, contain information that has been preselected, sorted, and processed for a particular use. Thus, the information contents are structured according to the targeted use. Yang *et al.* [YAN 04] described the use of annotation for commenting and for knowledge articulation in a collaborative environment. It has also been used as a formal description of Web pages to improve information retrieval [JÉR 02]. CritLink [YEE 02], an annotation tool, enabled users to attach annotations to any location in a Web page and to view the annotation on any page without installing any special software. Robert and David [ROB 06, ROB 07] viewed annotation, as a function of the user, document, and time in assisting economic actors to interpret retrieved information for solving decisional problems by providing a base for an enhanced information research.

Some works have also been done on annotating official sources. Bhatnagar *et al.* [BHA 07] defined data annotations that allow users to annotate relational data at five different levels of granularity – database level, relation level, column level, tuple level, and cell level. The models were implemented in XML. Geerts *et al.* [GEE 06] introduced annotation data model for manipulating and querying both data and annotation using the concept of block of colors to represent an annotated set of values. Bhagwat *et al.* [BHA 04] discussed annotation management system for relational database.

Several definitions of annotation exist in the literature. Annotation is defined in [BOD 07] as "a note, an explanation, or any other type of external remark that can be attached to a document without necessarily being inserted into the document". Two things can be deduced from the definition. Annotation is viewed as a separate document containing extra information to the existing information (object). Its purpose is for interpreting the underlying document (document interpretation). Brusilovsky [BRU 96] also defined it as "any object (annotation) that is associated with another object (document) by some relationship". This definition of annotation not only considers annotation as an object but also as an action involving *anchoring* the object with the concerned document. Of particular interest to us is the definition of annotation given by MacMullen [MAC 05]. He gave a tripartite definition of annotation, similar to Buckland's definition of information [BUC 91], that is, annotation-as-thing, annotation-as-process, and annotation-as-knowledge. He defines each part of the concept as follows:

Annotation-as-thing: *an annotation is an intentional and topical value-adding note linked to an extant information object.* Apart from viewing annotation as an object, the definition also states the purpose of annotation as value-added information.

Annotation-as-process: *an annotation is a process that has the function of creating or modifying an information object called annotation.*

Annotation-as-knowledge: *annotation is the intellectual component of an annotation, distinct from its physical manifestation.* Annotation as source of knowledge is very interesting especially when such knowledge is available to reduce uncertainty surrounding decision-making purposes. In [MEN 02], knowledge is the existence of a pattern relation and its implications resulting from processed information that is realized and understandable by the user of such patterns. The word "user" could be human or machine.

It can be deduced from the definitions above that annotation is an object created on an existing document; it is also the process of creating the object; the purpose of annotation creation could be for document interpretation, value adding, document comprehension, or as a source of knowledge. The study by Robert [ROB 07] dealt extensively with annotation-as-thing and annotation-as-process in the context of EI. In his work, annotation-as-thing and annotation-as-process refer, respectively, to annotation as an object and as an action. The aim of our work is to look at the semantics of annotation in relation to decision problems.

9.3. Annotation in EI

In this section, three areas of interest are identified: the use of annotation for eliciting necessary knowledge for proper formulation of decision problems, annotation for assisting actors for retrieving relevant information once sources have been identified, and the use of annotation for interpreting analyzed information.

9.3.1. *Annotation for knowledge elicitation*

The decision-making process is often based on available strategic information. Such information, however, has to be sought, collected, and processed with a view of eliciting knowledge relevant to the problem as well as representing both the collected information and elicited knowledge in a form that will facilitate information reuse. A decision based on such information alone may not be sufficient if the preferences of actors involved in problem resolution are not taken into consideration. Information of significance to one person may not be to another person depending on the individual's interest. Hence, availability of strategic information is as important as the person who needs it or interprets it. Annotation as knowledge is the expressed knowledge of annotator on the contextualized document. Knowledge elicitation is a process of obtaining, transforming, and documenting tacit knowledge from identified information source such as human experts to explicit knowledge. Actor's knowledge is elicited by capturing his/her interpretation on the document of interest. Such annotation is based on his/her intellectual capacity, experience, cultural background, and environment. Storing information on who annotates what and how personal characteristics influence annotations could serve as a source of knowledge on the annotator. Annotation patterns of an individual actor over time could reveal interesting patterns that could assist in discovering new knowledge about him/her.

9.3.2. Annotation in information retrieval

In information retrieval, the objective is to find information useful to the user's need. The process entails the user expressing his/her need as query, and the system maps the query to existing documents using keywords. In most cases, users have a long list of documents as the result of the query, to look through, most of which may not be relevant to their needs. The needs of a user may vary depending on so many factors. A major challenge in retrieving information automatically is that such retrieval is based only on the query submitted. Personalized Information Retrieval is aimed at improving the retrieval process by taking into consideration the interests of individual users based on their history of past search activity. A user may submit the same query at different times for different contexts. Using the history of past activities of a user for information retrieval may not meet the need of such user as his/her motive might be different. At any particular time, the motive behind submitting a query is only known to such a user. The user's query specifies *what* he/she is looking for. Documenting the *whys* he/she needs such information as well as the domain context in the form of annotation could prove very valuable in improving information retrieval.

9.3.3. Annotation as value-added information

Documents often contain information the author intended to pass across to readers. In most cases, such a document centers on a particular subject matter. Additional information that might not be known to the author or information the author might not have included in the document but which could prove valuable could be added in the form of annotation. Marshall [MAR 98] quoted Robert McCrum on the account of annotations found in the books of Graham Greene's library. The quotation revealed that Graham added extra information on the margins, flyleaves, and endpapers of those books. Such information may not have been provided in the books. The context could be totally different from the book context. Thus, annotation made becomes value-added information. Also, information system contains preselected, sorted, and processed information for a particular use. Thus, information contents are structured according to targeted end use. Given such structured information, users can express information needs more precisely. They can specify values in relation to attributes of the information. However, users could be faced with the following challenges. A user needs to have a minimum knowledge of his/her needs by specifying at least a value of the stored attributes, since the principle of information search is still content based. Problem arises where the user does not know what attribute to use for specifying his/her need or the attribute does not exist. Where a user specifies an attribute that does not exist, there would be a need for structural changes to accommodate new attributes. Such changes might be tedious, time-consuming, and costly. Adding such information through annotation is a means of resolving such problem.

9.3.4. Requirements for annotation model

We are of the opinion that, in designing an effective annotation model, the following questions should be considered:

Who makes an annotation? It is important to know who makes an annotation and the possibility of how his/her personal characteristics influence the annotation made. Annotation as knowledge is the expressed knowledge of an annotator on the contextualized document. Knowing the characteristics of the annotator is important. Annotation made may be based on his/her intellectual capacity, experience, cultural background, and environment. Storing information on who annotates, and what and how personal characteristics influence annotations made could serve as a form of knowledge on the annotator.

Annotation made concerns who? Annotation may be created to have implicit or explicit meaning depending on the targeted audience. Personal annotation could have implied meaning only to the annotator. With explicit annotation, the meaning of such annotation is expected to be unambiguous and have agreed understanding at least among community of users.

Why the annotation? The motive of making an annotation should be clear and expressly stated. The terms *type* and *objective* have been used to designate the reason for making an annotation. At any particular time, the motive for creating an annotation is only known to such an annotator. It is therefore necessary for the annotator to expressly state this.

When was annotation made? This concerns the date and time an annotation is created. In a collaborative environment, it can be used to determine the most recent annotation made concerning a decision problem resolution, for instance.

What document has been annotated? Annotation is made on an existing document. Such a document is referred to as an annotated object. The object may be the document itself or its content. Existing annotation made is also regarded as a document that can be annotated.

How is annotation anchored to the annotated object? This is relevant in determining the relationship between the annotation made and an annotated object. Annotation created can be anchored to the underlying document as inline annotation or as overlay depending on whether the actor has access rights to modify the document or not. Considering the wealth of information that resides in different sources of information, an annotation tool that does not take into consideration the structure of documents will prove more valuable.

In addition to providing answers to the above questions, the model should be able to satisfy the following functional requirements:

Ability to structure or restructure documents: We believe that annotation representation as attribute-value pair (AVP) for capturing an actor's observation and/or contextualizing document object of interest would improve significantly the effectiveness of such valued-added information as opposed to adding annotation as an atomic object only. It will provide a good basis for data restructuring, data mining, robust exploitation, and knowledge elicitation among others. Since the needs of actors are evolving, it becomes practically impossible to anticipate all possible attributes at the design stage, hence, the need for flexible and robust means of adding attributes and values as the need of actors arise. Actors should have the possibilities of expressing their views without restriction. They should be able to choose the word, phrase, or sentence that best suit what they intend to represent.

Ability to use annotation's object of mediation (communication): Annotation is being used to discuss topics of interest in different fora on the social Web. In Wikipedia (http://en.wikipedia.org/wiki/Main_Page), annotation is used for authoring documents. Tagging (annotation) is used in Delicious (http://www.delicious.com) for categorizing Web pages of interest to users. With Flickr (http://www.flickr.com/), group members can jointly annotate pictures of interest. The concern is the use of annotation as a mediation object for communicative acts among collaborators for sharing each other's perceptions in resolving a decision problem. Actors may share their perceptions of the decision problem or of any information through annotation in a collaborative environment. The conclusion arrived at about the object of deliberation (decision problem) could be added to the initial information source as annotation. The use of annotation as a platform for economic actors to share each other's perception could be done synchronously or asynchronously. With synchronous annotation, actors can communicate with one another in real time. It, however, requires all participating actors to be online. However, with asynchronous annotation, the actors need not communicate in real time. Electronic mail or any other form could be used in communicative acts. This, however, requires a means of notifying the involving actors about the pending message as time may be of essence.

Scalability: There should be the possibility of growth on annotation made. Annotations could become documents for further annotations.

Reusable: Previous annotations made should be reusable. Actors should be able to adapt previous annotations to similar problems without necessarily modifying it *provided problem contexts are similar*. A modified annotation becomes another annotation.

Granularity: Actors should be able to add annotation to a document or document object of interest at any level of granularity. No restriction should be placed on what to annotate and where to place such annotation. There should be the possibility of adding annotations both at coarse-grain level and fine-grain level. For example, annotation might be on the document title, paragraph, sentence, phrase, text, word, image section, and so on.

9.4. Proposition

We propose the use of annotation representation as AVP, a medium for capturing EI actors' interpretation of a document of interest. AVP is a data representation methodology that allows data elements to be represented with a set of attributes and values. The ability of an actor to express his/her observation and/or contextualize document objects as AVP annotation could improve significantly the effectiveness of such value-added information. A user query expressed as AVP will add semantic context to such a query. While most of the existing annotation models allow annotators to add annotation to a document of interest as an atomic object, it is believed that annotation represented as an AVP will offer enhanced interpretation functionalities. In annotation models where attributes are predefined, the structure of such models constrains users to choose one of the available attributes that may not adequately represent the user's objective. Therefore, the use of AVP will provide a good basis for data restructuring, data mining, robust exploitation, and knowledge elicitation, among others. The work focuses on two major areas: annotation creation and annotation exploitation.

9.4.1. *Annotation creation*

This is the process of capturing user annotation. It could be a new annotation or extension of annotation previously made on the same object. The process entails the user to identifying the object of interest, annotates the object, and then saves the annotation. Two *forms* of annotations can be inferred: annotations made on the entire document (referred to as A_{T1}) and annotations made on the objects of the document (referred to as A_{T2}). The objects of document such as terms, phrase, sentences, and so on will be called *document objects* (d_o). With d_o, the annotator might give the meaning or definition of each term identified: the synonyms of the term and the source in form of annotations. At this point, it is important to differentiate between the process of adding annotation to a document and the actual annotation added. While the former is regarded as an annotation process ($A_{process}$), the latter is annotation representation as AVP. This is denoted as A_{avp}. A_{T1} and A_{T2} are forms of A_{avp}. The set A_{avp} of annotation is defined as:

$$A_{avp} \subseteq id \times def \times attr \times val \times timestamp , \qquad\qquad [9.1]$$

where id is identifier, def is definition, attr is attribute name, and val is annotation value.

Figure 9.1 shows the logical view of annotation process.

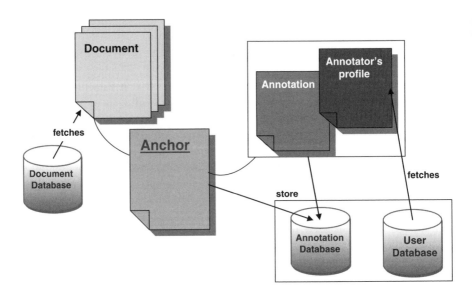

Figure 9.1. *Logical view of annotation process*

9.4.2. *Annotation exploitation*

Annotation exploitation in this context covers exploration and querying existing annotations. In annotation *exploration*, an user can explore stored information. Let A, D, and P represent the sets of all annotations, annotated documents, and annotators, respectively. An actor can explore:

– all annotations (A);

– all annotated documents (D);

– all annotators (P);

– all annotations made by a particular annotator in all annotated documents (AUDUp∈P);

– and all annotations contained in a particular document by all annotators (AUPUd∈D).

In *exploitation*, users may want to further refine their exploration to some specific information by querying the system. Querying operation may involve a homogeneous set of information or union of the sets of information. For instance, a user query operation may be on annotation, annotator, or document entities. The operation may also be a union of these entities. We also include a searching technique called AVP search for searching any information system based on the semantic context of the user. With AVP search, the user expresses his/her query as AVP. The attribute component is used for categorizing retrieved documents based on the user's objective of search. Figure 9.2 gives an overview of our approach. The stages involved are summarily described thus:

– User expresses his/her query as AVP.

– System computes semantic relation of user query and generates semantic patterns from the query and synonyms of the attribute.

– User selects patterns that best describe objective of his/her search.

– System queries search engine Application Programming Interface (API) (e.g. Google API) of choice with user-selected patterns.

– System retrieves documents ranked in the order of relevance based on documents with a greater number of matched patterns.

The importance of a user expressing his/her query as AVP is to serve two purposes: (i) categorizing such query and results obtained based on objective of search and (ii) obtaining results based on the semantic context of the user query. For example, a user who needs information on *causes of body odor* might search from the Web using any of the search engines or query any known information system. Such a user needs specific information on the likely causes of body odor. Search engines usually return results based on the user query terms. But user need, in most cases, is derived from the semantics of his/her query. In the above example, such a user needs information on *why* the body odor.

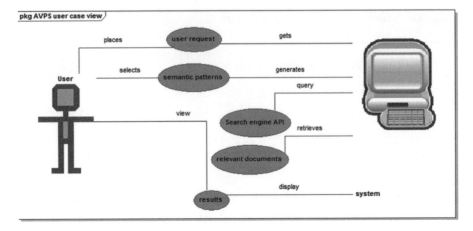

Figure 9.2. *AVP search uses case diagram*

9.5. Annotation model and architectural components

This section discusses the annotation model and annotation architecture. We used the architecture to develop a prototype called Annotation Model and Tools for Economic Actors (AMTEA).

Based on the annotation requirements stated above, the identified annotation components include the following: **Document, Annotator, Anchor,** and **Annotation.**

Document: This is written, printed, or recorded information representing the materialized knowledge of a person or group of persons, identified by actors and intended to be annotated or value-added. Each document is identified by its uniform resource locator (URL). Decision problems produced by decision makers are represented and stored in a document repository. The annotated object is the information source that may exist in the form of text, image, or voice. The object may be the document itself or its content. Existing annotation made is also regarded as a document that can be annotated.

Annotator: This is an actor that annotates (contextualizes) a document or document object of interest. Knowing the characteristics of the annotator is important. Storing information on who annotates what and how personal characteristics influence annotations could serve as a form of knowledge on the annotator regarding the decision problem. Annotations may be personal or shared collaboratively. For a decision problem, the annotation system should be able to keep track of changes made on the document. For example, if an annotator makes frequent changes on his/her annotation concerning a concept over a period of time, keeping a track of such modifications could serve as a form of knowledge on how diligent and meticulous the annotator is in giving value-added information.

Annotation: This is the actual information added by the actor to the document of interest. However, such annotation representation should be in AVP. Each annotation made will have a valid identifier called *annotation_id*, the annotation_ objective, mode of access – private, group, or public – annotation_date, and annotation body consisting of attribute and value.

Anchor: For annotation made to be anchored to the concerned document, there is the need to determine the position of the annotation with reference to the concerned document as well as the surrounding text. Taking the surrounding text of the annotated text into consideration will preserve the semantic context of the user.

The complexity of annotation as process ($A_{process}$) based on the above discussion can, therefore, be deduced. $A_{process}$ is defined over four tuples: annotator (U_{ann}), annotation-as-object (A_{object}), annotation anchor (A_{anchor}), and Document D, that is:

$$A_{process} \rightarrow (U_{ann}, A_{avp}, A_{anchor}, D)$$

9.5.1. *Annotation schema*

This section discusses annotation schema based on the identified annotation components. It explains the structure and interrelationship among the identified components that are annotator, annotation, document, and anchor.

A user may access any of the stored documents. If he/she finds any of it relevant, he/she may annotate the document or a section of the document using the annotation component. For the annotation component, the *anno_objectives* property captures the objective of the annotation being made. The *anno_access_mode* property enables annotators to specify whether the annotation made is private, protected (for a community of users), or for the public domain. The user's interpretation is contained in the *anno_description* property. The annotation created, the anchor information, and the information on the actor are stored in the annotation database. We have separated annotating the entire document from annotating parts of a document for the purpose of granularity. Anchoring an annotation to an entire document involves linking the annotation to the URL of the document. Annotation on a sectional part of a document (called the document object) requires the determination of both the positional and associational relations between the annotation and the document object. The concept component represents the abstract form of the document object. This is necessary as economic actors should be able to add values in the form of annotation with or without prior knowledge of the underlining document design. Information stored in both the annotation database and user database is a form of knowledge base. Knowledge on annotation pattern of an individual actor or annotations made concerning a decision problem can be extracted. The annotation schema is shown in Figure 9.3 where important attributes for each component are shown.

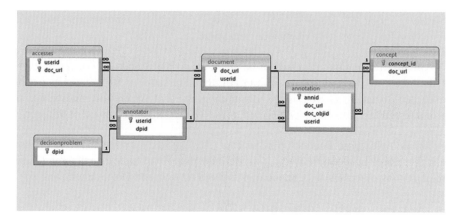

Figure 9.3. *The annotation schema*

9.5.2. *AMTEA architecture*

The general architecture of AMTEA is shown in Figure 9.4. It consists of four layers – database layer, application programming interface, software modules, and end-user interface.

End-user interface: this layer is divided into two functional components – annotation creation and annotation exploitation. Annotation generation components involve document uploading, creation of new annotation, or follow-up annotation. Annotation, document, or user's profile exploration through hyperlinks, querying, and annotation analyzer are contained in the exploitation components.

Capture and display modules: these are modules for capturing annotation and display of stored annotations. The capture module handles the login, registration of new users, and annotations created. The display module handles the necessary views of annotation, document, and user's profile.

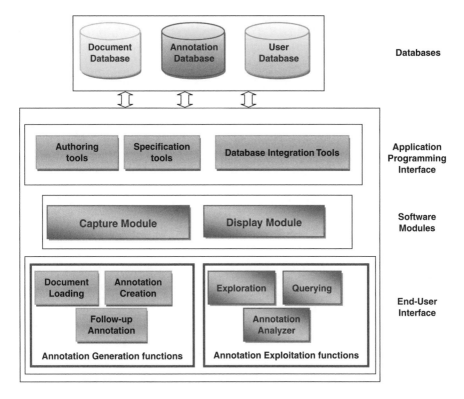

Figure 9.4. *General architecture of AMTEA*

The decision problem often starts from the decision maker who gives the initial demand as a document. This is stored in document repository. The watcher retrieves the document through the annotation tool provided. He/she then calls the annotation tool to add his/her annotation to the document. The user's interpretation is contained in *attribute and value* properties. Anchoring an annotation to an entire document involves linking the annotation to the Uniform Resource Identifier of the document. Annotations made are stored in the annotation repository. Figure 9.5 shows the screenshots of the display of annotation tool in AMTEA environment. In Figure 9.6, annotations made on the displayed document are indicated as A, and positions of the annotations and the actual annotation are indicated as B and C, respectively. EI actors can query stored documents, annotations, annotations on a particular document, annotations made by a particular actors, and so on. Explore, Query, Analyze, and Annotate (EQuA^{2}te) proposed in [DAV 03] is for exploiting the stored annotations, documents, and actors' information.

Figure 9.5. *Annotation tool in AMTEA environment*

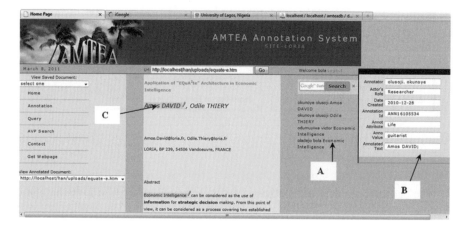

Figure 9.6. *Annotation creation and exploitation in AMTEA environment*

9.6. Bibliography

[BHA 04] BHAGWAT D., CHITICARIU L., TAN W.-C., VIJAYVARGIYA G., *An Annotation Management System for Relational Databases*, VLDB, Toronto, Canada, 2004.

[BHA 07] BHATNAGAR N., JULIANO A.B., RENNER R.S., "Data annotation models and annotation query language", *Proceedings of World Academic of Science, Engineering and Technology*, vol. 21, January 2007.

[BOD 07] BODAIN Y., ROBERT J.-M., "Developing a robust authoring annotation system for the semantic web", *Seventh IEEE International Conference on Advanced Learning Technologies (ICALT 2007)*, available online at http://ieeexplore.ieee.org/iel5/4280926/4280927/04281043.pdf, accessed on 20 October 2007.

[BRU 96] BRUSILOVSKY P., *Efficient Technique for Adaptive Hypermedia, Intelligent Hypertext: Advanced Techniques for the World Wide Web*, Lecture Notes in Computer Science, 1326, Spring-Verlag, Berlin, pp. 12–30, 1996.

[BUC 91] BUCKLAND M.K., "Information as thing", *Journal of the American Society for Information Science*, vol. 42, no. 5, pp. 351–360, 1991.

[DAV 03] DAVID A., THIERY O., "L'architecture EQuA²te et son application à l'intelligence économique", *Proceeding on the Conférence on Intelligence Economique: Recherches et Applications*, 2003.

[EUZ 02] EUZENAT J., "Eight questions about semantic web annotations", *Computer.org/intelligent IEE Intelligent Systems*, vol. 17, no. 2, pp. 55–62, 2002.

[GEE 06] GEERTS F., KEMENTSIETSIDIS A., MILANO MONDRIAN D., "Annotating and querying databases through colors and blocks", *Proceedings of the 22nd International Conference on Data Engineering (ICDE'06)*, Washington, DC, IEEE Computer Society, p. 82, 2006.

[MAC 05] MACMULLEN W.J., Annotation as process, thing, and knowledge: multidomain studies of structured data annotation, SILS Technical Report TR-2005-02, University of North Carolina, School of Information and Library Science, Technical Report Series, Chapel Hill, 2005.

[MAR 98] MARSHALL C.C., "The future of annotation in a digital (paper) world", *35th Annual GSLIS Clinic: Successes and Failures of Digital Libraries*, University of Illinois at Urbana-Champaign, 1998.

[MEN 02] MENÉNDEZ A., ATANES E., ALONSO J., MERINO C., BOURGOGNE P., GEFFROY P., POPKOWSKA M., CORNBILL J., DOBSON J., ISON K., NOBLE E., TURNER A., GIACHETTI C., CHERICONI S., DIANA V., AMATI L., MANCINI M.A., "Economic intelligence. A guide for beginners and practitioners", *CETISME Partnership*, 2002.

[ROB 07] ROBERT C.A., L'annotation pour la recherche d'informations dans le contexte d'intelligence économique, PhD thesis, University of Nancy 2, 2007.

[YAN 04] YANG, S.J.H., CHEN, I.Y.L., SHAO, N.W.Y. "Ontology enabled annotation and knowledge management for collaborative learning in virtual learning community", *Journal of Educational Technology & Society*, vol. 7, no. 4, pp. 70–81, 2004.

[YEE 02] YEE K., "CritLink: advanced hyperlinks enable public annotation on the web", *Demo to the CSCW 2002 Conference*, New Orleans, 2002, available online at http://zesty.ca/pubs/yee-critcscw2002-demo.pdf.

Chapter 10

Contribution of Cognitive Sciences to Document Indexing in Scientific, Technical, and Economic Watch for Competitive Intelligence

10.1. Introduction

We have observed that the economic concerns of businesses, or even states, are placing increasing pressure on aspects of scientific research in a strategic positioning approach to markets. The registration of patents in domains of high technology research allows companies or nations to be actively involved in tomorrow's technologies and their practical applications. Intellectual property has become a weapon for use in competitive intelligence.

It is now crucial that private or public organizations obtain tools and methods that allow them to "watch" the global environment in a given domain of research. Traditional keyword-based research does not provide sufficient exhaustivity or relevance, producing – paradoxically – "too much noise and too much silence".

In this chapter, we will present a new indexing method, different from traditional keyword-based indexing strategies; our method takes inspiration from theories found in cognitive sciences [ELD 00] to create a precise watch profile of the person receiving information. This method aims to supply value-added information for decision assistance in real time.

Chapter written by Elisabeth PAOLI-SCARBONCHI and Nadège GUENEC.

This contribution introduces a new dimension to information extraction, as it considers concepts and contexts linked to a research or watch problem and the various subsequent associations, whatever the discipline(s) or language(s) concerned, in an approach based on previous work relating to contextualization [MUC 05].

The proposed method allows us, thanks to "memory" indexing and coding in an interpretative pivot language [LAP 94], to produce value-added information from a large corpus of information. Thematic and personalized elaborated databases can then be constructed.

The aim of this chapter is to demonstrate the feasibility and interest of such a method using a computerized model made up of two main modules:

– *A memory indexing procedure*: (*mémoire évènementielle d'actualisation*, MEVA) developed by Christian Krumeich of the MAAG company.

– *A statistical analysis tool*: Matheo Analyzer, developed by Prof. H. Dou and his team at the CRRM, Aix-Marseille University, France [DOU 03a].

This platform has been used in the context of theses on scientific watch in various knowledge domains at the Paris-Est University, France [GUE 09, PAO 06].

The platform thus developed, named platform of elaborated information and technologies in applied research (*plate-forme d'information élaborée et technologies en recherche appliquée*, PIETRA) is able to carry out a set of processes in four steps:

– information capture;

– "memory" indexing;

– statistical processing; and

– the production of elaborated databases [PAO 06].

To illustrate this approach, we have chosen two subjects. The first is in the domain of regenerative medicine, and specifically applies to liver regeneration, a research theme addressed by Dr Mallet of the INSERM. Our second subject is on agricultural biotechnologies in China from a competitive intelligence perspective (the subject of an industrial doctoral thesis in partnership with the Limagrain Group).

10.2. Functionality of the PIETRA platform: general presentation

The PIETRA platform is made up of modules integrating capture, indexing, and analysis tools. Its structure is designed to be flexible to adapt to new problems and the processing of different languages.

The construction of a databank is a four-step process:

– *Capture*: capture of a wide information stream, using a classic research equation and logical operators. We thus obtain a first corpus, "corpus 1", using specialized capture tools.

– *MEVA suite*: use of the MEVA suite for targeted information retrieval based on memory indexing, which involves indexing meaning rather than graphical signs [RIC 00]. This method is used to target relevant information for knowledge creation through the coding of concepts, their contextualization, and associations. Using cognitive liaisons, it allows us to transform the research hypotheses of the watcher. Its thematic analysis profiles are expressed in a watch profile. This operation involves three phases:

- the construction of a watch profile;

- coding in the pivot language; and

- memory indexing.

After indexing, we obtain a new filtered corpus of knowledge, known as "corpus 2". This second corpus includes only those articles with contents suited to the aims of the watch process. A new documentary field may thus be created at the level of article metadata: the THM field, or the "theme of memory". A watch profile always includes several THMs in combination, for example, a "genome" THM and a "China" THM for research on biotechnologies in China.

– *Statistical processing*: statistical treatment of corpus 2 to create strategies for the analysis of metadata to obtain elaborated information [LEI 04]. This analysis leads to the production of a new corpus, with two additional fields: list of frequency (FREQ) and graph of the network (GRAPH) (list by order of frequency, highest first, and graphical representations). In this way, it is possible to create networks of information entities (authors, affiliations, keywords, etc.) associated with the THM field introduced in the previous phase.

– *Elaborated databases*: creation of elaborated databases through the successive enrichment of fields and their treatment.

10.3. Global usage strategy

An analogy can be made between the analysis strategy used for scientific watch or competitive intelligence (Figure 10.1) and the PIETRA analysis strategy, which follows successive enrichments using new fields and their processing (comments linked to arrows in Figure 10.1).

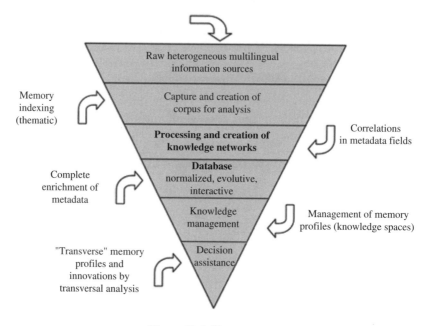

Figure 10.1. *Usage strategy*

This diagram shows that the final decision-making action is based on knowledge (concepts, association of concepts, and contexts) and not on the sets of keywords usually obtained through the use of traditional databases.

Based on memory indexing and not on indexing using graphical signs, the "decision level" of the expert or decision maker rises above traditional representations based on semantics, and knowledge creation increases in relevance.

10.4. Operation of the platform

The different phases of processing are as follows:

– *Phase 1: information source capture – "corpus 1"*: the strategy is to capture as wide a stream of information as possible. A traditional documentary approach would involve seeking the most relevant documents from the outset. Our approach, however, consists of obtaining the largest possible number of documents in the field of research or domain of study, using a generic research equation and various possibilities offered by traditional research, including keywords, Boolean operators, and so on.

– *Phase 2: memory indexing*: as an automated information retrieval system, the MEVA suite is used with the aim of reducing the density of the information collected, and has the advantage of using relevance, meaning that it can propose useful information that the expert may not have thought of. "Relevant" knowledge in this context is the knowledge not found through using large quantities of information or using mathematical sophistication, but which lies in the aptitude to contextualize and see relationships [MOR 04]. The method used by MEVA is different from traditional practices that work on creating an ontology, and makes use of resources produced by cognitive sciences for information seeking to precisely target relevant ideas in accordance with the wishes of the expert; the addition of synonyms extracted from databases does not allow us to improve performance in information [SAV 09]. For this reason, indexing is carried out before linguistic enunciation, at the level of concepts contained in the memory of the expert.

The whole approach of MEVA is based on the formalization of both the memory of the expert and their watch objectives. It is thus a "prereading" tool that is applied to the initial mass of information *as is*, and is part of recent advances in new technologies that, among other things, attempt to externalize cognitive functions [SER 07].

10.4.1. *Watch profiles*

MEVA therefore allows us to develop "watch profiles" and to carry out memory indexing. It acts as a workshop for information targeting in relation to a watch situation. The MEVA approach is not based on a linguistic approach, but on the identification and comprehension of cognitive elements that make up meaning. As a word cannot reflect a precise thought or an exact context, the watch process is based on thoughts before language. The watch profile is constructed in association with the expert to declare research themes and expected contexts, accounting for the implicit knowledge and knowledge associations of the researcher. This consists of listing elements of knowledge for each context. The choice of memory descriptors and links corresponds to the preoccupations of the expert and may be transposed into a new THM documentary field. This field constitutes a dynamically constructed qualitative contribution in terms of metadata.

The watch profile is then translated into a pivot language in the form of knowledge coding, the associations of which determine the THM. The pivot language is a language created to be as close as possible to the interpretative processes described by cognitive sciences. The coded units are not words, but units of meaning. The pivot language thus expresses concepts. The knowledge of the watcher, that is, what they know of their environment and their research hypotheses, is coded in conceptual terms by the pivot language. The watch profile thus created is then dynamized using the LISP[1] functions of the platform.

In this way, not only are concepts integrated into the information targeting approach, but also all possible associations between different concepts are included.

It is therefore important that the creation of the watch profile be done with the participation of the expert, as the expert alone declares the precise watch situation to enter into MEVA and the information targeting aims. It is this precision in the expression of demand that allows the research to be personalized.

10.4.2. The pivot language

The pivot language is a language for the symbolic expression of "knowledge", which allows us to code a watch profile in a file known as the base index.

Expression passes through:

– cognitive modalities;

– acquisition schemes;

– agents; and

– a spatio-temporal context.

We will now give a selection of modalities that express an action. Note that these are in French, as MEVA was developed in a French-speaking context, but a list of translations will be provided afterwards:

AVOIR: av	PERCEVOIR: pcv
AGIR: ag	POUVOIR: pv
DEVOIR: dv	VOIR: vr
ETRE: be	etc.

---

1 LISP: *List processing*, computing language often used in artificial intelligence applications.

Avoir, to have; *Agir*, to act; *Devoir*, to have to; *Être*, to be; *Percevoir*, to perceive; *Pouvoir*, to be able to; *Voir*, to see, etc.

Some operators used to link knowledge:

– > "implication";

– / in relation to (viewpoint);

– \ "in a context of".

To provide an illustration of use of the pivot language, we will take the example of a person traveling by bicycle. A traditional semantic translation of this might be: a person on a tool/a machine in movement. This creates a written or oral expression describing what we saw (a cyclist). The terms used for expression are external semiotic forms (ESF) that allow us to describe a situation. ESFs are the set of symbols used in human expression. They may, of course, be words, but also mathematical signs, chemical symbols, characters used in Asian languages, and so on.

To be able to express these terms, we start with the principle that an "interpretation phenomenon" [SEL 75] takes place between the moment we see the cyclist pass and the process that creates a written or oral situation at cognitive level. This situation is constructed by an individual in a subconscious manner, using our knowledge and in relation to our experience.

This is the point where we encounter the pivot language, used to code the process that reproduces the interpretation phenomenon. This interpretation consists of determining a cognitive situation that allows us to understand the observed phenomenon (I saw someone go by on something with two wheels that moves).

"A cyclist" would be coded in MEVA as follows:

be_tech=dpl/pers\ter

be_tech: existence of a technological entity

= linked to a scheme

dpl: movement (*déplacement*)

/in relation to

pers: person

\in a spatio-temporal context

ter: earth (*terre*)

In this way, we describe the different elements of knowledge implied in set contexts. We have thus created a "memory index". To fully take the watch profile into account, several indexes should be created. These indexes may be linked to other indexes depending on the context. It is from these indexes and their combinations that "memory indexing" is carried out. The combination of these indexes allows us to create a new documentary field, THM, as mentioned above.

10.4.2.1. *Functions*

The different functions used in the pivot language were developed in OpenLisp (ISO standardized LISP, created by Christian Jullien of the Eligis company), a variant of the LISP language generally used in artificial intelligence [SAV 09].

The coding essentially involves two types of functions: order 1 functions ("lex", "clex", and "syn") and the more complex order 2 functions, "ac" and "th".

The "lex" function is used to describe ESFs, that is, words, expressions, and symbols of all natures: chemical formulae, mathematical symbols, Chinese or Japanese characters, and so on – anything that may be used to translate a situation in relation to the knowledge of the expert.

The "syn" function is used to declare synonyms in relation to a particular context.

The order 2 "ac" function is the function that dynamizes memory indexing by activating associations between items of knowledge. In this way, different strategies are organized based on multiple combinations.

The "ac" function combines different elements describing a watch situation in relation to the contexts set out during the creation of the watch profile.

The use of these commands allows us to express a conceptualization of knowledge based on a reduced number of functions in OpenLisp.

Possible combinations are at the base of the constitution of the new THM indexing field.

Finally, the "th" function is used to define and clarify the interest of chosen themes.

10.4.3. *Memory indexing*

Corpus 1 is used to carry out memory indexing. The coding in the pivot language (index) is located in an "index block", and indexing is carried out by an indexing motor named memory indexing motor (*moteur mémoriel d'indexation*, MMI). During this indexing process, the set of "ac" combinations, each of which refer to an order 2 function, allows us to obtain relevant documents in relation to what was declared in the expert's watch profile.

The specificity of the pivot language is seen at the level of cognitive interpretation, which we call *internal semiotic forms* (ISF). The aim of indexing is to obtain a filtered corpus of knowledge in relation to a personalized research problem from a larger initial corpus.

10.4.4. *Validation*

A testing and validation phase must then be applied to the watch profile. As memory indexing is carried out using the MMI indexing motor, two types of interfaces developed within the framework of this application provide various possibilities of interactive combinations placed at the disposition of the expert.

A "combinatory mode" interface allows the expert to combine thematic elements, allowing the user to obtain new relevant documents for analysis.

The so-called "generic" interface (Figure 10.2) allows us to automatically generate documents corresponding to the watch profile (corpus 2).

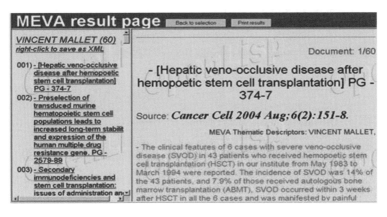

Figure 10.2. *Generic interface – presentation of results*

10.4.4.1. *Phase 3: statistical analysis*

From corpus 2, filtered in terms of knowledge and enriched with a new documentary field, THM, we can carry out statistical analysis and thus develop different analytical strategies. To do this, the PIETRA platform makes use of the Matheo Analyzer tool.

Using structured data sources, Matheo Analyzer allows statistical treatment and is able to produce different networks of authors, keywords, affiliations, and so on. The new field created by memory indexing, in combination with traditional documentary fields, allows us to enrich the treatment of traditional databases by adding a supplementary dimension of knowledge indexing (concepts, association of concepts, and contexts).

This statistical analysis allows us to add two additional fields to elaborated databases: FREQ and GRAPH. The first field produces lists by the decreasing order of frequency and the second provides graphical representations.

This process eventually creates a new elaborated database suitable for use in knowledge management. Using MEVA, we are able to genuinely manage knowledge, and not simply information.

10.4.4.2. *Examples of application: example 1*

Our aim is to carry out watch for an expert in the domain of regenerative medicine.

10.4.4.2.1. Creation of initial corpus

The research equation established for the creation of the initial corpus, in the domain of stem cell therapy, is as follows (using Boolean operators):

("stem cell"[All Fields] OR "stem cell"[MeSH Terms] OR "stem cell"[Text Word]) AND ("therapy"[Subheading] OR ("therapeutics"[All Fields]) OR "therapeutics"[MeSH Terms] OR therapy[Text Word])

This research equation is applied to the Medline database via Pubmed over the Internet, and allows us to obtain 12,648 notices (corpus 1). Document capture is carried out automatically as a continuous stream.

At this stage, we only have access to the traditional documentary fields provided by Medline.

Once this first corpus has been created, we must validate and refine the watch profile with the participation of the expert.

Following the intervention of the expert, a certain number of items of knowledge are expressed either implicitly or explicitly. In our study, the main issue concerns regenerative medicine as a future alternative to major surgery in the domain of innate or acquired liver disease with the aim of producing liver regeneration. The expert presents two important hypotheses for future experimentation: one in cell therapy and the other in liver gene therapy.

This may be expressed as follows: let K1 be an item of knowledge "liver regeneration", in a context of cellular therapy and gene therapy:

K1 -><K1/HYP1, K1/HYP2>

(K1: declaration of knowledge and HYP = elements of knowledge permitting the creation of hypotheses).

10.4.4.2.2. Memory indexing (corpus 2)

At each step, coding in the pivot language breaks down elements of the preoccupations of the expert: "find a way to increase the mass of therapeutic cells following both hypotheses":

be_tech=bio; *find a way…*

be_tech: technological entity, in the domain of knowledge, biology.

This would be translated as: "there is a technology in the domain of biology".

ag>be_fr_+; *to increase…*

Scheme of action involving a "make there be".

Translation: augment, increase, etc.

be_mes=phy/masse; *the mass…*

be_mes: a measurement in the domain of knowledge, physics.

Translation: the mass…

be_bio=gene/therap; *…of therapeutic cells,*

be_bio: biological entity in the domain of knowledge, genetics with connotations of applications, therapy (/therap).

Translation: gene therapy.

be_bio=cell/therap; *…of therapeutic cells* (Hyp1).

The same scheme as before, but in the domain of knowledge of cell biology.

Translation: … cell therapy.

be_loc=physio/org_foie; *in the liver (HYP2)*,

be_loc: a place in the domain of knowledge of physiology, and more precisely, the liver.

The "memory" combination in this case is expressed as follows:

(ac	be_tech=bio	ag>be_fr_+	be_mes=phy/masse
be_bio=gene/therapbe_bio=cell/therapbe_loc=physio/org_foie) K1)			

Each obtained document verifying K1 will now possess, in an "index block", a THM field of type THM/repop/foie/therap.

The set of codings declared in the watch profile constitutes an organized group known as the "memory thesaurus".

Once corpus 1 has been filtered by memory indexing, we obtain a new corpus of 478 notices (corpus 2). These 478 notices are said to be "relevant" in relation to the knowledge declared in the watch profile.

10.4.4.2.3. Statistical processing

Statistical analysis is then carried out on corpus 2. A series of processes may be envisaged, and may lead to the creation of a series of networks:

– Memory themes with memory themes, THM–THM: this intrafield combination allows us to discover networks of knowledge and research themes declared in the watch profile (Graph of Network).

– Cross-referencing of memory themes with authors (THM–AU) allows us to visualize the activity of each author, this activity being expressed in our THM field (Graph 2). AU–AU cross-referencing let us visualize different groups of authors.

We should remember that THMs are automatically generated and therefore develop over time, unlike MH terms.

The analytical situation consists of seeking references concerning the most cited author in relation to the theme of the watch profile (Figure 10.3):

thm/pvmedreg/asc/l/therap

(context of adult stem cells – asc – with the aim of therapy – therap – hepatic – liver –).

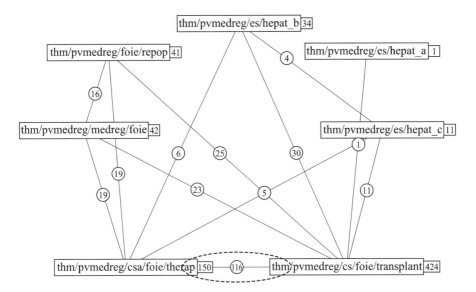

Figure 10.3. *Thematic networks: THM–THM*

We notice that Richard Poulsom is an author who appears four times in relation to the chosen theme (Figure 10.4). We can also see that this author appears five times in the whole set of articles.

We can then select the principal author, R. Poulsom, in connection with other authors (Figure 10.5) to identify cases of collaboration with other research groups.

We notice that three of the five appearances of this author are in association with the authors Alison and Wright, which is logical as these authors are members of the Poulsom's institute in England. By cross-referencing affiliations with authors, we see that Poulsom has only published with members of his own team.

In the list of selected articles, using memory indexing, we are able to see that of the five selected references concerning Richard Poulsom, two did not appear when using the classic keyword indexing process.

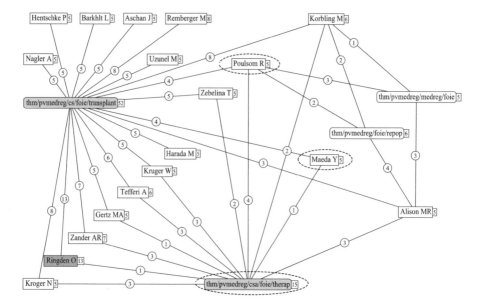

Figure 10.4. *THM–AU network*

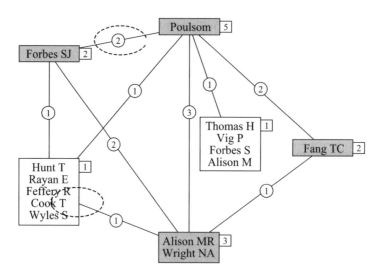

Figure 10.5. *Authors–authors' network*

In the following reference example, we show that a particular notice was discovered through the automatic generation of the THM field, which takes the "liver regeneration" context into account. As this information is not part of the MH descriptors in Pubmed, this notice would not have been found using the traditional methods. What follows is an extract from notice no. 12115866. Only the fields of interest for our study are included.

PMID – 12115866
DP – 2002 July
TI – Hepatic stem cells.
AB – The liver in an adult healthy body maintains a balance between cell gain and cell loss. Though normally proliferatively quiescent, hepatocyte loss such as that caused by partial hepatectomy, uncomplicated by virus infection or inflammation, invokes a rapid regenerative response to restore liver mass. This restoration of moderate cell loss and "wear-and-tear" renewal is largely achieved by hepatocyte self-replication. Furthermore, hepatocyte transplants in animals have shown that certain proportion of hepatocytes can undergo significant clonal expansion, suggesting that hepatocytes themselves are the functional stem cells of the liver. More severe liver injury can activate a potential stem cell compartment located within the intrahepatic biliary tree, giving rise to cords of bipotential so-called oval cells within the lobules that can differentiate into hepatocytes and biliary epithelial cells. A third population of stem cells with hepatic potential resides in the bone marrow; these hematopoietic stem cells can contribute to the albeit low renewal rate of hepatocytes, make a more significant contribution to regeneration, and even completely restore normal function in a Murine.
FAU – Forbes, Stuart
FAU – Vig, Pamela
FAU – Poulsom, Richard
FAU – Thomas, Howard
FAU – Alison, Malcolm
MH – Animals
MH – Cell Lineage
MH – Hematopoietic Stem Cell Transplantation/methods
MH – Hepatocytes/cytology/transplantation
MH – Humans
MH – Liver/*cytology
MH – Mice
MH – Mice, Transgenic
MH – Models, Animal
MH – Stem Cells/*cytology
SO – J Pathol 2002 July; 197(4): 510–8.
THM –
thm/pvmedreg/pvmedreg/repop/foie;thm/pvmedreg/cs/foie/transplant

This example shows that the theoretical and conceptual dimension of memory indexing refines the treatment of the problem presented by the expert by the use of his/her own knowledge and experience. It allows, moreover, greater efficiency in documentary research.

The final phase consists of the real-time creation of an elaborated database corresponding to a new type of indexing in terms of "knowledge".

10.4.4.3. Example 2

Our aim is to carry out watching in the domain of agricultural biotechnologies in China, in the particular case of hybrid wheat (in the context of a industrial conventions for research training (*Convention industrielle de formation par la recherché*) contract with the Limagrain Group).

The Chinese language is of particular interest to us in our approach to memory indexing of knowledge as it operates more directly based on cognitive representations (ISFs) than in the case of Indo-European languages, and in this it has similarities with the MEVA pivot language. A Chinese character corresponds to a syllable that already possesses a meaning, to a word or to part of a word. We might say that a Chinese character is a scheme of knowledge, which is more semiotically intense than a word. A word has a definition. A Chinese character is a construction based on cognitive operations that are linked, and in this way it is closer to ISFs than words are.

In this new example, the watch profile is built around four broad contextual themes (Th) (Table 10.1) and the use and interlinking of these themes will provide us with knowledge (Kn) in five broad domains.

Th 1	Th 2	Th 3	Th 4
Wheat	Scientific context	Chinese territory	Event
Increasing food needs Species threatened Market actors: businesses, professional associations, soft power, etc.	Hybridization phenomenon, major species *Fundamental research:* Chinese and international laboratories, researchers *Experimental research:* Tests, feedback, patents, COV	Provinces, decision centers, political power	Public and commercial actions, meetings, travel, mediatization

Table 10.1. *Contextual themes*

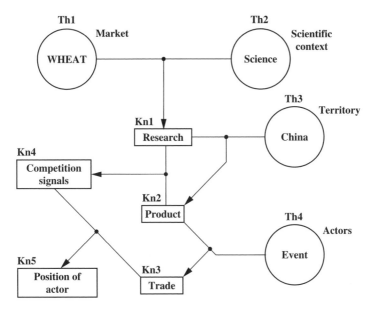

Figure 10.6. *Contextual themes and domains of knowledge*

The starting themes are broad outlines and work is carried out using a more detailed breakdown into subthemes. The only limit to this is the expert's need in terms of precision. Mixing between themes will allow us to access a second level of knowledge and touch on the dynamics of the system. This allows us to "prune" our lines of investigation and define a certain number of contexts.

10.4.4.3.1. Translation into the pivot language

The watch profile must be coded in the pivot language. A conceptual theme can be broken down into one or more subthemes that describe a precise concept. For example, the idea of wheat will be expressed by the concept of "a monocotyledon plant", which is the cereal "wheat". This can be translated as:

Pla/monocotyl/cer/fro/ble.

Behind each concept, we find ESFs that may, from a cognitive point of view, point to the idea of wheat for the expert. This means that, eventually, we will be able to provide the decision maker with documents concerning male sterility in cereals without the document needing to mention hybridization or wheat. It is in this way that a document will be considered "relevant" in relation to the watch profile of the expert, even if the classic research keywords do not appear in the document.

10.4.4.3.2. Presentation of an extract from the translation of the pivot language

```
;--------------------------------------------
; céréales (froment --> ble --> hybrides)
;--------------------------------------------

(lex cereal pla/monocotyl/cer)
(syn cereal cereales (谷 物) (良 种))
(lex caryopse pla/monocotyl/cer/car)
(syn caryopse caryopsis (颖 果))
(lex froment pla/monocotyl/cer/fro)
(syn (小 麦 属) (小 麦))
(lex wheat pla/monocotyl/cer/fro/ble)
(lex (epi de ble) pla/monocotyl/cer/fro/ble)
(lex (wheat head) pla/monocotyl/cer/fro/ble)
(lex  穗 pla/monocotyl/cer/fro/ble)
(lex (果 穗)  pla/monocotyl/cer/fro/ble)
(lex (穗 状 物) pla/monocotyl/cer/fro/ble)
(lex (winter wheat) pla/monocotyl/cer/fro/ble)
(lex  (冬 小 麦) pla/monocotyl/cer/fro/ble)
(lex (spring wheat) pla/monocotyl/cer/fro/ble)
(lex  (春 小 麦) pla/monocotyl/cer/fro/ble)
(lex (food wheat) pla/monocotyl/cer/fro/ble)
(lex  (粮 食 小 麦) pla/monocotyl/cer/fro/ble)
(clex-1 4 (white wheat) pla/monocotyl/cer/fro/ble)
(lex  (白 小 麦) pla/monocotyl/cer/fro/ble)
(lex (ble vitreux) pla/monocotyl/cer/fro/ble)
(lex (透 明 小 麦) pla/monocotyl/cer/fro/ble)
(clex 4 (hard wheat) pla/monocotyl/cer/fro/ble)
(lex (ble dur) pla/monocotyl/cer/fro/ble)
(lex (硬 粒 小 麦) pla/monocotyl/cer/fro/ble)
(clex 4 (soft wheat) pla/monocotyl/cer/fro/ble)
(lex (ble tendre) pla/monocotyl/cer/fro/ble)
(lex (软 质 小 麦)  pla/monocotyl/cer/fro/ble)
(lex (durete du ble) pla/monocotyl/cer/fro/ble)
```

Figure 10.7. *Presentation of the pivot language*

The specificity of Chinese is found at the moment of adoption of units declared in the watch profile by ESFs. Indo-European languages indicate a space of separation between semiotic elements. In Chinese, there is no gap between characters, and words are not distinguished using a graphical separator.

我的朋友是中国人。Without the knowledge of Chinese, it is impossible to know that this phrase, meaning "my friend is Chinese", is broken down into "words" as follows:

我的	朋友	是	中国人
My	friend	be	Chinese.

As characters are not separated in written Chinese, it is the reader who interprets and breaks down the different objects in a sentence to reconstitute the overall meaning.

This linguistic specificity is, in fact, beneficial in our approach. A Chinese character has meaning in and of itself and takes on this meaning outside of a constructed phrase. It is, effectively, a building block in combination as it is found at the level of ideas, contexts, associations, and semantics. For this reason, the pivot language is more accessible from Chinese writing. In the case of Chinese, the translation of the watch profile into the pivot language is almost direct; the Chinese language itself, by its means of expression, includes both semantic and conceptual levels.

10.4.4.3.3. Results

We will work using a large corpus preselected by a certain number of research projects. Our aim is to precisely define the business environment in the watch profile and to target the documents that respond to our watch objectives. The watch profile is created with the expert in the domain and a strong knowledge of the theme of study is needed for translation into the pivot language. The construction of a watch profile and its translation into the pivot language are operations that must be carried out rigorously and with attention to detail to obtain optimal results.

What follows is easier as the expert uses an interface in "combinatory" mode, which expresses the main themes of research. The experts must simply select new combinations to obtain the results window corresponding to their research aims.

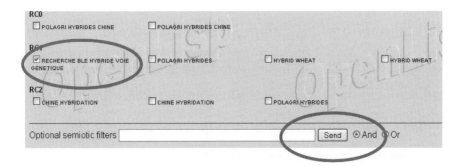

Figure 10.8. *Ergonomic visualization of research themes: user interface*

In this example, we selected a corpus of scientific articles extracted from an exclusively Chinese database, China national knowledge infrastructure (CNKI). For initial processing, the context in which we find this example, we chose to work on a restricted corpus to avoid "overloading" the analysis, as our aim was to demonstrate the feasibility of use of the MEVA tool to process a Chinese-language corpus. Corpus 1 contained 302 responses with references to male sterility in hybrid wheat for the period 2000–2008. From this corpus, we wish to extract articles dealing with techniques for cytoplasmic male sterility, one of the four possible techniques for male sterility.

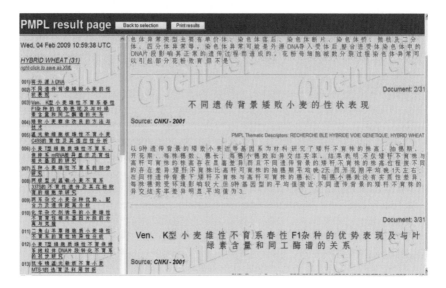

Figure 10.9. *Presentation of articles selected by the program*

The MEVA tool proposes 31 articles (Figure 10.9) corresponding to this technique out of the 302 articles offered in corpus 1. Without needing to translate all of the selected articles, the first four articles already show us that the aim of the watch process has been achieved.

Translation of the titles of articles suggested by MEVA:

– Observation of meiosis of mother pollen cells during the introduction of the exogenous DNA in common male-sterile wheat.

– Genetic differences in relation to trait performances in male sterility of dwarf wheat.

– Relationship between plant performance and chlorophyll density and isozymes in an F1 hybrid from a male-sterile strain of K-type spring wheat.

– Demonstration of differences between fertility genes in the preservation of mRNA molecules in a strain of wheat with cytoplasmic male sterility.

As the corpora used are relatively small, it is easy to go through corpus 2 "manually" to check the exhaustivity of the proposed selection. However, having proved the feasibility of our method for application in a Chinese-language context, we may now apply our approach to larger and multilingual corpora by fusing different sources, such as CNKI, Medline, and so on.

10.5. Elaborated databases

The processing approach and successive additions of fields allow us to obtain a new type of value-added database, through context-based indexing and graphical representations. These elaborated databases are particularly useful in "mapping" knowledge.

These elaborated databases have the following characteristics:

– personalized, as they refer to a watch problem encountered by an expert;

– flexible, as they take into account real-time developments in the concerns of the user;

– interactive, giving the possibility to produce thematic knowledge, THM, associated with other information entities in real time;

– may be integrated into graphical representations of results;

– usable by a collective network of experts.

Elaborated information needs, previously solved using mathematical (bibliometric), statistical, and linguistic processing of texts, may now be fulfilled using knowledge management capacities produced through the use of elaborated databases [PRA 00]. Among the possible developments in this domain [GUE 09], we find the use of new-generation bibliometric tools, such as data analysis [DOU 04], which will contribute via new forms of enrichment to the creation of elaborated databases.

10.6. Conclusion

We have tested a method of memory indexing based on the coding of cognitive representations of the knowledge of an expert during the creation of a watch profile in the context of the medical domain. Our second example, concerning the use of Chinese-language sources of information, provided additional validation of our methods.

The results obtained through the creation of a corpus, as part of the processing chain, show the efficiency and effectiveness of this method, which allows us to obtain only relevant documents in connection with a research problem encountered by an expert.

The MEVA method constitutes a significant contribution in terms of indexing, as it allows us to access the documents that were inaccessible using traditional methods (i.e. keywords – see the R. Poulsom example). Furthermore, when using multilingual sources, this method allows us to optimize a documentary research process by targeting relevant documents without needing to translate them. Only the documents suggested by MEVA, which target the decision maker's information need very precisely, may require translation. Given the cost of translation of a scientific article (around $300), this allows the users to order articles without the risk of error in relation to the strategic nature of the information contained within a document.

This experimentation, by bringing together different processing modules, allows us to obtain information with high added value (an elaborated database) from a wide spectrum of information sources. The relevance of this information is adapted to the specific concerns of an expert, with attention to concepts, associations, and the corresponding contexts, and it may be used to create personalized and interactive information seeking strategies.

This approach is likely to have numerous applications in the domain of competitive watching and in competitive intelligence as a whole. The PIETRA platform may also be put to good use in the establishment of thematic observatories taking account of scientific, economic, geostrategic data, and so on.

The consideration of the value of meaning in the interpretation of communications in information sciences, and particularly in indexing and analysis systems, presents us with new perspectives for the evolution of the information and documentation professions.

This new field of research, while still in its infancy, should produce numerous developments from a scientific point of view and in sectorial applications.

10.7. Bibliography

[DOU 03a] DOU H., ROSTAING H., LEVEILLE V., DOU J.M., MANINNA B., Systèmes d'analyse automatique de l'Information plates-formes de création de connaissance et travail à distance, Réseau TOPIK CNRS, 2003.

[DOU 03b] DOUSSET B., Intégration de méthodes interactives de découvertes de connaissances pour la veille stratégique, HDR, University of Toulouse III, 2003.

[DOU 04] DOUSSET B., GAY B., "Analyse par cartographie dynamique de l'effet de l'innovation sur la structure des réseaux d'alliances dans l'industrie des biotechnologies: application au domaine des anticorps thérapeutiques", 41ème Journée VSST, Toulouse, October 2004.

[GUE 09] GUENEC N., Méthodologies pour la création de connaissances relatives au marché chinois dans une démarche d'intelligence économique; application dans le domaine des biotechnologies agricoles, Thesis (work in progress), Paris-Est University, Marne la Vallée, 2009.

[ELD 00] ELDELMAN G., *Biologie de la Conscience*, Odile Jacob, Paris, 2000.

[LAP 94] LAPLACE C., *Théorie de la Traduction*, Didier Erudition, Paris, 1994.

[LEI 04] LEITZELMAN M., DOU H., KISTER J., Modélisation de connaissances et fouille d'informations par la cartographie dynamique: application de veille technologique avec Matheo Analyzer, 2004.

[MOR 04] MORIN E., Eduquer pour l'ère planétaire, in Economie et Humanisme, Lyon, available online at www.millenaire3.com/uploads/tx_ressm3/cahier31_01.pdf, 19 October 2004.

[MUC 05] MUCCHIELLI A., *Etudes des Communications – Approche par la Contextualisation*, Armand Colin, Paris, 2005.

[PAO 06] PAOLI-SCARBONCHI E., L'analyse mémorielle et statistique pour la création de Banques d'Information Elaborée (BIE). Application au travers d'une plate-forme de veille dans le domaine de la médecine régénératrice, Doctoral Thesis, Marne-La-Vallée University, November 2006.

[PRA 00] PRAX J.Y., *Le Guide du Knowledge Management*, Dunod, Paris, 2000.

[RIC 00] RICOEUR P., *La Mémoire, l'Histoire, l'Oubli*, Le Seuil, Paris, 2000.

[SAB 04] SABAH G., "Intelligence artificielle, linguistique et cognition, la linguistique cognitive", in FUCHS C. (ed.), *Cogniprisme*, Ophrys, Paris, 2004.

[SAV 09] SAVOY J., *The IR Group at Univ Neuchatel, Informer*, vol. 29, Winter 2009.

[SEL 75] SELESKOVITCH D., *Langage, langues et mémoire*, Lettres modernes, Paris, 1975.

[SER 07] SERRES M., Les nouvelles technologies: révolution culturelle et cognitive, Conference given for the 40th anniversary of the INRIA, 12/20/07, available online at http://interstices.info/jcms/c_33030/les-nouvelles-technologies-revolution-culturelle-et-cognitive.

PART 2

CI and Governance

Chapter 11

Integration of Competitive Intelligence and Watch in an Academic Scientific Research Laboratory

11.1. Introduction

Today, there is a perceptible malaise within research and teaching institutions, whether at university level or within research organizations themselves. This, in our opinion, is a symptom showing that simple academic aims (research, among other things) no longer allow us to anchor the work of research groups to reality. The recent financial crisis and its subsequent extension to the rest of the economy raises questions as to the way in which, in the short term (say 2 years), educational and research institutions should be involved in providing support to the production sector to maintain jobs. To put this aim into perspective, we look at research carried out some time ago by Porter [POR 90] and by the Dutch school [LEY 98]. Porter clearly showed that work in "clusters" generates increased innovation and improved performance through public–private sector partnerships. At the same time, the work of the Dutch school, focusing on the triple helix (analysis of public–private sector partnerships for increased rapidity in innovation), showed the solidity of Porter's vision and, at the same time, highlighted the fact that innovation, as the cornerstone of development, can only reach its full potential through the cooperation of State, research, and educational and industrial institutions.

Chapter written by Jacky KISTER and Henri DOU.

More recently, work carried out as part of European Union programs [INT 07] has shown that the innovation process consists of transforming competences and knowledge created in publicly funded research centers into money, that is, returns on investment. In our opinion, part of the current malaise can only be explained by the lack of real aims, the distancing of concrete applications from research and the lack of contact with the forces of production of a nation, or the lack of recognition given to finalized (applicable) research compared to the fundamental research sector. A number of countries have understood this new paradigm and established methods and tools to allow them to achieve such results. We may cite [DOU 07b] various reports that show this orientation: the Palmisano report (USA) [PAL 07], the Beffa report (France) [BEF 05], the Commonwealth report (Australia) [AUS 02], the Creativity report (Canada) [CAN 02], etc. and the work of Nagpaul and Roy [NAG 03, ROY 02] on the evaluation of Indian researchers.

11.2. Existing structures in universities and research organizations

Currently we see that, due to a lack of means, a majority of organizations create more or less varied indicators leading to the application of more or less valid labels. In this way, lists of journals (those accredited for publication) are created, authors are split into different groups depending on where they are placed in the author list in bibliographical references, and association with a given organization has effects on productivity. This rather controversial "bibliometric fever" [GIN 08] in some cases has become almost ridiculous [THO 09, CHA 09, FRI 09]. Moreover, through the fact that the career of a researcher is based on publication, these researchers are pushed to adapt their research strategies to the journals in which they should publish (according to rank and classifications developed in the United States). This should not be the case, but in France at least, the National Universities Council (*Conseil National des Universités*) and the National Center for Scientific Research (*Centre National de la Recherche Scientifique*, CNRS) push researchers in this way. The lists of "authorized" journals promote the development of research "adapted to the means of diffusion", and not the contrary. For example, multidisciplinary research would lead to publication in various journals, not necessarily focusing on the same theme. In this case, the index of dispersion would lead experts at the CNRS, for example, to say that a laboratory is too "dispersed" in its activity and does not focus its potential on a specific subject, where results would be published in even more specific journals with a constant and highly specialized readership, often involving peer review structures based on co-opted committees [CNR 09].

For the sake of good sense and to ensure that French research produces industrial applications that benefit the country, laboratories must establish study and validation systems for production at global level [DOU 93], allowing them to carry out high-quality research that also accords with the strategic needs of the country. By analyzing the problem – the basis of competitive intelligence (CI) and of the creation of knowledge through action – we see that several ingredients are needed to achieve these aims:

– a strategic vision: where do we want to go?

– reliable sources of information that can be analyzed and used to create bridges with industry;

– tools for increasing productivity in the collection and analysis of information;

– multidisciplinary groups of experts (public–private) who analyze relevant information in terms of strengths, weaknesses/opportunities, and threats (SWOT; see www.quickmba.com/strategy/swot/); and

– continuity in this course of action.

At the same time, we need to analyze the expertise of each individual, team, or laboratory to match up aims and means. The development of clusters and organizations such as regional centers for innovation and united economic development in France (*poles régionaux d' innovation et de développement économique solidaire*, PRIDES) is an example of this way of working, which leads to a *contract of aims associated with a contract of means over several years*. There is still a need for general recognition that, over time, these ingredients lead to increases in scientific potential, not only in the original target domain but also, by cross-fertilization, in other domains of collaboration, allowing other goals to be attained. The result of these processes is not a simple response to a specific industrial or societal question, but scientific progress, a source of new potential.

This model should allow us to optimize practical knowledge and competences created within laboratories, both to put them to use in the production sector and to direct their development by *setting out new problems to solve at fundamental level*. Laboratories, industrial players, and public powers would benefit from engagement in this "virtuous spiral" to create the dynamics necessary for research in France and elsewhere. As an example, we quote from a presentation made by Elias Zerhouni, director of the US National Institutes of Health [ZER 06]: "The success of American scientific research depends on the existing implicit partnership between academic research, the government and industry. The research institutions have the responsibility to develop the scientific capital. The Government finances the best teams by a transparent system of selection. Industry holds the critical role to develop robust products intended for the public. This strategy is the key of American competitiveness and must be maintained".

We will now examine the information sources on which the development of our propositions will be based. When we look at citations in published work from a research context (in this case, research in scientific disciplines), we see that patents are almost never cited. In the same way, patents have little or no place in laboratory evaluation criteria. However, the field of industrial property is vital for business development, moreover, that which is published within a patent is rarely published elsewhere. Patents are, therefore, key in attracting industrial interest in laboratories, not necessarily because the laboratory or the overarching organization holds patents, but because the laboratory will use and understand this information and apply it to create links between this work and their own research. This would lead to the creation of an attractive "space" promoting public–private sector dialog and bridging with competitiveness clusters.

11.3. Research structures, research actors and evaluation in the context of CI integration

Evaluation is currently at the heart of debates on research. One question raised involves which bibliometric indicators to use for which evaluation. This reflection was the subject of a forum retranscribed in the Life Science Research (*Vie de la Recherche Scientifique*) [VRS 07]. Using these indicators, not all sectors of science are equal; the blind application of indicators without knowledge of the domain of the fields of research, and even of subsectors within the same scientific domain, creates problems. This is the case with information and communication science and technologies (*sciences et technologies de l'information et de la communication*, STIC) and with human and social sciences, although, in France, the agency for the evaluation of research and higher education (*Agence d'évaluation de la recherche et de l'enseignement supérieur*, AERES) modulates its general principles for major research sectors (AERES evaluation grid, July 22, 2008). A report by the *Académie des sciences* (*Institut de France*) presented to the French minister for research and higher education on July 8, 2009 includes a very good critical overview of evaluation tools and criteria used in research and teaching of professional ethics and of the choice of evaluators and the relative positions of national and local evaluation [ACA 09]. This report highlights the frequency and format of these evaluations and their use. From our perspective, we consider that this report should be used as an element for internal reflection within institutions, or as a guide to avoid "bias and warping", intentional or unintentional errors driven by conflicts of personal interests on the part of direct or indirect experts. This is all the more relevant as the increasing autonomy of universities (in France) and the opening of competition between individuals, teams, research structures, universities and so on may lead to conflict situations and to individual or collective conflicts of interests. As an example, we note the possibility of "excellence bonuses": who will define the criteria for this, how, and with what transparency and durability of criteria? It is important to avoid situations where criteria are variable indicators that depend on a person or on a predetermined aim.

In domains with the greatest potential for business links, that is, those offering the greatest potential for value creation or returns on investment, the separation of individual evaluation and the evaluation of research organizations is a fundamental error. It is through the juxtaposition of fundamental researchers or teams and groups with a more "finalized" or technological focus that strong research dynamics emerge. We must, therefore, adapt this evaluation so that each may "find their place", without reference to "good" or "bad" research, and without certain unhelpful forms of reflection as seen on occasion within scientific departments of the CNRS, such as "that is not what you are paid to do", or "that is "feeder" research". If this is the case, we must avoid considering a research partnership exclusively as a source of finance or as a collective milk cow. If recurring donations to research units were sufficient, service provisions or "feeder" research would exist only for their specific individual interest and could easily be integrated in the framework of technical platforms. In the same way, considering research in industrial partnerships as "subresearch" shows a lack of consideration toward the economic world. *A priori*, ours is not a period where a company will participate in financing laboratory research "for fun". Obtaining industrial conventions for research training (*Convention industrielle de formation par la recherché*, CIFRE) contract is not an easy task and the same applies to industrial bursaries, the CNRS bursaries for doctors of engineering (*bourse de docteur ingenieur*) or multiannual contracts. Organizations need to maintain unity in their analysis of laboratory and businesses. This is particularly the case for the chemistry section of the CNRS, one of the first to depend on external funding. We cannot belittle this finalized research or research on contracts of aims and produce annual statistics on the number of contracts and patents in organizations. However, we must be careful, as it is rarely the institutions or organizations that are subject to review in such positions, but the representatives of these institutions who maintain outdated methods of working or are directly involved in collective or individual conflicts of interests.

Gingras [GIN 08], professor at the University of Quebec, Montreal, and director of the Observatory of Sciences and Technologies of the Interuniversity Center for Science and Technology Research, talks of "evaluative anarchy" [VRS 08]. For him, statistical indicators, through "their existence and their persistence", seem to "depend on a social law which states that "any number beats no number"". Quantitative indicators can, of course, be useful but only on the condition that they are replaced in the right context and not applied on a case-by-case basis depending on partisan interests. This quantitative aspect, moreover, is the basis of observatory of science and technology (*Observatoire des sciences et des techniques*) reports and is used for the comparison of data at national and international levels.

The recent multiplication of 'spontaneous' use of evaluation and creation of so-called 'quality' indicators have combined to create a certain chaos in the academic world which is not really able to evaluate these measurements. In spite of the multi-dimensional character of research, these indices use a single number to classify and evaluate the quantity of research produced by individuals and organizations. Those who claim to make decisions in light of these so-called 'objective' or 'international' indicators should leave the evaluation of research to scientists, who spend enough time doing this to be able to distinguish pseudo-metrics from robust indicators. This would probably diminish the risk of losses of control and the pernicious effects generated by measurements and classifications of research which are not worth the paper they are written on.

These same "non-experts" in the matter of indicators should at least apply the ethical principle that an indicator has no value except when it is placed in a broad context, applied to a large number of examples or to a community and validated by this community; consequently, the expert–evaluator must themselves take a position in this community, with the same tools (this remark appears in the report issued by the *Académie des Sciences* in July 2009 under the subject "choice of evaluators").

Reflections of this kind are not a recent development, as shown in an article by Thuillier [THU 83]. The conclusion of this article, on the state of evaluation in 1983, is still relevant: "is it not time to escape from a dilemma which, taken at the letter and interpreted in a completely individualistic spirit, may well lead to absurdity?" However, the financial environment of research has completely changed since 1983 and the biases and perversions seen in evaluation systems are even more flagrant.

It is clear that this evaluation parameter for individuals and structures is an aspect that determines the success of laboratory participation in clusters, PRIDES, the French national research agency (*Agence nationale de la recherche*, ANR) and FEDER. However, questions should be asked: at what moment should indicators, however reliable and robust, be used, and how can we take account of confidentiality clauses and economic interests?

The emergence of clusters has profoundly modified the relationships between public research institutions and businesses, by a change in scale in the financial volumes involved and by administrative setups mixing laboratories, businesses, regional government, the OSEO and the Interministerial Fund (*Fond unique interministériel*), among other things. Scientific and technico-economic expertise are now mixed and "value creation" is evaluated, estimated, and programmed, as with CIFRE contracts or the OSEO – National agency of research valorization (*Agence nationale de valoris ationde la recherche*, ANVAR). The system has shifted from a two-dimensional relationship between a laboratory or an expert and a business to a multidimensional setup based on the principle of sharing means and expertise to achieve a contract of aims and produce successful results. This setup may involve regional, national, or international, and therefore political, interests and gives small businesses or start-ups the chance to participate through the formation groups. The system has also become extremely competitive for laboratories, and the value of laboratories used in these programs is not simply analyzed using institutional indicators. Value may be based on the industrial experience, the reliability of engagements, the respect of timings, the notion of mutual respect, and a common goal of creation of value and of jobs. The role of the researcher in these programs is also greatly modified; the researcher becomes a direct actor in "value creation" and participates directly in the CI cycle.

11.4. Clusters and their power of attraction

Clusters are a major focus for development in France. They constitute a meeting place between public, research and industrial institutions, and should allow the creation of knowledge for action and thus considerably shorten the passage from research to production. This issue, which consists of creating a new dynamic, constitutes a beneficial boost for laboratories. However, inclusion in a cluster also involves acceptance by a different community, and candidates must submit themselves to judgment, effectively entering into the "real" world of competition where results are judged in relation to the solution of actual problems and not by publications destined for the international scientific community and for judgment of individual careers. This "publish or die" aspect leads certain individuals to work only for the impact factor of a journal, the level of citations or the "h" factor, in reference to an international system (ISI Web). This is part of the "biases and perversions of the evaluation system of the *Académie des Sciences* report". If scientific production must be placed at the disposal of the international community (already the subject of major debate), why not publish everything online with open access? This is the principle behind knowledge platforms, but access to this information is restricted to referenced actors who, by contributing to the platform themselves, generate progress for the whole community.

This community is often multidisciplinary in nature, being itself the sum of scattered expertise brought together in a contract of aims. This demands flexibility and a capacity to understand different languages and ways of working for pooling competences and the attainment of group objectives. In this, we also leave behind individual careerist aims to embrace collective working.

One role of clusters is to promote the development of small and medium businesses, to support them and to allow the development of new products through synergies. These businesses, involved in the creation of large numbers of jobs, often have good ideas (although sharing these ideas is difficult due to fears generated by competition), but also major gaps and difficulties in integrating the results of fundamental research into their development. This demands a two-pronged effort: research results must go through "mediation", in a manner of speaking, to be better understood and used by the business. In this domain, there is a form of "natural" mediation that consists of the creation of a patent. A patent clearly shows the transformation of research into ideas for new applications and/or products. Reading the patent generates awareness of competitors, their links, technologies, inventors, etc. The time constants of current patents, of those with decreasing use and reaching the end of their useful life and of those in the public domain, are also good indicators. In the same way, strategies developed by different companies or groups of companies are instructive, whether in terms of registration of patents, applications, or the technologies used. Thus, patents can be used to build a solid bridge between fundamental research, the competences of researchers, and the domain or domains of application.

We also note that, for a given territory or through collaboration, clusters promote network-based working. It is evident that synergies develop in this way and their existence requires no further proof. Thus, existing networks, whether in terms of intellectual property or in the framework of interlaboratory scientific collaborations, may now be detected relatively easily using bibliometric techniques. We can identify key subjects and collaborations from bibliographical descriptions found in existing publications or commercial or open-access databases,. There are, therefore, two complementary approaches in the domain of strategic information:

– an approach focused on seeking relevant information using existing resources: databases, the Internet, information from interpersonal networks, etc.

– an approach which, from a certain type of information and using appropriate tools, leads to the emergence of new information with great potential as a basis for reflection and which is suited to ulterior analysis of this information by experts (this is generally the part of the intelligence cycle that deals with the impact of information on the strategic orientations of the business). Extracting "decision information from a mass of scattered information" works using the same logic as that used in chemometrics by specialists in analytical sciences processing masses of information generated by complex equipment, obtained through the use of samples that are often very large. Data processing tools are used for visualization, to identify similarities and differences, and to show links between structural properties and rheological or industrial properties, while going beyond an interpretation based on characterization and identification alone. This parallel continues using the same logic of communication and presentation of results, which remains a task for experts in the domain.

These two approaches currently serve as a guide to a certain number of actors in the research domain in setting up work units to promote the development of public–private partnerships and which will allow the valorization of knowledge, expertise, and competences created in these laboratories. This is in addition to the valorization of products that already exist within these laboratories, which is important but not sufficient. In the following paragraph, we will look at three examples:

– the strategic unit established in the UMR 6239 workgroup, http://gicc. univ-tours.fr (genetics, immunology, chemistry, and cancer): StratéGICC;

– the laboratory of complex chemical systems (*laboratoire des systèmes chimiques complexes*, LSCC) www.umr6171.net, www.ism2.univ-cezanne.fr (analysis, aging, quality, and traceability of natural products and industrial derivatives) with the development of the strategic intelligence survey (SIS or information and innovation);

– the example of Thailand, with systematic patent analysis using automatic patent analysis (APA) in strategic domains.

11.5. Strategic analysis units, a support for the development of laboratories and of CI

As we have just stated, a critical analysis setting out information available at time "t" allows us to discover new orientations, possible partnerships, pitfalls to avoid, and orientations that should not be validated[1]. The three following examples, which show the reality and the development of this movement, highlight (looking at the development of the laboratories concerned) the fundamental contributions of this new approach. This orientation should not be confused with documentation. Through the use of different tools, experts and information sources, it provides a wider vision of the use of competences of the laboratory. In some ways, it acts as a powerful stimulus for changing mentalities and modifying behaviors. The new orientation leads to the shared management of knowledge within a team, to the notion of collaborative laboratories, and to the cross-fertilization, where innovation in one domain may be detected in or come from a different domain, whether or not the two domains are connected. It also leads to the establishment of scientific or technological observatories, shared over secure platforms or otherwise, and to the detection of potential partners and competitors. In all of these results, the temporal aspect is essential. The notion of evolution of reprocessed information places the notion of information for action at the heart of decision, with the result that "what is true at time t is not necessarily true at time $t+1$". This remark is particularly important in institutions where the time gap between the moment of decision and possible action, or simply the time needed for contractual implementation of the action, may block the innovative aspect entirely. This leads to reflection on modes

---

1 We might quote Sun Tzu in *The Art of War*: "if the enlightened Prince and the well-advised General are victorious each time they act, and if their feats are greater than the norm, this is due to prior information".

of management of laboratories involved in public–private sector partnerships, where the necessity for rapid decision is often barely compatible with systems of annual management where resources cannot be carried over, as in the case of recurring financial contributions, for example.

11.5.1. *GICC UMR*

This UMR is made up of eight teams under the direction of M. Yves Bigot. Team 8, made up of four people, is led by a doctoral student, M. Fabien Palazzi.

Figure 11.1. *GICC team no. 8*

Presentation: A strategic development cell was established in the GICC laboratory on 1st March 2008. This led to the creation of the StratéGICC team on 1st January 2009. Our team has a mission to create a valorization strategy for the laboratory in order to create favorable conditions for the establishment of a mixed public-private sector structure and to develop a research able to be transfered and used by industry a special unit was created to analyzed the patent production in the research field of the laboratory, this is illustrated in Figure 11.1.

The aims of the GICC UMR are as follows (for more information, see http://gicc.univ-tours.fr/laboratoire/presentation/equipe8.php?lang=fr&connect=0.):

– carry out strategic watch:

- implement technological watch on the four scientific themes of the laboratory: genetics, immunotherapy, chemistry, and cancer (including patents for different technologies concerned);

- identify public and private actors involved in these technologies;

- implement economic watch: identify local, national, and European sources of public finance;

– communicate: integrate and associate all actors concerned with the creation and establishment of the valorization strategy:

- communicate internally with scientists in the laboratory;

- communicate with the valorization services of the CNRS and the University of Tours;

- communicate externally: presentation of the laboratory at scientific and economic development events at local, national, and international level;

– seek partners:

- develop, select, and solidify existing contacts;

- locate and initiate contact with industrial and financial partners;

- provide operational monitoring of partnerships.

With the person in charge of coordinating work, we looked at the different problems posed by the development of public–private relationships in the laboratory. All aspects discussed in this chapter are concerned by this proactive approach and based on common sense. This strategic team will also benefit from our knowledge in the domain (increased productivity, bibliometric analysis, and APA) through the establishment of a synergy with the strategic analysis workshop of the ESCEM group (*Atelier d'intelligence stratégique du groupe ESCEM*, ATELIS) [DOU 08b] (For more information, see www.atelis.org.). ATELIS is located in Tours, France, and provides modular teaching on CI and the use of methods and tools for automatic information analysis, both to students and to businesses. ATELIS also delivers a European certificate of value management, but at present this is not a main priority.

11.5.2. *The LSCC: strategic intelligence survey unit*

We will now look at the way in which this structure was set up within the laboratory. The SIS unit was established at the beginning of 2009 as a result of 20 years of teaching and research experience [DOU 89, KIS 92, KIS 93, KIS 95, KIS 96] and 10 years of experience in the UMR CNRS 6171 complex chemical systems (*systèmes chimiques complexes*) directed by Jacky Kister (1998–2007) [BAR 06, DOU 08a, ROS 04], followed by the UMR CNRS 6263 bringing together the chemistry department of Paul Cézanne University, Marseille, team AD2EM-LSCC. The difference between this and the previous structure resides in the fact that the laboratory, already engaged in research in partnership with industrial or military institutions for over 25 years and with various national and international clusters, finances the SIS unit through contracts and a specific donation to the global secure communicating solutions (*solutions communicantes sécurisées*, SCS) center for the fuel quality sensor (FQS) project. This SIS unit is open to industrialists who participate in contracts. The role of the laboratory is to participate in "the design of new materials, products or processes for sustainable development". A particular feature of this laboratory, which is attached to the CNRS chemistry department (section 13 of the National Committee for Analytical Chemistry) and to the sustainable development department, is that it treats strategic information in the same way as information or measurements generated by analytical equipment in the domain of traceability, quality, and aging of natural or industrially transformed materials. The laboratory is organized into centers of industrial applications behind multidisciplinary competences in analytical chemistry, thermodynamics, experimental research methodology, chemometrics, and all aspects of formulation linked to aging phenomena (thermic, photochemical, bacterial, and ultimate stress factors). This leads to environmental and sustainable development concerns linked to quality control and traceability.

The SIS unit operates using internal expertise specific to major industrial and societal domains (petroleum products and industrial derivatives, the food and phytosanitary industries, cosmetology, galenics, and health products). The organization of this laboratory around watch and CI has been the subject of a number of international presentations in which it serves as a point of reference [KIS 07]. The SIS and its interface between strategic watch, chemistry, and galenic pharmacology won a prize in the national competition run by the French ministry of higher education and research with the OSEO and the ANR, in the *Emergence* (emerging) category for the year 2009. The award was collected by P. Prinderre on June 25, 2009 from Valérie Pécresse[2]. The award winning work corresponds to the CIFRE (industrial partnership for research) thesis of Christophe Sauzet, defended in March 2009, under the direction of J. Kisterand and P. Prinderre. This thesis, on the border between two disciplines (pharmacology and chemistry), led to the creation of a business youth innovative enterprise (Jeune Entreprise Innovante, JEI) within the inter-university Impulse "incubator", with assistance from Provence initiation equipment and the SIS [SAU 09]. However, most of the formalization of the SIS unit applies to the subject of "petroleum products and industrial derivatives".

The STIC cell, precursor of the SIS and initially placed under the responsibility of Mylène Leitzelman [LEI 04a, LEI 04c], a researcher at the ADEME in workgroup UMR 6171, worked on all aspects of strategic information, knowledge management (the CAGOLAB project), the establishment of cross-fertilization between centers of application, and the creation of scientific observatories or interactive platforms with the CEA and the ADEME (network of experts on fuel cells, http://veille.reseaupaco.org, network of sites of energy points in France,

---

2 French Minister for Higher Education and Research since 2002.

www.infoenergie.org) [LEI 04b]. This led to activity in non-presential or virtual scientific communities and to the development of a collaboration methodology, TCAO [LEI 07]. The whole project was self-financing. An active process of strategic information retrieval was also carried out, seeking innovative information through major participation in international congresses and exhibitions. The presentation given in the SIS unit is that produced at the time of its creation (for more information, see www.ciworldwide.org, June 2009). Figure 11.2 shows the logo of the SIS Unit which, for CNRS and University administrative considerations does not had the same name that the laboratory.

Figure 11.2. *Information, innovation, and CI platform*

The majority of small and medium businesses, industries, and clusters are currently operating in a hostile environment due to the financial crisis. In this difficult period, public research laboratories should use their competences and knowledge to assist companies in establishing processes for the creation of new products with the potential to conquer various parts of the market, principally through exports.

This situation led the LSCC to develop a platform, allowing small and medium companies, public research laboratories, and clusters to collect, process, and analyze strategic information in their domain.

This platform – a technical stage dedicated to strategic information – is available to all potential users of the LSCC.

11.5.2.1. Available facilities

Facilities provided include bibliographies on demand (subject to financial participation). The available tools may be used directly (and free of charge) by companies or after specific training given by experts in the domain (which must be paid for).

The platform also offers APA, Internet surveillance, analysis of structured information, automatic translation into various languages, Internet searches in different languages, international communications via Skype, and advanced Google products. This platform, which is now operational, is the result of collaboration between the LCSS (www.umr6171.net), CIWORLDWIDE (Prof. Henri Dou, www.ciworldwide.org), and two French companies, IMCS (www.imcsline.com) and Matheo Software (http://matheo-software.com).

11.5.2.2. Potential results and user references

Facilities of this kind are already in use by various companies and in various countries, including a wide range of European countries, Brazil, Indonesia, Thailand, etc. They have become part of the "traditional" tool set used for the development of CI through the collection and analysis of information. This platform is also part of various teaching programs developed in China (Shanghai), Malaysia (Kuala Lumpur), Indonesia (ITM Bandung), and France (IMPGT Marseille, Atelis ESCEM Tours Poitiers, and so on).

11.5.2.3. Industrial applications in France (extract)

Industrial applications of this in France include the FQS project, the SCS cluster (a cluster with international aims), QCARSPI (*in situ* measurement of fuel quality by near infrared (IR) spectrometry) in the context of the CAPENERGIES cluster, and the AIRCLAIR project (amelioration of environmental impact and reduction of consumption in heavy fuel motors using IR analysis) within the framework of the CAPENERGIES and MER-PACA clusters. The following bibliographical references provide a detailed description of the information analysis and the strategic information obtained [DOU 04, DOU 07a, DOU 08c, JOA 06 and LEI 04b].

11.5.2.4. Platform finance

This platform is financed by programs linked to clusters, such as FQS, linked to the SCS cluster, with the participation of the regional council of the Provence-Alpes-Côte d'Azur region and a CI program financed by the directors of the CNRS with the assistance of the Matheo Software company.

11.5.2.5. Example: Thailand

Systematic mapping of patent information is carried out using the Matheo Patent program in domains of interest for the development of Thai industry and for Thai clusters: www.toryod.com/publicationmapping.php.

From Figure 11.3, we see that different themes used in the development of clusters in Thailand are analyzed from the viewpoint of an industrial property perspective. For the cluster corresponding to tourism in the Phuket area, for example, the "Water Massage" aspect is taken into account. Starting from this analysis, we must simply go to the site and click to access the relevant text. We are thus able to see technical advances that may be used by local industries, patents still in operation in the domain along with those in the public domain, possible partnerships, etc. This method of approach takes all factors of the development of an aggressive cluster policy into account [KEN 03], a policy developed following the methodology set out by Porter and promoted by US AID [USA 09]. This shows that the concept of elaborated information, statistical treatment of information, and patent analysis is already integrated into clusters in developing countries. This example demands reflection, particularly in relation to the French situation. It is based on the use of the same tools as those used in the SIS platform, among other things in the domain of APA.

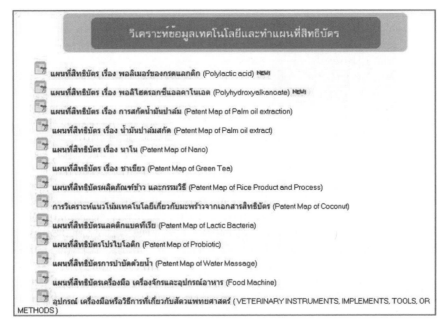

Figure 11.3. *Patent analysis using the Matheo Patent program (to access these works, for example "nano", see www.toryod.com/pdf/nano_mapping.pdf, June 2009)*

Thailand has an aggressive development policy in certain sectors and the country makes considerable use of that which it produces and protects to provide local industries (generally grouped into clusters, or candidates for future grouping) with information allowing them to direct their attention to economically profitable subjects. The process is simple. Based on the worldwide patent database accessible over the EPO server [EPO 09] (European Patent Office), systematic analysis is carried out on certain strategic subjects for the development of Thai industries. Figure 11.4 shows different domains for analysis [THA 09, TOR 09].

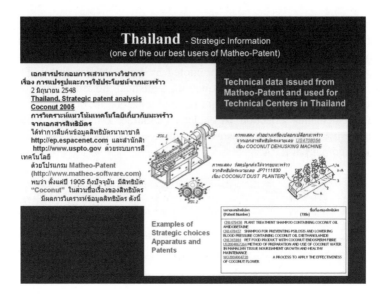

Figure 11.4. *Use of patent information resources in Thailand*

First, we carry out an analysis of the number of patents registered per year (to see whether or not the field is growing) and then we analyze different technologies using the international patent classification [WIP 09]. Then, based on matrices and/or networks, we select important elements for businesses involved in registering patents (whether registered in Thailand, extended to include Thailand, or registered only in other countries, etc.). Finally, we select patents, technologies, and aspects of interest for local industries. Figure 11.3 shows one aspect of the extracts produced in the domain of development of activities linked to coconuts as a basic commodity.

Organization at national level, valorization of information, and the use of clusters are highly sophisticated. By K.I.Asia platform [KIA 09], we can access different information, including a set of data concerning clusters.

The development of clusters in Thailand has been carried out with the same aims as the development of the cluster policy in France. In this way, the integration of research and development laboratories into clusters becomes a major issue. At the same time, governance, the strategic exploitation of information, and internal and external expertise allow us to follow the "route map" and to keep the initial objective in focus.

The steps of development of clusters are carried out following the classic model: geographic delimitation, contributors, route map, and evaluation (using the SWOT method, among others).

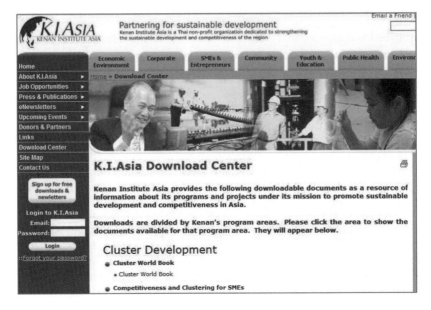

Figure 11.5. *K.I.Asia platform – "the download center"*

Six clusters are currently operational, out of the total 10 in development:

– multimedia and computer graphics,

– agricultural produce with high added value destined for western markets,

– tourism in Phuket,

– gemstones and jewelry,

– transport (cars and lorries), and

– silk.

11.6. Conclusion

We have seen how the development of research units for the processing and expert analysis of strategic information provides benefits for the development of research laboratories. We are now faced with a question: would units for the valorization and treatment of strategic information produce the same results at the level of a university, for example, or within a research organization? In our opinion, the answer to this question is clearly no. A CI unit, as we have described using a number of examples, remains linked to the strategic direction of the laboratory. The desire to deal globally with disparate subjects, often subjects not mastered by users who are not experts in the domain, will not produce scale economies but, instead, lead to dispersion and reduced efficiency. Currently, the success obtained by various units or high performing laboratories seems to be linked to the way in which information is integrated into the process of development of the research programs of these organizations. Although bibliography remains useful as a source of information for researchers, it can no longer be considered the be-all and end-all for strategic organizations and for decision making. The system must be organized in a different manner. Progress currently underway in information sciences, Internet communication, Web 1.0 and 2.0, in management and exchange platforms, and in tools for automatic transfer and analysis, allows us to organize CI units at the level of a research unit.

We thus find ourselves faced with an almost perfect break in alignment, between French national policy, where action is focused on introducing strategic watch and CI systems into small and medium businesses and industry, and the policy of research organizations and the national education establishment, that act in the opposite way, but with recognition accorded to those involved in these actions and to the essential practice of evaluation of the individuals and structures concerned [BIR 08].

11.7. Bibliography

[ACA 09] ACADEMIE DES SCIENCES, L'évaluation individuelle des chercheurs et des enseignants-chercheurs, 2009, available online at: www.academie-sciences.fr/actualites/textes/recherche_08_07_09.pdf.

[AUS 02] COMMONWEALTH OF AUSTRALIA, *Backing Australia's Ability: The Commonwealth Government's Commitment to Innovation*, June 2009, available online at: www.backingaus.innovation.gov.au/.

[BAR 06] BARTS N., ROSTAING H., KISTER J., "Système d'information d'aide au pilotage de la recherche", *VSST'2006, Séminaire Veille Stratégique Scientifique Technologique*, ENIC Télécom, Lille, France, 16–17 January 2006.

[BEF 05] BEFFA J.-L., *Pour une nouvelle politique industrielle de la France*, La Documentation Française, Paris, France, 2005.

[BIR 08] BIRRAUX C., ETIENNE J.C., Rapport sur l'évaluation de l'application de l'article 19 de la loi de programme pour la recherche France, Assemblée nationale, Sénat, Office parlementaire d'évaluation des choix scientifiques et technologiques, minutes of public session, 16 December 2008.

[CAN 02] GOVERNMENT OF CANADA, *Canadian Creativity and Innovation in the Next New Millennium*, June 2009, available online at: www.innovationstrategy.gc.ca/gol/innovation/site.nsf/fr/in05177.html.

[CHA 09] CHARLE C., "L'évaluation des enseignants-chercheurs", *Vingtième Siècle*, vol. 1, no. 102, April–June 2009.

[CNR 09] CNRS, Rapport du groupe de travail sur la caractérisation des unités de recherche, 2009, available online at: www.cnrs.fr/comitenational/doc/bilan/caracterisation.pdf.

[DOU 89] DOU H., HASSANALY P., QUONIAM L., KISTER J., "Clustering pluridisciplinary chemical papers to provide new tools for research management and trends. Application to coal and organic matter oxidation", *Journal of Chemical Information Sciences*, vol. 29, pp. 45–51, 1989.

[DOU 93] DOU H., HASSANALY P., ROUX M., KISTER J., "Stratégie de recherche et Veille Scientifique et Technique. Méthodologie et outils, application à la programmation de recherche", *Politique et Management public 1993, Actes du VI Colloque International Politique et management public*, University of Geneva, Switzerland, 25–26 March 1993.

[DOU 04] DOU H., "Benchmarking R&D and companies through patent analysis using free databases and special software: a tool to improve innovative thinking", *World Patent Information*, vol. 26, no. 4, pp. 297–309, December 2004, available online at: www.ciworldwide.org.

[DOU 07a] DOU H., MANULLANG S., DOU J.M. JR, *Competitive Intelligence and Technology Watch for Industry Development*, Departement Perindustrian, Indonesia, 2007. Part of this work is available as an Audiobook (in French) at www.ciworldwide.org.

[DOU 07b] DOU H., MANULLANG S., DOU J.M. JR, "Competitive intelligence, public private partnership, innovation, cluster policy and regional development", *Introductive Conference, Competitive Intelligence*, University Carlos III, Madrid, Spain, 2007.

[DOU 08a] DOU H., KISTER J., "Valorisation, synergies, innovation and development", *Proceedings of European Trans2tech Conference 06 03 2008 European Commission,* 6th framework Programme. Driving Innovation from science to Business, Paris, France, 2008.

[DOU 08b] DOU H., "Strengthening the private and public partnership in actionable knowledge. The case of ATELIS (Strategic Intelligence Workshop of the ESCEM Business School)", *Trans2Tech, Muenster, European Community Program*, Münster, Germany, 1–2 October 2008.

[DOU 08c] DOU H., Larrat P., "Strengthening the private and public partnership in actionable knowledge. The case of ATELIS (Strategic Intelligence Workshop of the ESCEM Business School)", *Trans2tech*, Muenster, 1–2 October 2008, Germany (European Community).

[EPO 09] European Patent Office http://ep.espacenet.com

[FRI 09] FRIDENSON P., "La multiplication des classements", *Le Mouvement Social*, vol. 2, no. 226, pp. 5–14, January–March 2009.

[GIN 08] GINGRAS Y., La Fièvre de l'évaluation de la Recherche. Du mauvais usage de faux indicateurs, Note de recherche, Centre de Recherche Universitaire sur la Science et la Technologie, Bibliothèques et Archives nationales du Québec, 2008, available online at: www.cirst.uqam.ca.

244   Competitive Intelligence and Decision Problems

[INT 07] INTERREG, Strategic Intelligence and Innovative Clusters – A Regional Policy Blueprint Highlighting the use of Strategic Intelligence in Cluster policy. Interreg III C (European Community), 2007.

[JOA 06] JOACHIM J., KISTER J., BERTACCHINI Y., DOU H., "Intelligence économique et systèmes d'information, Analyse à partir d'un sujet stratégique: HIV et formulation dynamique", *Information Sciences for Decision Making*, vol. 24, no. 336, 2006.

[KEN 03] KENAN INSTITUTE ASIA & J.E. AUSTIN ASSOCIATES, Thailand Competitiveness Initiative, Klongtoey, Bangkok, Special Project Section Competitiveness Public Information, version 22 July 2003

[KIA 09] K.I.ASIA, 2009, available online at: www.kiasia.org/EN/Myresume.asp?.

[KIS 92] KISTER J., RUAU O., HASSANALY P., DOU H., "Utilisation des analyses bibliométriques dans la détermination des stratégies de recherche", *Actes du colloque ADEST "La Scientométrie en action"*, M.R.T, Paris, France, 1–2 June 1992.

[KIS 93] KISTER J., RUAU O., HASSANALY P., DOU H.,"Utilisation des analyses bibliométriques dans la détermination des stratégies de recherche, Application au domaine des lourds pétroliers et du charbon", *Les cahiers de l'ADEST*, special edition, pp. 104–110, 1993.

[KIS 95] KISTER J., PIERI N., RUAU O., QUONIAM L., DOU H., "Stratégie de recherche et sciences de l'information en chimie analytique, Exemple de la fluorescence UV", *Analysis*, vol. 23, no. 10, pp. 518–522, 1995.

[KIS 96] KISTER J., "Stratégie de recherche et Veille Scientifique et Technique. Administrer les savoirs: leur production, leur administration, leur application, leur contrôle", *Bulletin du CIFFERSE*, Hors Série, vol II, pp. 328–333, October 1996.

[KIS 07] KISTER J., Applications des concepts de l'intelligence compétitive et de la veille stratégique à un laboratoire de recherche: Interactions Etat/Recherche/Industrie: une réponse aux questions sociétales et industrielles. Un modèle transférable à l'Indonésie, Puri Agung-Sahid Jaya Hotel, Jakarta, Indonesia, 11 April 2007.

[LEI 04a] LEITZELMAN M., KISTER J., BARBIER D., CLEMENT D., "Apport de la veille technologique sur une énergie de demain: La pile à combustible pour un développement durable", *Actes des 7es Journées Francophones des Jeunes Physico-Chimistes*, Shanes Palace, Monastir, Tunisia, 19–21 March 2004.

[LEI 04b] LEITZELMAN M., DOU H., KISTER J., "Système d'information de travail collaboratif assisté par ordinateur implémenté dans une UMR de recherche pluridisciplinaire et multisite", *Actes du colloque VSST'2004*, Veille Stratégique Scientifique et Technologique, Systèmes d'Information Elaborée, Bibliométrie, Linguistique, intelligence économique, Toulouse, France, 25–29 October 2004.

[LEI 04c] LEITZELMAN M., DOU H., KISTER J., "Modélisation de connaissances et fouille d'informations par la cartographie dynamique: applications de veille technologique avec le logiciel Matheo Analyzer™", *RIAO2004*, University of Avignon, France, 26–28 April 2004.

[LEI 07] LEITZELMAN M., LELOUP B., KISTER J., "Une approche centrée utilisateur pour la mise en place d'une plate-forme de TCAO (Travail Collaboratif assisté par Ordinateur): conclusions et perspectives", *Réunion nationale du GDR CNRS intelligence économique, session: information pour l'action*, Marseille, France, 6–7 December 2007.

[LEY 98] LEYDESDORFF L., ETZKOWITZ H., "The triple helix as a model for innovation studies" (Conference Report), *Science & Public Policy*, vol. 25, no. 3, pp. 195–203, 1998.

[NAG 03] NAGPAUL P.S., ROY S., "Constructing a multi-objective measure of research performance", *Scientometrics*, vol. 56, pp. 383–402, 2003.

[PAL 07] PALMISANO, Analysis of the Palmisano Report by Tamada Shumpeter, a fellow of the RIETI (Japan), June 2009, available online at: www.rieti.go.jp/en/columns/a01_0158.html.

[POR 90] PORTER M., *The Competitive Advantages of Nations*, Free Press, 1990.

[ROS 04] ROSTAING H., KISTER J., GIMNEZ TOLEDO E., "Système d'information pour l'aide à la gestion stratégique de la recherche dans un établissement public de recherché", *Actes du colloqueVSST'2004, Veille Stratégique Scientifique et Technologique, Systèmes d'Information Elaborée, Bibliométrie, Linguistique, intelligence économique*, Toulouse, France, 25–29 October 2004.

[ROY 02] ROY S., NAGPAUL P.S., "Structure and functioning of scientific personnel in CSIR: a quantitative appraisal", in MUNSHI U.M., KUNDRA R. (eds), *Information Management in New Millennium*, pp. 466–480, Allied, New Delhi, 2002.

[SAU 09] SAUZET C., PRINDERRE P., DOU H., KISTER J., "Policy cluster in technological research. Pharmaceutical applications: searching for a "cluster" by the use of cropwatch on two aspects: aspect technology (patents) and aspect fundamental research (scientific publications)", *Actes du VSST'2009, Veille Stratégique Scientifique et Technologique, Systèmes d'Information Elaborée, Bibliométrie, Linguistique, intelligence économique*, INIST-CNRS, Nancy, France, 30–31 March 2009.

[THO 09] THOMANN B., "L'évaluation de la recherche en question", *Histoire Moderne et Contemporaine*, 2009, available online at: www.laviedesidees.fr/L-evaluation-de-la-recherche-en.html.

[THU 83] THUILLIER P., "Publications scientifiques: comment fonctionne le jugement par les pairs", *La Recherche*, vol. 14, no. 143, pp. 520–523, April 1983.

[TOR 09] TORYOD, For more information, see www.toryod.com/publicationmapping.php, June 2009.

[USA 09] USAID, www.usaid.gov.

[VRS 07] VRS, *Vie de la Recherche Scientifique*, no. 370, pp. 48–50, September 2007.

[VRS 08] VRS, "Bibliométrie et évaluation de la recherche: le danger des mauvais usages des indicateurs", *VRS*, no. 374, pp. 38–40, September 2008.

[WIP 09] WIPO Resources, For more information, see www.wipo.int/classifications/ fulltext/new_ipc/ipcen.html, June 2009.

[ZER 06] ZERHOUNI E., "Intervention", *Congress organized by the American Society of Hematology*, December 2006, cited in PEREZ A., "Quel modèle pour la recherche publique française", *Les Echos*, 10 January 2007.

Chapter 12

E-Health and Societal and Territorial Intelligence in France: Collective Knowledge Production Issues and New Network Interface Organizations

12.1. Introduction

The World Health Organization (WHO) considered in 2000 the French healthcare system as the best in the world. However, in late 2008, 74% of French people surveyed considered that their healthcare system was worsening on a daily basis [TRO 08]. Healthcare systems are in crisis in all developed countries. This crisis is, first and foremost, linked to finance with growing budget deficits. In a context of new limited resources, healthcare systems have gained in weight in terms of national economies: 11.5% of gross domestic product in France in 2007 (compared with 5.4% in 1970), according to the organization for economic cooperation and development (*Organisation de coopération et de développement économiques*). The increasing cost of the healthcare system corresponds to underlying social changes, with an ageing population, the importance of chronic diseases and the increasing use of technology in medicine. The healthcare sector depends more and more on information and communication technologies (ICT) with the development of the concept of e-health. The issues involved are representative of those encountered in our society. This development is a response to the evolution of French-style competitive intelligence (CI) which, in its societal dimensions,

---

Chapter written by Christian BOURRET.

corresponds closely to the issues encountered in territorial intelligence. Interest in the healthcare sector is growing in information and communications sciences, as shown by the development of conferences and seminars over the last few years (GRESEC – CRAPE and EHESP, Rennes, October 2008, ACFAS, Ottawa, May 2009, etc.)[1].

The new applications of ICT in healthcare contribute to the development of a collective intelligence approach, with aspects of CI in its societal dimensions and aspects of territorial intelligence, particularly in new organizations of network interfaces.

In this chapter, we will first analyze the emergence of e-health as a response to the need to break down borders in the French healthcare system, particularly visible in the intentions of new interface organizations. We will then consider the new territorialization of healthcare management, which contributes to the convergence of the societal aspect of CI approaches with territorial intelligence. After this, we will look at the issues involved in collective knowledge production. We will conclude by showing how the establishment of regional information systems in healthcare may constitute a step toward the construction of societal and territorial intelligence systems for the domain.

12.2. E-health, the convergence of health issues, and ICT

12.2.1. Compartmentalization and crisis in health systems

A healthcare system is based essentially on the articulation between two sectors: primary care and hospital sector. In all developed countries, the cost of virtual barriers (corresponding to the weakness or absence of interactions) is seen as a major cause of the finance crisis in healthcare systems. This problem is particularly significant in France, where opposition exists between the health insurance sector and the state (ministry of health), and the primary care (private and "liberal") and the hospital sector (public or assimilated hospitals and private clinics). Opposition also exists between different professions: generalist/specialist doctors and treatment in relation to health and the medico-social sector (the relative positions of doctors/nurses/physiotherapists/social workers, and so on). Glouberman and Mintzberg [GLO 01] have shown that divisions exist within hospitals between the

---

1 GRESEC (*Groupe de recherche sur les enjeux de la communication,* research group on communication issues) – Université Stendhal Grenoble III, CRAPE (*Centre de recherche sur l'action publique en Europe,* research center on public action in Europe) – Rennes University 1, EHESP (*Ecole des hautes études en santé publique,* school of higher education in public health) – Rennes, ACFAS: *Association francophone pour le savoir,* French-speaking association for knowledge.

four separate worlds of treatment (doctors), care (nurses), administration, and management and highlight the need to improve cooperation.

These divisions are, for the most part, the result of a societal choice. The weight of individualism, the rejection of the German-style model of center-based medicine in favor of one-on-one dialog between doctor and patient, the freedom of installation given to private practitioners with payment for treatment (1927), and the "hospital-centric" system, where hospitals are responsible for almost 50% of expenditure, have shaped the French healthcare system.

In the United States, medical errors may be responsible for between 50,000 and 100,000 deaths per year [BLE 02]; this would be equivalent to between 10,000 and 20,000 deaths per year in France. According to Cordonnier [COR 01], 30% of these medical errors are the result of information management problems and particularly confusion in identification. In France, certain experts consider that the costs generated by divisions, assimilated to a lack of quality, may absorb up to 15% of the resources of the healthcare system. In the United States, Wennberg *et al.* [WEN 02] estimate that 20–30% of healthcare expenditure concerns treatments that produce no significant improvement in health are redundant or not applicable to the particular case of the patient. In the words of Grimson *et al.* [GRI 00] "the inability to share information across systems and between care organizations is just one of the major impediments in the healthcare business progress toward efficiency and cost-effectiveness".

12.2.2. The development of e-health

"Online health" constitutes one of the major concerns of the "information society". In 2000, the WHO considered that "the road to healthcare for all passes through information". The first use of computers in the healthcare sector was observed over 40 years ago, and the term e-health was first encountered over 15 years ago [SIL 03]. Since then, there have been considerable developments in the applications of e-health. In the context of a broad approach to e-health, Villac [VIL 04] cites G. Eysenbach, who states that "e-health is an emerging field, at the crossroads of medical information, public health and the economy, which concerns health services and facilitated access to information using the internet and associated technologies. In a wider sense, the term does not only characterize a technical development, but also a state of mind, a way of thinking, an attitude, and a sort of obligation for individuals working in networks to improve healthcare, locally, regionally or internationally, using information and communication technologies".

The IPTS report on e-health [IPT 04] gives an idea of the diversity of applications of e-health: computerized medical files, information systems, telemedicine, call centers, etc. E-health thus concerns three sectors: the hospital, where the development of ICT is a priority of the 2012 hospital plan in France (access to and transmission of medical information, payments, administrative and financial management, etc.), the primary care (long distance patient care, online appointment systems, computer programs for practice management), and the patients' homes (hospitalization and home stays, monitoring, and so on). It also applies to all ICT-based equipment, practices, and tools used to promote cooperation between the three sectors (telemedicine, call centers, and computerized medical files) along with access to new services linked to information and coordination (portals, service platforms, etc.).

12.2.3. *Evolution of medical practice, computerization, and ICT use*

The ways in which medicine is practiced have evolved considerably, a development accelerated by e-health. In 1995, B. Glorion, president of the French order of doctors, highlighted the passage toward more cooperative modes of working: "the reign of the soloist, no matter how talented, is over" [MAL 97]. This evolution corresponds to deep-lying modification in the composition of the medical profession and its representations. Doctors, including an increasing number of women, now wish to reconcile professional careers with family life. The aggravation of problems of medical demographics in certain zones (particularly in rural areas) and the importance of chronic illnesses, particularly linked to the aging population, have an influence on medical practices.

These changes also correspond to evolutions in the role of patients. The patients who have become better informed (largely thanks to Internet), have also become more demanding (with increased litigiousness, following the American model), demanding results and not just methods. We encounter the idea of the "utopia of perfect health", analyzed by Sfez [SFE 01]. These "new" patients group together in associations, most of which are federated into the inter-association collective for health (*collectif interassociatif sur la santé*) in France. This general movement can be observed in all countries. In the English-speaking world, we talk of patient empowerment. In France, patient rights were clarified by a law of March 4, 2002 on "patient rights and the quality of the healthcare system".

According to P. Bonet, president of the UNAFORMEC (continuous medical training), "all developments in our healthcare system pass through the mastery of medical information" [MAL 97]. Computerization constitutes a main response to the crisis in healthcare systems. For Carré [CAR 08], this corresponds to a decision made outside of the healthcare system, imposed in the United States in the 1980s by industrialists (particularly by the automobile industry, experiencing competition from Japan) who found that the cost of health insurance contracts was increasing the factory price. In Quebec, there was the *"computerized ambulatory bend"*, a move toward dehospitalization. From 1998, the United Kingdom established the ambitious *Information for Health* program [DEP 98]. In France, the reforms of August 2004 concentrated on three points, including new governance (while maintaining the separation between the health insurance and the ministry of health), use of ICT, particularly through the use of the "magic tool" represented by the personal medical record (*dossier médical personnel*, DMP), and an accentuation of regionalization in healthcare management.

These policies form part of the "informationalization" process discussed by Miège [MIE 04], corresponding to the extension of information use (and not just computer use) in all sectors of our society, including the private sphere. These data explosions, accelerated still further by the development of the Internet, pose a number of problems, particularly in relation to reliability as a basis for decisions and to the issue of hosting this information. Although these data have considerable economic significance, their use may also pose ethical problems and issues concerning the protection of privacy. For this reason, data have been the subject of particular legislation reflecting national specificities. The European directive of October 1995 considers healthcare data to be "sensitive" information. In France, a law on *"Informatique et Libertés"* (Computer science and freedoms) was passed in 1978, and the national commission for computer science and freedom (*Commission nationale de l'informatique et des libertés*) was created to control its application in the aim of protecting citizens from possible abuse in data use (particularly the creation of unauthorized files). The European directive extended this protection of personal rights. It introduced the notion of personal data any data that might be used to identify a person. Authorization to use these data depends on the aims of use (research, general interest) and on the nature of the data itself. France was slow to adapt its own legislation to the European directive (law passed August 6, 2004). In the United States, where freedom to use personal data is much more widespread and accentuated by competition between organizations, the risk of abuse is considerably higher. Congress made the Health and Human Services Department responsible for patient privacy, integrating it into the 1996 Health Insurance Portability and Accountability Act (Office for Civil Liberties). In Quebec (Canada), the Quebec Commission for Information Access plays a specific role.

12.3. Toward a new territorialization of healthcare management

12.3.1. *Reorganization of the health system by regionalization*

Attempts to respond to the healthcare crisis by developing the use of ICT are linked to the role attributed to regional powers in healthcare management. Unlike other countries, where a stronger tradition of decentralization exists (the Scandinavian states, Germany, Italy, Spain, Canada, Switzerland, etc.), a regionalized approach to healthcare management is a recent development in France. Regional unions of private doctors (*unions régionales de médecins libéraux*) appeared in 1993, followed by regional health insurance unions (*unions régionales d'assurance maladie*, URCAMs) and notably regional hospitalization agencies (*agences régionales d'hospitalisation*, ARHs) in 1996.

This evolution corresponds to developments in planning, particularly the establishment of hospitals and a better level of research: creation of health cards in 1970, and then regional plans for sanitary organization (*schemas régionaux d'organisation sanitaire*), in 1991. Initially only concerned with the hospital sector (rationalization and reduction of the number of beds), these plans were extended to cover the ambulatory sector, particularly with "territorial medical projects". These projects were linked to regional public health plans. The role of the regional health observatories (*observatoires régionaux de santé*, ORS) should also be mentioned. From 2004, regional healthcare projects (*missions régionales de santé*,) preceded the creation of regional healthcare agencies (*agences régionales de santé*, ARS), the "star" measure of a law on hospitals, patients, health, and territories promulgated on July 21, 2009. These agencies were established in the course of 2010.

12.3.2. *Affirmation of new organizations of innovative interfaces as sociotechnical forms, projects, and apparatus*

Morin [MOR 03] and Sainsaulieu [SAI 01] highlight the need for "reliance" throughout our society. This is particularly important in France in the healthcare sector. Experiments to break down divisions have taken the form of new interface organizations with more cooperative practices, often based on ICT use. These projects were particularly innovative, creating previously unknown organizational forms.

The first healthcare networks appeared in the mid-1980s, both in the form of coordinated care networks following the American Health Maintenance Organizations model and as health/social networks, often set up on the initiative of doctors in underprivileged zones seeking new ways of working, particularly in the context of the AIDS epidemic. Health networks, valorized by the law of March 4, 2002, which offered a synthetic description of these networks, are now widespread; around 1,000 such entities are present across France, caring for between 100 and 150,000 patients. The original opposition between health networks and coordinated care networks has given way to a distinction between pathology networks (at varying levels, but often at *departement* or regional level: diabetes, cancer, bronchiolitis, addictions, etc.) and generalist or "proximity" networks, which generally exist to promote care access for patients with complex pathologies or situations. We are now, in all likelihood, facing a new development: the construction of integrated territorial service networks [ACE 08] with the pooling of activities with other interface organizations in service platforms.

Health networks are no longer alone in their field. They are now subject to competition from local information and coordination centers (*centres locaux d'information et de coordination*), home-hospitalization establishments (*hospitalisation à domicile*, HAD), and especially *maisons de santé*, multidisciplinary healthcare centers, which appear to enjoy the favor of public powers. The *maison de santé* in Blettterans, in the Jura region of France, thus recently received a good deal of media attention. Since early 2009, the Groupama insurance company and the agricultural social mutual insurance (Mutualité Sociale Agricole, MSA) have joined together, as they had already done for certain healthcare networks, to propose a new territorial approach to healthcare in terms of *health districts* to respond to the dramatic reduction in the number of health professionals operating in rural areas. Two experiments are underway in the Dordogne and Ardennes regions.

These new interface organizations are all part of a global approach to healthcare envisaged as "complexity intelligence" (Morin and Le Moigne), with particular attention to "dialogies" or double logics (simultaneously opposing and complementary) [MOR 03] as, for example, not only between individual and collective approaches but also between pathology-based and proximity-based approaches, with issues of mixing competences and the creation of a new collective identity based around new cooperative practices. These new organizations constitute test forms with a focus on information and communication, in the sense of organized sharing. These organizations also constitute sociotechnical apparatus as proposed by M. Foucault, who envisaged them as the "network" which may be traced between different elements "of a resolutely heterogeneous group, with discourses, institutions, architectural setups, regulatory decisions, laws, administrative measures, scientific pronouncements, philosophical, moral and philanthropic propositions, in short: what is said and what remains unsaid" [BEU 06]. The "sociology of translation" and particularly the "sociology of the network actor", considering apparatus as "agents", fit well into the extension of M. Foucault's approach [AKR 06]. These interface organizations also constitute innovative project spaces, as seen by Alter [ALT 02] who considers innovation as a "constellation of ordinary activities", and a collective activity, with the emergence of new rationalities and actors. These organizations innovate by their position as an interface between primary care and hospital, medical and social, by the new cooperative practices developed, by the affirmation of new functions and new professions and through the development of new judicial and remunerative approaches (with payment by year rather than by intervention), and by the use of ICT.

The purposes of these new interface organizations, which correspond to the meeting of healthcare and ICT, are linked to two notions that are emblematic of our post-industrial society: the network and the project. Although the value of these notions is widely accepted, they are also subject to criticism due to their generality and obsessional character: Boutinet, for the project [BOU 01], and Musso, in the case of networks, have strongly criticized these notions, with Musso talking of "*rétiologie*", an "ideology of networks" [MUS 03]. D'Almeida [DAL 06] signals that a project corresponds to a focus on communication objectives. Information and communication sciences have highlighted its communicational dimensions. From this viewpoint, projects correspond to two types of operations: organizational and symbolic. This shows the meeting of project and network: "a man of projects is a man of networks and opportunities, a man of everywhere and nowhere whose actions are situated on an extendible canvas".

As interface spaces favorable to "situated coordination", these new organizational forms or apparatus participate in a new approach to a territory and may then be considered "as a construct, a result of the practices and representations of agents" [PEC 04]. In years to come, they may constitute the basic, local level for a new "territorialization" of healthcare management currently being established, followed by local hospitals, regional hospital centers, and national centers of excellence within the context of network-based working based on information sharing and new communication processes. The pooling operations (reception, logistics, etc.) and readability (single access point) of these organizations are currently under consideration, particularly through the use of ICT and especially Internet portals and shared tools (shared patient files). The system is moving toward a global range of services integrated in a local context. To improve the clarity of the offer and to improve service provision, these organizations are now faced with issues concerning collective knowledge construction, which broadly correspond to communication challenges through new uses of information and communications processes. For the hospitalization sector, the Larcher report [LAR 08] advises the creation of groups of "territorial hospital communities".

12.4. E-health and CI: societal dimensions and territorial intelligence

12.4.1. *E-health and CI*

Martre's report [MAR 95] defined CI as "the set of retrieval, processing and diffusion activities, with a view to use, of useful information to economic actors". This report constituted a concrete expression of reflections underway at the time on the subject of economic, or competitive, intelligence in France. This definition of CI promotes the notion of a cycle of information processing. In his preface to the collective publication *Les nouveaux territoires de l'intelligence économique* [DUV 08], A. Juillet, the long-serving head of CI, provided a redefinition of French-style CI. For Juillet, continuing the themes set out in Carayon's report [CAR 03],

CI exists to help with capitalizing on strong points while reducing weaknesses in a context of generalized competition, by knowing how to acquire necessary information. Theoretically, CI is "the mastery and protection of useful strategic information for decision makers". Practically, it is "a state of mind, a method and tools which allow us to collect and process all necessary information and data for decision making and to accompany implementation" [DUV 08]. Juillet also distinguishes between "French-style" CI and the approaches taken in the United States or the United Kingdom, considering that the latter use "overly economic" forms of targeting: CI in the United States is all too often reduced to a simple comparative benchmark, and British "business intelligence", although it has a wider field of action, does not give sufficient attention to the environment.

According to Fuchs [FUC 98], the main challenge confronting the US healthcare system – and those of all other developed countries – is "to devise a system of medical care that provides ready access at a reasonable cost", in a context of limited resources. The keywords in this context are *performance* and *efficiency*, or, to cite the title of a work by Moore, *Managing to do better* [MOO 00] through the use of new managerial approaches: total quality management, project management, process management, competence management, etc. with a resolutely client-centered approach. All these approaches are based on new uses of information and the development of interactions based on new communication processes.

Amos David [DAV 05], considering CI as a response to a decision problem, presented CI as a process made up of different phases:

– identification of a decision problem;

– transformation of the decision problem into an information problem;

– identification of relevant information sources;

– collection of relevant information;

– analysis of collected information to extract indicators for decision and interpretation of indicators;

– decision making.

With the increase in new uses of ICT, the healthcare sector is increasingly concerned with CI, the main aim of which is to assist stakeholders in decision making. This principally concerns pharmaceutical companies, medical equipment companies, and computer service providers (patent watch, industrial property, and so on). The development of personal medical records attracted the attention of major industrial groups (Orange, Thalès, etc.), which have since taken a step back. Google may also become involved. Web sites also play an important role. In February 2008, the Lagardère group bought the *Doctissimo* network. These development issues and acquisition strategies linked to CI also apply to another sector of e-health, that of online sale of medications (e-pharmacy), popular in the United states but banned in France, as is long-distance consultation of a doctor by a patient, something that is nevertheless widespread elsewhere (e.g. in Denmark). The development of e-health is influenced by national specificities and is thus connected to the history of mentalities and the evolution of representations.

12.4.2. The convergence of societal and territorial intelligence: a global intelligence approach to complexity

Flichy [FLI 04] puts forward the idea of "connected individualism". The contemporary individual is, indeed, often connected to multiple networks via the Internet, but is also often isolated. According to R. Debray, "a person only exists when fitted in a territory" [BEA 00], in an idea which insists on the importance of geographical territory as a "relevant context" for all policies, including healthcare. The approach to territories has developed a good deal [PEC 04]. In this spirit, we have looked at the construction of this approach around the synergy of local projects [BOU 08].

The diversity of territories is now widely recognized. In accordance with this evolution, the delegation for territorial development and competitiveness (*délégation à l'aménagement du territoire et à l'action régionale*, DATAR), created in 1963 in the context of voluntarism under the government of General de Gaulle, changed its name in 2005 to become the interministerial delegation for the development and competitiveness of territories (*délégation interministérielle à l'aménagement et à la compétitivité des territoires*, DIACT) but it may go back to being the DATAR. Beauchard [BEA 00] considers that a territory is constructed by the meeting of two approaches: the "patrimonial" territory (identity, mentalities, and representations) and the "transactional" territory (mobility and exchanges). As in the case of CI/territorial intelligence, individual/collective, local/global, order/disorder, static/dynamic articulations, etc., we can talk of "dialogues", or double logics, in a global perspective of "intelligence of complexity" [MOR 03] and sustainable development.

After analyzing the crisis of democracy, Rosanvallon [ROS 08] insists on the importance of proximity and citizen participation (participative democracy) in the creation of a new legitimacy. A few years ago, the author highlighted the need to refound the welfare state. Mucchielli [MUC 06] and Le Boterf [LEB 04] have shown the importance of context to action, and organizations may be seen as "a relevant context for action".

A. Juillet speaks of *Les nouveaux territoires de l'intelligence économique* (new territories for CI: judicial, in accounting and finance, cultural, societal or social, and so on). Territorial intelligence and competitive/economic intelligence (which A. Juillet suggests should be more globally envisaged as strategic intelligence) are thus led to converge, particularly through "social or societal intelligence", which could "become a pillar of the CI of tomorrow" with all the issues linked to sustainable development, "a fantastic opportunity for repositioning" in France [DUV 08]. For P. Clerc, social intelligence, or, in his own words, "societal" intelligence, "allows us to place any strategy in a richer context" [DUV 08].

Continuing the work begun by S. Dedijer, P. Clerc presents societal intelligence as the new territory *par excellence* of CI. This new approach, according to the author, involves rediscovering the state of mind of "world intelligence", which has always motivated humanity, first observed in the Sumerian culture, then *mètis* or cunning intelligence, practical intelligence, or the art of leadership used by the Greeks, symbolized by Ulysses and which, since work of Aristotle, has been largely supplanted by almost exclusive promotion of rational intelligence or *logos*.

In our opinion, CI in its societal aspects converges with territorial intelligence, as any societal intelligence approach is based in or on a territory. Bozzano (La Plata University, Argentina) defines territorial intelligence as follows: TI = CT + PTA/SDT, so territorial intelligence (IT) = comprehension of territory (CT) + participation of territorial actors (PTA) for sustainable development of the territory (SDT) [BOZ 08]. The participation of territorial actors and the implication of populations in a perspective of sustainable development contribute to the specificity of territorial intelligence with all issues linked to information sharing and the construction of collective intelligence [GIR 04].

For the authors of territorial intelligence, economic intelligence applied to a territory (Intelligence territoriale, l'intelligence économique appliquée au territoire) [FRA 08], there is no ambiguity: "territorial intelligence is an emerging concept which consists of applying the principles of economic intelligence at the level of a territory in order to improve competitiveness".

12.5. Issues in the production of collective knowledge

12.5.1. *Coordination: the complementarity of information and communication*

The improvement of coordination between actors, as the central aspect of the project, constitutes the *raison d'être* of healthcare interface organizations and corresponds to the tight interweaving of information and communication issues to build cooperative practices. The "territory" of these new organizational forms is built up by information sharing and by new communication processes, creating links from interactions. This complementarity contributes to the construction of meaning, and the organization corresponds to the creation of "generalized process-based communication" according to Mucchielli [MUC 06] and may be considered a "semiotic machine", according to Le Moënne [LEM 06].

From this perspective, negotiation takes on a crucial importance. These new organizational forms or apparatus constitute, first and foremost, places for negotiation between the primary and hospital care sectors and for the recreation of social links. For Bercot, a care network is an innovative process based on the construction of agreements. Its durability depends on the capacity for negotiation of the main actors on different levels: negotiating means a territory, a place, and a reputation [BER 06]. Grosjean *et al.* [GRO 04] see negotiation as "constitutive and institutive". It is not simply a source of regulation, but is at the heart of production of the proposed service and the fundamental resource for its definition and implementation to adjust and ensure compatibility between the various systems involved.

From our point of view, the uses of information (in the sense of formatting) and communication constitute "organizing" processes as expressed by the acronym CCO (Communication Constitutes Organization) in North America [PUT 09][2]. Communication corresponds to the establishment of relationships and the development of interactions, not just between human actors but also between sociotechnical apparatus. The main aim in promoting the use of information and communication processes is to move beyond the barriers that hinder interaction and limit cooperation.

12.5.2. *Information needs for decision assistance and new tools*

The information needs of these new interface organizations are found over three levels (micro, meso, and macro), which correspond to different issues. The "micro" level corresponds to relationships, care, and interactions between patients and healthcare professionals: care pathways with issues of traceability of actions and quality of care. The "meso" level concerns leadership of establishments and intermediary organizations, with, for example, T2A, a process for activity-based pricing. These levels are intrinsically linked: data collected to follow actions may also be used to evaluate the services provided by organizations. T2A, which makes use of analytical accounting data, is a tool for organizational management, but is

---

2 The work coordinated by Putnam and Nicotera (2009) looks at the constitutive role of communication in organizations: communication is what coordinates activities, creates relationships, and maintains cohesion in organizations. They also highlight the fact that organization is also formalization, and that communication and organization are not equivalent but mutually constitutive.

used more as a tool for the attribution of credits (the "macro" aspect of credit distribution and therefore of governance in the healthcare system).

The development of the position of the welfare state, undergoing a crisis and in need of "refoundation" [ROS 98], is based on contractualization and delegation, corresponding to new evaluation issues. The state acts in a less direct manner, becoming a "referee" and source of finance, responsible for evaluating the results obtained by delegated credits. The new objective-based management seen in all fields of activity of public powers supposes a comparison of results in relation to initial objectives (in France, conventions on aims and management (*conventions d'objectifs et de gestion*) for social security bodies and organic law of finance laws (*loi organique des lois de finances*) in the public sector and especially universities). Progressively, over 20 years or so, the logic of evaluation, coming from the private sector and the English-speaking world, has gained ground in the public sector, introducing notions of performance and efficiency.

These new strategies make use of new tools. Since 2004, the French have accorded great importance to the "miracle tool" constituted by the DMP, personal medical files, intended to ensure the traceability, quality, and non-redundancy of actions. These original ambitions have constantly been reviewed in a downward direction. The DMP is no longer compulsory and should return to shared status (the "personal" notion related to the dossier being the property of the patient, who was able to "hide" certain data). The position of the DMP needs to be determined in relation to other shared dossiers, such as the pharmaceutical dossier (a success), the cancer communication dossier (dossier communicant cancer, DCC), HAD records, health networks, and, from January 2009, the new project for employee health files, which will probably also take an electronic form. There is a real risk that all these files will contribute to the creation of new barriers. The main role of the new agency for shared information systems (*Agence des systèmes d'information partagés*, ASIP) will be to avert these risks, if the agency succeeds in defining its boundaries of action in relation to another new agency, the national agency for performance assistance in health and medico-social organizations (*Agence nationale d'aide à la performance des établissements de santé et medico-sociaux*, ANAP), and so on. Note that, in spite of more significant investment and better project management, the British electronic health record (EHR) is also experiencing difficulties. These computerized health records should now be integrated into shared portals [FIC 08], which will themselves form part of shared information systems, most probably at regional level [FIE 03].

Call centers such as the British NHS Direct or the Catalan *Sanitat Respon* contribute to patient orientation, unlike call centers known as service platforms (*plateformes de service*, PFS) provided by health insurance organizations in France, which merely inform users of their rights and are able to carry out simple administrative operations (certificates of cover, etc.). Alongside the various health portals, telemedicine is the most mediatized tool involved in e-health, with particular focus on telesurgery in zones with limited access. Telemedicine also covers telediagnosis and telesurveillance of sensitive patients at home. Databases have also undergone spectacular developments and can now be accessed via Internet portals. The Web sites of the National Institutes of Health (NIH) are among the most consulted in the world, particularly in the case of *Medline* (National Library of Medicine), available online since 1997. In France, the catalog and index of French-language medical sites (*catalogue et index des sites médicaux francophones*), run by the university hospitals of Rouen and launched in 1995, is appreciated throughout the French-speaking world. We should also mention the Orphanet site, a multilingual European portal for rare diseases, which operates with the assistance of 200 patient associations and the support of the INSERM. Certain states have developed Internet portals for health education. In Canada, we find the Canadian Health Network (*Réseau Canadien de la santé*, RCS), a pilot service run by Health Canada. The Scottish Health on the Web service has had considerable success in Scotland. The "Web 2.0", or social Web, as a support for collaborative networks, has undergone major developments in the healthcare sector.

12.5.3. *Evolution of professions and new professions*

New interface organizations thus contribute to the modification of positioning of professions and professional identities and to the emergence of new professions. The bronchiolitis network in the Ile-de-France region thus transformed the position of physical therapists, previously an "excluded profession", into major partners in working with doctors [CAB 05]. These organizations also contribute to the extension of the field of work of nurses.

The new functions or even new professions which emerge are, first and foremost, centered on negotiation and coordination, based on the development of information and communications capabilities, for example, case management nurses following a model used in Quebec to track the care path of complex patients (chronic pathologies and social difficulties) and especially coordinators in health networks. These coordinators act as "couriers" or "translators", helping to build the collective identity of the new interface organization through the multiplication of interactions, creating convergence between representations of all actors, to create collective meaning and identity, without underestimating the personal or institutional strategies of different actors and the importance of power struggles [CRO 77].

12.6. Shared information systems at regional level: a step toward societal and territorial information systems with a health component?

12.6.1. *Issues in the construction of regionalized information systems*

Information systems represent the activity of an organization and the interactions between actors. Durampart and Guyot [DUR 08] suggest that we should "examine the organization in the light of its information systems", based on the information and communications activities making up the work of the organization (what is said, what is known, and what is done) with emphasis on interactions. They perceive the organization as a set of evolving processes and not as a stable state. For them, the information systems constitute "a particular form of expression" (with the importance of the convergence of representations) … "it identifies, represents and formalizes an organization in movement".

Currently, we are observing a passage from information produced and exploited to individual ends, particularly in primary care medicine, toward information sharing to ensure the traceability of actions and cooperative practices with the intention of arriving at collective information production to improve patient services and control costs (efficiency). Information is no longer just a "source", but a "resource" abounding in new potential, as predicted by Levitan [LEV 82].

These issues concern the leadership of organizations and coordination. Ficatier envisaged "care coordination information systems" [FIC 08]. The computerization of care processes, and not just the DMP, is used to assist decision. The intention is to guarantee better coordination of healthcare professionals centered on the care path of the patient to ensure continuity and quality of care. Ensuring the interoperability of tools is a major challenge facing industrialists, national governments, and the European Union. In France, the companies responsible for sanitary and social information systems (*Les entreprises des systèmes d'information sanitaires et sociaux*) constitute a pressure group with the ability to highlight issues and provide criticism of questionable choices. At European level, we should mention the integrating of the healthcare enterprise activities, an initiative on the part of healthcare professionals and industrialists to improve information sharing, concentrating on the coordinated use of recognized standards such as DICOM and HL7.

Although healthcare is left to the care of individual member states, initiatives have been launched at European level. An e-health action plan was envisaged from 2004 with a route map for the adoption of new technologies up to 2010. The European Commission promotes improvements in interoperability between tools and services, establishing a guide for interoperability in e-health. The Commission Recommendation on cross-border interoperability of EHR systems (2008) constitutes a key point, and the interoperability of patient medical files is a first major step. As Fieschi's report [FIE 03] advises, solutions are mostly envisaged at regional level, notably through Internet portals promoting readability, interoperability, and pooling of proposed tools and services. A good example of this is the Franche-Comté Santé portal (Besançon). Semantic interoperability between data and knowledge is also essential. In a more recent report, Fieschi showed that "the governance of semantic interoperability is at the heart of the development of information systems in healthcare" [FIE 09], both to improve patient care and for decision making and the management of establishments.

12.6.2. Societal and territorial intelligence and building trust between actors around sociotechnical systems

The optimization of information systems is at the heart of the modernization of healthcare [REN 08]. In the context of a global approach, we are challenged to produce collective intelligence to improve the quality of patient-centered care and the efficiency of the healthcare system as a whole. This necessitates the use of new sociotechnical apparatus within interface organizations, allowing us to move beyond traditional divisions, particularly between the primary care and the hospital sectors.

C. Dupuy and A. Torre emphasize the relationship between notions of trust and proximity. "Trust constitutes one element for the comprehension of local dynamics" and is "the mother of action". Trust allows the construction of a collective future based on the convergence of representations of actors. Trust is built up over time through interactions [PEC 04]. The notion of proximity is also central for Rosanvallon. After explaining his ideas about *Counter-democracy, or the politics of the age of defiance*, the author seeks new foundations for *democratic legitimacy*, particularly in the notion of proximity, a word which, in his opinion, expresses the new type of relationships which citizens which to establish with governments. In 2002, a law made use of the term "democracy of proximity" [ROS 08]. From March 2002, in the healthcare sector in France, the term "*démocratie sanitaire*" has come into use, with increasing involvement of patients and recognition of their rights (patient empowerment).

The creation of trust is essential, both among human actors and in new uses of ICT (information systems, computerized medical files, protocols, best practice guides, and so on). Le Cardinal *et al.* [LEC 03] demonstrate the importance of a climate of trust between authors in complex projects, particularly in the establishment of information systems, promoting cooperation.

12.6.3. *Collective knowledge production: the core of new governance in the health system*

Information sharing and collective knowledge production are now at the heart of the new forms of governance currently being put into place in our healthcare system. This knowledge is, by definition, contextualized. The key measure of the law on hospitals, patients, health, and territories (July 2009) is the creation of ARS, which came into effect in 2010. The ARS bring together the ARH, URCAM, and regional delegations for sanitary and social action (*délégations régionales de l'action sanitaire et sociale*) and were prefigured, from 2004, by regional health missions.

The central question now concerns the tools to put into place to ensure the success of these new ARS. Two agencies have been established, the ASIP and the ANAP, by joining together existing entities. There is already a high authority on health (*haute autorité de santé*), which is responsible for the evaluation of establishments and the professional practices of private practitioners: this is a new development. Note that the decision was taken in August 2004 to create an institute of healthcare data (*Institut des données de santé*) to guarantee that these data will remain anonymous. In this context, we also find an inter-regime information system for health insurance (*système d'information inter-régimes de l'assurance maladie*), which is one of the largest data stores in the world, although the data it holds are used for reimbursement of patients and therefore the duration of storage is limited. The level of coherence of the whole set of entities remains to be seen.

We also encounter a watch dimension, with ORS and the institute for health watching (*Institut de veille sanitaire*). The URCAMs carried out analyses at regional level, as in the Ile-de-France region, using the territorial analysis of the healthcare system (*analyse territorialisée du système de santé*) approach.

The new interface organizations can play a role as levers in this evolution, through their role in the creation of links, implication of patients, protection of patient rights, and thus the emergence of "sanitary democracy" in the context of proximity and of entry points for social and territorial intelligence systems devoted to healthcare.

12.7. Conclusion

There is growing interest in the healthcare system in information and communications sciences, with the appearance of workshops and conferences on the subject. Miège has insisted on the importance of the articulation between information and communication on healthcare questions, accentuated by new uses of ICT [LAS 08].

The new uses of ICT in healthcare contribute to the development of a collective intelligence approach involving both economic intelligence, in its societal dimension, and territorial intelligence, particularly in new interface network organizations. The medicine of the future will most likely be based on networks around a patient. This constitutes a deep change, not only in terms of technology but also socially, by modifying the professional identity of different practitioners and particularly doctors, who must accept an external regard on increasingly cooperative practices.

In France, public bodies have been seeking the best interface organization to break down barriers in the healthcare system for the last 25 years. Healthcare networks, promoted by the law of March 2002, are now in competition with multiprofession health centers. Based on new uses of ICT, these new, innovative entities could become levers for the reorganization of the healthcare system. These interface organizations are "hologrammatic", bringing together all issues, intentions, stakes, and challenges of the whole healthcare system, or even of our society as a whole.

In particular, these issues concern information sharing and collective knowledge production. They are linked to both a new domain of economic intelligence [DUV 08] and to territorial intelligence, for which the implication of actors is essential, in an approach which also has links to sustainable development [GIR 04]. These are "cooperative transactions" as described by Zacklad [ZAC 09], who connects them to his approach of "an economy of conviviality".

This development is part of major current changes. These evolutions are not just linked to the healthcare sector, but concern our society as a whole. As Musso shows [MUS 03], they correspond to the ambivalence of technology, which may create either a society of knowledge or a society under previously unseen levels of control. The implication of citizens is essential to avoid drifting. In the context of proximity, this is connected to the idea of "sanitary democracy". This implication corresponds to needs for "reliance" and "social cohesion", which may be observed throughout our society. Territorial intelligence, with the importance of associations and local collectives, thus converges to the societal approach of economic intelligence, with the new role of the state as "strategist and partner" as suggested by Carayon [CAR 03] as a "reconfiguration" of the welfare state [ROS 98].

12.8. Bibliography

[ACE 08] Acef S., "Réseaux de santé et territoires", Informations sociales, vol. 147, pp. 72–81, 2008.

[AKR 06] Akrich M., Callon M., Latour B., Sociologie de la traduction. Textes fondateurs, Les Presses Ecole des Mines, Paris, 2006.

[ALT 02] ALTER N., "Les innovateurs du quotidien. L'innovation dans les entreprises", *Futuribles*, no. 271, January 2002.

[BEA 00] BEAUCHARD J., *La bataille du territoire. Mutation spatiale et aménagement du territoire*, Administration Aménagement du Territoire, L'Harmattan, Paris, 2000.

[BER 06] BERCOT R., "La coopération au sein d'un réseau de santé. Négociations, Territoires et dynamiques professionnelles", *Négociations*, vol. 1, pp. 35–49, 2006.

[BEU 06] BEUSCART J.S., PEERBAYE A., "Histoires de dispositifs", *Dispositif, Terrains & Travaux review*, vol. 11, pp. 1–7, 2006.

[BLE 02] BLENDON R.J., DESROCHES C.M., BRODIE M., BENSON J.M., ROSEN A.B., SCHNEIDER E., ALTMAN D.E., ZAPERT K., HERRMANN M.J, STEFFENSON A.M., "Patient safety. Views of practicing physicians and the public on medical errors", *The New England Journal of Medicine*, vol. 347, no. 24, pp. 1933–1940, 2002.

[BOU 08] BOURRET C., "Eléments pour une approche de l'intelligence territoriale comme synergie de projets locaux pour développer une identité collective", *International Journal of Projectics*, vol. 0, pp. 79–92, 2008, De Boeck, Brussels.

[BOU 01] BOUTINET J.P., *Anthropologie du projet*, PUF, Paris, 2001.

[BOU 06] BOUZON A. (ed.), *La communication organisationnelle en débat. Champs, concepts, perspectives*, L'Harmattan, Paris, 2006.

[BOZ 08] BOZZANO H., "Compréhension et développement du territoire/un nouveau réseau. Vrais problèmes, critères et développement de projets. Expériences en Amérique Latine", *6th International Conference of Territorial Intelligence organized by CAENTI (Coordination Action of the European Network of Territorial Intelligence)*, University of Franche-Comté, Besançon, France, 16 October 2008.

[CAB 05] CABE M.H. (ed.), "La santé en réseaux. Quelles innovations?", *Sociologie Pratique*, no. 11, PUF, Paris, 2005.

[CAR 03] CARAYON B., Rapport de la commission présidée par Intelligence économique, compétitivité et cohésion sociale, La Documentation française, Paris, 2003.

[CAR 08] CARRE D., "Trois postures communicationnelles en santé: désingularisation, culpabilisation et imposition", *1er colloque international francophone: La santé: communiquer pour qui, pourquoi, avec quels enjeux? Spécificités et défis*, Lille Catholic University, France, 15 February 2008.

[COR 01] CORDONNIER E., "Communication dans la santé. Vers la connectivité médicale multimedia", in LE BEUX P., BOULLIER D. (eds), *L'information médicale numérique*, Les cahiers du numérique, Hermès, Paris, pp. 13–36, 2001.

[CRO 77] CROZIER M., FRIEDBERG E., *L'acteur et le système. Les contraintes de l'action collective*, Le Seuil, Paris, 1977, new edition by Points-Essais, Le Seuil, Paris, 1992.

[DAL 06] D'ALMEIDA N., "Les organisations entre projets et récits", in BOUZON A. (ed.), *La communication organisationnelle en débats. Champs, concepts et perspectives*, L'Harmattan, Paris, pp. 145–158, 2006.

[DAV 05] DAVID A., "L'intelligence économique et les Systèmes d'Information: problématiques et approches de solutions", *Conférence"Veille stratégique: mise en œuvre et valorisation de la veille stratégique en entreprise*", Algérie-Télécom, Alger, Algeria, June 2005.

[DEP 98] DEPARTMENT OF HEALTH, *Information for Health. An Information Strategy for the Modern NHS 1998-2005*, NHS Executive, London, 1998.

[DOO 08] DOOR J.P., LE GUEN J.M. (chairs), Rencontres parlementaires sur les systèmes d'information de santé, L'optimisation des systèmes d'information au cœur de la modernisation de la santé, Maison de la Chimie, Paris, France, 4 November 2008.

[DUR 08] DURAMPART M., GUYOT B., "Interroger l'organisation à la lumière des systèmes d'information", *Actes du XVIe congrès de la Société Française des Sciences de l'Information et de la Communication (SFSIC)*, University of Technologie of Compiègne, Compiègne, France, June 2008.

[DUV 08] DUVAL M.A. (ed.), *Les nouveaux territoires de l'intelligence économique*, preface to A. JUILLET, ACFCI, IFIE Editions, Paris, 2008.

[ELL 01] ELLUL J., *La technique ou l'enjeu du siècle*, Economica, Paris, 2001.

[FIC 08] FICATIER T., "Système d'information de la coordination des soins: levier de performance", *Revue hospitalière de France*, vol. 521, pp. 30–33, March–April 2008.

[FIE 03] FIESCHI M., Les données du patient partagées: la culture du partage et de la qualité des informations pour améliorer la qualité des soins, rapport au ministre de la Santé, Paris, 2003.

[FIE 09] FIESCHI M., La gouvernance de l'interopérabilité sémantique est au cœur du développement des systèmes d'information en santé, report, ministre de la Santé et des Sports, Paris, 2009.

[FLI 04] FLICHY P., "L'individualisme connecté: entre la technique numérique et la société, Nouvelles réflexions sur l'internet", *Réseaux*, vol. 22, no. 124, pp. 17–52, 2004.

[FRA 08] FRANÇOIS L. (ed.), *Intelligence territoriale, l'intelligence économique appliquée au territoire*, Tec & Doc, Lavoisier, Paris, 2008.

[FUC 98] FUCHS V.R., *Who Shall Live? Health, Economics, and Social Choice*, World Scientific, Singapore, 1998.

[GIR 04] GIRARDOT J.J., "eIntelligence territoriale et participation", *Actes Journée nationale TIC et Territoire: quels développements?*, Lille, France, May 2004.

[GLO 01] GLOUBERMAN S., MINTZBERG H., "Managing the care of health and the cure of disease", *Health Care Management Review*, vol. 26, no. 1, pp. 56–84, 2001.

[GRI 00] GRIMSON J., GRIMSON W., HASSELBRING W., "The SI challenge in health care", *Communications of the ACM*, vol. 43, no. 6, pp. 49–55, 2000.

[GRO 04] GROSJEAN M., HENRY J., BARCET A., BONAMY J., "La négociation constitutive et instituante. Les co-configurations du service en réseaux de soins", *Négociations*, vol. 2, pp. 75–90, 2004.

[IPT 04] IPTS, INSTITUT DE PROSPECTIVE TECHNOLOGIQUE, The IPTS Report. Numéro spécial: aspects de l'e-santé, no. 81, European Commission Joint Research Center, Seville, February 2004.

[LAR 08] LARCHER G., *Rapport de la commission de concertation sur les missions de l'hôpital*, La Documentation française, Paris, April 2008, available online at http://lesrapports.ladocumentationfrancaise.fr/BRP/084000209/0000.pdf.

[LAS 08] Colloque *La santé dans l'espace public*, GRESEC (Grenoble 3) – CRAPE (Rennes 1), Rennes, EHESP, 23–24 Octobre 2008.

[LEB 04] LE BOTERF G., *Travailler en réseau. Partager et capitaliser les pratiques professionnelles*, Editions d'Organisation, Paris, 2004.

[LEC 03] LE CARDINAL G., GUYONNET J.F., POUZOULLIC B., "La concertation: la clé du success", in BALANTZIAN G. (ed.), *Les systèmes d'information. Art et pratiques*, Editions d'Organisation, Paris, pp. 413–442, 2003.

[LEM 06] LE MOËNNE C., "Les communications d'entreprise entre médias, réseaux et recompositions organisationnelles", in BOUZON A. (ed.), *La communication organisationnelle en débat. Champs, concepts, perspectives*, L'Harmattan, Paris, pp. 103–121, 2006.

[LEV 82] LEVITAN K.B., "Information resource(s) management – IRM", *Annual Review of Information Science and Technology*, vol. 17, pp. 227–266, 1982.

[MAL 97] MALAVOY V., *Réseaux et Filières de soins. Mieux comprendre*, Unaformec, Paris, 1997.

[MAR 95] MARTRE H. (ed.), *Intelligence économique et stratégie des entreprises*, Commissariat Général du Plan, La Documentation française, Paris, 1995.

[MIE 04] MIÈGE B., *L'information-communication objet de connaissance*, De Boeck, Bruxelles, 2004.

[MOO 00] MOORE G.T., *Managing to do Better: General Practice in the 21st Century*, Office of Health Economics, London, 2000.

[MOR 03] MORIN E., LE MOIGNE J.L., *L'intelligence de la complexité*, L'Harmattan, Paris, 2003.

[MUC 02] MUCCHIELLI A., *Approche Systémique et Communicationnelle des Organisations*, Armand Colin, Paris, 2002.

[MUC 06] MUCCHIELLI A., "Le contexte organisationnel: essai de définition d'un concept nécessaire pour les études sur les organisations", in BOUZON A. (ed.), *La communication organisationnelle en débat. Champs, concepts, perspectives*, L'Harmattan, pp. 131–143, Paris, 2006.

[MUS 03] MUSSO P., *Critique des réseaux*, PUF, Paris, 2003.

[PEC 04] PECQUEUR B., ZIMMERMANN J.B., *Economie de proximités*, Hermès, Paris, 2004.

[PUT 09] PUTNAM L.L., NICOTERA A.M. (eds), *Building Theories of Organization. The Constitutive Role of Communication*, Routledge, New York, 2009.

[REN 08] Rencontres parlementaires sur les systèmes d'information de santé, DOOR J.-P. and LE GUEN J.-M. (chairs), *L'optimisation des systèmes d'information au cœur de la modernisation de la santé*, Paris, Maison de la Chimie, 4 Novembre 2008.

[ROS 98] ROSANVALLON P., *La nouvelle question sociale. Repenser l'Etat-providence*, Le Seuil, Paris, 1998.

[ROS 08] ROSANVALLON P., *La légitimité démocratique. Impartialité, réflexivité, proximité*, Le Seuil, Paris, 2008.

[SAI 01] SAINSAULIEU R., *Des sociétés en mouvement. La ressource des institutions intermédiaires*, Desclée de Brouwer, Paris, 2001.

[SFE 01] SFEZ L., *L'utopie de la santé parfaite*, PUF, Paris, 2001.

[SIL 03] SILBER D., "The case for eHealth", *European Commission Conference on eHealth*, Brussels, Belgium, 2003.

[SIL 05] SILBER D., "L'e-santé est-elle source d'économies?", *Les Tribunes de la santé*, no. 9, Presses de Sciences Po, Paris, pp. 75–82, 2005.

[TRO 08] TROUVELOT S., "Santé, les prix fous et les arnaques", *Capital*, vol. 206, pp. 51–55, November 2008.

[VIL 04] VILLAC M., "La "e-santé": Internet et les TIC au service de la santé", in CURIEN N., MUET P.A. (eds), *La société de l'information*, La Documentation française, Paris, pp. 277–299, 2004.

[WEN 02] WENNBERG J.E., FISHER E.S., SKINNER J.S., "Geography and the debate over medicare reform", *Health Affairs*, 2002, available online at http://content.healthaffairs.org/cgi/content/abstract/hlthaff.w2.96.

[ZAC 09] ZACKLAD M., "Les économies de la convivialité dans les sociétés de l'information et du service", *Inaugural Lecture*, CNAM, Paris, 17 June 2009.

Chapter 13

Governance and Short-Term Product Development in Clusters – An Example: The FIRE Application

13.1. Introduction

The development of clusters in France, after selection and the establishment of governance, has followed different trajectories, as shown by a recent evaluation of these clusters by an auditing company [KPM 06] (the results of this evaluation are due for publication in 2011). However, a certain number of articles and discussions have led us to think that, in certain cases, the development of clusters has led to "drifting". The appropriation of various projects by big businesses has led to a certain degree of abandonment of the primary function of clusters, which was the establishment of relationships and actions contributing to the comfort and development of small and medium industries and businesses present in clusters [DOU 06].

At the outset, the creation of clusters was supposed to lead to the development of new synergies through public–private partnerships brought about by the different players involved in the cluster: the state (or regional governments), research and education, and industry. These aspects have received attention in various publications, including the work of Michael Porter and the Dutch school (triple helix) (Figure 13.1) [LEY 98].

Chapter written by Henri Dou.

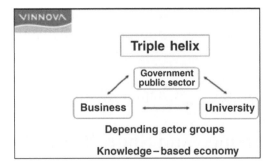

Figure 13.1. *Triple helix [INT 07]*

We should also remember that the development of clusters was intended to save time and create high-performance clusters as quickly as possible, entities which, in a normal system of development (without voluntarist state intervention), would only have reached such levels of performance in 10 or 15 years or even longer (see the examples of Sophia Antipolis in Nice, France, and Triangle Park in the United States).

Job creation, another aim of clusters, was meant to become one of the principal elements in the dashboard. In this chapter, we will use an example (the FIRE project, developed by the secure communicating solutions (SCS) cluster in Provence-Alpes-Côte d'Azur (PACA)) to highlight those points we consider to be most important in creating the conditions for shared development among actors in the cluster and among small and medium businesses and industries.

13.2. Considerations on the development of clusters

In the development of competitiveness clusters, public–private sector partnerships have developed around different research orientations, which follow the pattern set out below:

– in the majority of cases, development of generic technologies over a span of 5 years or more. In this case, most interest comes from large companies and from groups of laboratories (National Scientific Research Center (CNRS, Centre National de la Recherche Scientifique), universities, etc.). These actions are, in most cases, characterized by the purchase of heavy material. The problem in such cases is that the initial aim of the cluster, to establish a relatively rapid dynamic, is not attained;

– in the best of cases (which is, alas, rare), the aim is to develop industrially viable products in the short term, using synergy between the competences of the various actors involved in the cluster, with, if necessary, the development of rapid fundamental research to increase the industrial robustness of the product.

The latter case attracts our attention, as it illustrates how development and innovation within clusters should operate:

– The state finances research and education, facilitating the creation of knowledge and competences (first step). To stop here would be to carry out only half of the work.

– The second step consists of transforming these competences and knowledge into action, i.e. into commercial, exportable products. This step is crucial, and it should be the major concern of clusters, which, unfortunately, is far from being the case.

This definition of innovation, set out in different projects carried out on the initiative of the European Community (Interreg III) [ERI 06], highlights the importance of this approach. It must, clearly, be accompanied by fine analysis of the competences already present, an analysis which will lead to brainstorming, evaluations using strength, weaknesses, opportunities, threats (SWOT) analysis terms, etc. This prefigures the activities to be carried out by the competitive intelligence (CI) unit associated with the cluster; the CI unit must act not only in terms of CI but also in terms of technical CI (this term is preferred to that of economic intelligence in this case, as the latter term has no real meaning at international level). This last orientation is very different from traditional technological watch as it associates technical analysis with the introduction of this analysis into the development strategy. Note that the sole function of information supply, without organizing the creation of actionable knowledge, is not the aim of the CI unit [DOU 07a]. Actionable knowledge cannot be found; it must be created. This is why the stages of creation of actionable knowledge become fundamental in economic development processes, and the reason we have highlighted the importance of creating conditions for the analysis of information obtained by a CI unit (technical or otherwise) in light of competences already present in the cluster. This *modus operandi* is fundamental and renders the development of a center for the simple diffusion of information to companies in the cluster obsolete. However, this is unfortunately what happens in certain poles. The practice is born of the fact that partners in the cluster may not wish to exchange or discuss information of strategic importance to their business, the result of which has been the transformation of what should have been CI units into simple documentation centers (centers already present within the major companies of the cluster).

13.3. Grievances of small businesses and industries

Clusters were initially designed to generate contacts between varied actors: large companies (including multinationals) with small and medium businesses and industries, in addition to public and political actors. In this context, grievances have emerged, particularly from small businesses and industries:

– Too much talking and sharing too much information can lead to ideas being "captured" by entities with greater power and speed in development than that found in the small company responsible for the original idea. For this reason, information exchanges remain limited and do not go "to the bottom of things", rendering the innovative dynamic which should emerge in the cluster sterile, at least in part. In this context, we cite the example (without giving the name) of a cluster that established an information exchange platform but where, by prior accord, it is not possible to know what has been consulted and by whom in this platform, even for members of the cluster! In this simple example, we see all the difficulty of establishing a propitious climate for intercompany innovation in such conditions.

– Lack of a judicial framework for project development. Who participates, and how will profits, if profits are generated, be distributed between project actors, etc.? As an illustration, we might cite the example of an aviation technology cluster in the Lorraine region of France, where simplified joint-stock companies (*sociétés par action simplifiées*) are created for particular projects [BOU 06]. These are simple to implement and present the advantage of fixing "rules" for actors, rendering exchanges more fluid and allowing more rapid attainment of objectives. Other systems have been developed, for example, in Australia with the creation of initially fictitious entities (e.g. the distribution of one hundred "parts" among actors), with pro rata distribution of parts in relation to work carried out or to carry out (this distribution is reviewed each year). Once the product is finalized, this allows immediate passage, as far as judicial protection is concerned, to the creation of a real company for exploitation of the product. We can also cite the approach often used by businesses in the domain of initial discussions before the exchange of licenses or the creation of partnerships: non-disclosure agreements.

– The projects developed are too long term, creating, in the best of cases, generic technologies which generally will not be useable by small businesses and industries as it is far from certain that, in 5 years, the entities concerned will still be involved in the cluster, or even still be in activity.

– Big businesses have a large number of people available to participate in governance of the cluster, but these individuals remain attached to their company and are either person which are representative of the company, or which are retired from the company on "non-operational career end pathways" or are present to gain benefits for their employer from possible advances, with no guarantee of sharing the results.

– The research or R&D projects developed or presented by the majority of clusters are too complex and, in case of success, produce results too late.

13.4. The context of the SCS cluster, PACA, France

Before any detailed description of the project and before discussing the factors which allowed its development, it is interesting to know that the FIRE project is the only commercial product developed in a relatively short time span within the SCS cluster (a cluster with international ambitions) involving small industries and businesses as well as medium-sized entities.

We will now provide a brief reminder of the structure of the SCS cluster. The SCS cluster was created in the PACA region by actors including businesses, associations, and laboratories, which shared knowledge in microelectronics, software, and telecommunications. The set of key competences present in the domain was intended to lead, after market analysis, to the creation of new and innovative products. At the outset, the cluster was made up of 44 companies, 10 laboratories, and 7 associations for the promotion of technologies, often financed by regional or national government institutions.

Figure 13.2 allows us to visualize the cluster, with its two main geographical sites: the Rousset region (near Marseille), with a pronounced industrial character, and the region of Sophia Antipolis, near Nice, which has a clearer "research" character.

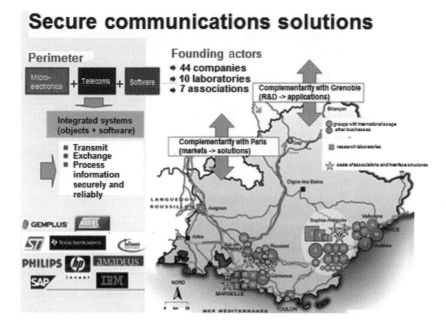

Figure 13.2. *Structure of the SCS cluster*

Modeling the cluster shows the desired effects of synergy: it allows market analysis (of what exists) then, using the set of competences present in the cluster, develops the innovation and creation of products likely to conquer international markets. We note the existence of a double mechanism: creation of competences with state assistance and then, from these competences, development and innovation of new industrial products.

Thus, the value chain of the SCS cluster may be represented as shown in Figure 13.3.

Figure 13.3. *The SCS value chain [CHA 07]*

13.5. Origins of the FIRE project

The FIRE project [GUS 09] was born of a simple idea to create an application allowing the use of multiple, relatively simple sensors at reduced cost due to mass production. The domain of this application needed to respond to a social or industrial demand in order to generate finance.

The analysis of existing products based on the knowledge of participants brought up the traditional domains of security, protection, information transfer, geographic localization, etc. The markets linked to these applications were already taken by products with which it would be hard to compete, and thus a new idea was needed. This idea emerged following unplanned brainstorming sessions and informal discussions between companies involved in sensor development. This highlights the necessity not of *a priori* valorization but of creating the right conditions for exchanges and meetings leading to the production of innovative ideas. In this way, various valorization cells developed by public organisms (research organizations or universities) have very little impact, as their practices are based on the valorization of existing attributes rather than the creation of exchange conditions promoting innovation. Following on from these discussions and after reviewing possible domains of protection and detection, an individual wondered if it would be possible to apply or create a system for protection against forest fires. In this case, note the influence of mental preconditioning: the PACA region is subject to serious forest fires in summer, producing environmental degradation and with disastrous effects on certain economic activities, particularly tourism. This preconditioning certainly played a part in the emergence of the idea.

13.5.1. *From idea to creation*

An idea to create a system to monitor forest fire using RFID captors, which emerged in the Smart Packaging Solution (SPS) Company, which then became, by consensus, the project manager, competences were sought within the cluster. This then led to the constitution of a consortium for carrying out the project, including SPSs (packaging, sensors, and low-cost industrial production), Cryptiris (development of secure RF communication systems), the Paul Cézanne University/CNRS (IM2NP laboratory) (design and optoelectronic characterization of IR sensors), the Université de Provence/CNRS (IUSTI laboratory) (fire modeling, optimization of sensor networks on-site), CEREN (experimental validation on different scales and testing (fire tunnel and smoldering)), SDIS 13 (tests, feedback on real fires), and Protection Civile 06 (institutional and operational expertise).

13.5.2. *Industrial aims of the project*

The industrial aim of the project was to create a low-cost system allowing large scale and long distance:

– transmission of alerts in prevention phase (crossing temperature, hygrometric thresholds and wind speed) and in crisis phase (fire detection);

– rapid and precise detection and localization of the source of a fire;

– prediction of the arrival of a fire in a sensitive area and anticipation of its evolution;

– continuous information provision on the intensity of the fire and its spatio-temporal evolution.

A concomitant aim was the development of a volatile organic compound (VOC) sensor in order to detect local increases in VOCs, intoxication, generalized wildfire, and signaling, using an alarm, the threshold for the lower limit of inflammability.

13.6. From design to creation and commercialization

The FIRE project is now operational. It uses general packet radio service (GPRS) transmission over a secure mobile infrastructure, geolocation using current population survey (CPS), digital terrain models, vegetation maps, calculation of average winds, and information retrieval and processing. It is presented commercially in the form of modules: a FIRE cell (20 ha) or a basic kit (<20 ha), where the density of sensors varies depending on the local fire risk.

13.6.1. General event sequence from an idea to a commercial product

In this project, it is remarkable to look back at the sources of creation of clusters. Initially, it associated small industries and companies and was born of the convergence of a set of competences present in the cluster. The complementary research projects carried out to finalize the product were of short duration, simply focusing competences already present in a university laboratory on a precise aim. The operational FIRE product is a good example of the creation of a robust and internationally exportable product with high added value. The time taken for its creation, relatively short, constitutes an ideal toward which clusters should aim. The development of base technologies linked to long-term research (of the order of 5 years) should also be part of the aims of a competence cluster, but this should be counter-balanced by the valorization of competences and knowledge toward accepted market products. This is the very definition of innovation and of the triple helix: the government finances research and training, which develops knowledge and competences, from which innovations may develop leading to the creation of internationally marketable products. In this way, a virtuous spiral is created and synergies and development created by clusters reach their full potential.

The application has been presented internationally through trade fairs or "B-to-B" contacts: Italy, Chile, Morocco, Tunisia, Greece, and the United States have all either been approached by, or have spontaneously approached, the cluster following international communications. The interest expressed by each country is clear and significant.

The project to establish a pilot in the PACA region, financed by the European fund of regional development (FEDER) and the region, should be supported by the SCS cluster and would be a determining and trigger element for the commercialization phase. The cluster would also be responsible, in the case of exemplary projects, for maintaining a technological "shop window", participating in the international outreach desired by the state.

To return to one of the aspects of the KPMG study of competitiveness clusters, the FIRE project seems exemplary in terms of its responses to the different criteria set out by KPMG. Figure 13.4, an extract from this study, presents these criteria.

The six main statements

---

1 - International strategy and competitor management are not enough mastered

- The international impact of the project generated by the poles are a key factor for the perception of the poles

- The succeed of the projects depends upon the knowledge of these markets of their size of their trend. These aspects are strategic

- If the poles did their first strategic positioning in 2005, the determination of their position on the international market is not yet a routine aspect of their functioning

- Market survey as well as the competor survey and concurrential survey are not sufficiently mastered. The advantages links to these analysis are still missing in precision

- The SWOT analysis developed in the candidature in 2005 must be reinforced at the international level and maintained

Figure 13.4. *Extract from the six main statements – KPMG analysis (http://www.kpmg.com/global/en/pages/default.aspx)*

13.7. Conclusion

It is therefore possible, if a cluster is well structured from the outset and if the actors involved meet and exchange, to create new products from existing competences requiring adjustment with limited research input. A fundamental aspect is highlighted in the KPMG study: "this (the success of the cluster) is incontestably centered on economic results: turnover, margins, and the development of new markets. Common sense!". These are the applications that create solid links between authors and indubitably constitute a base from which other shared projects may develop. The initial idea was not "captured" by a third party; it was, however, shared with each actor bringing their own competences to the creation, but, essentially, a project manager was chosen by common accord, meaning that possible returns on investment could be shared equitably between different actors. Furthermore, a company was created to commercialize the "FIRE product", leading to the creation of jobs.

Note, too, that relatively simple methodologies exist which allow us, from a set of competences, to decline these competences in already created applications, allowing us to create a basis for reflection that promotes innovation. The use of industrial property and Automatic Patent Analysis within this framework is an example of this; various works have been published in this context to describe both applications and subjacent ideas [DOU 04, DOU 07b].

It is thus clear that the operation of clusters should not focus strictly on preexisting methodologies at organizational level and the "dominant thought". These organizations must be open, leaving as much place as possible for innovation and exchange, and must also facilitate fluidity in contacts and support the ethics of exchanges and information sharing [CIW 09].

13.8. Bibliography

[BOU 06] BOURGOGNE P., The StratinC project, European Community (Intelligence and Innovative Cluster), 2006, www.competitivite.gouv.fr/spip.php?article25.

[CHA 07] CHARAI H., Presentation given in the course of an AMIE meeting, Casablanca, Morocco, 2007.

[CIW 09] CIWORLDWIDE, Various pieces of information published on the subject, June 2009, www.ciworldwide.org.

[DOU 04] DOU H., "Benchmarking R&D and companies through patent analysis using free databases and special software: a tool to improve innovative thinking", *World Patent Information*, vol. 26, no. 4, pp. 297–309, 2004.

[DOU 06] DOU H., "Competitive intelligence accelerator of cooperation", *Intelligencia Economica defensa y seguridad – Que desafíos por el siglo XXI*, Military College, Santiago du Chili, Chile, 21–22 November 2006, www.ciworldwide.org.

[DOU 07a] DOU H., "La Inteligencia Competitiva, hoy – competitive intelligence today", *Conference Internationale, Competitive Intelligence*, Carlos III University, Madrid, Spain, 28–29 November 2007, www.ciworldwide.org.

[DOU 07b] DOU H., MANULLANG S.D., DOU J.M., JR, *Competitive Intelligence and Technology Watch for Industry Development*, Department of Industry, Indonesia, 2007.

[ERI 06] ERIKSON P., Regional Center of formation and training, Guiseppe Zanardelli, Azienda speciale de la provincia de Brescia, Interreg III C, Aalborg, Denmark, 13 February 2006.

[GUS 09] GUSTINI G., FIRE project, June 2009, guy.gustini@orange.fr, www.pole-scs.org/scs_project20146.fr.htm.

[INT 07] INTERREG III, Strategic intelligence and innovative clusters – a regional policy blueprint highlighting the use of strategic intelligence in cluster policy, Interreg III C (European Community), 2007.

[KPM 06] KPMG, Poles of Competitiveness in France: promising but defects of youth to be corrected, December 2006, www.kpmg.fr/FR/Publication/Documents/Communications/EtudeKPMGPolesCompetitivite07.pdf.

[LEY 98] LEYDESDORFF L., ETZKOWITZ H., "The triple helix as a model for innovation studies (Conference Report)", *Science &* Public *Policy*, vol. 25, no. 3, pp. 195–203, 1998.

Chapter 14

Competitive Intelligence and the Development of Corporate Universities

14.1. Introduction

In light of the new entrepreneurial context, organizations must reconsider their strategies, field of action, margins for maneuver, and the means at their disposition. More than ever, this new paradigm demands an innovative vision of problems and a different perspective in order to guarantee higher levels of competitiveness. This innovative vision is intimately linked to knowledge, the ethics of knowledge, and knowledge sharing – three inseparable aspects.

Economic intelligence and competitive intelligence (CI) play a growing role within this global framework and are becoming essential instruments for business success in a highly competitive economy. It is only by anticipation of results and access to innovative strategies for the application of renewed solutions that businesses may now emerge victorious.

Work within a cooperative network, with the aim of increasing and differentiating productivity and the creation of new contracts, must be made more dynamic. Businesses working within such networks obtain benefits which increase their competitive advantage [POR 98].

Chapter written by Cláudia CAMELO, Miguel Rombert TRIGO, Luc QUONIAM, João Casqueira CARDOSO.

In this chapter, we will consider CI as a tool for decision assistance. We will also analyze the relationship between CI and corporate universities by studying the ways in which these establishments can play a role in the provision of economic impetus.

To summarize, the relationship between CI and corporate universities may take different forms. Upstream, CI is an integral part of the design and execution process. Later, it is seen as a service which a corporate university offers to businesses or other institutions.

14.2. Competitive intelligence

In its limited sense, CI is defined by many authors as a systematic process for the collection, processing, analysis, and breakdown of information on competitors. It should aim to provide information on technologies and general commercial tendencies in order to facilitate the decision-making process, helping to achieve the strategic goals of the company. In this process, the time needed for execution is of crucial importance, as, in cases of short- or medium-term work, decision making depends on a vast quantity of information.

This precise lack of time available to process an unpredictable volume of information, with selection of only that which is useful for decision making, can reasonably be seen as one of the main challenges encountered in CI.

Furthermore, we might see CI as a way of attempting to avoid brutal changes and economic or social disturbances, through anticipated knowledge of tendencies and social behaviors. In the Western world, CI is also seen as a necessity in response to what has been done in Japan, leading to the resurgence of the country [COE 00].

The concept of technological watch (systematic surveillance based on the aims of the company and the associated technologies and centers of research) first appeared in France. According to the authors cited above [COE 00], this concept, initially centered on technical aspects, developed to take on a more global form, producing the idea of economic intelligence.

This evolution led France to define CI as a national objective. Thus, the report produced by the Plan Commission [COM 94] defines CI as a set of coordinated research, processing, distribution, and protection actions concerning information of use to economic actors, obtained in a legal manner. It is intended to supply those responsible for decision processes within businesses or state bodies with the necessary knowledge for comprehension of their environment in order to adjust their individual or collective strategies [TAR 06b].

According to Coelho and Dou [COE 00], a similar process also occurred in the United States in a more aggressive form from around 1984, leading to the creation of technological CI.

As an operational system for the collection, processing, and transmission of implicit and explicit knowledge to those responsible for strategic decision making, CI must supply precise information at a precise moment in a precise form to a specific person, allowing this person to make a precise decision [QUE 06]. Thus, CI plays an important role in an increasingly competitive market, motivating decisions which often have effects on the continuity of a business.

We noted that 90% of the information needed for organizations to understand markets, gain knowledge of their competitors, and make strategic decisions is accessible in the public domain [QUE 06]. This facilitates the practice of CI, which is not a tool limited to certain users but an instrument accessible to all; Internet access is sufficient to enable the use of CI. This transversality means that any type of company or organization, however small, may use CI without unreasonable financial outlay.

Note that CI is not a simple market analysis approach. It is a process of research, focused on the environment of the organization, where important data for competitiveness are identified and lead to a determined action [ETT 95]. The larger and more dispersed the business environment, the more complex CI will be.

This learning process, motivated by competition and based on information allowing the optimization of short- and long-term strategy, is of great or even crucial importance for the success of organizations.

The world in which we live is increasingly complex; Coelho and Dou [COE 00] recognize this fact, as we have moved from a world of quasi-certainties to a much more complex system of quasi-uncertainties which must be controlled. We live in what is known as the "information society", where the Internet and all its applications and associated technologies play an increasingly active role; economic actors born of concentrations and reorganizations become more powerful than "sovereign" states. Ideologies are ceasing to exist, and the gap between rich and poor is growing. In this context, the importance of CI is becoming increasingly clear.

The growing role of CI is not limited to the fact that, faced with the current global situation, it is increasingly urgent to attempt to predict changes so that they do not excessively disturb the life of the country, the business, or the institution. The attention paid to information must therefore be permanent, as stated by Taylor [TAY 06]. If we only become aware of a modification when the first signs become apparent, it is already too late.

CI certainly goes further; in the context of globalization, CI has been used to find responses to problems presented by the organizational and information context, by making it possible to optimize the internal operation of the various services of the organization, offering solutions to develop decision making [QUE 06].

At a time when information production seems unlimited and its diffusion is increasingly simple and instantaneous, it is important to assist companies investing in new technologies to create more wealth than more traditional structures. The mechanisms found for the processing of produced information then become essential in assisting in the practice of CI.

As Coelho and Dou stated [COE 00], mankind owes its wealth to new technologies and to the creation of knowledge, and no longer to crude oil alone. They added that businesses must, in order to truly become stronger, take a gamble on processes for internal knowledge creation and not just apply management practices in the strictest sense of the term.

Knowledge is different from any other resource in that it is constantly obsolete; knowledge considered to be advanced today will be outdated tomorrow. Knowledge production is not the sole factor involved in global economic competition, but it is the deciding factor.

All the tools made available by the Internet contribute to the diversification of products and services on offer, with a significant effect on the *modus operandi* of companies. Nowadays, communication is no longer simply the process of transmission from one entity to another. With information coming from various sources and circulating in different directions, communication has been transformed into a sort of collective intelligence.

Information, knowledge, and intelligence are, moreover, distinct concepts. Information is transformed into knowledge only when processed by a user. Intelligence appears as a set of knowledge. Thus, information cannot become knowledge without being used. Additionally, no element of knowledge can be called intelligence without the association of other knowledge [BAT 05, IDE 08].

Moving away from the circulation of information between two entities, we now observe the development of a circuit between one entity and n others, increasing efficiency in knowledge sharing through communication. The Internet plays an essential role in this development. Web 2.0 has added a new way of developing this communication process and of sharing knowledge, enlarging the information circuit by transforming it into a circuit between n entities and n entities. The preexisting linear action thus gives way to a cycle of information sharing between all actors involved: the senders and the receivers of information.

It is also interesting to consider the opinions expressed by Fuld [FUL 06], who believes that information has a tendency to repeat itself, meaning that, if organizations succeed in creating an information memory, through the constant collection of information relevant to their sector, it is possible to facilitate the decision-making process.

For a company, knowledge must go beyond technological knowledge or technical knowledge of processes, in that the analysis and comprehension of the environment in which the business operates should constitute its main aim. It is, indeed, essential to be aware of the internal and external environment simultaneously [COE 00].

Thus, by possessing knowledge of all interactions, a business may gradually develop a global supraintelligence which can be used to successfully analyze situations and act more efficiently.

The response to all these new demands comes through the creation of CI systems. Companies must develop ways of obtaining the strategic information needed for decision-making processes, either through training or through the implementation of new working practices.

The methods used are based on a strategy for the collection of information, followed by an information management phase designed to allow experts to work collectively on the information, in accordance with a shared vision of the future of the company [COE 00].

As Kotler [KOT 00] reports, faced with current competitive markets, it is no longer enough to understand clients. Companies must now pay much more attention to their competitors. Successful businesses have been developed by using intelligence systems to obtain continuous information on their competitors.

No organization can ignore the existence of the strategies of their competitors without running the risk of failing to obtain good products from their intelligence activities, weakening strategy and leading to bad decisions [FUL 06].

CI operations also need to concentrate on consumers and suppliers as, by satisfying their needs, it becomes possible to control the market and, consequently, competitors. The intelligence process then appears relatively simple, involving observation from our intelligence perspective, paying attention to the teaching of management and to signs, and attempting to obtain information directly from its source [FUL 06].

By introducing a CI process, the organization creates, in an environment of uncertainty, a mechanism able to reduce the element of surprise present in markets. This allows decision makers to question the "absolute truths" which they previously believed without hesitation. By being able to satisfy and fulfill needs and by contributing to the existence of users with a greater awareness of their own role, we create durable market advantages [TOM 03].

According to Tomé [TOM 03], CI should be seen as a process able to produce an action, predicting market developments which may, in one way or another, have an impact on the activity of the business. In this way, CI constitutes a value creation process for businesses and leads to strategic reflection and processes. CI contributes to decision making by focusing this strategic reflection and process on priority needs, posing critical questions, and identifying the best course of action to take.

Organizations must become visionary so that, with the capacity for anticipation, they may succeed in identifying transformations requiring action – for example, by identifying future or emerging markets [FUL 06]. This question is accompanied by a preoccupation concerning the creation of a clear distinction between CI and monitoring systems which often exist but concern only the analysis of existing competition and the threats and opportunities it represents.

14.3. Corporate universities

Corporate universities are a support structure for the practice of corporate education within a company. They provide a set of strategic learning solutions applicable to the essential competences of organizations [PER 03].

Company-based education allows the development of a set of actions which aim to broaden knowledge and competences adapted to the strategic interests of the organization and, consequently, suitable for the development of its competitive potential [MAR 05]. Thus, in addition to the fact of promoting the qualification of the human resources of the company, company-based education promotes "[...] the development and establishment of business and human competences, seen as critical for the viabilization of commercial strategies" [EBO 04].

The creation of corporate universities is only meaningful if it is effectively linked to an overriding economic strategy. We must remember the essential character of results and of periodic evaluation of the objectives initially defined for each action. This allows us not only to check whether strategic goals are really being implemented but also to identify possible needs for reformulation of the plan being followed, permitting continual improvement of processes.

A corporate university may have various characteristics, which vary between countries and between organizations. These characteristics, as set out by Pereira [PER 03], are as follows:

– proactiveness;

– centralized organization;

– targeting of specific sectors;

– a desire to deepen forms of actions;

– growing use of new technologies;

– essentially strategic objectives;

– an entrepreneurial perspective linking commercial development and continued training;

– aims integrating the strategy of a specific organization;

– those responsible for the organization are the managers and instructors involved in the teaching process;

– aims involving the creation and democratization of knowledge and encouragement of organizational learning;

– operation as a business center;

– the target public is made up of workers, clients, suppliers, and the community as a whole;

– the teaching body is constituted of internal executives and experts and external lecturers and consultants;

– increasing the social responsibility of the company.

By implementing company-based learning, corporate universities establish themselves as educational establishments with a strategic function: they aim to assist their partner organization in the attainment of a mission and in carrying out activities which create a culture of knowledge, at both individual and collective level [ALL 02].

From a historical viewpoint, corporate universities appear as the result of an evolution of training activities promoted by human resources departments. Initially, their main aim, "... in the United States, was employee training, seeking the improvement of professional competences and excellence in their activity within the company (development of expertise)" [TAR 06b]. In this respect, corporate universities have proven to be the best way for companies to instruct their employees and guarantee competitiveness in markets.

Meister [MEI 98] indicated that corporate universities are the sector in which the increase in offer in higher education is largest and highlighted the following particular aspects, which he considers to be essential to the success of a corporate university:

– unite aims of training development with the strategic needs of organizations;

– implicate decision makers, students, and teachers;

– choose an executive to be responsible for institutional training – known as a Chief Learning Officer;

– consider employee training as a strategic and continuous process and not as an isolated phenomenon;

– link employee salaries to learning;

– extend the reach of the corporate university beyond training employees of the company. Training may also apply to clients and to the supply chain:

– pilot the corporate university as a business center within the company;

– develop a series of new, innovative alliances or partnerships with the higher education sector;

– demonstrate the value of the teaching infrastructure of the corporate university;

– develop the corporate university as an instrument for obtaining competitive commercial advantages and as a business center.

According to Martins [MAR 05], the factors that explain the exponential increase in corporate universities are as follows:

– increased competition for market positions at national and international level;

– increased demand for training and professional qualifications on the part of the workforce;

– awareness of the need to improve the image of organizations, both for the outside public and within the organization;

– a vital need to develop, diffuse, and perpetuate relevant knowledge for the essential competences of the organization.

The greatest concentration of creations of corporate universities took place in the United States in the 1980s. Since 1988, there were around 400 such institutions in the United States; 10 years later, there were around 1,200 and 1,600 in the 2000s. Corporate universities have never been as present in Europe as in the United States; in 2001, there were around 100, mostly in France, where there were around 30 [TAR 06a].

Over the last 15 years, the number and visibility of corporate universities has increased considerably. During this period, the number of conferences, consultations, and publications on teaching practices in businesses and associated subjects has undergone continuous growth. Nevertheless, company-based teaching is not the exclusive domain of corporate universities; this is, indeed, far from being the case. A significant number of companies, particularly large businesses, have invested considerable amounts in this kind of initiative, at business level, and these units are not specifically listed as corporate universities. Others, on the other hand, use the term when in reality they only offer training and development through departments of units focused exclusively on trade [PAT 09].

In the majority of cases, corporate universities emerge within and on the initiative of companies or institutions, with the mission of carrying out educative actions in order to promote individual and collective development. This aspect essentially summarizes the history of corporate universities throughout 30 years in which they have been active. Examples of corporate universities include the General Electric Corporate University [GEC 09] and those of the Bank of Brazil [UNI 09d], the Petrobras University [UNI 09c], the Motorola University [MOT 09], the UCUF [UNI 09a], and others.

In 2007, Fernando Pessoa University (UFP), a Portuguese higher education institution, after implementing CI actions internally, decided to advance toward previously unseen perspectives of a national-level implementation of a corporate university, affirming that, following its conception, "[...] a corporate education program will always begin with the existence of a partnership between Fernando Pessoa University and an organization (company, state, community, association representing a sector, etc.) which is convinced of the importance of qualification for its employees as a way of gaining in competitiveness" [EDU 09].

This association, aside from the fact from being able to link practical knowledge with knowledge obtained through university research, guarantees that educational programs will be geared toward practical operations. These programs follow the three main axes of company-based education:

– in-depth knowledge of the organization (culture, values, traditions, and vision);

– analysis of the environment surrounding the organization (contracts, clients, competitors, tendencies, and best practice of other organizations);

– the acquisition of basic competences linked to organizational and individual competitiveness (learning to learn, effective communication, collaboration, creativity and problem solving, reading competence, information technologies).

The practical result of this work was the appearance of the first Portuguese corporate university, the CEVAL business university, establishing a partnership between Fernando Pessoa University and the chamber of commerce of the Vales do Lima e Minho region, created in January 2007 [UNI 09b].

The UFP's work in company-based education did not stop there, and in November 2008, the UFP Academy, a corporate university specific to the UFP, was created [ACA 09a], dedicated to the qualification of current and former employees and students and to the development of organizational competences.

At a time when competitiveness and innovation are essential elements for the survival of organizations, it is important to develop capacities for learning, especially to create new knowledge. As Tarapanoff [TAR 06a] indicates, for this to occur, organizations and their employees must learn to become organizations with a focus on learning.

We consider that the interest in company-based education is naturally connected to the major changes currently underway in the geography of production and consumption linked to the value of knowledge in post-industrial societies [FER 06].

In parallel with the development of corporate universities, four factors emerged which have had an effect on the economic world, education, and society as a whole [PAT 05]:

– the appearance of an economy of knowledge and training organizations;

– the rapidity and frequency of restructuring in companies, leading entrepreneurs to center their action on shared principles and practices;

– the constant and developing presence of ICT (information and communication technology) and its application in training and development;

– the growing diversification of education systems, replacing models centered on training plans by models centered on functions, models centered on a campus by diffused learning systems, and the standardized path of knowledge progression by multiple access routes to knowledge.

The phenomenon of corporate universities is situated at the center of these four important factors in the current economy.

14.4. The role of CI in the creation of corporate universities

For company-based education to become an effective instrument for competition and excellence, a company must first prepare the ground to welcome it. Second, this preparation makes use of the existence of a flexible and adaptable organizational structure, combined with a business culture centered on personal evaluation and investment in training. Third, it passes through the use of CI to try and predict the future and guarantee innovative change to the project, becoming the necessary means for attainment of the final aim: the creation of a corporate university. It is only then that management may progress in a sure and credible manner, reducing the part played by uncertainty in future strategic decisions.

Fuld [FUL 09] describes the CI process as shown in Figure 14.1.

Figure 14.1. *CI process*

In the planning phase, we identify questions that guide the collection process. When dealing with public information, we check that the information source is sufficiently large to enable attainment of predefined objectives. Next, we collect primary sources, including data often extracted from direct contact with individuals. The analysis and production phase aims to convert retrieved data into relevant information. Finally, we proceed to the creation and diffusion of reports. These reports should produce critical intelligence in a format corresponding to the needs of the decision maker.

These steps may lead to the implementation – or avoidance of the implementation – of a CI process with a view to creating a corporate university. One thing is certain: on reaching the final stage of report production, the decision maker must be able to suggest different options based on various anticipated possible scenarios.

Thus, through the use of CI techniques, organizations will be able to predict contract opportunities, possible constraints, and strategies, allowing them to remain a step ahead of their competitors and become more competitive. CI thus accords a fundamental role to the sustainable development of a company education project, while also reducing the degree of uncertainty of directors in decision making.

14.5. Corporate universities and potential domains of action

The sectors of activity of corporate universities vary from one organization to another. There is no standard model for a corporate university; models are created according to need and based on the strategic aims of the founding entity. These models are also influenced by the economic and financial situation of the surrounding organization or country. The analysis of internal and external context is, in this respect, one of the main aspects to consider when designing a corporate university. This analysis must cover not only consumers and suppliers but also competitors.

In this phase of design and choice of the most suitable model for a corporate university, CI plays an extremely important role. CI contributes to the processing of information produced during the analysis of the surrounding environment, identifying constraints and appropriate solutions for each situation, allowing the avoidance of sudden changes through forward planning.

Rowley *et al.* [ROW 98] presented the first corporate universities as education centers, created internally, within companies responsible for continuous education and training. Their initial intentions were as follows:

– To provide employees with the ability to work with new techniques and updated practices.

– To develop a suitably trained and prepared workforce, which will necessarily give the company a competitive advantage.

– To change the first education centers and adopt structures similar to those of higher education institutions.

There are now various corporate universities throughout the world which assist their parent companies in developing a base of collaborators with access to strategic information. This allows the company to remain competitive.

Over the years, corporate universities have progressively taken on other roles, enlarging their sphere of action. Currently, corporate universities are developing around three main possible axes:

– in-depth knowledge of the organization (culture, values, traditions, and vision);

– analysis of the environment of the organization (business, clients, competitors, tendencies, and best practices of other organizations);

– basic competences for organizational and individual competitiveness (research preparation, effective communication, collaboration, creativity, problem solving, reading competences, and information technologies).

Based on these three axes, the corporate university divides its activity into different projects and activities, whether in training or in simple organizational improvements. The Accor Latin America Academy [ACA 09b] is an example illustrating this type of actions.

Another way of working consists of creating strong associations between corporate education and the management of people and competences, dividing the actions of the corporate university into three main operational programs, each oriented toward the three phases of the relationship between an individual and a company or institution: recruitment, development, and departure. The operational welcome program aims to integrate individuals into the business through various welcoming actions destined for target publics. The operational development program is devoted to relations between the company, its employees, and external partners. This program may have aims ranging from performance management to updating and developing knowledge through lifelong training, to promoting the enrichment of the organizational culture, and to the preparation for change processes, among other aspects. The organizational program for departure aims to accompany those leaving the company or institution, using various mechanisms to discover the reasons for this departure and seeking occasions for new relations in the future. The idea that predominates in this case is not to limit interaction to the last moment of contact with the institution but to maintain points for resuming contact. The UFP Academy [ACA 09a] is one example of a corporate university based on this strategy of action.

We would do well to remember that there is no preformatted model for a corporate university, and each must adapt to the real needs of the founding entity, independently of the form in which it distributes its sectors of action, the names it gives to its programs, the lessons it gives, and the individuals it involves in its work. The quality of the model of the corporate university is measured not by its form but by the results achieved and associated success stories.

By analyzing the theoretical propositions of these initiatives and their respective activities, we conclude that the corporate university tag refers, finally, to a new generation of strategic teaching initiatives [PAT 09]. This new generation of initiatives is as valuable as its impact on the individual and collective development of those involved, i.e. the sustainable development of organizations.

14.6. Integrated CI services in corporate universities

The actions of corporate universities are inevitably linked to the training and development of human resources, but are not completely identical to these tasks. The corporate university also presupposes a role in integrating different sectors of the company, through the implementation of transversal projects, such as policies for welcoming and integrating new employees. This policy may be extended to welcoming suppliers, clients, or partners, with the constant aim of creating an immense network of multifunctional contacts to concretize the position of the company in the relevant market.

In company-based learning, CI may presuppose a perspective of provision of services to the mother company. These services are structured in different ways: either on the initiative of the corporate university itself through diagnosis of sectors where CI might support decision making, or at the request of managers who, at moments of strategic decision making, may use CI services to predict actions and decisions which would put the company in an advantageous situation.

How, then, can CI services be applied in a corporate university?

In our opinion, we must begin by raising awareness of the importance of such services among managers, by demonstrating the ways in which CI allows users to preempt the plans of the competition. An engagement of this kind should focus on the potential effects of the practice of CI, demonstrating its effectiveness through the construction of a pilot project.

The employees of the organization must also be made aware of the importance of CI and be supplied with tools to allow them to play an active part in its implementation, practicing CI on a daily basis in the course of their work. As Fuld [FUL 06] reminds us, CI *can* be taught, and all members of an organization may therefore put it to practical use to improve results.

One form of action would be to create small-scale CI training courses. As an alternative, or in addition, we might include more occasional and specific training actions in the course of sectorial actions, for example a "CI hour". This would be made easier by the fact that CI is a completely transversal subject which complements other subjects. Initiatives of this kind might result in the implementation of small CI projects in the context of the day-to-day work of personnel, allowing employees to gain understanding of the use of this tool.

After carrying out engagement and awareness tasks, we must define general aims for the CI project and a timeline for its implementation. Of course, these aims will always require organizational supervision, in direct association with the strategic aims of the company.

A project group must then be set up, based on a multicompetent team created to respond to the needs of the specific project. This group does not need to be particularly large: three to five elements suffice. It must, however, be sufficiently diversified to cover different perspectives of the same reality, thus enriching the results produced. The group must operate with sufficient autonomy to manage its own work and suggest actions and must have access to sufficient human and material resources and a calendar of actions.

Based on the predefined general objectives, the project group will be responsible for the definition of specific aims and the implementation of the CI process in its different phases.

After carrying out CI work, the group must report on a proposed plan of action. This report will act as a support for the decision to be made.

Once a decision has been made based on the CI work carried out, the results must be evaluated in order to identify the real effects of the CI procedure behind the decision. This evaluation of results may lead to a redefinition of the initial general aims, entering into a new project cycle where each phase will be repeated and reevaluated at the end of the process.

Figure 14.2 summarizes the possible phases of application of CI services in a corporate university.

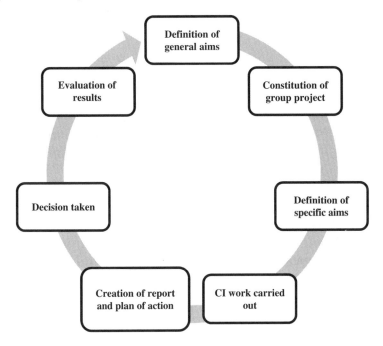

Figure 14.2. *CI services in a corporate university*

CI services attempt to provide a response to various questions [TOM 03], such as:

– What are the characteristics of the sector in which the organization operates?

– Who are, or who might be, its competitors?

– What are the strengths and weaknesses of these competitors?

– What are the likely tactics of these competitors?

– What anticipated action should the organization take in relation to the predicted tactics of its competitors?

14.7. Conclusion

We live in a world with an increasingly global and competitive economy where only the most attentive can survive. This kind of scenario does not allow us to continue using conservative action strategies, insufficiently open to new action mechanisms. Information and knowledge are produced at incredible speed, demanding increased perspicacity.

CI is an essential analytical tool when confronted with today's economic challenges, used with the aim of maintaining the economic competitiveness of businesses and of society as a whole. We are faced with a world dominated by the power of information, where strategic information management, using CI, has become not only essential for the survival and development of human societies, but also a specific issue for the maintenance of power and independence by states [JUI 09].

In our opinion, corporate universities could have a deciding role in the reinforcement, diffusion, and use of CI practices in operations, in that they are able to implement actions relating to awareness and engagement on the part of managers and collaborators, acting as a catalyst for the individual and collective development of all employees of an organization, teaching them to look beyond the small, closed world of their daily activities and to find new action mechanisms. It is only in this way that it will be possible to maintain an active organization through a constant learning process.

In summary, we can say that there is a common denominator between CI practices and the actions of corporate universities: innovation. With the presence of this shared element, both play a key role in the takeoff of societies and institutions. We can only hope that CI and corporate universities will work together to further these aims.

14.8. Bibliography

[ACA 09a] ACADEMIA UFP, Universidade Fernando Pessoa, February 2009, www.ufp.pt.

[ACA 09b] ACADÉMIE ACCOR LATIN AMERICA, February 2009, http://academie.accorbrasil. com.br/.

[ALL 02] ALLEN M., *Corporate University Handbook: Designing, Managing, and Growing a Successful Program*, Amacon, New York, 2002.

[BAT 05] BATES M.J., "Information and knowledge: an evolutionary framework for information science", *Information Research*, vol. 10, no. 4, p. 239, 2005.

[COE 00] COELHO G.M., DOU H., "Inteligência competitiva e a formação de recursos humanos no Brasil", *Revista de Biblioteconomia de Brasília*, vol. 23/24, no. 4, pp. 455–472, 2000.

[COM 94] COMMISSARIAT GÉNÉRAL AU PLAN, Intelligence économique et Stratégique des Entreprises, report of a workgroup led by MARTRE H., La Documentation Française, Paris, 1994.

[EBO 04] EBOLI M., "Educação Corporativa", *Revista T&D – Inteligência Corporativa*, vol. 137, no. 12, p. 48, November 2004.

[EDU 09] EDUCAÇÃO CORPORATIVA, Universidade Fernando Pessoa, February 2009, www.ufp.pt.

[ETT 95] ETTORE B., "Managing competitive intelligence", *Management Review*, vol. 84, no. 10, pp. 15–19, 1995.

[FER 06] FERREIRA J.R., BENETTI G., "O futuro da indústria: educação corporativa – reflexões e práticas: coletânea de artigos", *MDIC/STI: IEL*, Brasília, Brazil, p. 213, 2006.

[FUL 06] FULD L.M., *The Secret Language of Competitive Intelligence: How to See Through and Stay Ahead of Business Disruptions, Distortions, Rumors, and Smoke Screens*, Crown Business, New York, p. 309, 2006.

[FUL 09] FULD L.M., Fuld & Company – The global leader in competitive intelligence, February 2009, www.fuld.com/.

[GEC 09] GE CORPORATE UNIVERSITY, February 2009, www.ge.com/careers/life_at_ge/index.html.

[IDE 08] IDEHEN K.U., "The difference between information and knowledge", *Kingsley Idehen's Blog Data Space*, November 2008, www.openlinksw.com/blog/~kidehen/index.vspx?id=650.

[JUI 09] JUILLET A., El concepto y el dispositivo publico de la inteligencia economía, February 2009, www.intelligence-economique.gouv.fr/.

[KOT 00] KOTLER P., *Administração de Marketing*, Prentice Hall, São Paulo, 2000, www.netsaber.com.br/resumos/ver_resumo_c_3015.html.

[MAR 05] MARTINS H.G., "Para Aonde Vai a Universidade Corporativa? Notas Para Uma Agenda da Educação Corporativa Brasileira", *O Futuro da Indústria: Educação Corporativa: Coletânea de Artigos, MDIC/STI: IEL/NC*, Brasilia, Brazil, p. 192, 2005.

[MEI 98] MEISTER J., *Corporate Universities: Lessons in Building a World Class Workforce*, McGraw Hill, New York, 1998.

298 Competitive Intelligence and Decision Problems

[MOT 09] MOTOROLA, Motorola University, February 2009, http://intrarts.com/Motorola/index.shtml.

[PAT 05] PATON R., PETERS G., STOREY J., TAYLOR S., *Handbook of Corporate University Development*, Gower Publishing, London, p. 285, 2005.

[PAT 09] PATON R., PETERS G., QUINTAS P., Estratégia de educação corporativa: universidades corporativas na prática, February 2009, http://www.educor. desenvolvimento.gov.br/public/arquivo/arq1229431109.pdf.

[PER 03] PEREIRA C.S., "Educação Corporativa na Era do Conhecimentoé", *Gestão de empresas na era do conhecimento*, Edições Sílabo, Lisbon, vol. 1, p. 551, 2003.

[POR 98] PORTER M., "Clusters and the new economics competitions", *Harvard Business Review*, pp. 77–90, November/December 1998.

[QUE 06] QUEYRAS J., QUONIAM L., "Inteligência Competitiva", *Inteligência, Informação e Conhecimento*, IBICT/UNESCO, Brasília, Brazil, p. 456, 2006.

[ROW 98] ROWLEY D.J., LUJAN H.D., DOLENCE M., *Strategic Choices for the Academy: How Demand for Lifelong Learning Will Re-Create Higher Education*, Jossey-Bass, San Francisco, p. 309, 1998.

[TAR 06a] TARAPANOFF K., *Inteligência, Informação e Conhecimento*, IBICT/UNESCO, São Paulo, Brazil, 2006.

[TAR 06b] TARAPANOFF K., FEREEIRA J.R., "Aprendizado Organizacional: Panorama da Educação Corporativa no Contexto Internacional", *Inteligência, Informação e Conhecimento*, IBICT/UNESCO, Brasília, Brazil, p. 456, 2006.

[TAY 06] TAYLOR J., "Leonard Fuld interview with Jeff Taylor. Factiva CI Center, 2001", *The Secret Language of Competitive Intelligence*, Crown Business, New York, p. 309, 2006.

[TOM 03] TOMÉ F., "A Inteligência nos Negócios", *Gestão de empresas na era do conhecimento*, Edições Sílabo, Lisbon, vol. 1, p. 551, 2003.

[UNI 09a] ÚNION FENOSA – UNIVERSIDAD CORPORATIVA, February 2009, www. unionfenosa.es/webuf/wcm/connect/ufwebcontenidos/WebUF/Conocenos/RecursosHuma nos/UniversidadCorporativaUCUF/.

[UNI 09b] UNIVERSIDADE CORPORATIVA CEVAL, Conselho Empresarial dos Vales do Lima e Minho, February 2009, http://www.ceval.pt/userfiles/files/publicacoes%20ceval/24813.pdf.

[UNI 09c] UNIVERSIDADE PETROBRÁS, February 2009, www2.petrobras.com.br/Petrobras/portugues/empregos/emp_gestao_index.htm.

[UNI 09d] UNIVERSIDADE CORPORATIVA DO BANCO DO BRASIL, February 2009, www44.bb.com.br/appbb/portal/bb/unv/index.jsp.

Chapter 15

Emerging Functions for Driving Competitive Intelligence at Regional Level

According to Gonnot [GON 94], competitive intelligence (CI) offers a new way for the state to act in relation to businesses and offers new perspectives for the definition of development strategies of industries and service businesses. Consisting of research, the use and the protection of economic information, "CI aims to establish a new 'partnership' between the State and businesses, a partnership made possible by breaking down barriers to the circulation of information". This initiative is linked to the defense of national interests: "for the State, support for economic information is also an aspect of the defense of national interests, while preserving the principles of a liberal economy open to outside competition". To assist and to structure this partnership between state and businesses, CI structures have been established little by little in France, beginning in the period 1997–2000. Clerc and Pautrat define CI structures as follows: "a national competitive intelligence structure is conceived as a combination of practices and knowledge for the production and interpretation of knowledge, developed at national level with the participation of different institutions (the State, administrations, businesses, universities, networks of chambers of commerce, professional unions, etc.). A structure of this kind is distinguished by three aims:

– to develop specific and specialized teaching to increase collective capacities for the interpretation and comprehension of environments. Organizations uniting members of professions linked to competitive intelligence (watchers, coordinators,

Chapter written by Audrey KNAUF.

analysts, marketing experts etc.) play a role in the diffusion and maintenance of knowledge;

– to produce knowledge suited to the issues of globalization and useful in fine-tuning individual or collective strategies (between the State and businesses, or between different businesses, for example);

– to implement influence actions supporting these strategies, based on the promotion of the national cultural, economic and political model" [CLE 99].

One key issue in each of these approaches is that of collective efficiency which must be created and reinforced not only through suitable and innovative governance and management but also through the establishment of innovative and robust organizations, processes, methods, technologies, and tools. Anticipation and rapid action in a context where time is of essence, mastery of complexity, the evaluation and deepening of knowledge, pooling resources and contents, accelerating innovation, accelerating individual learning, and optimization of watch are all conditions that, with others, constitute a basis for the success of clusters and regional CI apparatus. Whether in small, medium, or large businesses, universities, or territorial institutions concerned with reinforcing competitiveness and attractiveness, identity, cohesion and social links, context and shared reference points, and trust become essential "activators" for the flow of knowledge, the source of innovation, and the value creation. These values must respond to issues of delocalization of companies, the globalization of markets, reduction in industry and the opening and extension (release) of Europe, factors which raise questions for public authorities concerned with French industry, its visibility in global markets, its competitiveness and durability, and the attractiveness of the territory. One of the essential aims of the establishment of such systems is to render an attractive territory.

In this chapter, we provide a definition for these structures, which we limit to regional structures for CI (*dispositifs régionaux d'intelligence économique*, DRIE) and competitiveness clusters. These are systems that lead to networking of competences and knowledge as much as resources, promoting innovation and value creation in the context of a growing global "economy of knowledge". We have studied these entities through the means of a national survey carried out between 2005 and 2008. Based on our results and on-the-ground observations, we propose a definition of a new profession useful for piloting CI structures: that of coordinator.

15.1. Regional systems for CI

Among the organizations we consider as being CI structures, we find the DRIE. These have the particularity of facilitating exchanges of knowledge and competences (theoretical and practical knowledge) in a given territory, between public and private sector actors. CI is not exclusively used by large groups as a means of organizing their economic defense. It should be within reach of all companies participating in the creation of national wealth and the maintenance and creation of jobs. One of the strong points of the coordinator, the actor necessary for the implementation of this kind of structure, is to act as a relay point between these two entities (public/private) and to create not just a shared vocabulary, but a climate of trust. Among the responsibilities attached to this post, we find the protection of knowledge, the anticipation of relevant markets, the defense of interests, etc.

15.1.1. *History*

In the 1994 Plan report, H. Martre already spoke of CI structures: "Businesses are now forced to adjust their strategies based on a new reading grid, taking into account the growing complexity of the realities of competition on different global, national and local stages. The effectiveness of such an approach is based on the use of competitive intelligence systems, which institute strategic information management as a major lever serving economic performance and employment".

In March 1995, R. Pautrat sent a letter to a number of prefects in the Midi-Pyrénées and Rhône-Alpes regions of France to inform them of the Prime Minister's agreement to the constitution "of an effective CI structure", continuing the work begun by the Plan Commission, and to announce the forthcoming launch of pilot operations. He requested that they welcome Philippe Caduc and Philippe Clerc[1] who were to present projects and experiments to launch in their regions and *départements* (counties). These projects were "based on actions to raise awareness of competitive intelligence in businesses, training in management of networks and information streams, influence strategies and technological watch". These initiatives applied propositions for a single access point, necessary for the company, and the development of collaborative CI platforms.

Regional CI programs were then launched from 1997. The intention was no longer to bring together central administrations, national politicians, and representatives of large companies, but to unite regional actors involved in economic development and the diffusion of public information linked with the company: devolved state services, services linked to territorial collectives, universities, engineering schools or research centers, professional syndicates and employers' unions, technopoles, regional associations, and some well-installed businesses.

---

1 Project executive on the Plan Commission within the workgroup presided by Henri Martre before being placed at the SGDN then, in 1997, responsible for working with the prefect of the Basse-Normandie *département* to implement one of the first regional CI systems.

Among these regional actors, chambers of commerce and industry are placed in a central position as their status[2] and position within regions gives them a ready-made role as intermediaries between businesses and public powers. Thus, following the first *Assises* organized in the Basse-Normandie region, other regions followed suit. The Centre region launched its regional program[3] during *Assises* held at Tours on October 23, 1998 and the Franche-Comté region [WER 99] launched a similar program on March 12, 1999 in Besançon. CI thus made its entry into state-region planning contracts (CPER).

Six years later, in his report (p. 90), [CAR 03] stated that: "in state-region planning contracts from 2000 to 2006, almost all of the chapters concerning economic development and attractiveness express the intention, more or less clearly defined, to make use of competitive intelligence structures.

The competitive intelligence measures set out in the CPERs correspond, for certain regions, to the pursuit of programs already begun under the previous contract. This was notably the case for the Basse-Normandie and Centre regions. For the majority, however, these programs or actions were either partly or completely new. The most widely envisaged concrete interventions involved awareness, training and advice seminars, and the implementation of collective competitive, technological and regulatory watch actions. Just over half of the CPERs considered make more or less explicit reference to these two types of action. On the other hand, fewer contracts included strategic watch approaches aimed at an increase in the added value of the territory. In this respect, the CPER of the Lorraine region represents one of the most successful examples of a territorial valorization approach".[4]

---

2 Their status and missions are defined in a law of April 3, 1898 *relating to chambers of commerce and consultation chambers of arts and manufacturing*. They are public establishments with an administrative character. These institutions have a dual inter-professional role, both representative and consultative in relation to public powers. They also participate in the socioeconomic development of their area (teaching, information, creation, development, and management of public and commercial establishments). See NOUVION A.P., *L'Institution des chambres de commerce, pouvoirs et contrepoids*, Bibliothèque des sciences administratives, LGDJ, Paris, pp. 1–23, 1992.

3 Regional prefecture, Conseil régional du Centre, Secrétariat général aux affaires régionales, DRIRE, DRCE, CRCI, ANVAR, Trésorerie générale de la région Centre, Centre Tech, DRRT, DST, University of Orléans. The European Commission participated financially. See *Intelligence économique en région Centre. Orientations pour un plan d'action régional*, CRCI Centre, October 1998.

4 Source: DATAR, March 2000.

Other initiatives based on the same model have been developed at European level. This is the case with STRATegic Intelligence and Innovative Clusters (STRATINC), a European project carried out within the framework of the INTERREG IIIC program (2003–2006), which aimed to boost the competitiveness of territories, local businesses, and industrial clusters by reinforcing strategic intelligence and prospecting, allowing them to manage innovation and face the challenges of globalization.

Thus, the CI approach, now led by the state, would doubtless not have taken concrete form without the action carried out over several years by "pioneers" who promoted the diffusion of CI practices within businesses and the creation of CI structures on the initiative of prefectures of pilot regions such as Basse-Normandie, the Nord-Pas-de-Calais, or Lorraine. In this, conciliar and professional networks played a central and historical role by their participation in the implementation of territorial intelligence approaches in these pilot regions, comprising aspects such as economic security, the protection of industrial knowledge and assets, and support to the competitive potential of host companies and territories.

15.1.2. *Definition of regional systems for CI*

Starting out as a national approach, CI necessarily extends to operational approaches at regional level. Business prosperity does not only concern large groups but also concern – and especially – small and medium businesses and industries that make up a major part of the economic fabric of France. The primary aim and vocation of CI are therefore to promote local development, ensuring the relevance of territorial intelligence.

These approaches and structures have several aims: to produce and share knowledge among the socioeconomic actors of a territory, to protect knowledge, and to create networks linking not only private sector decision makers but also, and especially, between private and public sector actors. This comes down to improving understanding between the two entities, with mutual enrichment through sharing experiences, working together, and pooling competences to increase the potential attractiveness and competitiveness of their region. In this way, these structures and approaches promote a new model for regional economic development, providing the region with means of anticipation which give local decision makers the capacity to develop new activities, thus creating jobs and wealth for the area.

Regional structures, placed under the responsibility of prefects, have two main orientations:

– competition: anticipation and accompaniment of economic transformations;

– economic security: concerns the management of scientific and technological assets and the identification and treatment of threats to businesses.

The approach taken is as follows:

– definition of a strategic perimeter at regional level, or in other terms, establish or update a map of businesses concerned;

– provide training in, and raise awareness of, CI: train individuals in competition issues, knowledge sharing and asset protection, directing decision makers toward competent structures in each of the given domains;

– establish state–business networks and networks between businesses to improve the circulation of useful information among economic actors.

15.1.3. *System actors*

Most state service provision at regional and departmental level is carried out in direct connection with businesses, and in this way, it plays a relevant role in the territorial application of CI: SGAR, fiscal services, DRCE, DRIRE, DRCCRF, DIREN, etc. Other establishments or agencies also maintain regular contracts, including the ADIT, INSEE, OSEO, etc.

Thus, we may distinguish between major groups of actors contributing to knowledge sharing within a region:

– Public:

- The prefect of a region: intermediary between central and local administrations, the prefect applies government policy in the domains of economic and territorial development. The prefect also plays a central role in the organization of economic defense. The prefect is the decision maker who chooses to initiate a project, such as a territorial information system or a DRIE.

- The regional council: regional councils are active in the economic development of regions, reinforced by new laws on decentralization.

- Chambers of commerce and industry: the extremely high number of small businesses and industries linked to chambers of commerce and industry gives these organizations an advantage in the relevant implementation of CI within a region. They share a culture and common language within professional representative bodies and industrial technical centers.

- Devolved state services: the DRIREs, directly concerned by this project, are mobilized through their mission of environmental protection and monitoring. Defense (*direction de la protection et de la sécurité de la défense*, DPSD) and

Interior (*direction du Renseignement Intérieur*, DRI) services have a dual mission, including promotion of the defensive aspect of CI and the diffusion of information collected during their actions to generate awareness. Agents of devolved state services and of public establishments carry out part of their actions around the prefect, within a strategic context of CI at territorial level.

– Private: small and medium businesses and industries.

15.2. Competitiveness clusters

Clusters are, by nature, structures for networking knowledge and competences, with the aim – among other things – of bringing together research and businesses to create products and processes which may be developed and commercialized, potentially on an international level. This type of structure allows small companies to gain a foothold in the market and allows research projects to contribute in a concrete and applicable manner to the industrial sector. We consider this form of organization, and the associated approach, to be a form of CI structure which benefits a territory (including businesses, laboratories, and universities).

In the context of globalization and heightened competition, the presence of specific competences and knowledge is an essential vector, both for attracting investors and for developing the internal capacities of a territory. This factor defines levels of economic attractiveness which are very unequal depending on local contexts. A certain number of regions have announced international ambitions, thanks to a dense distribution of resources and high-tech or very specialist companies. In terms of competition, competitiveness creates new qualitative demands that companies must satisfy in terms of organization, training, and research. The competitiveness of an industry is based mainly on "immaterial investments" in the domain of human resources, product quality, or the valorization of scientific and technological experience. Moreover, the competitiveness of a national economy is a function of the development of its industry, taking account of international exchanges linked to industrial products and the importance of productivity gains. However, since the mid-1980s, these parameters no longer seem sufficient to explain the economic superiority of one country over another. To adapt, companies would benefit from means and advantages accorded by governments. Although the internal management of competition must be handled by businesses themselves, the engagement of the collectivity is a powerful and indispensable motor for external forms of competition. Based on this realization, the French government launched a call for proposals for the development of clusters (www.competitivite.gouv.fr; see also http://polescompet.canalblog.com/).

15.2.1. *What is a cluster?*

On September 14, 2004, the interdepartmental committe on planning and development of the land (*Comité interministériel de l'aménagement et du développement du territoire,* CIADT) characterized a cluster as the combination, in a territory, of:

– three ingredients (businesses, training centers, and research units) involved in a partnership approach with the aim of creating synergies based on shared and innovative projects, with the critical mass needed for international visibility;

– three deciding factors (partnership, R&D projects, and international visibility).

Thus, the main aims of competitiveness clusters "are to reinforce the competitiveness of the national territory, dynamize economic development, create or maintain industrial jobs and attract investment and competences at European and global level"[5] [LER 05].

Two main types of cluster have been defined:

– essentially *technological* clusters (importance of research activities and strength of interactions between research centers and businesses, working on the development of a technological domain);

– essentially *industrial* clusters (concentration of businesses with more "applied" R&D activities, closer to immediate markets).

15.2.2. *The contribution of CI to clusters*

The French state aims to help businesses to comprehend essential technologies to develop and master using a reference document covering 40 "key technologies", created in 2006 following two prior studies carried out in 1995 and 2000. We note that, in this new generation, the "way in" is not only technological; organizational and economic aspects are also covered.

To understand these complex questions, a large number of small companies need methodological accompaniment. Once again, small businesses must take their place in a cooperative framework to gain access, through shared platforms, to watch tools suited to their activity. This is an important aspect of competitiveness clusters, which should, among other things, allow the identification and diffusion of good practice in CI.

---

5 Fabrice Leroy is a project executive, member of the "poles de compétivité" workgroup, company direction, MINEFI.

Clusters are the result of an association among research, training, and industry at territorial level. This new articulation shows the contribution made by CI at regional level. We should remember that CI, in a region, is seen as a veritable territorial development policy, allowing analysis of markets in a territory and detection of the associated threats and opportunities.

CI is also the creation of network actor strategies with the aim of creating, directing, and motivating links created between actors to serve as a common project. Thus, the ambitions of competitiveness clusters are clearly strategic, in that they promote regional CI.

The distribution of the 71 projects across all regions may be seen as a political aim on the part of France to strengthen each territory, using networks of actors mobilized along common aims of competitiveness and attractiveness. Competitiveness clusters are centered on the notion of networks: inter-company networks (small companies and large groups), public/private sector networks (companies, local organizations, research), and networks including businesses, research centers, and training organizations; the aim is that all partners will collaborate on projects of technological cooperation to improve competitiveness.

The approach taken by clusters demonstrates similar ambitions and the same cultures as CI. Innovation, pooling, surveillance, anticipation, and networking are all shared aims. The VigIE letter of March 2007 [AUF 07] includes a dossier on CI in clusters: "according to the first feedback collected, it seems that a number of clusters do not yet have a real competitive intelligence approach, although all are considering the possibility. Interns have, on occasion, made attempts. But there is a lack of real human and financial means for the development of this strategic function. Among the reasons cited, we find the slow takeoff of clusters, but also the difficulty for companies of pooling strategic functions. The "coopetition" (cooperation-competition) which clusters wish to develop to increase the competitiveness of our territories has met with a cool reception from small businesses. Larger groups, at times the driving force behind these clusters, often have their own CI services and do not see the need to share this with the network. Nevertheless, a few initiatives have emerged".

Lintignat [LIN 07], director of KPMG, states in the February 2007 edition of RIE that "almost one in two actors considers competitive watch to be insufficient in their cluster. It is the lack of dedicated human resources and the absence of method which limit access to competitive watch techniques. The cost is seen as considerable, and the tools badly known [...]; few 'pooled' actions exist for the moment".

Following these approaches, the government proposes to allocate 2 million euros per year to facilitate the development of a watch and CI system suited to the main economic, technological, and commercial issues available to all competitiveness clusters, allowing them to develop specific information tools.

15.2.3. *Evaluation of centers*

In December 2006, KPMG[6] produced a short, first overview of competitiveness clusters in France, based on a series of interviews with actors, which indicates a number of "teething problems" and recommends concentration on good practices for rapid progress. The advice and audit bureau noted six main points:

– International strategy and competitive watch are insufficiently mastered.

– While inter-company partnerships and those with research units have been well integrated, those involving training are not yet at this point. KPMG noted, in particular, the lack of presence of business schools within clusters.

– Success will be measured by turnover and the development of new, and especially international, markets. On the other hand, actors do not consider job creation or territorial impact as high priority aims of clusters.

– After a year of operation, businesses feel insufficiently involved in clusters and fairly distanced from academic actors; they consider the economic results to be "very insignificant".

– Companies are reluctant to cooperate in the domain of innovation, whereas the effects of cooperation constitute "one of the key advantages of a cluster".

– Points for improvement: appropriation of strategy, rapidity of instruction of assistants, relationships between actors, and international communications.

Several key factors for the success of clusters have been identified: industry/research/training cooperation, the launch of projects on the market, reactiveness, critical size, the quality of governance, financial engineering and intellectual property, and marketing. Indicators for success have been defined for following four axes: the creation of projects with high economic value, real federation of actors, employment levels, and economic performance.

Nevertheless, participants remain optimistic about the applications of the concept and 50% of the 158 companies, institutions, and research actors questioned considering that clusters should increase their international visibility.

---

6 Firm specializing in audit and management consultancy. KPMG, *Les pôles de compétitivité français: Prometteurs mais des défauts de jeunesse à corriger*, 2006.

A second evaluation was carried out between November 2007 and June 2008 by the Boston Consulting Group and CM International. This evaluation covered both the national approach and a detailed evaluation of each of the 71 clusters. It was passed on a broad approach of interviews and information collection with all the competitiveness clusters and with actors involved in the approach (state, collectivities, companies, research institutions, universities, etc.) and French and international public policy experts concerned with the field of innovation and competition.

At national level, the report discusses five clear priorities for action:

– Consolidate and render durable the positive dynamics of cooperation surrounding innovation-based cooperation created from 2005 by competitiveness clusters.

– Increase the responsibility of actors in competitiveness clusters, evolving toward a logic of contractualization and *a posteriori* control, in a simplified local environment (state and territorial collectivities).

– Reaffirm the state's engagement in competitiveness clusters and develop the dimension of strategic piloting of the approach.

– Maintain finance for collaborative R&D projects and pursue the optimization of finance circuits in projects by reinforcing their global coherence.

– Integrate the policy of competitiveness clusters more firmly in all research and innovation support practices.

15.2.4. *Review of the first phase of cluster support: 2006–2008*

Since 2005, *455 R&D projects* have benefitted from public finance of a total of 929 million euros, 620 million euros of which came from the state. These projects represent more than 2.8 billion euros of R&D expenditure and involve almost 10,000 researchers. Moreover, in 2006 and 2007, 1,343 projects received assistance from state agencies (ANR and Oséo-AII) to the tune of 770 million euros.

At international level, almost 4 million euros was attributed by the direction générale des entreprises (DGE) in 2006 and 2007 for international cluster development, of which 2.35 million euros was to promote the accompaniment of international partnerships of small companies involved in clusters. Fourteen projects were accepted, half of which were destined to promote the participation of businesses involved in competitiveness clusters in European clusters.

15.2.5. *Launch of the second phase of cluster support: 2009–2011*

Following evaluation of the first phase of cluster policy, the French president indicated in June 2008 that government support for competitiveness clusters would be maintained for a second period of 3 years (2009–2011), with a budget of 1.5 billion euros.

On September 24, 2008, the prime minister announced new directions to be taken in cluster policy, and the broad outline of this second phase, called "clusters 2.0".

During the fourth national day for competitiveness clusters, held at Bercy on October 1, 2008, the different approaches for the implementation of this new policy were detailed, based around three main axes:

– Reinforce the coordination and leadership of clusters, notably through the creation of "performance contracts".

– Implement new means of finance, particularly for innovation platforms.

– Develop the growth and innovation ecosystem of each cluster, notably by encouraging the use of private sector finance.

In the short term, competitiveness clusters benefitted from measures protecting the revenues of small businesses and industries, with guarantees given as to the confidentiality of their competences in relation to other partners involved in the approach and to external risks.

15.3. Survey of CI systems

This survey was developed with the aim of obtaining a clearer vision of CI structures established within regions (DRIES and clusters) and to better understand their approach to CI. The three main orientations of the survey were CI actions, actors, and tools used. Our panel was selected based on the age of the approach, its general function, and its visibility in France or, in other terms, notoriety (the approach works, is durable, and applies to a large and diverse panel of socioeconomic actors). We also wished to compare structures operating in different ways due to their status, origins, and public. These interviews were carried out between 2005 and 2008, by email and telephone, and each lasted around one and a half hours. This was added to by reading articles, press releases, and the Web sites of various organisms. The structures concerned can be divided into three groups: DRIEs, *pôles de compétitivité* (competitiveness clusters recognized by the French state), and other clusters of businesses and associated networks.

The first group concerns DRIEs, regional CI approaches. This group includes COGITO, DECiLOR, and IE BN. COGITO[7], in the Alsace region, aims to assist businesses in carrying out CI, to support the creation of collective watch platforms, and to encourage the use of consultancy firms. The DECiLOR structure[8], in Lorraine, consists of making the whole business support system (CRITT, technical centers, technological centers, council chambers, university establishments, private consultants, etc.) integrate CI methods and tools. It has the particularity of being structured according to different fields. The regional CI portal of the Basse-Normandie region[9] raises awareness of CI, creates exchange networks between public and private actors, identifies key technologies for the regions, and aims to valorize the territory in relation, for example, to scientific and technical competences.

The second group concerns competitiveness clusters (*pôles de compétitivité*). Examples include SYSTEM@TIC and *Véhicule du futur*. SYSTEM@TIC[10] aims to consolidate the leadership of major participants to anchor their R&D activities durable in the Ile-de-France region, to contribute to the emergence of new companies, and to the development of small technology companies so as to reinforce the attractiveness of the Ile-de-France in the digital domain. The *Véhicule du futur*[11] cluster aims to increase the international visibility of the territory of Franche-Comté, raise awareness of its contribution, and propose and implement solutions at European level in the field of vehicle manufacture and future means of mobility. It thus aims to "mesh" the competences present in the territory in the transport and automobile sectors.

Finally, we find the category of business clusters and associated networks, represented by AERIADES (an aerospace cluster in Lorraine) and OPERA. AERIADES[12] seeks to promote a regional offer in the aeronautics and space sectors using regional actors in research, industry, and training. The industrial aim is to make competences and capabilities converge using a shared network, to exploit complementarities to respond to invitations to tender for full system equipment. The OPERA[13] collective intelligence network offers a frame of reference and

---

7 With the participation of D. Munck, formerly responsible for COGITO.
8 With the participation of all members of the network (administrator, infomediaries, consultants, etc.) over 4 years.
9 With the participation of F. Chardin, responsible for the Basse-Normandie network.
10 With the participation of François CUNY, former permanent secretary, now head of relations with small businesses, www.systematic-paris-region.org/.
11 With the participation of B. Morgullis, general secretary, www.vehiculedufutur.com/.
12 With the participation of C. Jungers, general administrator of the cluster.
13 With the participation of Ludovic Guizzi, animator of the *process* network, www.oppra.net.

a space for exchange on the management of organizational processes through the identification, sharing, and construction of good practice based on a network of industrialists, consultants, and academics in the Rhône-Alpes region. The actions of the *process* network are based on monthly workshops with expert presentations, and termly training actions led by experts to facilitate benchmarking within the group. The results of our survey are presented in Table 15.1.

15.3.1. *Results of the survey*

Regional CI system/ center	Actions								
	Watch	Capitalization	Awareness/training			Animation/ cooperation assistance	Protection	Advice/ accompaniment	Influencing actions
			IR	Protection	KM				
COGITO	▒		▓	▓		▓		▓	▓
B. Normandie			▓	▓		▓		▓	▓
IAAT	▓		▓	▓		▒		▒	▓
DECiLOR	▓		▓	▓		▒	▓		▓
OPERA	▓					▓	▓	▒	
SYSTEM@TIC		▒	▓			▓			
Véhicule du Futur	▓					▓			
AERIADES		▓				▓			

Note: A white box indicates that the action has not been established. A light gray box indicates that the action is in progress or part of the minor actions of the group. Dark gray indicates that the action exists.

Table 15.1. *Actions of CI systems*

15.3.2. *Comments*

The "watch" column corresponds to the watch process as a service provided (from need analysis to the provision of information, via collection, processing, validation, and qualification). The "awareness" column includes three main components of CI, including watch, which we will limit in this case to information retrieval (IR). Decision makers and other CI actors will essentially be made aware of means of collecting information (tools and methods for retrieving information from different supports). Cooperation assistance is seen in the form of exchange networks between businesses involved in or exterior to the structure. Finally, protection includes the security dimension of information structures.

We note that one of the main missions of these structures is the development of collaboration between companies, the constitution of *networks*, to facilitate knowledge exchange between these companies and across the territory (between the public and private sectors). Raising *awareness* of information seeking and retrieval and of asset protection is also an essential mission. *Influence* and *knowledge management* aspects, however, are not always taken into account; only the DECILOR structure includes them, and this is a recent development. We also note that *watch* is not offered as a service by all structures; half of these structures consider that watch is not the direct role of their organization. They limit themselves to raising awareness and to accompaniment without going as far as offering watch services. To do this, they position themselves as intermediaries, directing those requiring watch activities (decision makers in small companies) toward organizations offering watch services (ARIST, CCI, private firms, etc.). At DECiLOR, watch services remain by far and away the main focus, with the central objective of providing small companies with personalized watch services and the fields covered with collective watch. However, the structure tends to more global services, integrating the RELIE network[14], namely advice, raising awareness, and cooperation. Finally, the majority of these structures play a role providing advice and accompaniment to companies.

Towards the actions (shares) led within the poles and clusters, we note that the most important concern coordination, cooperation, accompaniment, and protection (which we will limit, for the moment, to economic security aspects). We also note that, in most recent actions, the part played by influence or communications actions is much larger than that seen in DRIEs. Watch is, first and foremost, sectorial. SYSTEM@TIC very occasionally offers personalized watch on specific studies. The capitalization dimension is hardly taken into account, but this is work in progress. Watch actions are not part of the dominant activities of clusters. Where they do exist, they mostly concern sectorial, so collective, watch. This observation leads us to the following conclusion: the watcher is not the unique and essential resource person in this type of configuration, and, often, coordination and leadership actions are left to the delegate/administrator/correspondent of the structure (DRIE or cluster). If the watcher was indispensable to all CI actions, then his/her actions could not be subcontracted or reduced to the strict minimum (occasional information seeking). Consequently, other CI actors than the watcher may take a place in CI actions, as the simple watch aspect is not necessarily inseparable from a CI structure.

---

14 CI network for the Lorraine region.

Finally, the fundamental difference which exists between DRIEs and clusters and which explains our results is that DRIEs offer CI actions, whereas clusters make use of CI in the course of their own actions. We carried out another survey in late 2008–early 2009[15] among the 71 French *pôles de compétitivité* and the five organizations of this type found in Belgium. Our results are based on the analysis of a panel of 49 clusters, with information obtained by email and via cluster Web sites. Figure 15.1 shows the services offered by these centers.

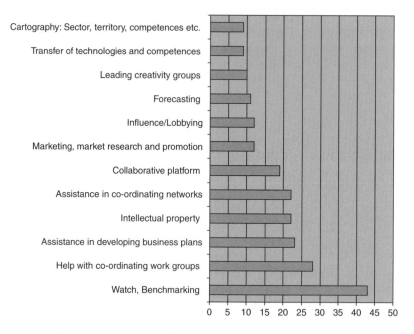

Figure 15.1. *Services offered by centers by number of instances*

We see that 12 types of services are offered at least nine times (representing ~18% of the panel of 49). Among these service types, the watch-benchmarking service arrives in first place, and four others are offered more than 20 times: workgroup coordination, assistance in developing business plans or seeking finance, awareness and management of intellectual property, and coordination of business networks.

---

15 The details of the survey are published in [GOR 09].

15.4. The role of coordinator

Following the evaluation of CI structures, surveys, and on-the-ground observation between 2003 and 2008, we identified weaknesses and needs[16] at various levels. We were able to observe the weaknesses remaining in the CI approach integrated into these structures. These weaknesses are the result of essential needs not covered by structures, which have not found a response from CI actors, either through a lack of time, resources, or experience or due to choices made upstream of these structures based on a political environment which may have since developed.

These observations have made us aware of the importance of proposing a new position necessary for piloting approaches involving relations between the public bodies and the private sector. This type of structure requires new operatives (inexistent until now), able to understand the two entities and their issues, to create a common language, and to coordinate the different CI projects developed with the participation of small businesses and state services.

We have chosen the title of "coordinator" for this post, but the title is not fixed and could easily be replaced by "CI delegate" or "CI project coordinator". Our choice of the term "coordinator" aims to show the dimension of coordination of actors and the leadership role involved in the position. We will now provide a more precise definition of the roles and competences of this individual and his/her influence on other actors involved in a CI approach.

15.4.1. *Roles and activities of the coordinator*

15.4.1.1. *Ten strategic roles of the coordinator*

The coordinator must fulfill 10 (non-fixed) strategic roles in conformity with, and dependent on, dimensions of CI. These strategic roles assist in the process of organizational learning which targets the development of organizational competences and the emergence of innovative projects, all of which leads to the effective conduct of the CI process.

1) *Synthesizer*: the coordinator acts as a channel for communications and information sources; with access to several internal and external information sources, he/she is responsible for interpreting information, giving it strategic

---

16 These weaknesses and needs are listed in [KNA 07].

meaning and thus added value, then sharing this information. He/she thus integrates this new information into existing thought, adding to the knowledge base shared by all actors in the process and influencing shared strategic understanding in the organization.

2) *Facilitator*: the facilitator assists the adaptation of process actors through concrete encouragement toward creativity, the execution of projects enabling organizational learning, and the development of new skills.

3) *Manager* (of skills): the manager aims to increase the repertoire of organizational competences, either by providing new competences to the organization or by using existing competences in a different way. To do this, the coordinator may use a forward-looking jobs and skills management policy to make professions more attractive, reduce absenteeism, solve problems of badly executed work, restart motivation, reduce staff turnover (one of the weak points highlighted in the DECiLOR structure, with a high rate of departure among infomediaries), adjust effectives to the needs of developments in the approach (readjust depending on the evolution of needs, professions, and the sector in general), and establish a training plan. A manager intervenes at several levels. The manager operates in connection with the exterior (as spokesperson, a representative of the organization, creating a link between the organization and the environment); he/she also interacts with information (diffusion, relay, and capture) and decision (distribution of resources depending on aims) and, finally, interacts with individuals and groups as a leader, coordinator, adviser, trainer, evaluator, etc. Thus, the manager has an influence on tasks, relationships, and organization.

4) *Controller* (direction, evaluation): to ensure that activities are carried out and that goals are attained.

5) *Coordinator* (organization, regulation, liaison, and networking): "coordinating" means that operations are in interaction, that is, activities are mutually interdependent[17]. Coordination allows avoidance of conflicts where there is overlap between the competences of different actors, whether within structures or "on the ground"; it is a specific approach allowing methodical and progressive structuring of a future approach. Coordination consists of "articulating" tasks. The coordinator organizes the context of work based on organizational aims. Moreover, he/she acts as a liaison agent by creating and maintaining networks of contacts (it is important to maintain good relations with other socioeconomic actors, to facilitate the exchange of information essential to good supervision of operations).

---

17 Leplat, in [BOU 08a].

The coordinator also plays a role as a relay point within these networks, maintaining equilibrium in the process (between public and private sector actors) and continuity in operations, creating bridges between actors and their different roles. As regulator, the coordinator maintains the group, with attention to time constraints, but does not intervene at basic level, avoiding giving personal opinions or attempting to manipulate the group.

6) *Mediator* (moderator, communicator): the mediator does not take sides. He/she accompanies the reflection of both parties, allowing them to reach an agreement. While the mediator must deal with problems arising, for example, in the course of operations, work conflicts or interpersonal relations, in certain situations he/she must also act as a mediator with different authorities within the organization or with different external pressure groups. Occupying a central position between public authorities, public and private decision makers, and CI actors, the coordinator communicates information, decisions, and projects from one level to another according to circumstances. To be effective in mediation (and in transmitting knowledge), the individual must respond to two demands:

– be sufficiently reassuring for both partners; that is, *belong to both spaces;*

– provide enrichment of meaning for both partners; relationships are important in the process of development and progress.

The mediator obliges each party to listen to the other, using reformulation techniques. The mediator obtains the input of "silent" partners, promoting participation and interactions. We may also speak of information mediation, the fruit of social interactions transmitted through a tool.

Finally, there are three psychological "truths" which the mediator must account for and manage within a workgroup context, the interactions of which play the role of a regulation system. These "truths" are: (1) the need to act, (2) interest in the designated task, and (3) the respect of the individual.

7) *Advisor*: this role requires the coordinator to have the necessary experience to render their judgment on a subject credible and to be able to support and justify their opinion and the conclusions of their interventions. The coordinator thus provides an objective vision of the situation of a company, benefits from a wide range of experience (new approaches, etc.), creates a dynamic where internal resources cannot or will not mobilize themselves sufficiently (hierarchy, sympathy or adhesion issues, etc.), and provides knowledge and techniques not mastered internally. The coordinator proposes methodologies for managing information and expertise. A strong audit dimension is also present.

8) *Trainer* (awareness): the coordinator must master the necessary communications and pedagogic technologies for strong transmission of knowledge, possess knowledge of the CI structure and approach as a whole, and be able to base his/her actions on a coherent theoretical base. The coordinator can then train targets in CI, providing basic tools and methods for the integration of good information management practices, identification and use of the corresponding technical tools, and organization of decision structures. At the conclusion of this objective, targets owe be capable of defining in a autonomous way or with a help, their information and knowledge management strategy, watch domains and profiles, improvements in information management and to clarify the role they may play in the structure.

9) *Security guarantor* (protection): by implementing procedures (with the person responsible for the information system, if one exists) and ensuring their application, providing warning of risks, coordinating shared actions among those in charge of IS security and users (watchers, decision makers, etc.). In addition to this, the coordinator should have a global vision of information assets and be aware of the potential risks of security breaches. As a trusted individual, the coordinator must also raise awareness of information and knowledge protection (information and intellectual assets) as a whole, not just through tools, for all actors involved in a CI approach.

10) *Leader*: the abilities of the leader are based on his/her own expertise, mediation capacities, and the ability to detect motivation in group members (for group participation). The leader aims to avoid strong oppositions and overly quick consensus decisions which may "kill" a debate. The leader created and leads debates and may also seek to enter into contact with other networks. This leadership role involves a number of tasks:

– Promotion: the leader must promote the structure in which he/she is involved to other socioeconomic actors.

– Conviction: the leader must influence the behavior of actors to create cooperation.

– Creation of a dynamic: by making actors the "engine" of a CI approach. For this, regular motivation is required.

– Communication: communicating ceaselessly with individuals with very different activities, hierarchical positions, cultures, professional jargon (public/private), etc., the leader must find a common language and ensure comprehension between group members. In a pragmatic way, communication is an integral part of raising awareness and must allow identification, readability, and visibility of regional CI actions.

– Coordination: see role no. 5.

The leader creates procedures, guarantees the right function of the CI structure, leads networks, supports actors involved in the CI activity in terms of methods and organization, and ensures the coherence of work produced.

These 10 strategic roles are linked to change: understanding the need for change, preparing for change, promoting change, and, finally, implanting change, improving organizational performance while promoting learning and the development of new skills.

Table 15.2 provides a synthesis of these roles and activities.

The collective level corresponds to a set (or group) of decision makers. Individual level refers to the direct intervention of the coordinator with a decision maker. The aspects of CI are CI actions developed within a CI structure. These aspects are not all found in every CI structure, meaning that the coordinator will not necessarily need to fulfill the 10 different roles listed above.

Aspects of CI	Role at collective level	Role at individual level
Watch	4) Controller 5) Coordinator 8) Trainer 9) Security guarantor 10) Leader	1) Synthesizer 7) Advisor 9) Security guarantor
Capitalization	2) Facilitator 3) Manager 4) Controller 5) Coordinator 6) Mediator 8) Trainer 9) Security guarantor 10) Leader	7) Advisor
Protection	4) Controller 10) Leader	2) Facilitator 7) Advisor
Influence	7) Advisor	6) Mediator 7) Advisor

Table 15.2. *Classification of roles of the coordinator in different aspects of CI*

Based on this table, we can summarize the roles of the coordinator as follows; the coordinator is responsible for *mediation* between all actors in a CI structure and interacts with the structure as a whole (IS and actors). He/she *coordinates, supervises, controls,* and monitors operations. He/she is responsible for the implementation if CI awareness and training activities and also offers possibilities for inter-company meetings, to dynamize the network and pool the competences of the companies involved. Finally, as the *central person* in the structure, he/she has a global and precise vision of the sector(s) of activity and/or the territory covered, not just at regional but at national or international level, allowing him/her to predict the evolution of the structure.

Thus, the coordinator acts as a *relay point*, linking companies which may have the same type of information needs or encounter similar information problems and thus creating relationships. He/she also acts as a link between companies and public authorities. This new mission was born of our observations within the different fields involved in regional CI structures. We noted that companies within the same network do not necessarily "know" each other, or at best lack precise knowledge of the activities of others, information which could provide them with answers to questions concerning the development of their sector and of their abilities. We also noticed a level of incomprehension between different structures involved in approaches due to the absence of a common language.

The aim of these three central functions (coordination–leadership–mediation) is to create synergy and good dynamics within a group, ensuring that members of structures pool certain knowledge and competences to be more competitive within their territory and in global markets and ensuring that actors from both spheres (public and private) understand each other and are able to collaborate on federated projects.

15.4.2. *Competences of the coordinator*

Based on the needs we have identified and the type of CI personnel involved in a CI structure, we will now establish a list of desirable knowledge and skills for a coordinator. This is, however, an "ideal" list, in which we have chosen to highlight the competences needed for effective management of a CI structure. However, some of these attributes are not essential but might be advantageous depending on context, the domain, the needs of decision makers, existing experience, etc. Moreover, these competences and roles vary depending on the CI action developed by the structure. Given that the presence of all types of action is rare, the coordinator does not need to possess all the skills or competences listed.

In terms of skills, we look for the capacity to implement information cycles, the CI process, and the watch process and the ability to use information seeking methods, benchmarking, prospection, etc. The coordinator should know and use information systems and integrated tools (portals, motors/directories, databases, watch agents, collaborative tools, knowledge management tools, etc.).

In terms of knowledge, the coordinator should have a general knowledge of CI structures (their organization and *modus operandi*) and of the local network (or fabric) – actors, operations, finance, policies, sectors of activity, etc. The daily activities of the coordinator also require general knowledge of law (as it relates to information and communications), knowledge management, quality procedures, innovation, business knowledge, project management (cost, time, human, and material resources), tendering (specifications), crisis communication and risk management, etc. All of these knowledge are required by the fact that the CI process and the context of a CI structure (region, actors with different statuses, multiple needs, etc.) demand a global vision of the surrounding environment. Thus, in a territorial framework, this means taking account of parameters of various forms, including legislative, commercial, and security aspects.

The coordinator must also understand the working of public authorities: their principles, operations, etc. Among the list of essential skills, some are mundane, for example, those linked to judicial, economic, or methodological aspects (dossier creation, establishment of business cooperation); others may be seen as complementary, for example, those linked to the management of human and information networks. This last point is where the role of coordinator takes on its fullest meaning. This role involves the organization of human resources (pooling means, capitalization of experience, federating initiatives, etc.), but also of information (optimization of watch practices and circulation of information by the establishment of rules and "good practice guides"). The principle is to allow actors from the public and private sectors, working on shared projects, to share and pool knowledge and to have access to all information necessary for their projects, information which must be "proportionally" held by both parties. The coordinator plays a role of moderator in this case, ensuring that each party "opens up" equally for the benefit of the project by the regular provision of information needed for success.

The coordinator must be able to direct organizations toward service providers in accordance with their needs, toward state support, particularly in terms of finance (or toward other sources of finance, at local level or from the European Community, requiring knowledge and monitoring of different types of finance proposed by the EC and to monitor calls to tender (PCRD, Interreg, etc., depending on the sectors involved), etc.). The coordinator must maintain a directory of contacts likely to respond to varying types of request linked to the needs of public or private sector actors to ensure operations run smoothly.

We have also created a non-exhaustive list of desirable aptitudes in a coordinator: open-mindedness, curiosity, teaching skills, ability to synthesize, faculties of adaptation, sense of management and organization, etc.

This profession is, in some ways, similar to one in a completely different domain, that of GP: the doctor is able to diagnose a patient and direct them toward a specialist for treatment of their specific problem. The GP has a global vision of diseases which may affect a patient but cannot, by any means, cure all of them. His/her essential role lies in the capacity to identify the problem and find the right person to respond to it.

We do, however, still need responses to some aspects of this new profession:

– *Status* of the new staff member. We are not yet in a position to say who might be responsible for recruiting for this position and, consequently, what the status of the coordinator would be. The political orientations of different regions, for example, may have an effect on this type of position, if the position is dependent on public bodies.

– *Experience.* Given the multiple aspects of this new profession, a certain level of experience is desirable. However, the creation of a new position, with new needs, new constraints, new issues, and new organizations, means that it would be difficult to find candidates with experience in this type of configuration. We would suggest, nevertheless, that the person chosen should have a certain level of experience in the dominant aspects (orientations and tendencies) of the structure. For example, if the structure focuses on watch and economic security, the new staff member should have a minimum of experience in these domains.

– *Knowledge of the local fabric.* The individual concerned should ideally have knowledge of the region in which the structure is located. Nevertheless, this raises questions as to the limits we apply to the knowledge itself: does the candidate need to possess historical, cultural, and political knowledge of the region?

– *Public/private gap.* This type of structure, federating state services and small businesses/industries, demands thorough knowledge of the workings of these organizations and their "politics". In short, the new worker must master the administrative vocabulary and "spirit" of public powers along with the vocabulary and "character" of private partners (paying attention to double messages often due to relatively heavy hierarchical structures). Moreover, as a mediator and a figure of trust, the coordinator must be able to dose and moderate the contributions of each party, establish cooperation, and manage behavior which may be ambivalent (paying attention to overly ambitious individuals), as the stakes involved are certain to be radically different. Essentially, the coordinator must be able to show both parties (public/private) that the approach is equally advantageous to both groups and that neither party will suffer. This demands a certain strength of character which is difficult to formalize and evaluate during recruitment.

– *Cost.* We are not in a position to measure the real cost associated with the creation of this post: salary, operational costs, cost of training, and who should be responsible for these costs (this is linked to the status problem).

– *Budgetary management.* We have not taken this aspect into account. We feel that the coordinator should have a specific budget for management of their activity, but in a public or semi-public context, this may not be possible. The response to this question is unlikely to be found before status questions have been resolved.

– *Development perspectives of the coordinator in relation to the CI approach.* Does the coordinator become a "prisoner" of the position, or, building on knowledge and experience gained in the function, will it be possible to transfer to similar positions in domains other than CI? This question is also important as development prospects are a subject of negotiation during the recruitment of qualified personnel.

15.5. Conclusion

The coordinator therefore operates on three levels:

– The *human* level (individual and collective, private and public) to manage CI actors (and their relationships) and competences within a CI structure, and by providing advice and expertise to actors.

– The *information* level, capturing signals from outside the structure, analyzing, and centralizing them in preparation for capitalization. Through the role of communicator, the coordinator acts as the "nerve center" of their organization, providing validated and qualified information and checking information provided by third parties.

– The *organizational* level, by managing the structuration of actors and tasks, ensuring interactions, and coordinating exchange networks.

This approach provides a first response to the development of CI professions according to needs felt by decision makers federated within organizations (the principle of DRIEs and clusters) and according to the evolution of these organizations themselves, as some are still very recent.

It also gives us a perspective on a profession based on the reinforcement of increasingly clear and necessary links between public powers and the private sector around federating projects in which CI occupies an important place.

This study looked first and foremost at the French model, but we feel that it may be applied to other areas, particularly abroad, as clusters and centers of competition are, by their very nature, organizations with an international aspect and do not only operate using French models and mechanisms.

15.6. Bibliography

[AMB 08] AMBASSADE DE FRANCE EN ALLEMAGNE (FRENCH EMBASSY IN GERMANY), La politique des clusters en France et en Allemagne: Pôles de compétitivité, Kompetenznetze allemands et clusters bavarois – Coopération franco-allemande entre clusters d'innovation, 2008, available online at www.wissenschaft-frankreich.de.

[AUF 07] AUFORT S., "L'intelligence économique dans les poles", *VigIE*, pp. 8–10, March 2007.

[BOU 06] BOUABDALLAH K., THOLONIAT A., "Pôle de compétitivité et Intelligence économique territoriale: contours et enjeux d'une nouvelle politique industrielle territorial", *Actes du 8ᵉ Forum Européen IES 2006 Intelligence économique, Veille et Innovation*, Nice, France, pp. 8–10, 2006.

[BOU 08a] BOURRET C., "Eléments pour une approche de l'Intelligence Territoriale comme système de synergie de projets locaux pour développer une identité collective", *Projectics*, no. 2008/1, De Boeck University, pp. 79–92, 2008.

[BOU 08b] BOUZON A., MEYER V., *La communication des organisations, entre recherche et action*, L'Harmattan, Paris, 2008.

[CAP 03] CAPPELIN R., "Territorial knowledge management: towards a metrics of cognitive dimension of agglomeration economies", *International Journal of Technology Management*, vol. 26, no. 2/3/4, pp. 303–325, 2003.

[CAR 03] Carayon B., *Intelligence économique, compétitivité et cohésion sociale*, La Documentation française, Paris, France, 2003.

[COL 05] COLLETIS G., "Entreprises et territoires: proximités et développement local", *Entreprises, réseaux et territoires*, 22 March 2005.

[CLE 99] CLERC P., PAUTRAT C., *Intelligence économique, Encyclopédie de la gestion et du management* (E.G.M), Dalloz, Paris, 1999.

[GON 94] GONNOT J.M., "Eléments pour l'allocution d'ouverture du colloque sur l'intelligence économique", *Actes du colloque "L'intelligence économique, l'information au service de la compétitivité"*, Assemblée nationale, Paris, France, pp. 7–8, 30 June 1994.

[GOR 07] GORIA S., KNAUF A., "Composite picture to help to study and to define a regional economic intelligence device", *The Fifth Annual International Conference of Territorial Intelligence*, CAENTI, Huelva, Spain, pp. 148–164, 2007.

[GOR 09] GORIA S., KNAUF A., "Présentation d'une étude fonctionnelle de diverses formes d'intelligences territoriales mises en œuvre par les pôles de compétitivité", *Pôles de compétitivité et développement économique régional*, Liège, Belgium, March 2009.

[KNA 07] KNAUF A., Caractérisation des rôles du coordinateur-animateur, émergence d'un acteur nécessaire à la mise en pratique d'un dispositif régional d'intelligence économique, Doctoral thesis in ICT, University of Nancy 2, Nancy, October 2007.

[KNA 08] KNAUF A., GORIA S., "Spécification des métiers et compétences impliqués dans le dispositif d'intelligence économique: identification d'un métier émergent pour le pilotage et l'animation des actions dédiées à l'intelligence économique en region", in FRANÇOIS L. (ed.), *Intelligence territoriale – L'intelligence économique appliquée au territoire*, Lavoisier, Paris, pp. 71–86, 2008.

[LER 05] LEROY F., "Pôles de compétitivité: de l'appel à projets à la labellisation", *Entreprises, réseaux et territoires*, 22 March 2005.

[LIN 07] LINTIGNAT J., "Pôles de compétitivité: quel bilan?", *Regards sur l'intelligence économique*, no. 18, January/February 2007.

[WER 99] WERNER E., "La Franche-Comté lance un programme ambitieux et original", *Technologies internationales*, no. 52, pp. 42–44, March 1999.

Chapter 16

Attractiveness of Territories and Territorial Intelligence: Indicators

16.1. Introduction

Globalization, a phenomenon supposed to break down borders and make distances disappear, brings attention back to the idea of "territory", not as an element of cultural differentiation but as an element of competitive differentiation. Globalization has resulted in a polarization of economic activities into agglomerations, districts, or clusters, depending on the theoretical angle taken in discussing the matter. Globalization is not, therefore, a sort of homogenization but results in the creation of competition between territories. This new factor means that territories must be "attractive", and competitive intelligence (CI) can be used to help them achieve this goal.

The time when simply raising awareness of a territory was sufficient to make it attractive is now past. It is difficult, if not foolish, to attempt to "sell" a territory before increasing its visibility and readability, making it economically, socially, and territorially coherent [CAM 05]. Before this, CI, and territorial intelligence (TI) in particular, has an essential role to play in showing that an attractive territory is a reasoned construct regrouping competitive actors to respond to the complexification of the international environment and to the concerns of the "society of knowledge".

The notion of territory, in the economic sense of the term, has been interpreted in extremely varied ways during different periods, from "state" to "region" to "localized system" [BRY 06]. For the classical economists Adam Smith and David

Chapter written by Nathalie FABRY and Sylvain ZEGHNI.

Ricardo, the territory, in the state-region sense of the term, is the source of differences and serves as a basis for the commercial specialization of countries[1]. Other actors focus on explaining industrial localization and the spatial concentration of activities, such as Marshall [MAR 90] for *industrial districts* or Perroux [PER 50, PER 55, PER 61] for *centers of growth and development*. These authors consider the territory more as a market, a space for production, transactions and profit creation – thanks to scale economies and externalities – rather than as a reasoned construction. More recently, with the development of geographic economy [FUJ 99], the territory has become not just a place for the agglomeration of activities but a place for the accumulation of knowledge and an endogenous source of growth. We thus move from an extensive vision of the territory to a more localized reading of economic activity. With globalization and the multiplicity and heterogeneity of actors, the notion of territory takes on a certain analytical relevance. Understanding how a territory develops becomes a major concern and generates two legitimate questions for research: what is the "attractiveness" of a territory, and how can this "attractiveness" be measured?

The aim of this chapter is to provide a response to these questions and to clarify the logic of attractiveness of a territory associated with TI. First, we will look at the theoretical basis for this attractiveness. We feel that this will be found in the concept of "territorial value". Second, we will attempt to identify relevant indicators for territorial attractiveness and propose a TI approach destined to ensure the durability of this attractiveness.

16.2. Attractiveness and value of a territory: elements of analysis

An attractive territory, be it a state, a region, a county, a rural area, an urban center, or even a town, is able to attract businesses and capital for industrialization, modernization, growth, and prosperity. In such cases, we speak of "productive attractiveness". This may be brought by the presence of foreign companies, by more local actors or a combination of the two. The attractiveness of a territory takes on a more social and residential dimension when we take into account the ability of a territory to accommodate various populations [GAU 05]. We feel that the attractiveness of a territory will be "fuller" and more durable if it combines these two aspects.

Before going further, we must establish the position of attractiveness in relation to competitiveness. The two terms are fairly close, and both are forms of results. However, competitiveness is "instant" and resumes performance *ex post* (parts of the market, degree of openness); attractiveness applies not just to the intrinsic quality of

1 According to the principle of absolute advantage (Smith) or comparative advantage (Ricardo).

the territory (offer) but especially to the way in which this offer is suited to the needs and projects of actors. In other terms, competitiveness validates the potential of a territory (natural and constructed resources), while attractiveness validates the choice of localization of actors. A territory will become more attractive by attracting and harnessing resources and revenues from external sources.

Attractiveness is, in fact, the fruit of a process of synergizing heterogeneous actors. It owes its durability and coherences to an organized and well thought out construction. The key to analyzing the attractiveness of a territory is understanding the distinction between creating and harnessing wealth (section 16.2.1). In this context, TI contributes greatly to understanding the mechanisms of attraction (section 16.2.2).

16.2.1. *Attractiveness of territories: creating and harnessing value*

We must distinguish between attractiveness based on attracting companies to a territory, on the one hand, and the attractiveness that comes from the capacity to valorize the territory which results from harnessing resources on the other. We thus go from a logic of value creation to a logic of harnessing value.

16.2.1.1. *Using attractiveness to create value*

The attractiveness of countries has been a particular subject of study in international economics to understand the implications of implantations of offshoots of foreign companies[2] or foreign direct investment (FDI). According to Dunning [DUN 93], three advantages must be present simultaneously for FDI to occur: ownership advantage, including all the elements of superiority of a company in relation to its competitors; localization advantage, relating to the advantages offered by a host territory to foreign companies; and internalization advantage, which makes the FDI more interesting from a strategic point of view than a simple market transaction (subcontracting)[3]. Among these three advantages, the localization advantage has taken on increasing importance in the current context of globalization.

This localization advantage was first seen from the angle of natural resources. A territory is attractive because it has exploitable natural resources, reliable infrastructures (telecommunications, ports, airports, roads), an available qualified and productive workforce, technologies, public services, and, more generally, a favorable socioeconomic and political environment. Attractiveness in this way is

---

2 This is particularly the case since the opening up of "transition" countries (China and the East).
3 The OLI paradigm: ownership advantage, localization advantage, and internalization advantage.

based on what a territory has to offer. Criteria relating to demand and the potential for growth reinforce the localization advantage of an area. A company investing in a territory wishes to develop parts of the market in this territory. The size and growth of the market, the tastes and preferences of consumers, and their per capita income are major factors in FDI in a territory. Attractiveness is thus linked to demand.

The densification of international competition pushes companies to adopt an efficiency seeking strategy, combining cost optimization with the exploitation of new leads. In this context, on top of the advantages already mentioned, the legislative environment, macro-economic and institutional stability, and the presence of local and international competitors creating external and network effects all contribute to the attractiveness of a territory [FAB 06, ROD 03]. Attractiveness is carried by constructed advantages. The move from natural to constructed advantages gives each territory a potential margin for manoeuver in drawing the contours of its attractiveness. Thus, a territory will be attractive if it is able to welcome FDI, implying that companies wish to invest in the territory. There is an implicit relationship of seduction and retention which tempers the attractiveness of a territory by business opportunities offered to companies, their aversion to risk, and more generally the "image" put forward by the territory.

This idea acts as a basis for most attractiveness indicators [CUS 08, ERN 08a, ERN 08b, ERN 08c]. However, an extraverted reading based on the capacity to welcome foreign businesses is not sufficient to measure the attractiveness of a territory. We must consider all actors, without distinctions based on provenance, and envisage the territory as a complex socioeconomic architecture validated not only by the choices of companies but also by local and immigrant populations. Publications on the subject all too often forget that territorial attractiveness is based on dual foundations: attractiveness for businesses and attractiveness for populations (residents and tourists). At this point, CI, and TI in particular, plays an important role in helping territories to respond to the renewed challenge of attractiveness.

Attractiveness is considered from the perspective of the choice of localization of companies, so jobs, and not residency. The "production" dimension is highlighted at the expense of the "consumption" aspect. Although this approach is important, it remains limiting. Use of economic base analysis can allow us to surpass these limits.

16.2.1.2. *Using attractiveness to harness value*

The notion of attractiveness for harnessing value has its origins in the theory of economic bases, developed by Cantillon in around 1725 and, more recently, by Sombart [SOM 54]. Using the example of a fortified medieval village, Sombart first distinguishes a population group with exterior revenues due to wealth, authority, or practicing a particular trade (taxes, rents, allocations, and industry) [KRU 68]. These are the "Städtegründer" or town founders. This population category – the "base" – will be able to employ other individuals in their service or make use of the services of independent workers, seen as "passive" individuals or "secondary founders". Sombart divides this group into two categories: the "unmittelbare Brotnehmer" (direct breadwinners) and the "mittelbare Brotnehmer" (indirect breadwinners). The first group is made up of servants and employees of the "founders", whereas the second group is made up of independent workers (traders, bankers, transporters, craftsmen, etc.). Sombart deduced that the larger the base, the more it will be able to generate, through a multiplication effect, urban growth, and the concentration of skills, showing, in passing, that the growth of the town is based on the development of services.

Thus, originally, economic base theory is built on the distinction between a local residential economy and an external economy. Local economic development consists of developing the territory by attracting businesses, "indirect or derived" jobs, but also migrants who will add to the base by bringing in revenues from outside. Economic base theory is particularly interesting nowadays when looking at the effects of migration [GON 06]. Over the last 10 years, in industrial countries, we have observed a disconnection of the territories where wealth is produced and those where the possessors of this wealth reside. This dissociation removes an entire aspect of attractiveness from the territory, as the aim of attractiveness is not just to produce value but also to harness value produced elsewhere through individual migrations (residents, workers, and tourists) [DAV 08].

One of the main difficulties is thus to quantify human and financial circulation between territories, linked to harnessing value. As Davezies indicates [DAV 08, p. 55]: "the economic reading of a territory remains exclusively dependent on the representation of a territory supporting activities and generating revenues, and not on a territory supporting populations with revenues which may be independent of local activity". In this way, TI can contribute to understanding attractiveness.

16.2.2. *TI and attractiveness: measuring the value of a territory*

For Bruneau [BRU 04, p. 31], TI is "the capacity for anticipation, the mastery of all forms of information, and the organized use of networks of influence and actions by elected representatives and territorial executives to benefit the territory for which they are responsible". Bruté de Rémur [BRU 06, p. 93] distinguishes two levels of TI: the territorialization of CI, which consists of the local application of CI measures taken at national level without distinguishing between actors (businesses and local government), and intelligence based on the territory, an "autonomous" action taken at local level "for the determination of specific objectives and the implementation of actions specific to the space concerned, in accordance with policies adopted at larger, higher levels".

Gaucherand [GAU 05], taking a different approach, identifies three levels of TI:

– Territorial CI, which consists of "creating products and leading CI services for actors involved in economic innovation". This may take the form of pooled watch platforms or the installation of a CI portal (sectorial syntheses, competence mapping, etc.), for example.

– Strategic TI, which consists of creating strategic watch infrastructures hosting permanent diagnosis tools (dashboards, development analysis, identification of strong tendencies, and major changes).

– Management of territorial communities, particularly in the domain of information and communications technology (ICT) (digital territories) or more generally by motivating actors through the creation of social links.

From these various and non-exhaustive points of view, we retain the fact that there is no stable definition of TI. One thing, however, is certain: TI cannot be reduced to the local transposition of national CI, to a simple watch policy [BER 06], or to territorial marketing. It always involves a strategic and prospective dimension while using CI tools [FRA 08].

From a TI perspective, a territory is attractive not only because of its natural and/or created resources but because it offers the following possibility resources:

– diagnosing and taking account of what exists (competences, advantages, resources, etc.);

– *expertise on and valorization of the territory.* This involves understanding local production dynamics, innovations, and, more generally, socioeconomic relationships, which generate synergies and give flesh to the emergence of a localized social capital. This relational aspect, often based on networks and information pooling, reduces opportunism, and consequently incertitude, and may facilitate the emergence of a learning and knowledge sharing process [BER 06, CAM 05];

– *anticipation and determination of priority axes and establishment of federating projects.* This applies to the establishment of local governance, bringing together public actors (local public administrations, communities), institutions and private actors (businesses) responsible for identifying the needs of actors, offering projects and proposing solutions [CAM 05];

– *creation of a strategy to ensure the durability of attractiveness* by seeking to understand ongoing transformations, anticipate ruptures and threats, and seize opportunities. This relates to the facilitation of renewal of the economic fabric in the medium and long term and to its inclusion in a system of international competition between territories.

The attractiveness issue consists of bringing together the actions of heterogeneous actors, promoting their complementarities/interdependences and revealing synergies, without losing sight of a durable development project [PEL 08]. In the next section, we will see that a TI approach allows the introduction of a new model for action and decision within a territory to serve aims of attractiveness.

16.3. Attractiveness and implementation of a TI approach

The articulation between territorial dynamics, population dynamics, and company dynamics must be at the heart of the construction of a TI approach. This is why we propose the implementation of a participative approach to the construction of territorial attractiveness, with true coproduction of attractiveness by all involved (section 16.3.2). This coproduction of territorial attractiveness is based on the creation and sharing of decision assistance tools among actors. This supposes genuine investment in an information database, a tool for shared anticipation (section 16.3.3). Beforehand (section 16.3.1), we will show the necessity of looking at the criteria of territorial attractiveness, as there is no definite response on the choice of relevant indicators, as shown by the example of the Ile-de-France (IDF), a region with a particular attachment to the notion of its own attractiveness.

16.3.1. *Territorial attractiveness: comparison of studies on the IDF region*

The question of criteria of attractiveness may be tackled in various ways, depending on the size of the territory and its geographic situation, and in practice, the response is found in a "bundle" of interconnected variables. Without attempting to provide exhaustive coverage of the question, we will examine the matter of criteria through a number of recent studies carried out on the IDF region.[4]

For regional development agency (ARD) [AGE 05, p. 5], attractiveness, or "the capacity of a region to attract and retain all types of resources, whether human, financial or technological", is seen through five main components: the analysis of the IDF region, based on surveys carried out by various organizations (DATAR, DIACT, Cushman & Wakefield, Healey & Baker, IMD), FDI, financial and property investment, assets, tourism, and major international manifestations. The study

---

4 For more global studies concerning major global centers, see the City Mayors Web site (www.citymayors.com) or the Global City Index in *Foreign Policy* published at www.foreignpolicy.com/story/cms.php?story_id=4509&page=0. We might also use the European Attractiveness Scoreboard, published at www.gtai.com/uploads/media/ European_ Attractiveness_Scoreboard_2008.pdf. To compare the IDF with another major region, such as Greater Montreal, we can use the following address: www.montrealinternational.com/ fr/accueil/index.aspx.

concludes that the IDF is beaten by London in terms of FDI, the level of investment in commercial property, stock market capitalization, and the presence of foreign talent. On the other hand, Paris (the center of the IDF region) overtakes London in terms of quality of life, the presence of decision centers, the profitability of property investment and tourism (for business or leisure).

For Floret [FLO 04, p. 16], "attractiveness is a heterogeneous mass measuring subjective social factors as much as considerations of pure economic competitiveness (trade GDP, average individual wealth, costs and charges, etc.). This subjectivity is thus a fundamental aspect of data on attractiveness and relates to the shared values of a nation. It includes both constructed and inherited values. Thus, for many visitors, Paris and the Ile-de-France are more a representation of the past (allowing the development of high-level tourism) than carriers of future values. As each individual has their own interpretation of attractiveness, political work on the subject should use mechanisms supporting competitiveness – an 'objective' value – while imagining elements showing the subjective part of attractiveness."

Attractiveness may be tackled by taking two groups into account: businesses that participate in the region's production and thus its material wealth and workers in the IDF who participate in the processes of local life (industrial or associative). Each group exercises meaningful functions (independent variables). Thus, for *companies*, we apply criteria such as research potential, training systems, economic potential, the labor market, implantation criteria, quality of life, networks, the fiscal and regulatory framework, the social climate, and the effectiveness of administrative and political structures. For *residents*, we use criteria of urbanism and housing, communications networks, cultural, sport and leisure potential, other collective equipment, the quality of life (and the cost of living), the social environment, the labor market, economic potential, and the training system. In fact, we attempt to identify possible developments and to identify criteria for territorial attractiveness in a prospective fashion.

Concerning the observed attractiveness of the IDF, three domains require rapid decisions although the effects of these decisions will only be felt in the long run. These include *the infrastructure and urbanism* for the construction and/or support of a polycentric region in a limited space, welcoming young populations important for future professions and new activities, *governance* to give unity to the region and reduce spatial inequalities, and *research and training* to "reposition the region in the world of knowledge (social, technical, and artistic) and research".

The European Cities Monitor report [CUS 08] presents strong criteria for the implantation of companies in a territory/town and analyses attractiveness from an economic point of view, using quantitative and qualitative data. Among these criteria, we can identify the access to markets, consumers, or clients, the availability of qualified labor, the quality of infrastructures and the density and interconnection of communications' infrastructures, the cost of labor, the business climate (taxes, etc.), the supply of business premises (availability and cost), the use of foreign languages, the quality of life, and the quality of the environment. The indicators used are divided into five categories: demographics, labor (availability, quality, and price), business costs (property), access to markets, and the environment.

The Greater Paris Investment Agency [PAR 06, PAR 08] in collaboration with Ernst and Young, surveyed the economic attractiveness of the region through the strategic functions of the metropole. This involves taking account of the number of company headquarters implanted in the region, R&D centers, and service centers dedicated to internal clients (the back-offices of companies, shared service centers, etc.) and to external clients (client relation centers, call centers, etc.). According to Ernst and Young, these strategic functions play a positive role in the creation of value and thus the attractiveness of the region. We should, however, add decision and technological functions to this list as a basis for diagnosis and comparison of territorial attractiveness.

Sources	Links
Paris IDF region	*Paris Région* www.paris-region.com/ IDF Economic and Social Council www.cesr-ile-de-France.fr/cesr_htm/commun/theme_jf.asp
Ernst and Young	European attractiveness survey (various countries and issues): http://www.ey.com/DLResults?Query=[CountryCode]=FR~[LanguageCode] =fr~[T_Issues]=%28Issues\Business%20environment%29
Cushman and Wakefield	European cities monitor and other reports http://www.cushwake.com/cwglobal/jsp/kcLanding.jsp?Country=GLOBAL &Language=EN
Foreign policy	The 2010 global cities index http://www.atkearney.com/index.php/Publications/global-cities-index.html
Saffron consultants	The Saffron European City Brand Barometer: revealing which cities get the brands they deserve http://saffron-consultants.com/wp-content/uploads/Saff_CityBrandBarom.pdf

Table 16.1. *The attractiveness of the Paris Area according to major sources*

This non-exhaustive presentation shows that the attractiveness of a territory may be approached from different angles, both quantitative and qualitative in nature. Nevertheless, a number of reports have resulted from isolated initiatives and act as a support for lobbying, while it would be more relevant to establish an approach associating all actors in the construction of attractiveness. All analyses highlight the advantages of the IDF region but indicate weaknesses and risks of losing ground to other major European cities to differing degrees. It is therefore reasonable to look at the importance of motivation of all actors in creating attractiveness in a territory[5].

16.3.2. *The participatory method*

We have chosen to develop a method that takes account of the diversity of local actors, inspired by the method created by the French Agency for Tourism Engineering (Agence Française de l'Ingénierie Touristique, AFIT) [PER 03] for the establishment of a durable tourism policy. This method makes use of a participatory approach. In this model, indicators are not an end unto themselves, but situated at the center of a set of steps, the aim of which is to pilot attractiveness in the territory. The proposed method is broken down into four phases: inspection of the current situation, diagnosis, the definition of strategic axes, and the action plan. The first two steps are crucial, as the definition of strategic axes and the action plan depend on these phases (see Figure 16.1).

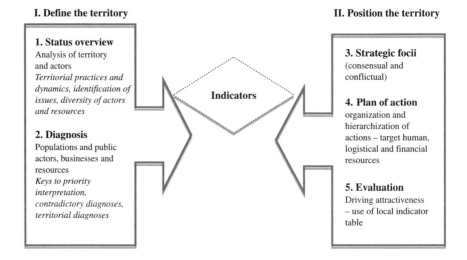

Figure 16.1. *The five steps of the participative method*

---

5 This importance of mobilization of actors seems to have been integrated little by little by the ARD which, in early 2008 and at the request of the regional council of the IDF, launched an "Attractiveness" action plan to accompany the implementation of priority axes in the regional economic development plan. The partners involved were *départements* and their agencies or expansion committees, the main intercommunal bodies, council chambers, professional organizations, and competitiveness clusters.

In the first phase (inspection of the situation), we must analyze local realities, based on documentary resources and meetings with different local actors. The aim is to identify the diversity of public and private actors, their practices, and spontaneous territorial dynamics. Existing orientations and actions are evaluated at this stage. This identification stage is carried out on two levels: the first is a "territory" analysis, allowing us to understand the impact of public policy on the attractiveness of a territory and to identify issues present in the territory. We also seek to gather information on the diversity of approaches taken by territorial actors linked to local policies (local policy decision makers). The second level is a "business" analysis, used to identify the desires and expectations of businesses.

The second phase is the diagnosis phase and is carried out with the aim of interpreting signs and tendencies observed during the previous stage to identify exploitable fields for progress. This phase is based on a well-known operational marketing technique, SWOT (strengths, weaknesses, opportunities, and threats) applied to a given territory, taking account of businesses operating locally and the resources available for the development of activity. This phase has three main goals: first, to identify and validate priority keys for interpretation to see whether the attractiveness policies analyzed respond to the priority issues of the territory.

Second, we aim to promote the elaboration of contradictory diagnoses expressing the variety of points of view, also dynamizing the participative approach.

Finally, we aim to produce a diagnosis of the territory using shared bases for interpretation – the issues linked to the territory and the local table of attractiveness indicators. This diagnostic work helps identify the strengths and weaknesses of different types of policies implemented by actors to respond to the development issues of the territory.

The third phase is given over to the definition of strategic axes. It aims to project sufficiently stable axes over a duration of 3–5 years, collectively defining and prioritizing strategic axes for the territory. For this, the local coordination group must synthesize the results of previous debates. The proposition of strategic axes must take account of the set of elements validated during diagnosis in the previous phase. It must also prioritize and validate strategic axes using a temporal approach. This should result in the definition of consensual strategic axes and the identification of conflicting axes, which, in the latter case, are only shared by one section of the actors involved.

Finally, the action plan must organize and prioritize actions, in terms of time, which correspond to main developmental aims, identified in the strategic plan. The central aim is to make the proposed actions respond correctly to the desired attractiveness objectives.

This participatory method is based on the establishment of networks of relationships and moves toward an integrated interpretation of territorial attractiveness. From this perspective, information constitutes one of the pillars for the establishment of an attractiveness policy.

16.3.3. *Information and attractiveness*

Territories should no longer be approached by decision makers as the product of an unconscious trajectory, but as a space for the sharing of information and knowledge. In this way, territorial actors should be better able to understand the reasons for cooperation in the framework of territorial attractiveness. We therefore move from a situation where actors are "subjected" to a development strategy to one with a reasoned and shared development strategy. Within this context, we must consider the specificities of a territory, its social and institutional organization, the proximity and accessibility of resources, etc.

The development of an attractiveness strategy passes through shared access to knowledge of the territory, on the one hand, and, on the other, by durable structuring of the territory from a social, economic, technological, intellectual, environmental, and cultural point of view. This supposes the maintenance of a dynamic of "localized innovative performance" as shown by Massard and Mehier [MAS 04]. For Dou and Bertacchini [DOU 01], the role of TI is the establishment of a Territorial Managing System, with the aim of acquisition and redistribution of information to local actors and the demonstration of territorial potential in the domains of transfer and valorization of information through networks. In the same spirit, Herbaux and Bertacchini [HER 03, p. 4] state that "territorial intelligence is a culture of organization based on the pooling and treatment of signals from economic actors, destined to provide those in command positions with decisive information at the ideal moment".

The establishment of collective, participatory tools is necessary in the context of appropriation of TI by actors in the territory. At the center of this collective appropriation, we find the question of accessibility of knowledge and information [MAS 05]. The notion of accessibility should not be understood in a purely geographic sense but in a more complex way that brings together three dimensions: the spatial, human, and structural dimensions, while taking the transversal temporal dimension into account. The spatial dimension refers as much to the notion of movement as to that of relationships or connectivities between individuals. The human dimension should be envisaged as the potential for connectivity between individuals and the territory. It forms part of an approach to the appropriation of a territory by an individual. The structural dimension consists of the potential for connectivity of units of production and public actors in the territory with populations. The temporal dimension is transversal and allows us to distinguish the level of engagement of authors in relation to the territory. Thus, in the short term, an employee seeks a job in a territory; in the long term, the fact of staying within the territory will depend on social networks, educational infrastructures, and housing. Different actors in a territory see their relationship with that territory according to the temporal space in which they find themselves.

We can thus define the territorial capital as the relational capital representing the potential for connectivity between actors in this territory: the existence of social networks and links, both between businesses and with public actors, inhabitants, and other businesses. In Figure 16.2 and Appendix A, we propose an attempt at modeling the territory using the three dimensions described above. Our reading of the territory adds to the traditional model, too often limited to an analysis of the geographic situation, the infrastructure, and the presence of companies. We add population indicators and take particular notice of immaterial resources as an attractiveness factor. Essentially, we look at indicators relating to education, training, and access to ICT, and more generally to the valorization of local heritage. Moreover, we consider these resources not just as short-term "stock", but also in a dynamic (forward-looking) and historical perspective.

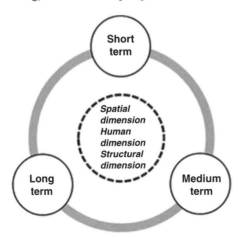

Figure 16.2. *Attractiveness of a territory*

Reading the territory in this way necessarily leads to the establishment of "aggressive" attractiveness, based on endogenous resources specific to the territory which allow it to capitalize on specific skills and specializations. The analysis of territorial attractiveness thus involves seeking adequate indicators to measure the true position of the territory concerned, while taking into account temporal horizons and the dimension involved.

16.4. Conclusion

At the end of this analysis, and in accordance with the analysis carried out by the DIACT [DIA 05], it seems necessary to highlight some major issues linked to the attractiveness of a territory. Economic base theory allowed us to show that an attractive territory accommodates both value creation activities and populations with revenues which may be independent of local activity (allocations, retirement, tourism, etc.). The territory is thus considered a support for both created and harnessed value.

The contribution of TI as we see it allows us to move beyond three weaknesses of the notion of attractiveness present in traditional literature on the subject. First, attractiveness is not exclusively based on companies, but on three "pillars": the *economic*, the *residential*, and the *tourism aspect* of a territory, which is all too often neglected [FAB 08]. Second, as attractiveness is a relative notion, studies have a tendency to underestimate benchmarking for positioning a territory, but this tool is essential when comparing the relative performance of territories in the context of competition. Finally, attractiveness is a temporal notion. From this point of view, existing studies too often concentrate on the present situation without placing the territory in a historical perspective. In the same way, future prospects are often neglected.

Furthermore, actors have representations of territories which vary depending on their temporal horizon. These representations affect their level of engagement in a territory. A territory seeking durable attractiveness must not only attract but also retain populations and businesses. It is at this point that TI should be considered a transversal method for "reading" a territory.

16.5. Bibliography

[AGE 05] REGIONAL DEVELOPMENT AGENCY PARIS ILE-DE-FRANCE, an attractive region, 2005, available online at www.europinvest-paris.info/FR/Document/Publications/ IDF_une%20région%20attractive.pdf.

[BER 06] BERTACCHINI Y., GIRARDOT J.J., GRAMMACIA G., "Territorial intelligence: theory, position, hypothesis, and definitions", *5th Conference ICT and Territory: Which Development?*, University of Franche-Comté, 9–10 June, 2006.

[BRU 04] BRUNEAU J.M., "Territory intelligence: what is it?", *Veille Magazine*, no. 80, December 2004.

[BRU 06] BRUTE DE REMUR D., *What Business Intelligence Means*, Editions d'Organisation, Paris, 2006.

[BRY 06] BRYKOVA I., "The international competitiveness of national regions: conceptual and practical dimensions", *Journal of International Economic Policy*, vol. 4, pp. 31–56, 2006.

[CAM 05] CAMAGNI R., "Attractivité et compétitivité: un binôme à repenser", *Territoires* vol. 2030, no. 1, pp. 11–15, 2005.

[CUS 08] CUSHMAN ET WAKEFIELD, European Cities Monitor, 2008, available online at www.cushwake.com/cwglobal/jsp/kcReportDetail.jsp?Country=GLOBAL&Language= EN&catId=100006&pId=c17500010p.

[DAV 08] DAVEZIES L., *The Republic and Its Territories*, coll. La république des idées, Le Seuil, Paris, 2008.

[DIA 05] DIACT (INTERMINISTERIAL DELEGATION TO REGIONAL DEVELOPMENT AND COMPETITIVENESS), "Regional attractiveness in urban projects", *Les notes de l'Observatoire*, April 2005.

[DOU 01] DOU H., BERTACCHINI Y., "The territorial competitive intelligence. A network approach", *Actes du colloque VSST*, Barcelona, Spain, 2001.

[DUN 93] DUNNING J., *Multinational Enterprises and the Global Economy*, Addison-Wesley, Wokingham, 1993.

[ERN 08a] ERNST & YOUNG, European attractiveness survey, 2008, available online at www.ey.com/global/content.nsf/France/attractiveness-europe-2008-EN.

[ERN 08b] ERNST & YOUNG, France attractiveness Survey – Liberté, créativité, attractivité?, 2008, available online at www.ey.com/global/content.nsf/France/attractiveness-form-France-2008.

[ERN 08c] ERNST & YOUNG, Global cities attractiveness, 2008, available online at www.ey.com/global/content.nsf/France/Global-Cities-Attractiveness-Survey-2008_EN.

[FAB 06] FABRY N., ZEGHNI S., "How former communist countries of Europe may attract inward foreign direct investment? A matter of institutions", *Communist and Post-Communist Studies*, vol. 39, pp. 201–219, 2006.

[FAB 08] FABRY N., "Tourism clusters, actors competitiveness and regional attractiveness", in FRANÇOIS L. (ed.), *Regional Intelligence, Business Intelligence Applied to Territory*, Lavoisier, Paris, 2008.

[FLO 04] FLORET C., Ile-de-France attractiveness towards 2025, Economical and social council of the Ile-de-France Region, report presented by the prospective department, May 2004, available online at www.cesr-ile-de-france.fr/cesr_doc/magazine/magazine 41-attractivite.pdf.

[FRA 08] FRANÇOIS L., "Business intelligence in support of the economic competitiveness of territories: regional intelligence", in FRANÇOIS L. (ed.), *Intelligence territoriale, l'intelligence économique appliquée au territoire*, Lavoisier, Paris, 2008.

[FUJ 99] FUJITA M., KRUGMAN P., VENABLES A.J., *The Spatial Economy: Cities, Regions and International Trade*, MIT Press, Boston, 1999.

[GAU 05] GAUCHERAND A., "Introduction to the regional intelligence concept", *I-expo Conference on the Theme "Information and Competitiveness"*, Paris, France, 2005, available online at www.i-expo.net/documents/actes2005/A2-AurelienGaucherand.pdf.

[GON 06] GONNARD S., Interregional migration flows: new links between internal migrations and regional development?, Doctoral Thesis, University of Paris 12, Val-de-Marne, 2006.

[HER 03] HERBAUX P., BERTACCHINI Y., "Mutualization and regional intelligence", *International Journal of Information & Communication Sciences for Decision Making*, vol. 9, pp. 1–9, 2003, available online at http://isdm.univ-tln.fr/PDF/isdm9/isdm9a73_herbaux.pdf.

[KRU 68] KRUMME G., "Werner Sombart and the economic base concept", *Land Economics*, vol. 48, pp. 112–116, 1968.

[MAR 90] MARSHALL A., *Principles of Economics, an Introductory Volume*, MacMillan, London, 1920, 8th edition, vol. 4, chap. 10, 1890, available online at http://socserv2.socsci.mcmaster.ca/~econ/ugcm/3ll3/marshall/prin/index.html.

[MAS 04] MASSARD N., MEHIER C., "Knowledge externalities, intellectual assets and localised and innovant performances. First interdisciplinary workshop on performance and intangible", *Première journée Interdisciplinaire de recherché Performance et Immatériel*, Angers, France, October 2004, available online at http://leshumas.insa-lyon.fr/stoica/page.php4_fichiers/Publications_AXE_1/2004_06_NMASSARD_CMEHIER_ANGERS.pdf.

[MAS 05] MASSARD N., MEHIER C., "Proximity, accessibility to knowledge and innovation", *Regional Studies Association International Conference*, Aalborg, Denmark, 28–31 May 2005.

[PAR 06] PARIS-ILE-DE-FRANCE, CAPITALE ÉCONOMIQUE ET ERNST & YOUNG, 2005 survey on international investment in the 15 most attractive european metropolis. L'Ile-de-France prend la tête du classement, 2006, available online at www.europinvest-paris.com/FR/Document/Benchmarking/E&Y/Nouveau%20dossier/Etude%20IDE%20IDF%202006.pdf.

[PAR 08] PARIS-ILE-DE-FRANCE, CAPITALE ÉCONOMIQUE ET ERNST & YOUNG ET CSA, Global cities' attractiveness survey 2008, Paris et ses principales concurrentes européennes dans la compétition mondiale, 2008, available online at www.ey.com/Global/assets.nsf/France/Global_Cities_Attractiviveness_2008/$file/Global_Cities_Attractiveness_2008_VF.pdf.

[PEL 08] PELISSIER M., "The origin and fundaments of regional intelligence: a simple variation of business intelligence at the territory level?", in FRANÇOIS L. (ed.), *Intelligence territoriale, l'intelligence économique appliquée au territoire*, Lavoisier, Paris, 2008.

[PER 50] PERROUX F., "Economic space: theory and applications", *The Quarterly Journal of Economics*, vol. 64, no. 1, pp. 89–104, 1950.

[PER 55] PERROUX F., "Note on the concept of growth poles", *Economie appliquée*, vol. 7, no. 1, pp. 307–320, 1955.

[PER 61] PERROUX F., *The 20th Century Economy*, PUF, Paris, 1961.

[PER 03] PERRRET J., TEYSSANDIER J.P., MARETTE C., "Managing sustainable tourism in region and firms", *Cahiers de l'AFIT - Guides de savoir-faire*, La Documentation Française, Paris, 2003.

[ROD 03] RODRIK D., SUBRAMANIAN A., "The primacy of institutions", *Finance and Development*, vol. 40, no. 2, pp. 31–34, 2003.

[SOM 54] SOMBART W., *The Economics of Location*, Yale University Press, New Haven, 1954.

16.6. Appendix A: grid for territorial analysis by aspect

Spatial dimension
Short term: Public transport, accessibility of equipment and jobs from living spaces, accessibility of healthcare provision from living spaces, part played by secondary residences in all movements, number of migrants between urban areas, section of employees with jobs outside their territory of residence, coverage by cell phone networks, number of operators offering broadband in the territory, number of broadband technologies in the territory, proportion of population with broadband coverage, coverage of the main road network, coverage by other transport networks (ports, airports, rail), average daily/annual traffic on major road axes, cultural provision per capita, sports equipment per capita.
Medium term: Development of digital infrastructures, economic orientation of living spaces, balance of arrivals and departures by age and qualification, development of road coverage, development of coverage by other transport networks (ports, airports, rail), development of average daily/annual traffic on major road axes.
Long term: Development of environmentally friendly means of transport, section of cultural heritage on national lists.

Human dimension
Short term: Crime levels, proportion of job prospects linked to FDI among the working population, total number of R&D researchers, proportion of researchers working in administration, jobs linked to FDI, proportion of jobs in fragile sectors, weight of establishments with 20–99 employees, unemployment, activity levels by age and gender.
Medium term: Housing, accessibility of healthcare services from living spaces, arrival of tourists, development of the qualification index, development of the active population, structuring of living spaces by healthcare provision, structuration of living spaces by education equipment, index of work qualification, development of salaried activity, development of unemployment rates, structure of jobs by CSP, structure of qualifications for 15–59 year olds, average spending per child in first degree education, average spending per child in second degree education, average spending per student in higher education, number of university students.
Long term: Development of structuring of living spaces by healthcare provision, development of structuration of living spaces by education equipment, number of risk prevention plans.

Structural dimension
Short term: Territorial expenditure, infrastructure and public services, regional fiscal pressure, proportion of researchers working in administration, import/export as a proportion of exchanges, weight of establishments with 20–99 employees, proportion of activity considered in regional added value, proportion of R&D expenditure in the public sector and higher education, number of patents registered, business creation, total exports, total imports, existence of competitiveness clusters, weight of first five sectors in salaried employment, weight of the four largest companies.
Medium term: Existence of complementary businesses (industry/services), 5-year survival rate of business creations, financial potential per capita, fiscal potential per capita, structuring of living spaces by services and jobs, economic orientation of living spaces, development of regional GDP, regional GDP per job, regional GDP per inhabitant, average 5-year survival rate of business creations, development of weight of first five sectors in salaried employment, development of weight of four largest companies.
Long term: Development of inter-territory networks, competitiveness clusters, development of territorial expenditure.

List of Authors

Christian BOURRET
Paris Est Marne la Vallée University
France

Cláudia CAMELO
Fernando Pessoa University
Porto
Portugal

João Casqueira CARDOSO
Fernando Pessoa University
Porto
Portugal

Amos DAVID
University of Nancy 2
France

Henri DOU
Atelis (Groupe ESCEM)
Tours
France

Bernard DOUSSET
Paul Sabatier University
Toulouse
France

Gérald DUFFING
ICN Business School Nancy-Metz
France

Nathalie FABRY
Paris-Est Marne-La-Vallée University
France

Ilhème GHALAMALLAH
Toulouse 1 Capitole University
France

Nadège GUENEC
Paris-Est Marne-La-Vallée University
France

Philippe KISLIN
University of Paris 8
France

Jacky KISTER
Aix-Marseille 3 University
Marseille
France

Audrey KNAUF
Nancy 2 University
France

Eloïse LOUBIER
Paul Sabatier University
Toulouse
France

Hanène MAGHREBI
Nancy 2 University
France

Victor ODUMUYIWA
Nancy 2 University
France

Olusoji B. OKUNOYE
University of Lagos
Nigeria

Bolanle OLADEJO
University of Ibadan
Nigeria

Olufade F.W. ONIFADE
University of Ibadan
Nigeria

Adenike O. OSOFISAN
University of Ibadan
Nigeria

Elisabeth PAOLI-SCARBONCHI
Paris-Est Marne-La-Vallée University
France

Luc QUONIAM
Laboratoire Paragraphe
University of Paris 8
France

Odile THIERY
Nancy 2 University
France

Miguel Rombert TRIGO
Fernando Pessoa University
Porto
Portugal

Lise VERLAET
Montpellier 3 University
France

Charles O. UWADIA
Department of Computer Sciences
University of Lagos
Nigeria

Sylvain ZEGHNI
Paris-Est Marne-La-Vallée University
France

Index